Rick

VENI

200

Rick Steves & Gene Openshaw

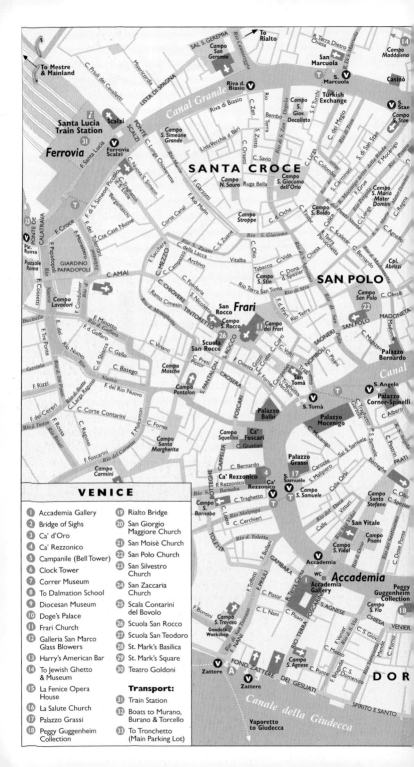

VENICE

1. Accademia Gallery
2. Bridge of Sighs
3. Ca' d'Oro
4. Ca' Rezzonico
5. Campanile (Bell Tower)
6. Clock Tower
7. Correr Museum
8. To Dalmation School
9. Diocesan Museum
10. Doge's Palace
11. Frari Church
12. Galleria San Marco Glass Blowers
13. Harry's American Bar
14. To Jewish Ghetto & Museum
15. La Fenice Opera House
16. La Salute Church
17. Palazzo Grassi
18. Peggy Guggenheim Collection
19. Rialto Bridge
20. San Giorgio Maggiore Church
21. San Moisè Church
22. San Polo Church
23. San Silvestro Church
24. San Zaccaria Church
25. Scala Contarini del Bovolo
26. Scuola San Rocco
27. Scuola San Teodoro
28. St. Mark's Basilica
29. St. Mark's Square
30. Teatro Goldoni

Transport:

31. Train Station
32. Boats to Murano, Burano & Torcello
33. To Tronchetto (Main Parking Lot)

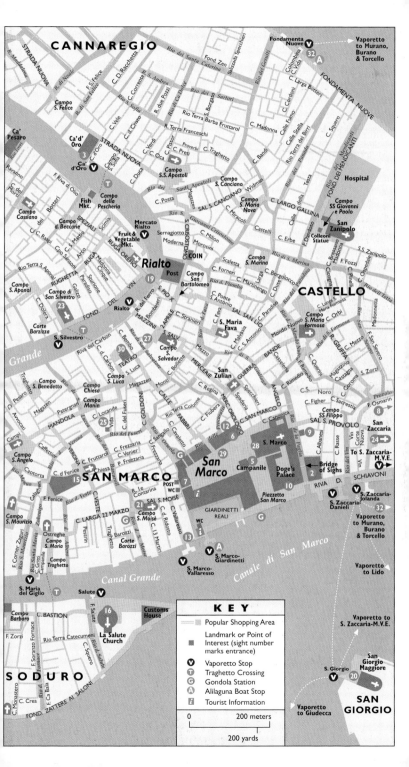

Rick Steves'
VENICE
2008

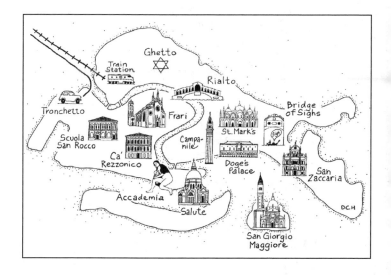

AVALON
TRAVEL

CONTENTS

Venice Overview

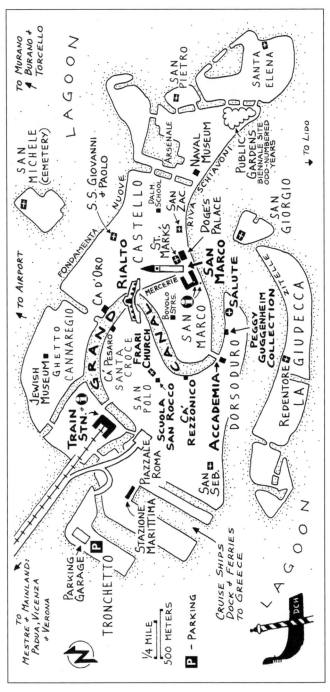

INTRODUCTION

Engineers love Venice—a completely man-made environment rising from the sea, with no visible means of support. Romantics revel in its atmosphere of elegant decay, seeing the peeling plaster and seaweed-covered stairs as a metaphor for beauty in decline. And first-time visitors are often stirred deeply, awaking from their ordinary lives to a fantasy world unlike anything they've ever seen before.

Those are strong reactions, considering that Venice today, frankly, can also be an overcrowded, prepackaged, tacky tourist trap. But Venice is unique. Built on a hundred islands with wealth from trade with the East, its exotic-looking palaces are laced together by sun-speckled canals. The car-free streets suddenly make walkers feel big, important, and liberated.

By day, it's a city of museums and churches, packed with great art. Everything's within a half-hour walk. Cruise the canals on a vaporetto water-bus. Climb towers for stunning seascape views. Shop for local crafts (such as glass and lace), high fashions, or tacky souvenirs for your Uncle Eric. Linger over lunch, trying to crack a local crustacean with weird legs and antennae. Sip a spritz at a café on St. Mark's Square while the orchestra plays "New York, New York."

At night, when the hordes of day-trippers have gone, another Venice appears. Dance across a floodlit square. Glide in a gondola through quiet canals while music echoes across the water. Pretend it's Carnevale time, don a mask—or just a clean shirt—and become someone else for a night.

About This Book

Rick Steves' Venice 2008 is a personal tour guide in your pocket. Better yet, it's actually two tour guides in your pocket: The co-author of this book is Gene Openshaw. Since our first "Europe

Introduction

through the gutter" trip together as high school buddies 35 years ago, Gene and I have been exploring the wonders of the Old World. An inquisitive historian and lover of European culture, Gene wrote most of this book's self-guided museum tours and neighborhood walks. Together, Gene and I will keep this book up-to-date and accurate (though for simplicity, from this point "we" will shed our respective egos and become "I").

The book is organized this way:

Orientation includes tourist information, tips on public transportation, local tour options, and other helpful hints. The "Planning Your Time" section offers a suggested schedule for how to best use your limited time.

Sights provides a succinct overview of the most important sights, arranged by neighborhood, with ratings:

▲▲▲—Don't miss.

▲▲—Try hard to see.

▲—Worthwhile if you can make it.

No rating—Worth knowing about.

The **Self-Guided Tours** lead you through Venice's most important sights, with tours of the Grand Canal, St. Mark's Square, St. Mark's Basilica, Doge's Palace, Correr Museum, Accademia, Scuola San Rocco, Frari Church, Ca' Rezzonico (Museum of 18th-Century Venice), Peggy Guggenheim Collection, La Salute Church, San Giorgio Maggiore, and the islands in Venice's lagoon: Cimitero, Murano, Burano, and Torcello.

The **Self-Guided Walks** take you through Venice's back streets. The walk from St. Mark's to Rialto (with an optional extension to the Frari Church) follows a less touristy route between these two major landmarks. The walk from St. Mark's to San Zaccaria explores the area behind the basilica, featuring a historic church and a seldom-seen view of the famous Bridge of Sighs.

Sleeping is a guide to my favorite budget hotels, conveniently located near St. Mark's Square, the Rialto Bridge, and the Accademia—all handy to the sights in this compact city.

Eating offers restaurants ranging from inexpensive eateries to splurges, with an emphasis on good-value places with memorable ambience.

Venice with Children, Shopping, and **Nightlife** contain my best suggestions on these topics.

Transportation Connections covers connections by train, bus, and plane, laying the groundwork for your smooth arrival and departure.

Day Trips covers nearby destinations: Padua, Vicenza, and Verona.

Venetian History fills you in on the background of this fascinating city.

The **appendix** is a traveler's tool kit, with a handy packing checklist, recommended books and films, a climate chart, detailed instructions on how to use the telephone, useful Italian phone numbers, Italian survival phrases, and lots more.

Throughout this book, when you see a ✪ in a listing, it means that the sight is covered in much more detail in one of my tours (a page number will tell you where to look to find more information).

Browse through this book and choose your favorite sights. Then have a great trip! Traveling like a temporary local, you'll get the absolute most out of every mile, minute, and euro.

PLANNING

Trip Costs

Six components make up your trip costs: airfare, surface transportation, room and board, sightseeing/entertainment, shopping/miscellany, and gelato.

Airfare: A basic, round-trip United States–Venice (or even cheaper, Milan) flight should cost $700 to $1,500, depending on where you fly from and when (cheapest in winter). Always consider saving time and money in Europe by flying "open jaw" (into one city and out of another).

Surface Transportation: Venice's sights are within walking distance of each other, but vaporetto boat rides, while expensive ($8), are fun and save time. For a one-way trip between Venice's airport and the city, allow about $4 by bus, $12 by speedboat, or $120 by water taxi (for details, see Transportation Connections, page 261).

The cost of round-trip, second-class train transportation to day-trip destinations is affordable and depends on the speed of the train (about $8 to Padua, about $15–25 to Vicenza, and about $20–40 to Verona).

Room and Board: You can easily manage in Venice in 2008 on an overall average of $120 a day per person for room and board. This allows $10 for lunch, $5 for snacks, $25 for dinner, and $80 for lodging (based on two people splitting the cost of a $160 double room that includes breakfast). If you've got more money, I've listed great ways to spend it. Students and tightwads can enjoy Venice for as little as $50 a day ($25 for a bed, $25 for meals and snacks).

Sightseeing and Entertainment: Figure about $9–14 per major sight (Accademia, Doge's Palace, Guggenheim), $4–8 for smaller ones (museums, climbing church towers), and $25–30 or more for splurge experiences (e.g., tours and concerts). A gondola ride costs $95–100 (by day) or $120–135 (at night); split the cost by going with a pal. An overall average of $30 a day works for most. Don't skimp here. After all, this category is the driving force behind your trip—you came to sightsee, enjoy, and experience Venice.

Shopping and Miscellany: Figure a minimum of $2 per postcard, coffee, soft drink, or gelato. Shopping can vary in cost from nearly nothing to a small fortune. Good budget travelers find that this category has little to do with assembling a trip full of lifelong, wonderful memories.

When to Go

Venice's best travel months (and busiest, most expensive months) are May, June, September, and October. Between November and April you can usually expect mild winter weather, some flooding (particularly March and Nov), shorter lines, and generally none of the sweat and stress of the tourist season (except during the Carnevale festival in mid–late Feb).

Venice's summers are more temperate than Italy's scorching inland cities. Venetian temperatures hit the high 70s and 80s in summer and drop to the 30s and 40s in winter. Most mid-range hotels come with air-conditioning—a worthwhile splurge in the summer—but usually available only from May (at the earliest) through September. Spring and fall can be cool, and many hotels do not turn on their heat until winter. For specific temperatures, see the climate chart on page 350 of the appendix.

Off-Season Travel: Here are several things to keep in mind if you visit Venice off-season, roughly November–March.

- Certain sights close early (Doge's Palace, Correr Museum, Scuola San Rocco, San Giorgio Maggiore, Ca' Rezzonico, and Ca' Pesaro close at 17:00). Many sights stop selling tickets an hour before closing. The lace and glassmaking demonstrations on Burano and Murano also close early in winter.
- The orchestras in St. Mark's Square may stop playing at 18:00 (and may not play at all in bad weather or during their annual vacations, usually in March).
- Vaporetto #2 (the Grand Canal fast boat) may have limited off-season hours (approximately 9:15–20:30).
- Expect the occasional *acqua alta* (flooding), particularly at St. Mark's Square and along Zattere (southern edge of Venice, opposite Giudecca Island).

Venice has two main weather patterns: Wind from the southeast (Bulgaria) brings cold and dry weather, while the scirocco wind from the south (Egypt) brings warm and wet weather, pushing more water into the lagoon and causing the *acqua alta*. This shouldn't greatly affect your sightseeing plans. Tobacco shops and some souvenir shops sell boots to keep your feet dry. Elevated wooden walkways are sometimes set up in the busier, more flooded

Know Before You Go

Plan ahead! As soon as you have your itin[erary],
review this list for what you might want to ch[eck]
in advance:

Because **airline carry-on restrictions** are always
changing, visit the Transportation Security Administration's
website (www.tsa.gov/travelers) for an up-to-date list of what
you can bring on the plane with you...and what you have to
check.

Call your **debit and credit card companies** to let them
know the countries you'll be visiting, so that they'll accept
(and not deny) your international charges. Confirm what your
daily withdrawal limit is; consider asking to have it raised so
you can take out more cash at each ATM stop.

Be sure that your **passport** is valid at least six months
after your ticketed date of return to the US. If you need to get
or renew a passport, it can take up to three months (for more
on passports, see www.travel.state.gov).

Check to see whether you'll be visiting during any **holidays,** when rooms can cost more and get booked up quickly
(see page 7).

To avoid long lines at the **Accademia,** Venice's top art
museum, make reservations at least a day beforehand. In
Padua, reservations are mandatory to visit the **Scrovegni
Chapel** (known for its frescoes by Giotto), so book well in
advance.

If you plan to hire a **local guide,** it's smart to reserve
ahead by email. Popular guides can get booked up in high
season.

If you're taking an **overnight train** and you need a
couchette or sleeper—and you must leave on a certain
day—consider booking it in advance, even though it may
cost more. Other Italian trains, like the high-speed ES trains,
require a seat reservation, but for these it's usually possible to
make arrangements in Italy just a few days ahead. (For more
on train travel, see page 261.)

If you're planning on **renting a car** in Italy, you'll need an
International Driver's Permit (available at your local AAA office
for $15 plus the cost of two passport-type photos; see www
.aaa.com).

Intro

Just the FAQs, Please

Whom do I call in case of emergency?
Dial 113 for English-speaking police help. To summon an ambulance, call 118.

What if my credit card is stolen?
Act immediately. See "Damage Control for Lost Cards," page 344, for instructions.

How do I make a phone call to, within, and from Europe?
For detailed dialing instructions, refer to page 337.

How can I get tourist information about my destination?
See page 333 for a list of tourist information offices (abbreviated **TI** in this book) located in the US.

What's the best way to pack?
Light. For a recommended packing list, see page 351.

Does Rick have other materials that will help me?
Thanks for asking. For more on my guidebooks, public television series, free audio tours, public radio show, guided tours, travel bags, accessories, and railpasses, see page 334.

Are there any updates to this guidebook?
Check www.ricksteves.com/update for changes to the most recent edition of this book.

Can you recommend any good books or movies for my trip?
Sure. For suggestions, see pages 336–337.

squares to keep you above the water. And it's worth a trip to St. Mark's Square to see waiters in fancy tuxes and rubber boots.

Travel Smart

Many people travel through Italy thinking it's a chaotic mess. They feel any attempt at efficient travel is futile. This is dead wrong—and expensive. Italy, which seems as orderly as spilled spaghetti, actually functions well. Only those who understand this and travel smart can enjoy Italy on a budget.

Really, this book can save you lots of time and money. But to have an "A" trip, you need to be an "A" student. Read it all before your trip; note the days when museums are closed and whether reservations are mandatory. If you save St. Mark's Basilica for Sunday morning (when it's closed), you've missed the gondola. You can sweat in line at the Doge's Palace, or you can buy your Museum Card at the nearby Correr Museum and zip right though the palace

Do I need to speak some Italian?
Many Italians—especially those in the tourist trade, and in big cities—speak English. Still, you'll get better treatment if you learn and use the Italian pleasantries. For a list of survival phrases, see page 353.

Do I need to carry my passport in Italy?
Yes. Anti-terrorism regulation requires you to show your passport whenever you go online at an Internet café. Carry it in your money belt.

How much do I tip?
For pointers on tipping, see page 344.

Will I get a student or senior discount?
Not likely. Discounts for sights are not listed in this book because they are generally limited to European residents and countries that offer reciprocal deals (the US does not).

How can I get my VAT taxes back on major purchases?
For information on how to get a Value Added Tax refund on major purchases, see page 345.

How do I calculate metric amounts?
Europe uses the metric system. A liter is about a quart, four to a gallon. A kilometer is six-tenths of a mile. I figure kilometers to miles by cutting them in half and adding back 10 percent of the original (120 km: 60 + 12 = 72 miles, 300 km: 150 + 30 = 180 miles). For more metric conversions, see page 349.

turnstile. Day-tripping to Verona or Vicenza on Monday, when most sights are closed, is bad news. A smart trip is a puzzle—a fun, doable, and worthwhile challenge.

Reserve your hotel room well in advance if you'll be in Venice on a major holiday, festival (see page 346), or weekend. Hotels usually get booked up on Carnevale (Jan 25–Feb 5 in 2008), Easter and Easter Monday (March 23–24), April 25, May 1, November 1, and on Fridays and Saturdays year-round. Religious holidays and train strikes can catch you by surprise anywhere in Italy.

Saturdays are virtually weekdays, with earlier closing hours. Sundays have the same pros and cons as they do for travelers in the US: Sightseeing attractions are generally open, while shops and banks are closed. Rowdy evenings are rare on Sundays.

Be sure to mix intense and relaxed periods in your itinerary. Every trip (and every traveler) needs at least a few slack days. Pace yourself. Assume you will return.

Plan ahead for laundry, picnics, and Internet stops. Get online at Internet cafés or your hotel to research transportation connections, confirm events, check the weather, and get directions to your next hotel. Buy a phone card and use it for reservations, reconfirmations, and double-checking hours.

Enjoy the friendliness of the local people. Slow down and ask questions—most locals are eager to point you in their idea of the right direction. Keep a notepad in your pocket for organizing your thoughts. Wear your money belt, and learn the local currency and how to estimate prices in dollars. Those who expect to travel smart, do.

PRACTICALITIES

Red Tape: You need a passport but no visa or shots to travel in Italy. You may be denied entry into certain countries if your passport is due to expire within six months of your ticketed date of return. Get it renewed if you'll be cutting it close. Pack a photocopy of your passport in your luggage in case the original is lost or stolen.

Time: In Italy—and in this book—you'll use the 24-hour clock. It's the same through 12:00 noon, then keep going: 13:00, 14:00, and so on. For anything over 12, subtract 12 and add p.m. (14:00 is 2:00 p.m.).

Italy, like most of continental Europe, is generally six/nine hours ahead of the East/West Coasts of the US, except for the beginning and end of Daylight Saving Time: Europe "springs forward" the last Sunday in March (two weeks after most of the US), and "falls back" the last Sunday in October (one week before US). For an online converter, try www.timeanddate.com/worldclock.

Business Hours: Traditionally, Italy uses the siesta plan. Nowadays, however, many businesses have adopted the government's recommended 8:00 to 14:00 workday. In tourist areas, shops are open longer. People usually work from about 8:00 to 13:00 and from 15:30 to 19:00. Some stores and restaurants close on Sunday. Banking hours are generally Monday through Friday 8:30 to 13:30 and 15:30 to 16:30, but they can vary wildly.

Watt's Up? Europe's electrical system is different from North America's in two different ways: the shape of the plug (two round prongs) and the voltage of the current (220 volts instead of 110 volts). For your North American plug to work in Europe, you'll need an adapter, sold inexpensively at travel stores in the US. As for the voltage, most newer electronics or travel appliances (such as hair dryers, laptops, and battery chargers) automatically convert the voltage—if you see a range of voltages printed on the item or its plug (such as "110–220"), it'll work in Europe. Otherwise, you can buy a converter separately in the US (about $20).

News: Americans keep in touch with the *International Herald Tribune* (published almost daily via satellite throughout Europe). Every Tuesday, the European editions of *Time* and *Newsweek* hit the stands with articles of particular interest to European travelers. Sports addicts can get their daily fix online or from *USA Today*. Good websites include www.europeantimes.com and http://news.bbc.co.uk.

MONEY

Banking

Throughout Europe, cash machines (ATMs) are the standard way for travelers to get local currency. Bring plastic—credit and/or debit cards—along with several hundred dollars in hard cash as an emergency backup. It's smart to bring two cards, in case one gets demagnetized or eaten by a temperamental machine. Traveler's checks are a waste of time (long waits at slow banks) and a waste of money (in fees).

Cash from ATMs

To use a bank machine (ATM) to withdraw money from your account, you'll need a debit card (ideally with a Visa or MasterCard logo for maximum usability), plus a PIN code. Know your PIN code in numbers; there are only numbers—no letters—on European keypads.

Before you go, verify with your bank that your card will work overseas, and alert them that you'll be making withdrawals in Europe; otherwise, the bank may not approve transactions if it perceives unusual spending patterns.

Try to take out large sums of money to reduce your per-transaction bank fees. If the machine refuses your request, try again and select a smaller amount; some cash machines won't let

---

Exchange Rate

1 euro (€) = about $1.30

To convert prices in euros to dollars, add about 30 percent: €20 = about $26, €50 = about $65. Just like the dollar, one euro is broken down into 100 cents. You'll find coins ranging from €0.01 to €2, and bills ranging from €5 to €500.

Look carefully at any €2 coin you get in change. Some unscrupulous merchants are giving out similar-looking, gold-rimmed old 500-*lire* coins (worth $0) instead of €2 coins (worth $2.60). You are now warned!

you take out more than about €150 (don't take it personally). Also, be aware that some ATMs will tell you to take your cash within 30 seconds, and if you aren't fast enough, your cash may be sucked back into the machine...and you'll have a hassle trying to get it from the bank.

To keep your cash safe, use a money belt—a pouch with a strap that you buckle around your waist like a belt, and wear under your clothes. Thieves target tourists. A money belt provides peace of mind, allowing you to carry lots of cash safely. Don't waste time every few days tracking down a cash machine—change a week's worth of money, stuff it in your money belt, and travel!

Credit and Debit Cards

For purchases, Visa and MasterCard are more commonly accepted than American Express. Just like at home, credit or debit cards work easily at larger hotels, restaurants, and shops, but smaller businesses prefer payment in local currency (in small bills—break large bills at a bank or larger store).

Credit and debit cards—whether used for purchases or ATM withdrawals—often come with additional, tacked-on "international transaction" fees of up to 3 percent plus $5 per transaction. To avoid unpleasant surprises, call your credit-card company before your trip to ask about these fees.

If your cards are lost or stolen, see page 344 for advice on what to do.

TRANSPORTATION

Your public transportation concerns in Venice are limited to vaporetto boats, covered in the Orientation chapter. For a private ride, you can hire a gondola or a pricey, speedy water taxi. For more information on boating, see "Getting Around Venice" in the Orientation chapter. If you have a car, stow it at a parking lot at Tronchetto (in Venice) or Mestre (on the mainland). For arrival and departure information, see the Transportation Connections chapter. For advice on travel agencies in Venice, see page 22. If you'll be traveling throughout Italy by train or car, consider *Rick Steves' Italy 2008.*

TRAVELING AS A TEMPORARY LOCAL

We travel all the way to Italy to enjoy differences—to become temporary locals. You'll experience frustrations. Certain truths that we find "God-given" or "self-evident," such as cold beer, ice in drinks, bottomless cups of coffee, hot showers, and bigger being better, are suddenly not so true. One of the benefits of travel is

How Was Your Trip?

Were your travels fun, smooth, and meaningful? If you'd like to share your tips, concerns, and discoveries, please fill out the survey at www.ricksteves.com/feedback. I value your feedback. Thanks in advance—it helps a lot.

the eye-opening realization that there are logical, civil, and even better alternatives. A willingness to go local ensures that you'll enjoy a full dose of Italian hospitality.

If there is a negative aspect to Italians' image of Americans (apart from our foreign policy), it's that we are big, loud, aggressive, impolite, rich, and a bit naive. Given our reluctance to work with the world on climate change issues, Europeans don't respond well to Americans complaining about being too hot or too cold. To encourage conservation, the Italian government limits when air-conditioning or central heating can be used. (Generally, heat is turned off in early April and air-conditioning isn't allowed until May.) Bring a sweater in winter, and in summer, be prepared to sweat a little like everyone else. Also, Americans tend to be noisy in public places, such as restaurants and trains. Our raised voices can demolish Europe's reserved and elegant ambience. Talk softly.

While Italians, flabbergasted by our Yankee excesses, say in disbelief, *"Mi sono cadute le braccia!"* ("I throw my arms down!"), they nearly always afford us individual travelers all the warmth we deserve.

Judging from all the happy feedback I receive from travelers who have used this book, it's safe to assume you'll enjoy a great, affordable vacation—with the finesse of an independent, experienced traveler.

Thanks, and *buon viaggio!*

BACK DOOR TRAVEL PHILOSOPHY
From *Rick Steves' Europe Through the Back Door*

Travel is intensified living—maximum thrills per minute and one of the last great sources of legal adventure. Travel is freedom. It's recess, and we need it.

Experiencing the real Europe requires catching it by surprise, going casual..."Through the Back Door."

Affording travel is a matter of priorities. (Make do with the old car.) You can travel—simply, safely, and comfortably—nearly anywhere in Europe for $100 a day plus transportation costs. In many ways, spending more money only builds a thicker wall between you and what you came to see. Europe is a cultural carnival, and, time after time, you'll find that its best acts are free and the best seats are the cheap ones.

A tight budget forces you to travel close to the ground, meeting and communicating with the people, not relying on service with a purchased smile. Never sacrifice sleep, nutrition, safety, or cleanliness in the name of budget. Simply enjoy the local-style alternatives to expensive hotels and restaurants.

Extroverts have more fun. If your trip is low on magic moments, kick yourself and make things happen. If you don't enjoy a place, maybe you don't know enough about it. Seek the truth. Recognize tourist traps. Give a culture the benefit of your open mind. See things as different but not better or worse. Any culture has much to share.

Of course, travel, like the world, is a series of hills and valleys. Be fanatically positive and militantly optimistic. If something's not to your liking, change your liking. Travel is addictive. It can make you a happier American as well as a citizen of the world. Our Earth is home to six and a half billion equally important people. It's humbling to travel and find that people don't envy Americans. Europeans like us, but, with all due respect, they wouldn't trade passports.

Globe-trotting destroys ethnocentricity. It helps you understand and appreciate different cultures. Regrettably, there are forces in our society that want you dumbed down for their convenience. Don't let it happen. Thoughtful travel engages you with the world—and it's more important than ever these days. Travel changes people. It broadens perspectives and teaches new ways to measure quality of life. Rather than fear the diversity on this planet, travelers celebrate it. Many travelers toss aside their hometown blinders. Their prized souvenirs are the strands of different cultures they decide to knit into their own character. The world is a cultural yarn shop, and Back Door travelers are weaving the ultimate tapestry. Join in!

ORIENTATION

The island city of Venice is shaped like a fish. Its major thorough-fares are canals. The Grand Canal winds through the middle of the fish, starting at the mouth where all the people and food enter, passing under the Rialto Bridge, and ending at St. Mark's Square (Piazza San Marco). Park your 21st-century perspective at the mouth and let Venice swallow you whole.

Venice is a car-less kaleidoscope of people, bridges, and odor-less canals. The city has no major streets, and addresses are hope-lessly confusing. There are six districts (see map on page 17): San Marco (most touristy), Castello (behind San Marco), Cannaregio (from the train station to the Rialto), San Polo (other side of the Rialto), Santa Croce (the "eye" of the fish, east of the train station), and Dorsoduro (the belly of the fish and southernmost district of the city). Each district has about 6,000 address numbers.

To find your way, navigate by landmarks, not streets. Many street corners have a sign point-ing you to *(per)* the nearest major landmark, such as San Marco, Accademia, Rialto, and Ferrovia (train station). Obedient visitors stick to the main thoroughfares as directed by these signs...and miss the charm of back-street Venice.

Planning Your Time

Venice is remarkably small. You can walk across it, from head to tail, in about an hour. Nearly all of your sightseeing is within a 20-minute walk of the Rialto Bridge or St. Mark's Square. Remember

Orientation

Daily Reminder

Need a calendar? See the appendix.

Sunday: The Church of San Giorgio Maggiore (on an island near St. Mark's Square) hosts a Gregorian Mass at 11:00. The Church of San Polo is closed today, and these sights are open only in the afternoon: St. Mark's Basilica (14:00–16:00), Frari Church (13:00–18:00, closed Sun in Aug), and the Church of San Zaccaria (16:00–18:00). Today, the Rialto open-air market consists mainly of souvenir stalls (fish and produce sections closed). It's a bad day for a pub crawl, as most pubs are closed.

Monday: All sights are open except for the Rialto fish market, Dalmatian School, Ca' Pesaro, and Torcello Museum (on Torcello Island). The Accademia and Ca' d'Oro close at 14:00. Don't side-trip to Verona or Vicenza today, as most sights in these towns are closed.

Tuesday: All sights are open except the Peggy Guggenheim Collection, Ca' Rezzonico (Museum of 18th-Century Venice), and the Lace Museum (on Burano Island).

Wednesday: All sights are open except the Glass Museum (on Murano Island).

Thursday/Friday: All sights are open.

Saturday: All sights are open except the Jewish Museum.

Notes: The Accademia is open earlier (daily at 8:15) and closes later (19:15 Tue–Sun) than most sights in Venice. Some sights close earlier off-season (such as the Doge's Palace, Correr

that Venice itself is its greatest sight. Make time to wander, explore, shop, and simply be.

Two key considerations: Maximize your evening magic, and avoid the midday crowds around St. Mark's Basilica and the Doge's Palace.

Note that the Museum Card and the pricier Museum Pass cover the popular Doge's Palace and less-visited Correr Museum (both on St. Mark's Square). Because the Doge's Palace has longer lines, it makes sense to buy your Card or Pass at the Correr Museum (for more tips on crowd control, see the "Daily Reminder" sidebar).

If you're heading from St. Mark's Square to the Frari Church via the Rialto Bridge, consider taking the less-traveled, more interesting route outlined in my St. Mark's to Rialto self-guided walk (see page 192).

You'll have to juggle the itineraries below, depending on when you're visiting. Refer to the "Daily Reminder" above for details on when sights are open and closed.

Museum, Campanile, and St. Mark's Basilica).

Churches: Modest dress is recommended at churches and required at St. Mark's Basilica—no bare shoulders, shorts, or short skirts. Some churches are closed to sightseers on Sunday morning (including St. Mark's Basilica, Frari Church, Church of San Zaccaria, and San Giorgio Maggiore), and many are closed from roughly 12:00 to 14:30 or 15:00 Monday through Saturday (this includes La Salute and San Giorgio Maggiore).

Crowd Control: Crowds can be a serious problem at the Accademia (to minimize crowds, go early or late, or call 041-520-0345 to reserve tickets in advance); St. Mark's Basilica (try going early or late, or you can skip the line if you have a bag to check—see page 67); Campanile (go early or late—it's open until 21:00 July–Aug; or skip it entirely if you're going to the similar San Giorgio Maggiore bell tower); and the Doge's Palace. For the Doge's Palace, you have three options for avoiding the ticket-sales line: Buy your Museum Card or Museum Pass at the Correr Museum (then step right up to the Doge's Palace turnstile, thus skipping the long line); visit at 17:00 (if it's April–Oct), when lines disappear; or book a Secret Itineraries Tour (see page 86). The sights that have crowd problems (St. Mark's Basilica, Doge's Palace, and Accademia) get even more crowded when it rains.

Venice in One (Busy) Day

9:00	Walk from St. Mark's Square to Frari Church (following my self-guided walk), taking time to enjoy the Rialto market action.
11:00	Tour Frari Church.
12:00	Lunch near the Frari, then catch the vaporetto (boat) back to St. Mark's to wander and shop.
14:30	Correr Museum.
15:30	St. Mark's Basilica.
16:30	Doge's Palace.
18:00	Go up the Campanile for city view.
18:30	Pub dinner (crawl, or stay put and munch).
20:00	Gondola ride (or take my self-guided Grand Canal Cruise).
21:00	Enjoy the dueling orchestras with a drink on St. Mark's Square.

Venice in Two Days
Day 1
9:00   Walk from St. Mark's Square to Frari Church (following my self-guided walk). Stop along the way at the Rialto market to browse.

11:00   Tour Frari Church.

12:00   Tour Ca' Rezzonico or Scuola San Rocco (if you prefer Tintoretto to Casanova).

13:00   Lunch in Dorsoduro neighborhood, then take the vaporetto back to St. Mark's Square to wander and shop.

15:00   Correr Museum.

16:00   St. Mark's Basilica.

17:00   Doge's Palace.

19:00   Go up the Campanile for city view (in Sept–June, the tower closes at 19:00; get here by 18:00, or skip the tower).

20:00   Dinner.

22:00   Enjoy the dueling orchestras with a drink on St. Mark's Square.

Day 2
9:00   Shopping or exploring.

11:00   Take my self-guided Grand Canal Cruise by vaporetto.

13:00   Lunch (pizza near Accademia Bridge?).

14:00   Tour Accademia, explore Dorsoduro neighborhood, visit La Salute Church or Peggy Guggenheim Collection.

17:00   Commence pub crawl, eating dinner along the way.

20:00   Gondola ride.

Venice in Three (or Four) Days
Day 1
9:45   St. Mark's Basilica and Square.

11:00   Correr Museum.

12:00   Shop, wander, and have lunch in St. Mark's area.

16:00   Doge's Palace.

18:00   Ascend Campanile.

19:00   Gondola ride.

20:00   Dinner.

Day 2
9:00   Walk from St. Mark's Square to Frari Church (following my self-guided walk), allowing time to experience the Rialto market scene.

11:00   Tour Frari Church.

12:00   Tour Scuola San Rocco for Tintoretto.

Venice's Districts

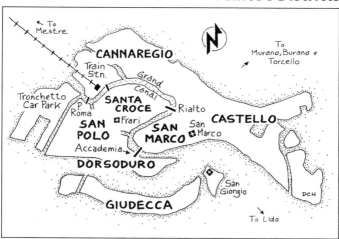

13:00 Lunch.

14:00 Tour Ca' Rezzonico.

15:00 Explore Dorsoduro, the neighborhood around the Accademia.

17:00 Tour the Accademia.

18:00 Hop on a vaporetto for my self-guided Grand Canal Cruise.

Day 3

9:00 Explore the lagoon by vaporetto or tour boat, visiting Burano and Torcello.

15:00 Take my self-guided walk from St. Mark's to San Zaccaria, then catch a vaporetto to visit the Church of San Giorgio Maggiore for a superb view of Venice (see photo).

17:00 Start pub crawl.

21:00 Savor a drink while listening to the dueling orchestras on St. Mark's Square.

Day 4

Side-trip to Padua and/or Verona.

OVERVIEW

Tourist Information

There are TIs at the **train station** (daily 8:00–20:00, crowded and surly); at **St. Mark's Square** (daily 9:00–15:30; with your back to St. Mark's Basilica, it's at the far-left corner of the square); and near the **St. Mark's Square vaporetto stop** on the lagoon (daily 10:00–18:00, sells vaporetto tickets). Smaller offices are at **Piazzale Roma** and the **airport** (daily 9:00–20:00). For a quick question, save time by phoning 041-529-8711. The TI's official website is www.turismovenezia.it.

At any TI, confirm your sightseeing plans. Pick up the two free pamphlets that list museum hours, exhibitions, and musical events (in Italian and English), and ask for the fine brochures outlining three offbeat Venice walks.

The free monthly entertainment guide *Un Ospite di Venezia* (a listing of events, nightlife, museum hours, train and vaporetto schedules, emergency telephone numbers, and so on) is available at fancy hotel reception desks (www.aguestinvenice.com).

Maps: Of all places, you'll need a good map in Venice. Hotels give away lousy freebies, and the TI sells a simple one that isn't much better. Bookshops, newsstands, and postcard stands sell a wider range of maps; the €3 maps are pretty bad, but if you spend €5, you'll get a map that shows you everything. Invest in a good map and use it—this can be the best €5 you'll spend in Venice.

Arrival in Venice

For a rundown on Venice's train station and airport, see Transportation Connections, page 261.

Passes for Venice

To help control (and confuse?) its flood of visitors, Venice offers cards and passes that cover some museums and/or transportation. For most visitors, the simple Museum Card or Museum Pass will do. Both of these passes are sold at all of the sights they cover.

The **Museum Card** is really just another name for the (mandatory) combo-ticket you must buy to visit the Doge's Palace or the Corer Museum. It covers admission to both of those sights, plus the two museums accessed from within the Correr—the National Archaeological Museum and the Monumental Rooms of Marciana National Library (€13, called *"Museum Card per i Musei di Piazza San Marco,"* valid for 3 months; to bypass long line at Doge's Palace, purchase card at Correr Museum, then enter Doge's Palace).

The pricier **Museum Pass** includes the St. Mark's Square sights listed above, plus Ca' Rezzonico (Museum of 18th-Century

Venice; see tour on page 145), Mocenigo Palace (textiles and costumes), Casa Goldoni (home of the Italian playwright), Ca' Pesaro (modern art), and museums on the islands—Murano's Glass Museum and Burano's Lace Museum (€18, valid for 6 months). The pass pays for itself if you see the Doge's Palace, Correr Museum, and Ca' Rezzonico.

The **Chorus Pass** gives you access to 16 of Venice's churches (including San Polo and the Frari, covered in this book) and their works of art (€8, €5 with a Venice Card—see below, or pay €2.50 per church; Chorus Family Pass costs €16 for 2 adults and kids 18 and under). You'd need to visit four churches to save money.

No cards or passes cover these top attractions: Accademia, Peggy Guggenheim Collection, Scuola San Rocco, Campanile, and the three sights within St. Mark's Basilica that charge admission.

Venice Cards: The Blue and Orange Venice Cards are transit passes (good for 1–7 days) that include the use of public toilets—not worth considering unless you have diarrhea.

"Rolling Venice" Youth Discount Pass: To those under age 30, this worthwhile pass (€4/1 day, €15/3 days) gives discounts on sights and transportation, plus information on cheap eating and sleeping. It's sold at the train station (both inside at the TI, and outside at the Vela kiosk).

Helpful Hints

Get Lost: Accept the fact that Venice was a tourist town 400 years ago. It was, is, and always will be crowded. While 80 percent of Venice is, in fact, not touristy, 80 percent of the tourists never notice. Hit the back streets. Venice is the ideal town to explore on foot. Walk and walk to the far reaches of the town. Don't worry about getting lost. In fact, get as lost as possible. Keep reminding yourself, "I'm on an island, and I can't get off." When it comes time to find your way, just follow the directional arrows on building corners or simply ask a local, *"Dov'è San Marco?"* ("Where is St. Mark's?") People in the tourist business (that's most Venetians) speak some English. If they don't, listen politely, watch where their hands point, say, *"Grazie,"* and head off in that direction. If you're lost, pop into a hotel and ask for their business card—it comes with a map and a prominent "You are here."

Be Prepared to Splurge: Venice is expensive for locals as well as tourists. The demand is huge, supply is limited, and running a business is costly. Things just cost more here; everything must be shipped in and hand-trucked to its destination. Perhaps the best way to enjoy Venice is just to succumb to its charms and blow a lot of money.

Warning: The dark, late-night streets of Venice are safe. Even so, pickpockets (often elegantly dressed) work the crowded main streets, docks, and *vaporetti* (wear your money belt and carry your day bag in front). Your biggest risk of pickpockets is actually inside St. Mark's Basilica. A service called Counter of Tourist Mediation handles complaints about local crooks, but does not give out information (tel. 041-529-8710, complaint.apt@turismovenezia.it). Immigrants selling items such as knock-off handbags on the streets are doing so illegally—if you buy goods from them, you'll risk getting a big fine.

Medical Help: Venice's S.S. Giovanni e Paolo hospital (tel. 118) is a 10-minute walk from both the Rialto and San Marco neighborhoods, located on Fondamenta dei Mendicanti toward Fondamenta Nuove. Take vaporetto #41 from San Zaccaria-Jolanda to the Ospedale stop.

Take Breaks: Venice's endless pavement, crowds, and tight spaces are hard on the tourist. Schedule breaks in your sightseeing. Grab a cool place to sit down, relax, and recoup—meditate on a pew in an uncrowded church, or stop in a café.

Etiquette: Walk on the right and don't loiter on bridges. Picnicking is forbidden (keep a low profile). On St. Mark's Square, a "decorum patrol" admonishers snackers and sunbathers. The only place for a legal picnic is in Giardinetti Reali, the small park along the waterfront west of the Piazzetta near St. Mark's Square.

Dress modestly. Men should keep their shirts on. When visiting St. Mark's Basilica or other major churches, men, women, and even children must cover their shoulders and knees (or risk being turned away). Remove hats when entering a church.

Pigeon Poop: If bombed by a pigeon, resist the initial response to wipe it off immediately—it'll just smear into your hair. Wait until it dries, and it should flake off cleanly.

Public Toilets: There are handy public WCs (€1) near St. Mark's Square (one behind the Correr Museum, another at the waterfront park Giardinetti Reali), near Rialto, and at the Accademia Bridge. You'll find public pay toilets near most major landmarks. Use free toilets—in a museum you're visiting or a café you're eating in—when you can.

Water: Venetians pride themselves on having pure, safe, and tasty tap water piped in from the foothills of the Alps. You can actually see the mountains from Venice's bell towers on crisp, clear winter days.

Lingo: *Campo* means square, *campiello* is a small square, *calle* is street, *fondamenta* is the road running along a canal, *rio* is a small canal, *rio terra* is a street that was once a canal and has been filled in, and *ponte* is a bridge.

Services

Money: The plentiful ATMs are the
easiest way to go. If you must
exchange currency, be aware that
bank rates vary. The American
Express exchange desk is just off
St. Mark's Square (see "Travel
Agencies," on page 22). Non-
bank exchange bureaus, such as
Exacto, will charge you $10 more
than a bank for a $200 exchange.

Internet Access: You'll find handy,
if pricey (€5/hr), little Internet
places all over town. Every hotel knows a place nearby.

Post Office: A large post office is just outside the far end of St.
Mark's Square (the end farthest from the basilica; Mon–Fri
8:30–14:00, Sat 8:30–13:00, closed Sun, shorter hours off-
season). The main P.O. is near the Rialto Bridge (on the St.
Mark's side, Mon–Sat 8:30–18:30, closed Sun). Use post
offices only as a last resort, as simple transactions can take
45 minutes if you get in the wrong line. You can buy stamps
from tobacco shops and mail postcards from any of the red
postboxes around town.

Bookstores: Libreria Mondadori is a gorgeous bookstore carrying a huge selection of Venice books, local guidebooks,
and even my guidebooks (the tourist-oriented books are on
the ground floor). This is the biggest bookstore in town,
with plenty in English and three Internet terminals (daily
May–Oct 10:00–23:00, Nov–April 10:00–20:00, across from
American Express a block behind Piazza San Marco at 1345
Complesso del Ridotto, tel. 041-522-2193). **Libreria Studium**
stocks all the English-language guidebooks (including mine)
just a block behind St. Mark's Basilica (Mon–Sat 9:00–19:30,
shorter hours Sun, Calle de la Canonica, tel. 041-522-2382).

Laundry: These two laundry options are near San Marco, but your
hotelier can direct you to one near your hotel: A modern **self-
service** *lavanderia* is on Ruga Giuffa at #4826 (wring clothes
before drying, or you'll bring them home damp; June–Sept
daily 8:30–20:00, shorter hours Oct–May, next to recommended Hotel al Piave—see page 217, mobile 347-870-6452,
run by Massimo). **Lavanderia Gabriella** offers full service
(€15/load wash and dry, Mon–Fri 8:00–12:30, closed Sat–Sun;
with your back to the door of San Zulian Church, go over
Ponte dei Ferali, then take first right down Calle dei Armeni,
then first left on Rio Terra Colonne to #985; tel. 041-522-1758,
Elisabetta).

Tips for Tackling My Self-Guided Tours

Sightseeing can be hard work. The self-guided tours in this book are designed to help make your visits to Venice's finest museums meaningful, fun, fast, and painless. To get the most out of the tours, read the tour the night before your visit.

When you arrive at the sight, use the overview map to get the lay of the land and the basic tour route. Expect a few changes—paintings may be on tour, on loan, out sick, or shifted at the whim of the curator. To adapt, pick up any available free floor plans as you enter, or ask an information person to glance at this book's maps to confirm they're current. If you can't find a particular painting, just ask any museum worker. Point to the photograph in this book and ask, *"Dov'è?"* (doh-VEH, meaning "Where?").

The tours cover the highlights. You might want to supplement with an audioguide, a dry-but-useful recorded description in English (about €5).

Museums have their rules. For security reasons, you're often required to check even small bags, and every museum has a free checkroom at the entrance. They're safe. If you have

something you can't bear to part with, be prepared to stash it in a pocket or purse. Cameras are normally permitted in museums, but no flashes or tripods (without special permission). Video cameras are usually allowed. Many sights have "last entry" times 30–60 minutes before closing. Guards usher people out before the official closing time.

At the museum bookshop, thumb through a guidebook to be sure you haven't overlooked something of particular interest to you. If there's an on-site cafeteria, it's usually a good place to rest and have a snack or light meal. Museum WCs are free and generally clean.

And finally, every sight or museum offers infinitely more than the few stops I cover. Use these tours as an introduction—not the final word.

Travel Agencies: If you need to get train tickets, make seat reservations, or arrange a *cucetta* (koo-CHET-tah—a berth on a night train); you can avoid a time-consuming trip to the crowded train station by using a downtown travel agency. They can also give advice on cheap flights. Note that you'll get a far better price if you're able to book at least a week in advance. Consider booking flights for later in your trip while you're here.

American Express books flights, sells train tickets, and makes train reservations (Mon–Fri 9:00–17:30, closed Sat–Sun, about 2 blocks off St. Mark's Square en route to Accademia at Salizada San Moisè, 1471 San Marco, tel. 041-520-0844). Avoid their €5 phone card, which only buys you about a third as many minutes as similar cards sold by corner newsstands—one more thing to erode the trust they've earned over the decades.

Oltrex, just one bridge past the Bridge of Sighs, sells train and plane tickets and happily books train reservations for a €2 fee (daily 9:00–19:00, Riva degli Schiavoni 4192, tel. 041-524-2828).

English Church Services: The **San Zulian Church** (the only church in Venice that you can actually walk around) offers a Mass in English (generally Mon–Fri at 9:30 and Sun at 11:30 May–Sept, Sun only Oct–April, 2 blocks toward Rialto off St. Mark's Square).

Haircuts: I've been getting my hair cut at **Coiffeur Benito** for 16 years. Benito has been keeping local men and women trim for 26 years. He's an artist—actually a "hair sculptor"—and a cut here is a fun diversion from the tourist grind (€20 for women, €18 for men, Tue–Fri 8:30–13:00 & 15:30–19:30, Sat 8:30–13:00 only, closed Sun–Mon, behind San Zulian Church near St. Mark's Square, Calle S. Zulian Già del Strazzariol 592a, tel. 041-528-6221).

Getting Around Venice

On Foot: Navigate by major landmarks. There are signs on street corners all over town pointing to San Marco, Accademia, Ferrovia (train station), and Piazzale Roma (the bus stop behind the train station). Determine whether your destination is in the direction of a major signposted landmark, then follow the signs through the maze of squares, lanes, and bridges.

By Vaporetto: The public-transit system is a fleet of motorized bus-boats called *vaporetti*. They work like city buses except that they never get a flat, the stops are docks, and if you get off between stops, you might drown.

For most travelers, only two lines matter: #1 is the slow boat, which takes 45 minutes to make every stop along the entire length of the Grand Canal (leaves every 10 min); #2 is the fast boat that zips down the Grand Canal in 25 minutes (leaves every 10 min), stopping at Tronchetto (parking lot),

Piazzale Roma (bus station), Ferrovia (train station), Rialto Bridge, San Tomà (Frari Church), Accademia Bridge, San Marco (west end of St. Mark's Square), San Zaccaria (east end of St. Mark's Square), and on to San Giorgio Maggiore. Some #2 boats go only as far as Rialto *(solo Rialto)*—check with the conductor before boarding.

It's a simple system, but there are a few quirks. Some stops have just one dock for boats going in both directions, so make sure the boat you get on is pointing in the direction you want to go. Larger stops have two docks side by side (one for each direction), while some smaller stops have docks across the canal from each other (one for each direction). Check the signs to find the right dock. Electronic reader boards on busy docks display which boats are coming next and when. Signs on board indicate upcoming stops.

Some lines don't run early or late. For example, off-season the #2 fast vaporetto doesn't leave the San Marco–Vallaresso dock (at St. Mark's Square) until 9:15 (and runs only until 20:30); if you're trying to get from St. Mark's Square to the train station to catch an early train, you'd need to take a different fast boat that loops outside the Grand Canal. If there's any doubt, ask a ticket-seller or conductor. If you plan to ride a lot of *vaporetti*, consider picking up the most current ACTV timetable (free at ticket booths, in English and Italian, www.actv.it).

Standard single **tickets** are €6 each (a few shorter runs are only €2, such as the route from San Marco to Vallaresso to San Giorgio Maggiore and La Salute). Tickets are good for 60 minutes in one direction; you can hop on and off at stops during that time. Technically, you're not allowed a round-trip (though in practice, a round-trip is allowed if you can complete it within a 60-minute span). Buy tickets at the dock from ticket booths or from a conductor on board (do it before you sit down, or you risk being fined €30). Oversized luggage can cost a second ticket—but light packers have no worries.

You can also buy a **pass** for unlimited use of *vaporetti* and ACTV buses (sold in 12-hour increments—€13/12 hrs, €15/24 hrs, and so on up to €30/72 hrs). Because single tickets cost a hefty €6 a pop, these passes can pay for themselves in a hurry. And it's fun to be able to hop on and off spontaneously. On the other hand, many just walk and rarely use a boat—so before buying a pass, look at a map to see how far afield your likely destinations are.

Passes must be stamped before the first use. Tickets generally come already stamped, but if for whatever reason, your ticket lacks a stamp, stick it into the time-stamping yellow machine before boarding. Riding free? There's a one-in-ten chance a conductor will fine you €30.

For vaporetto fun, take the Grand Canal Cruise (see page 44). During rush hour (about 9:00 from the Tronchetto parking lot and train station toward St. Mark's, about 17:00 in the other direction), boats are jam-packed. If you like joyriding on *vaporetti*, ride a boat around the city and out into the lagoon, then over to the Lido, and back. Ask for the circular route—*circulare* (cheer-koo-LAH-ray). It's usually the #51 or #52, leaving from the San Zaccaria–Danieli vaporetto stop (near the Doge's Palace) and from all the stops along the perimeter of Venice.

By *Traghetto*: Only four bridges cross the Grand Canal, but

traghetti (gondolas) shuttle locals and in-the-know tourists across the Grand Canal at seven handy locations (see map on page 46; routes also marked on pricier maps sold in Venice). Most people stand while riding (€0.50, generally run 6:00–20:00, sometimes until 23:00, though a few run only until 14:00).

By Water Taxi: Venetian taxis, like speedboat limos, hang out at most busy points along the Grand Canal. Prices, which average €60, are a bit soft (about €60 to the train station or €90 to the airport for up to four people, extra fees for very early or late runs). Negotiate and settle on the price before stepping in. For travelers with lots of luggage or small groups who can split the cost, taxi rides can be a worthwhile and time-saving convenience—and skipping across the lagoon in a classic wooden motorboat is a cool indulgence. For €90 an hour, you can have a private taxi-boat tour.

By Gondola: To hire a gondolier for your own private cruise, see the Nightlife chapter, page 255.

TOURS

Avventure Bellissime Venice Tours—This company offers a selection of two-hour walks, including the basic St. Mark's Square introduction called the "Original Venice Walking Tour" (daily at 11:00; 45 min on the square, 15 min in the church, 60 min along back streets). Their other walks are Cannaregio and the Jewish Ghetto; San Polo and Dorsoduro (called "Original Hidden Venice Walk"); Doge's Palace (includes secret itinerary); Ghosts and Legends; and Secret Gardens (€20–25/person, cheaper for returnees and students,

Orientation

Floods

Venice floods about 100 times a year—but not because of tides (which are miniscule in the Mediterranean). It normally happens in March and November, when the winds blowing from the south (Egypt) combine with high barometric pressure over the southern Adriatic Sea to push water toward the sea's northern end.

Floods start in St. Mark's Square (the entry of the church is nearly the lowest spot in town). You might see stacked wooden benches in the square; during floods, the benches are placed end-to-end to create elevated sidewalks. If you think the square is crowded now, when it's flooded it turns into total gridlock, as all the people normally sharing the whole square jostle for space on these narrow wooden walkways. From a distance, it's quite a sight.

There are measuring devices at the outside base of the Campanile (near the exit, facing St. Mark's Square) that show the current sea level (livello marea). Find the mark that shows the high-water level from the terrible floods of 1966 (waist-level, at Campanile exit). When the water level rises one meter above mean sea level, a warning siren sounds, and it repeats if a serious flood is imminent. Imagine being a Venetian and hearing the alarm. You rush home to remove your carpets and raise your furniture above the incoming saltwater. Many doorways have three-foot-high wooden or metal barriers to block the high water (acqua alta), but the seawater still seeps in through floors and drains, rendering the barriers nearly useless. After the water recedes, you have to carefully clean everything it touched to minimize the damage caused by the corrosive seawater.

In 2006, the pavement around St. Mark's Square was taken up, and the entire height of the square was raised by adding a layer of sand, and then replacing the stones. If the columns along the ground floor of the Doge's Palace look stubby, it's because this process has been carried out many times over the centuries. Venice has been battling rising water levels since the fifth century. But today, with global warming, the water is winning.

€5 discount in 2008 for Rick Steves' readers who book online or call direct, group size 8–20, most tours last 2 hours and run rain or shine, English-language only, tel. 041-520-8616, mobile 340-050-2444, see www.tours-italy.com for details, info@tours-italy.com, Monica or Jonathan). The company also runs day trips to the Dolomites, Veneto hill towns, and Palladian villa tours (8-person maximum, varying prices, €10 discount if you say "Rick sent me").

Their 70-minute Grand Canal boat tour, offered daily at 16:30 (€40), is good. Tours are limited to about eight passengers. You'll enjoy a fascinating, relaxing look at the wonders of the Grand Canal as well as the intimate back canals with a motor-mouthed (and interesting) guide. The departure is timed to give photographers the best possible light.

Classic Venice Bars Tour—Debonair local guide Alessandro Schezzini is a connoisseur of Venetian *bacari*—classic old bars serving traditional *cicchetti* (local munchies). He offers evening tours that include sampling a snack and a glass of wine at three different *bacari*, and he'll answer all of your questions about Venice (€30/person with this book in 2008, March–Nov, generally Mon, Wed, and Fri at 18:00, other evenings and off-season by request and with demand, 6–8 per group, meet at top of Rialto Bridge, call or email a day or two in advance to confirm, mobile 335-530-9024, venische@libero.it).

Venicescapes—Michael Broderick's private theme tours of Venice are intellectually demanding and beyond the attention span of most mortal tourists. Rather than a "sightseeing tour," consider your time with Michael a rolling, graduate-level lecture. Michael's objective: to help visitors gain a more solid understanding of Venice. For a description of his various itineraries, see www.venicescapes.org (book well in advance, tours last 4–6 hours: €275 for 2 people, €50/person after that, plus admissions and transportation, tel. 041-520-6361, info@venicescapes.org).

Local Guides—Licensed guides are carefully trained and love explaining Venice to visitors. The following companies and guides give excellent tours to individuals, families, and small groups. If you organize a small group from your hotel at breakfast to split the cost (€65/hr with 2-hour minimum), the fee becomes quite reasonable.

Elisabetta Morelli is reliable, personable, and informative, giving good insight into daily life in Venice (€65/hr with this book in 2008, tours last 2–3 hours, tel. 041-526-7816, mobile 328-753-5220, bettamorelli@inwind.it).

Venice with a Guide is a co-op of 10 equally good guides (www.venicewithaguide.com).

Walks Inside Venice is a group of three women enthusiastic about teaching (€75/hr per group, 3-hour min; Cristina: mobile

348-341-5421; Roberta: mobile 347-253-0560; Sara: mobile 335-522-9714; www.walksinsidevenice.com, info@walksinsidevenice.com).

Alessandro Schezzini isn't a licensed Italian guide (and is therefore unable to take you into actual sights), but he does a great job getting you beyond the clichés and into offbeat Venice. He offers a relaxed, two-hour, back-street "Rick Steves" tour (€15/person, March–Nov, generally Mon, Wed, and Fri, meet at 16:00 at top of Rialto Bridge, call to confirm, mobile 335-530-9024, venische@libero.it). You can take this offbeat walk, and then join Alessandro for the pub crawl immediately afterwards (see "Classic Venice Bars Tour," above). Alessandro also gives private tours to groups of any size at any time (€90/2.5 hrs).

SIGHTS

Venice's greatest sight is the city itself. As well as seeing world-class museums and buildings, make time to wander narrow lanes, linger over a meal, or enjoy evening magic on St. Mark's Square.

In this chapter, don't judge a listing by its length. Some of Venice's most important sights have the shortest listings and are marked with a ✪ (and page number). These sights are covered in greater detail in one of the tours included in this book.

One of Venice's most delightful experiences—a gondola ride, worth ▲▲▲—is covered under Nightlife (see page 255).

San Marco District

▲▲▲**St. Mark's Square (Piazza San Marco)**—This grand square is surrounded by splashy, historic buildings and sights (each one described in more detail in the next few pages): St. Mark's Basilica, the Doge's Palace, the Campanile (bell tower), and the Correr Museum. The square is filled with music, lovers, pigeons, and tourists by day, and is your private rendezvous with the Venetian past late at night, when Europe's most magnificent dance floor is *the* romantic place to be.

For a slow and pricey evening thrill, invest about €15 (including the cover charge for the music) in a glass of wine or coffee at one of the elegant cafés with the dueling orchestras (see "Cafés on St. Mark's Square," page 63). For an unmatched experience that offers the best people-watching, it's worth the small splurge. But if all you have is €1, buy a bag of pigeon feed and become popular in a flurry. (To control the poopulation, the city adds bird birth control to the feed.) To get the flock to flutter airborne, toss your sweater in the air.

The **Clock Tower** (Torre dell'Orologio), built during the Renaissance in 1496, marks the entry to the main shopping drag,

Venice

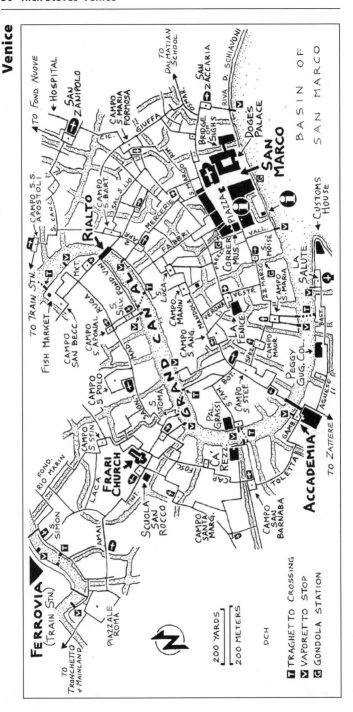

TO FOND NUOVE
TO HOSPITAL
SAN ZANIPOLO
CAMPO S. MARIA FORMOSA
TO DALMATIAN SCHOOL
SAN ZACCARIA
RIVA D. SCHIAVONI
GIUFFA
OSMAR.
CIC.
BRIDGE OF SIGHS
DOGE'S PALACE
SAN MARCO
BASIN OF SAN MARCO
CAMPO S.S. APOSTOLI
S. CANC.
CAMPO S. BART.
S. SAL.S. LIO
MERCERIE
S. MARCO
PIAZZA
RIALTO
CUSTOMS HOUSE
TO TRAIN STN.
MKT.
FISH MARKET
CORRER MUS.
FRESC.
VALL.
S. MOISE
LA SALUTE
FABBR.
APR.
S. LUCA
VERONA
VESTE
22 MARZO
CAMPO S. MARIA
BAST.
S. SILV. FOND. VIN.
CAMPO S. AFONAL RUGA
CAMPO SAN BECC.
CAMPO MANIN
MANDOLA
CAMPO S. ANG.
LA FENICE
CAMPO MAUR.
SPEZ.
PEGGY GUG. COL.
TO TRAIN STN.
TO ZATTERE
MAD.
CAMPO S. POLO
S. TOMA
GRAND CANAL
S. SAM. BOT.
CAMPO S. STEF.
PAL. GRASSI
AGUESE
ACCADEMIA
RIO FOND. MARIN
FOND. MARIN
S. SIMON
LACA
AMAI
FRARI CHURCH
TINT.
FOSC.
CA' REZZ.
GAMB.
TOLETTA
CAMPO S. STIN
CAMPO SANTA MARG.
SCUOLA SAN ROCCO
CAMPO SAN BARNABA
FERROVIA (TRAIN STN.)
TO TRONCHETTO & MAINLAND
PIAZZALE ROMA

200 YARDS
200 METERS

DCH

T TRAGHETTO CROSSING
V VAPORETTO STOP
G GONDOLA STATION

called the Mercerie, which connects St. Mark's Square with the Rialto. From the piazza, you can see the bronze men (Moors) swing their huge clappers at the top of each hour. In the 17th century, one of them knocked an unsuspecting worker off the top and to his death—probably the first-ever killing by a robot. Notice one of the world's first "digital" clocks on the tower facing the square (with dramatic flips every five minutes). The Clock Tower, with guided tours in English by reservation only, is not worth the headache to visit (€12, includes Correr Museum, Mon–Wed mornings and Thu–Sun afternoons; for details on reserving a visit, see page 100).

Venice's best **TI** is in the far-left (southwest) corner of the square (daily 9:00–15:30), and a €1 WC is 30 yards beyond St. Mark's Square (see *Albergo Diorno* sign marked on pavement, WC open daily 9:00–17:30). Another TI is on the lagoon (daily 10:00–18:00, walk toward the water by the Doge's Palace and go right, €1 WCs nearby).

For more about the square, ✪ see the St. Mark's Square Tour on page 56.

▲▲▲**St. Mark's Basilica (Basilica di San Marco)**—Built in the 11th century to replace an earlier church, this basilica's distinctly Eastern-style architecture underlines Venice's connection with Byzantium (which protected it from the ambition of Charlemagne and his Holy Roman Empire). It's decorated with booty from returning sea captains—a kind of architectural Venetian trophy chest. The interior glows mysteriously with gold mosaics and colored marble. Since about

A.D. 830, the saint's bones have been housed on this site.

Cost, Hours, Information: Basilica entry is free, open Mon–Sat 9:45–17:00 (until 16:30 off-season), Sun 14:00–16:00, tel. 041-522-5205. Lines can be long, the dress code is strictly enforced, and bag check is mandatory, free, and can save you time in line; for details, see page 67. No photos are allowed inside. Three separate exhibits inside each charge admission: the **Treasury** (€2, includes audioguide, same hours as church), the **Golden Altarpiece** (€2, same hours as church), and the **San Marco Museum** (€3, Mon–Sat 9:45–16:30, Sun 9:45–16:00). The San Marco Museum has the original bronze horses (copies overlook the square), a balcony offering a remarkable view over St. Mark's Square, and various works related to the church.

✪ See St. Mark's Basilica Tour on page 66.

Venice at a Glance

▲▲▲**St. Mark's Square** Venice's grand main square. **Hours:** Always open.

▲▲▲**St. Mark's Basilica** Cathedral with mosaics, saint's bones, treasury, museum, and viewpoint of square. **Hours:** Basilica— Mon–Sat 9:45–17:00 (until 16:30 off-season), Sun 14:00–16:00; San Marco Museum—Mon–Sat 9:45–16:30, Sun 9:45–16:00.

▲▲▲**Doge's Palace** Art-splashed palace of former rulers, with prison accessible through Bridge of Sighs. **Hours:** Daily April–Oct 9:00–19:00, Nov–March 9:00–17:00.

▲▲▲**Rialto Bridge** Distinctive bridge spanning the Grand Canal, with a market nearby for locals and tourists. **Hours:** Bridge—always open; market—souvenir stalls open daily, pro- duce market closed Sun, fish market closed Sun–Mon.

▲▲**Correr Museum** Venetian history and art. **Hours:** Daily April–Oct 9:00–19:00, Nov–March 9:00–17:00.

▲▲**Accademia** Venice's top art museum. **Hours:** Mon 8:15–14:00, Tue–Sun 8:15–19:15.

▲▲**Peggy Guggenheim Collection** Popular display of 20th- century art. **Hours:** Wed–Mon 10:00–18:00, closed Tue.

▲▲**Frari Church** Franciscan church featuring Renaissance mas- ters. **Hours:** Mon–Sat 10:00–18:00, Sun 13:00–18:00 (closed Sun in Aug).

▲▲**Scuola San Rocco** "Tintoretto's Sistine Chapel." **Hours:** Daily April–Oct 9:00–17:30, Nov–March 10:00–17:00.

▲**Campanile** Dramatic bell tower on St. Mark's Square with elevator to the top. **Hours:** Daily July–Aug 9:00–21:00, Sept–June 9:00–19:00.

▲**Bridge of Sighs** Famous enclosed bridge, part of Doge's Palace, near St. Mark's Square. **Hours:** Always viewable.

▲**San Giorgio Maggiore** Island across the lagoon featuring church with Palladio architecture, Tintoretto paintings, and fine views back on Venice. **Hours:** Daily May–Sept 9:00–12:00 & 14:30– 18:30, Oct–April 9:30–12:45 & 14:30–17:00, closed to sightseers Sun 11:00–12:00 during Mass.

closed *Tue* **Fortuny Museum** = The Birth of
Campo San Beneto
Art Deco.

Vaporeto stops Sant'Angelo or SanSamuele
#1   #2

▲**La Salute Church** Striking church dedicated to the Virgin Mary. **Hours:** Church—daily 9:00–12:15 & 14:30–17:30; Sacristy—Mon–Sat 10:00–12:00 & 15:00–17:00, Sun 15:00–17:00.

▲**Ca' Rezzonico** Posh Grand Canal palazzo with 18th-century Venetian art. **Hours:** April–Oct Wed–Mon 10:00–18:00, Nov–March Wed–Mon 10:00–17:00, closed Tue.

▲**Ca' Pesaro** International modern art gallery in a canalside palazzo. **Hours:** April–Oct Tue–Sun 10:00–18:00, Nov–March Tue–Sun 10:00–17:00, closed Mon.

▲**Dalmatian School** Exquisite Renaissance meeting house. **Hours:** Tue–Sat 9:15–13:00 & 14:15–18:00, Sun 9:15–13:00, closed Mon.

Church of San Zaccaria Final resting place of St. Zechariah (San Zaccaria), plus a Bellini altarpiece and an eerie crypt. **Hours:** Mon–Sat 10:00–12:00 & 16:00–18:00, Sun 16:00–18:00 only.

Church of San Polo Ninth-century church with works by Tintoretto, Veronese, and Tiepolo. **Hours:** Mon–Sat 10:00–17:00, closed Sun.

Jewish Ghetto Neighborhood and Jewish Museum. **Hours:** Museum open June–Sept Sun–Fri 10:00–17:00, Oct–May Sun–Fri 10:00–16:30, closed Sat and Jewish holidays.

Ca' d'Oro Venetian Gothic palace with temporary exhibits, fronting the Grand Canal. **Hours:** Mon 8:15–14:00, Tue–Sun 8:15–19:15.

Murano Island famous for glass factories and glassmaking museum. **Hours:** Glass museum open April–Oct Thu–Tue 10:00–18:00, Nov–March Thu–Tue 10:00-17:00, closed Wed.

Burano Sleepy lacemaking island with lace museum. **Hours:** Lace museum open April–Oct Wed–Mon 10:00–17:00, Nov–March Wed–Mon 10:00–16:00, closed Tue.

Torcello Near-deserted island with old church, bell tower, and museum. **Hours:** Most sights open daily March–Oct 10:30–18:00, Nov–Feb 10:00–16:30, museum closed Mon.

▲▲▲**Doge's Palace (Palazzo Ducale)**—The seat of the Venetian government and home of its ruling duke, or doge, this was the most powerful half-acre in Europe for 400 years. The Doge's Palace was built to show off the power and wealth of the Republic. The doge lived with his family on the first floor near the halls of power. From his once-lavish (now sparse) quarters, you'll follow the one-way tour through the public rooms of the top floor, finishing with the Bridge of Sighs and the prison. The place is wallpapered with masterpieces by Veronese and Tintoretto. Don't worry much about the great art. Enjoy the building.

Cost and Hours: €13 for Museum Card, also includes admission to the Correr Museum (both sights also covered by €18 Museum Pass). If the line is long at the Doge's Palace, buy your ticket at the Correr Museum across the square; then you can go directly through the Doge's turnstile without waiting in the long line. Open daily April–Oct 9:00–19:00, Nov–March 9:00–17:00, last entry 1 hour before closing.

Tours: Consider the €5 audioguide or the Secret Itineraries Tour, which takes you into palace rooms otherwise not open to the public (€16; in English at 9:55, 10:45 and 11:35; 75 min, call 041-291-5911 to reserve tour same day or a day in advance, or call 041-520-9070 if more than 2 days in advance, www.museiciviciveneziani.it).

❂ See Doge's Palace Tour on page 85.

▲▲**Correr Museum (Museo Civico Correr)**—This uncrowded museum gives you a good overview of Venetian history and art. The doge memorabilia, armor, banners, statues (by Canova), and paintings (by the Bellini family and others) re-create the festive days of the Venetian Republic. There are English descriptions and breathtaking views of St. Mark's Square throughout the museum.

Cost and Hours: Covered by €13 Museum Card, which also includes the Doge's Palace (both are also covered by €18 Museum Pass). Open daily April–Oct 9:00–19:00, Nov–March 9:00–17:00, last entry 1 hour before closing, enter at far end of square directly opposite basilica, tel. 041-240-5211, www.museiciviciveneziani.it.

❂ See Correr Museum Tour on page 100.

▲**Campanile (Campanile di San Marco)**—This dramatic bell tower replaced a shorter lighthouse, once part of the original fortress/palace that guarded the entry of the Grand Canal. The lighthouse crumbled into a pile of bricks in 1902, a thousand years after it was built. Ride the elevator 300 feet to the top of the reconstructed bell tower for the best view in Venice. For an ear-shattering experience, be on top when the bells ring (€6, daily July–Aug 9:00–21:00, Sept–June 9:00–19:00). The golden angel at the top always faces into the wind. Lines are longest at midday; beat the crowds and enjoy crisp morning air at 9:00, or try in the early evening (around 18:00).

A Dying City?

Venice's population (62,000) is half what it was 30 years ago, and people are leaving at a rate of a thousand a year. Of those who stay, 25 percent are 65 or older.

Sad, yes, but imagine raising a family here: Apartments are small, high up, and expensive. (A 1,000-square-foot studio can sell for up to a million dollars.) Humidity and occasional flooding make basic maintenance a pain. Home-improvement projects require navigating miles of red tape, and you must follow regulations intended to preserve the historical ambience. Everything is expensive because it has to be shipped in from the mainland. You can easily get glass and tourist trinkets, but it's hard to find groceries or get your shoes fixed. Running basic errands involves lots of walking and stairs—imagine crossing over arched bridges while pushing a child in a stroller and carrying a day's worth of groceries.

With over 12 million visitors a year, on any given day, Venetians are likely outnumbered by tourists. Despite government efforts to subsidize rents and build cheap housing, the city is losing its locals. The economy itself is thriving, thanks to tourist dollars and rich foreigners buying second homes. But the culture is dying. Even the most hopeful city planners worry that in a few decades, Venice will not be a city at all, but a museum, a cultural theme park, a decaying Disneyland.

For more on the Campanile, ✪ see the St. Mark's Square Tour on page 56.

La Fenice Opera House (Gran Teatro alla Fenice)—During Venice's glorious decline in the 18th century, this was one of seven opera houses in the city. A 1996 arson fire completely gutted the theater, but La Fenice ("The Phoenix") has risen from the ashes, thanks to an eight-year effort to rebuild the historic landmark according to photographic archives of the interior. To see the results at their most glorious, attend an evening performance. If you visit, you'll see a grand lobby and the theater itself—saccharine and bringing sadness to locals who remember the richness of the place before the fire (€7 entry fee includes 45-minute audioguide, generally open daily 10:00–16:00, may be closed for practice or performance, concert box office open daily 9:30–18:30, www.teatrolafenice.it).

Behind St. Mark's Basilica
Diocesan Museum (Museo Diocesano)—This little-known museum circles a peaceful Romanesque courtyard immediately behind the basilica (just before the Bridge of Sighs). It's filled with

plunder from the Venetian Empire that never found a place in St. Mark's (€1 for cloister but the good stuff upstairs comes with an €8 fee, daily 10:00–18:00, tel. 041-522-9166).

▲**Bridge of Sighs**—Connecting two wings of the Doge's Palace high over a canal, this enclosed bridge was popularized by travelers in the Romantic 19th century. Supposedly, a condemned man would be led over this bridge on his way to the prison, take one last look at the glory of Venice, and sigh. While overhyped, the bridge is undeniably tingle-worthy—especially after dark, when the crowds have dispersed and it's just you and floodlit Venice. It's around the corner from the Doge's Palace: Walk toward the waterfront, turn left along the water, and look up the first canal on your left. You can actually cross the bridge (from the inside) by visiting the Doge's Palace.

❍ See St. Mark's to San Zaccaria Walk on page 202; also see Doge's Palace Tour on page 85.

Church of San Zaccaria—This historic church is home to a sometimes-waterlogged crypt, a Bellini altarpiece, a Tintoretto painting, and the final resting place of St. Zechariah, the father of John the Baptist (free, €1 to enter crypt, €0.50 coin to light up Bellini's altarpiece, Mon–Sat 10:00–12:00 & 16:00–18:00, Sun 16:00–18:00 only, 2 canals behind St. Mark's Basilica).

❍ See St. Mark's to San Zaccaria Walk on page 202.

Across the Lagoon from St. Mark's Square

▲**San Giorgio Maggiore**—This is the dreamy island you can see from the waterfront by St. Mark's Square. The striking church, designed by Palladio, features art by Tintoretto and good views of Venice (free entry to church, daily May–Sept 9:00–12:00 & 14:30–18:30, Oct–April 9:30–12:45 & 14:30–17:00, closed Sun 11:00–12:00 to sightseers during Mass, Gregorian Mass sung Mon–Sat at 8:00, Sun at 11:00). The church's bell tower costs €3 and is accessible by elevator until 30 minutes before the church closes. To reach the island from St. Mark's Square, take the five-minute vaporetto ride (€2, 6/hr) on #2 from the San Zaccaria–M.V.E. stop (the San Zaccaria dock farthest from the Bridge of Sighs, 50 yards past the big equestrian statue).

❍ See San Giorgio Maggiore Tour on page 175.

Dorsoduro District

▲▲**Accademia (Galleria dell'Accademia)**—Venice's top art museum, packed with highlights of the Venetian Renaissance, features paintings by the Bellini family, Titian, Tintoretto, Veronese, Tiepolo, Giorgione, Canaletto, and Testosterone. It's just over the wooden Accademia Bridge from the San Marco action (€6.50, Mon 8:15–14:00, Tue–Sun 8:15–19:15, last entry

30 min before closing, no photos allowed, info tel. 041-522-2247, www.gallerieaccademia.org). Expect long lines in the late morning, because they allow only 300 visitors in at a time; visit early or late to miss the crowds, or make a reservation at least a day in advance (call 041-520-0345 or visit www.gallerieaccademia.org and click "Prenotazione"). The dull audioguide costs €4 (€6 for double set or Palm Pilot). One-hour guided tours in English are €5 (€7/2 people, Sat–Sun at 11:00).

✪ See Accademia Tour on page 114.

At the Accademia Bridge, there's a decent canalside pizzeria (Pizzeria Accademia Foscarini—see page 241) and a public WC at the base of the bridge.

▲▲Peggy Guggenheim Collection—The popular museum of far-out art, housed in the American heiress' former retirement palazzo, offers one of Europe's best reviews of the art of the first half of the 20th century. Stroll through styles represented by artists whom Peggy knew personally—Cubism (Picasso, Braque), Surrealism (Dalí, Ernst), Futurism (Boccioni), American Abstract Expressionism (Pollock), and a sprinkling of Klee, Calder, and Chagall (€10, generally includes temporary exhibits, Wed–Mon 10:00–18:00, closed Tue, last entry 15 min before closing, audioguide-€7, mini-guidebook-€5, free and mandatory baggage check, pricey café, photos allowed only in garden and terrace—a fine and relaxing perch overlooking Grand Canal, near Accademia, Dorsoduro 704, tel. 041-240-5440, www.guggenheim-venice.it). The place is staffed by international interns working on art-related degrees.

✪ See Peggy Guggenheim Collection Tour on page 157.

▲La Salute Church (Santa Maria della Salute)—This impressive church with a crown-shaped dome was built and dedicated to the Virgin Mary by grateful survivors of the 1630 plague (church—free, daily 9:00–12:15 & 14:30–17:30; sacristy—€1.50, Mon–Sat 10:00–12:00 & 15:00–17:00, Sun 15:00–17:00; tel. 041-274-3928 to confirm). It's a 10-minute walk from the Accademia Bridge; the Salute vaporetto stop is at its doorstep (the San Marco–Vallaresso to Salute vaporetto hop is €2). While the dome will likely be covered in scaffolding in 2008, the interior is marvelous.

✪ See La Salute Church Tour on page 170.

▲Ca' Rezzonico (Museum of 18th-Century Venice)—This grand Grand Canal palazzo offers the best look in town at the life of Venice's rich and famous in the 1700s. Wander under ceilings by Tiepolo, among furnishings from that most decadent century, enjoying views of the canal and paintings by Guardi, Canaletto, and Longhi (€6.50, April–Oct Wed–Mon 10:00–18:00, Nov–March Wed–Mon 10:00–17:00, closed Tue, last entry 1 hour before closing, audioguide-€4 or €6/double set, free and mandatory baggage check, at Ca' Rezzonico vaporetto stop, tel. 041-241-0100).

✪ See Ca' Rezzonico Tour on page 145.

Santa Croce District

▲▲▲**Rialto Bridge**—One of the world's most famous bridges, this distinctive and dramatic stone structure crosses the Grand Canal with a single confident span. The arcades along the top of the bridge help reinforce the structure...and offer some enjoyable shopping diversions, as does the **market** surrounding the bridge (souvenir stalls open daily, produce market closed Sun, fish market closed Sun–Mon).

✪ See St. Mark's to Rialto Walk on page 192.

▲**Ca' Pesaro International Gallery of Modern Art**—This museum features 19th- and early-20th-century art in a 17th-century canalside palazzo. The collection is strongest on Italian (especially Venetian) artists, but also presents a broad array of other well-known artists. The highlights are in one large room: Klimt's beautiful/creepy *Judith II,* with eagle-talon fingers; Kandinsky's *White Zig Zags* (plus other recognizable shapes); the colorful *Nude in the Mirror* by Bonnard that flattens the 3-D scene into a 2-D pattern of rectangles; and Chagall's surprisingly realistic portrait of his hometown rabbi, *The Rabbi of Vitebsk.* The adjoining Room VII features small-scale works by Matisse, Max Ernst, Mark Tobey, and a Calder mobile. Admission also includes an Oriental Art wing (€5.50, April–Oct Tue–Sun 10:00–18:00, Nov–March Tue–Sun 10:00–17:00, closed Mon, last entry 1 hour before closing, located a 2-minute walk from the San Stae vaporetto stop, tel. 041-524-0695).

18th-Century Costume Museum—The Museo di Palazzo Mocenigo offers a walk through six rooms of a fine 17th-century mansion with period furnishings, family portraits, ceilings painted (c. 1790) with family triumphs (the Mocenigos produced seven doges), Murano glass chandeliers in situ, and a paltry collection of costumes with sparse descriptions (€4, Tue–Sun 10:00–17:00, closed Mon, a block in from the San Stae vaporetto stop, tel. 041-524-0695).

San Polo District

▲▲**Frari Church (Chiesa dei Frari)**—My favorite art experience in Venice is seeing art in the setting for which it was designed—as it is at the Frari Church. The Franciscan "Church of the Brothers" and the art that decorates it is warmed by the spirit of St. Francis. It features the work of three great Renaissance masters: Donatello, Giovanni Bellini, and Titian—each showing worshippers the glory of God in human terms (€2.50, Mon–Sat 10:00–18:00, Sun 13:00–18:00, closed Sun in Aug, last entry 15 min before closing, audioguide-€1.60 or €2.60/double set, modest dress recommended,

San Polo District

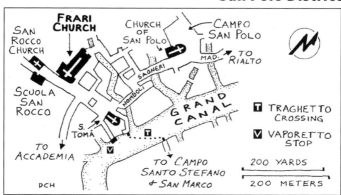

tel. 041-272-8618). The church often hosts evening concerts (€15, buy ticket at church; for concert details, look for fliers, call 041-272-8611, or check www.basilicadeifrari.it).

○ See Frari Church Tour on page 137; if you'll be walking to the church from the Rialto Bridge, see the St. Mark's to Rialto Walk on page 192.

▲▲Scuola San Rocco—Sometimes called "Tintoretto's Sistine Chapel," this lavish meeting hall (next to the Frari Church) has some 50 large, colorful Tintoretto paintings plastered to the walls and ceilings. The best paintings are upstairs, especially the *Crucifixion* in the smaller room. View the neck-breaking splendor with one of the mirrors *(specchio)* available at the entrance (€7, includes informative audioguide, daily April–Oct 9:00–17:30, Nov–March 10:00–17:00, last entry 30 min before closing, or see a concert here—tickets run €15-30—and arrive 30 min early to enjoy the art as an evening bonus, tel. 041-523-4864, www .scuolagrandesanrocco.it).

○ See Scuola San Rocco Tour on page 127; also see St. Mark's to Rialto Walk on page 192.

Church of San Polo—This nearby church, which pales in comparison to the two sights just listed, is worth a visit for art-lovers. One of Venice's oldest churches (from the ninth century), San Polo features works by Tintoretto, Veronese, and Tiepolo and son (€2.50, Mon–Sat 10:00–17:00, closed Sun, last entry 15 min before closing).

○ See St. Mark's to Rialto Walk, page 192.

Cannaregio District

Jewish Ghetto—In medieval times, Jews were grudgingly allowed to do business in Venice, but only starting in 1385 were they allowed to live there (subject to strict laws and special taxes).

Anti-Semitic forces tried to oust them from the city, but in 1516, the doge compromised by restricting Jews to a special (undesirable) neighborhood. It was located on an easy-to-isolate island near the former foundry *(geto)*, coining the word "ghetto" for a segregated neighborhood.

The population swelled with immigrants from Germany, reaching 5,000 in the 1600s, the Golden Age of Venice's Jews. Restricted within their tiny neighborhood (the Ghetto *Nuovo*, or "New Ghetto"), they expanded upward, building six-story "skyscrapers" that still stand today. The community's five synagogues were built atop the high-rise tenements. (As space was very tight and you couldn't live above a house of worship, this was the most practical use of precious land.) Only two synagogues are still active. You can spot them (with their five windows) from the square, but to visit them you have to book a tour through the Jewish Museum (listed below).

The island's two bridges were locked up at night, when only Jewish doctors—coming to the aid of Venetians—were allowed to come and go. Eventually the ghetto community outgrew its original island, and the ghetto spread to adjacent blocks.

Getting There: It's a five-minute walk from the train station. Exiting the station, turn left and walk along the main route (Lista di Spagna). Immediately after crossing the first bridge, turn left and walk 50 yards to a small covered alleyway (Sottoportego del Ghetto) between the *farmacia* and the Gam-Gam Kosher Restaurant. This is your entrance to the Ghetto.

◉ **Self-Guided Tour:** Walk down Sottoportego del Ghetto past a few kosher-food places and Jewish-themed stores, cross a canal, and enter the main square.

Campo di Ghetto Nuovo must have been quite a scene in the past, ringed by 70 shops and with all of Venice's Jewish commerce compressed onto this one spot. As late as the 1930s, 12,000 Jews called Venice home, but today there are only 500—and only a few dozen live in the actual Ghetto. The square is still surrounded by the six-story "skyscrapers" that once made this a densely packed neighborhood.

Today the square, with its three cistern wells, is quiet. You'll see the large Jewish senior center/community center (Casa Israelitica di Riposo), flanked by two different Holocaust memorials by the Lithuanian artist Arbit Blatas. The barbed wire and bronze plaques remind us that it was on this spot that the Nazis rounded up 200 Jews for deportation (only eight returned). At #2884A is the Chabad, a welcome center that helps visiting Jews find places to pray, get kosher food, and so on. The Locanda del Ghetto is the city's only kosher hotel. At the far end of the square (near #2900, to the right of the Jewish Museum) is an old plaque in Hebrew.

Water, Water Everywhere, but...

As you explore Venice, notice the wells that grace nearly every square. Well water in the middle of the sea? Venice, surrounded by water, originally had no natural source of drinking  water. For centuries, locals collected water from the mainland with much effort and risk. Eventually, in the ninth century, they devised a way to collect rainwater by using town squares as catchment systems. The rain falls into the square, flows down through the slightly sloped pavement, drains through the limestone grates, and filters through sand into a large clay tub under the pavement. Citizens could drop their buckets down the "well" to draw up fresh rainwater. With a safe local source of drinking water, Venice's population began to grow. Several thousand of these cisterns provided lagoon communities with drinking water right up until 1886, when an aqueduct was built (paralleling the railroad tracks across the lagoon) to bring in water from nearby mountains. Since then, the clay tubs have rotted out and the wells have been capped. Now, with a high tide, the floods show first on these limestone grates, which mark the low point of each town square.

The **Jewish Museum** (Museo Ebraico) offers two things: a museum and a synagogue. The humble two-room museum has silver menorahs, cloth covers for the Torah scrolls, various religious objects, artifacts of the old community, and scant English explanations (€3, June–Sept Sun–Fri 10:00–17:00, Oct–May Sun–Fri 10:00–16:30, closed Sat and Jewish holidays, Campo di Ghetto Nuovo, tel. 041-715-359, small café and bookstore). To see the **synagogue,** you must sign up for a half-hour English tour (€8.50, tours run hourly June–Sept Sun–Fri 10:30–17:30, Oct–May Sun–Fri 10:30–16:30, closed Sat and Jewish holidays).

Exiting the square through Sottoportego de Ghetto Nuovo (a different street from the one you came in on), you'll cross the main road that runs between the train station and San Marco. Just beyond that is the San Marcuola vaporetto stop.

Ca' d'Oro—This "House of Gold" palace, fronting the Grand Canal, is quintessential Venetian Gothic (Gothic seasoned with Byzantine and Islamic accents). Inside, there's little to see aside from special exhibitions (€5, Mon 8:15–14:00, Tue–Sun 8:15–19:15, free peek through hole in door of courtyard, Calle Ca' d'Oro 3932).

❂ See Grand Canal Cruise on page 44.

Castello District

▲Dalmatian School (Scuola Dalmata di San Giorgio)—This "school" (which means "meeting place") is a reminder that Venice was Europe's most cosmopolitan place in its heyday—the original melting-pot community. There were about a hundred such "schools" for various ethnic, religious, and economic groups in the city. The government supported these gathering places for foreigners, because they could then keep an eye on them.

It was here that the Dalmatians (from the southern coast of present-day Croatia) worshiped in their own way, held neighborhood meetings, and worked to preserve their culture. The chapel on the ground floor happens to have the most exquisite Renaissance interior in Venice, with a cycle of paintings by Carpaccio ringing the room; be sure to pick up the English descriptions to the right of the entrance.

The scenes tell a fascinating story about St. George, the patron saint from the Croatian hometown of this brotherhood living together in Venice. On the far left, George jams a spear through the skull of a dragon, to the relief of the damsel in obvious distress. Notice half a damsel on the ground—good thing George got there in time. Next, George is shown with the defeated dragon (spear still in his head) before the thankful, wealthy mom and dad. In the third panel (left of altar), mom and dad—also the queen and king of a pagan tribe—convert to Christianity (€3, Tue–Sat 9:15–13:00 & 14:15–18:00, Sun 9:15–13:00, closed Mon, last entry 30 min before closing, between St. Mark's Square and Arsenale, on Calle dei Furlani, 3 blocks southeast of Campo San Lorenzo, tel. 041-522-8828).

Santa Elena—For a pleasant peek into a completely non-touristy, residential side of Venice, walk or catch vaporetto #1 from St. Mark's Square to the neighborhood of Santa Elena (at the fish's tail). This 100-year-old suburb lives as if there were no tourism. You'll find a kid-friendly park, a few lazy restaurants, and beautiful sunsets over San Marco.

La Biennale—Every odd year (next in 2009), Venice hosts a world's fair of contemporary art. Countries around the world send their best and most outrageous art to be displayed in buildings and pavilions scattered over the Giardini park and the Arsenale. Some artists convert entire buildings into a single installation, creating a weird wonderland of colors, video images, stage fog, laser lights, and piped-in sound. The festival is an excuse for temporary art

Sights

exhibitions, concerts, and other cultural events around the city (take vaporetto #1 or #2 to Giardini–Biennale stop; for the latest—including a calendar of events—see www.labiennale.org).

Venice's Lagoon

With more time, venture to some nearby islands in Venice's lagoon. While still somewhat touristy, they offer an escape from the crowds, a chance to get out on a boat, and some enjoyable museums for fans of glassmaking and lace. For more on all of these sights, ✪ see Venice's Lagoon Tour on page 182.

Murano—This island, famous for its glassmaking, is home to several glass factories and the **Glass Museum** (Museo Vetrario), which traces the history of this delicate art (€5.50, April–Oct Thu–Tue 10:00–18:00, Nov–March Thu–Tue 10:00–17:00, closed Wed, tel. 041-739-586).

Burano—This island's claim to fame is lacemaking, and the easiest one-stop opportunity to learn more is at the **Lace Museum** (Museo del Merletto di Burano, €4, closed for renovation through fall of 2008, then likely open April–Oct Wed–Mon 10:00–17:00, Nov–March Wed–Mon 10:00–16:00, closed Tue, tel. 041-730-034).

Torcello—This sparsely populated island features what's claimed to be Venice's oldest church. With impressive mosaics, a climbable bell tower, and a modest museum of Roman sculpture and medieval sculpture and manuscripts, the church is worth a wander (€3 for any one sight, €5.50 for any two sights, or €8 for all sights plus an audioguide; most sights open daily March–Oct 10:30–18:00, Nov–Feb 10:00–16:30, museum closed Mon; museum tel. 041-730-761, church/bell tower tel. 041-730-119).

GRAND CANAL CRUISE

Take a joyride and introduce yourself to Venice by boat. Cruise the Canal Grande all the way to San Marco, starting from Tronchetto (parking lot), Piazzale Roma (where the airport bus stops), or Ferrovia (train station).

If it's your first trip down the Grand Canal, you might want to stow this book and just take it all in—Venice is a barrage on the senses that hardly needs a narration. But these notes give the cruise a little meaning and help orient you to this great city.

While the Grand Canal is done in 25 minutes on boat #2, this tour is designed to be done on the slow boat #1 (which takes about 45 minutes). If you can, grab a seat in the front of the boat (unfortunately, a few #1 boats have no public access to the bow). If you find yourself stuck on the side, that works, too—but you'll be standing and walking back and forth at times (the left side is a bit better). Try to avoid sitting in the back, only because you'll miss the wonderful forward views.

To help you enjoy the visual parade of canal wonders, I've organized this tour by boat stop, pointing out both what you can see from the stop and what to look forward to as you cruise to the next stop.

ORIENTATION

Cost: €6 for a 60-minute vaporetto ticket (or covered by a pass; see page 24).

Hours: Enjoy the best light and the fewest crowds by riding late in the day. Sunset bathes the buildings in gold. After dark, chandeliers light up building interiors. "Rush hour" in the direction of this tour (heading toward San Marco) is morning, when local workers and tourists staying on the mainland commute into town. In the evening, the crowds head home and you'll find boats going toward San Marco relatively empty. Boats run every 10 minutes.

Getting There: Start at Tronchetto (the bus and car park), Piazzale Roma (buses from the airport), or Ferrovia (the Santa Lucia train station). When catching your boat, confirm that you're on a "San Marco via Rialto" boat (some boats finish at the Rialto Bridge while others take a non-scenic outside route). The conductor announces *"Solo Rialto!"* for boats going only as far as Rialto. Those boarding at Tronchetto and Piazzale Roma are most likely to find empty seats. Wherever and whenever you board, make a bee-line for the front, as that's where tourists generally go first.

Stops to Consider: You can break up the tour by hopping on and off at various sights you'll pass along the way—most of them are described in greater depth elsewhere in this book (but remember, your vaporetto ticket is good for only 60 minutes). These are all worth considering as hop-off spots: San Marcuola (near the Jewish Ghetto), Mercato Rialto (for a look at the market and a walk across the famous bridge), Ca' Rezzonico (for its Museum of 18th-Century Venice), Accademia (for the Accademia art museum and the nearby Guggenheim Collection), and Salute (to check out the huge and interesting La Salute church).

Information: Some city maps (on sale at postcard racks) have a handy Grand Canal map on the back.

Length of This Tour: Allow 45 minutes on vaporetto #1, or 25 minutes on vaporetto #2.

Starring: Palaces, markets, boats, bridges—Venice.

THE TOUR BEGINS

While you wait for your boat, here's some background on Venice's "Main Street."

At more than two miles long, nearly 150 feet wide, and nearly  15 feet deep, the Grand Canal is the city's largest, lined with its most impressive palaces. It's the remnant of a river that once spilled from the mainland into the Adriatic. The sediment it carried formed barrier islands that cut Venice off from the sea, forming a lagoon.

Venice was built on the marshy islands of the former delta, sitting on pilings driven nearly 15 feet into the clay (alder was the

Grand Canal

Grand Canal

Vaporetto Stops

1. Ferrovia
2. Riva de Biasio
3. San Marcuola
4. San Stae
5. Ca' d'Oro
6. Mercato Rialto
7. Rialto
8. San Silvestro
9. Sant'Angelo
10. San Tomà
11. Ca' Rezzonico
12. Accademia
13. Santa Maria del Giglio
14. Salute
15. San Marco
16. San Zaccaria

preferred wood). About 25 miles of canals drain the city, dumping like streams into the Grand Canal. Technically, Venice has only three canals: Grand, Giudecca, and Cannaregio. The 45 small waterways that dump into the Grand Canal are referred to as rivers (e.g., Rio Nuovo).

Venice is a city of palaces, dating from the days when Venice was the world's richest city. The most lavish palaces formed a grand chorus line along the Grand Canal. Once frescoed in reds and

blues, with black-and-white borders and gold-leaf trim, they made Venice a city of dazzling color. This cruise is the only way to truly appreciate the palaces, approaching them at water level, where their main entrances were located. Today, strict laws prohibit any changes in these buildings, so while landowners gnash their teeth, we can enjoy Europe's best-preserved medieval city—slowly rotting. Many of the grand buildings are now vacant. Others harbor chandeliered elegance above mossy, empty (often flooded) ground floors.

❶ Ferrovia

The **Santa Lucia train station,** one of the few modern buildings in town, was built in 1954. It's been the gateway into Venice since

1860, when the first station was built. "F.S." stands for "Ferrovie dello Stato," the Italian state railway system.

More than 20,000 people a day commute in from the mainland, making this the busiest part of Venice during rush hour. To alleviate some of the congestion and make the commute easier, a new **bridge** (slated to be finished by 2008) will span the Grand Canal between the train station and Piazzale Roma, behind you (see sidebar).

Opposite the train station, atop the green dome of **San Simeone Piccolo** church, St. Simeon waves *ciao* to whomever enters or leaves the "old" city. The pink church with the white Carrara-marble facade, just beyond the train station, is the **Church of the Scalzi** (Church of the Barefoot, named after the shoeless Carmelite monks), where the last doge (Venetian ruler) rests. It looks relatively new because it was partially rebuilt after being bombed in 1915 by Austrians aiming (poorly) at the train station.

❷ Riva de Biasio

Venice's main thoroughfare is busy with all kinds of **boats:** taxis, police boats, garbage boats, ambulances, construction cranes, and even brown-and-white UPS boats. Somehow they all manage to share the canal in relative peace.

About 25 yards past the Riva de Biasio stop, you'll look left down the broad **Cannaregio Canal** to see what was the **Jewish**

A New Bridge over the Grand Canal?

Venice's new **Calatrava Bridge,** slated for completion by 2008, is a modern structure of glass, steel, and stone. Only the fourth bridge to cross the Grand Canal, it links—or will link—the train station with Piazzale Roma. Many Venetians wonder whether it'll be done on time...if at all. Sections of the bridge are being constructed in a nearby warehouse and, when completed, will be ferried to their place and assembled. Skeptics doubt that some sections of the span of the bridge (just under 310 feet total) will be able to squeeze through Venice's narrow canals and tight corners.

The bridge was designed by Spanish architect Santiago Calatrava, whose other projects include the City of Arts and Sciences Museum in his hometown of Valencia, Spain; the twisting torso skyscraper in Malmö, Sweden; and the Olympic Sports complex in Athens, Greece.

This controversial bridge draws snorts from Venetians, who've been waiting two years for its inauguration while construction was delayed by politics and finances. With an original price tag of €4 million, the cost is currently around €6.5 million. The modern design of the bridge is also a sore point for a city with such rich medieval and Renaissance architecture—but Calatrava's structure is intended to "bridge" the old traditions of the city with modern forms, using local Istrian stone to smooth the transition.

Adding fuel to the controversy is the fact that the sleek form does not allow for wheelchair access, which would clutter up the lines of the bridge. Critics also question whether it'll withstand the daily hordes of tourists. Time will tell.

ghetto (see page 39). The twin, pale-pink, six-story "skyscrapers"—the tallest buildings you'll see at this end of the canal—are reminders of how densely populated the world's original ghetto was. Set aside as the local Jewish quarter in 1516, this area became extremely crowded. This urban island developed into one of the most closely knit business and cultural quarters of all the Jewish communities in Italy, and gave us our word "ghetto" (from *geto*, the copper foundry located here).

❸ San Marcuola

At this stop, facing a tiny square just ahead, stands the unfinished church of San Marcuola, one of only five churches fronting the Grand Canal. Centuries ago, this canal was a commercial drag of expensive real estate in high demand by wealthy merchants. About 20 yards ahead on the right stands the stately gray **Turkish "Fondaco" Exchange,** one of the oldest houses in Venice. Its

horseshoe arches and roofline of triangles and dingleballs are reminders of its Byzantine heritage. Turkish traders in turbans docked here, unloaded their goods into the warehouse on the bottom story, then went upstairs for a home-style meal and a place to sleep. Venice in the 1500s was very cosmopolitan, welcoming every religion and ethnicity, so long as they carried cash. (Today the building contains the city's Museum of Natural History—and Venice's only dinosaur.)

Just 100 yards ahead on the left, Venice's **Casinò** is housed in the palace where German composer Richard *(The Ring)* Wagner died in 1883. See his distinct, strong-jawed profile in the white plaque on the brick wall. In the 1700s, Venice was Europe's Vegas, with casinos and prostitutes everywhere. Casinòs ("little houses") have long provided Italians with a handy escape from daily life. Today they're run by the state to keep Mafia influence at bay. Notice the fancy front porch, rolling out the red carpet for high rollers arriving by taxi or hotel boat.

❹ San Stae

The San Stae Church sports a delightful Baroque facade. Opposite the San Stae stop, look for the peeling plaster that once made up **frescoes** (scant remains on the lower floors). Imagine the facades of the Grand Canal at their finest. As colorful as the city is today, it's still only a faded sepia-toned remnant of a long-gone era, a time of lavishly decorated, brilliantly colored palaces.

Just ahead, jutting out a bit on the right, is the ornate white facade of **Ca' Pesaro.** *"Ca'"* is short for *casa* (house). Because only the house of the doge (Venetian ruler) could be called a palace *(palazzo),* all other Venetian palaces are technically *"Ca'."*

In this city of masks, notice how the rich marble facades along the Grand Canal mask what are generally just simple, no-nonsense brick buildings. Most merchants enjoyed showing off. However, being smart businessmen, they only decorated the side of the buildings that would be seen and appreciated. But look back as you pass Ca' Pesaro (which houses the International Gallery of Modern Art—see page 38). It's the only building you'll see with a fine side facade. Ahead, on the left, with its glorious triple-decker medieval arcade (just before the next stop) is Ca' d'Oro.

❺ Ca' d'Oro

The lacy **Ca' d'Oro** (House of Gold) is the best example of Venetian Gothic architecture on the canal. Its three stories offer differ-

ent variations on balcony design, topped with a spiny white roofline. Venetian Gothic mixes traditional Gothic (pointed arches and round medallions stamped with a four-leaf clover) with Byzantine styles (tall, narrow arches atop thin columns), filled in with Islamic frills. Like all the palaces, this was originally painted

and gilded to make it even more glorious than it is now. Today the Ca' d'Oro is an art gallery (see page 41).

Look at the Venetian chorus line of palaces in front of the boat doing an architectural can-can. On the right is the arcade of the covered **fish market** with the open-air **produce market** just beyond. It bustles in the morning but is quiet the rest of the day. This is a great scene to wander through—even though European hygiene standards recently required a remodeling job that left it cleaner...but less colorful. Find the *traghetto* gondola ferrying shoppers—standing like Washington crossing the Delaware—back and forth. There are seven *traghetto* crossings along the Grand Canal, each one marked by a classy

low-key green-and-black sign. Make a point to use them. At €.50 a ride, they are one of the best deals in Venice.

❻ Mercato Rialto

In 2007, this new stop was opened to serve the busy market (boats only stop here from 8:00 to 20:00). The long and officious-looking building at this stop is the Venice court house. Straight ahead, in the distance, rising above the huge post office, you can see the tip of the Campanile (bell tower) crowned by its golden angel at St. Mark's Square, where this tour will end. The **post office** (100 yards directly ahead, on left side, often with *servizio postale* boats moored at its blue posts) was the German Exchange, the trading center for German metal merchants in the early 1500s.

You'll cruise by some trendy and beautifully situated wine bars on the right, but look ahead as you round the corner and see the impressive Rialto Bridge come into view.

A major landmark of Venice, the **Rialto Bridge** is lined with shops and tourists. Constructed in 1588, it's the third bridge built

on this spot. Until the 1850s, this was the only bridge crossing the Grand Canal. With a span of 160 feet and foundations stretching 650 feet on either side, the Rialto was an impressive engineering feat in its day. Earlier Rialto Bridges could open to let big ships in, but not this one. When this new bridge was completed, much of the Grand Canal was closed to shipping and became a canal of palaces.

When gondoliers pass under the fat arch of the Rialto Bridge, they take full advantage of its acoustics. *"Volare, oh, oh..."*

❼ Rialto

Rialto, a separate town in the early days of Venice, has always been the commercial district, while San Marco was the religious and governmental center. Today, a winding street called the Mercerie connects the two, providing travelers with human traffic jams and a mesmerizing gauntlet of shopping temptations. This is the only stretch of the historic Grand Canal with landings upon which you can walk. They unloaded the city's basic necessities here: oil, wine, charcoal, iron. Today, the quay is lined with tourist-trap restaurants.

Venice's sleek, black, graceful **gondolas** are a symbol of the city (for more on gondolas, see page 256). With about 500 gondoliers joyriding amid the churning *vaporetti,* there's a lot of congestion on the Grand Canal. Pay attention—this is where most of the gondola and vaporetto accidents take place. While the Rialto is the highlight of many gondola rides, gondoliers understandably prefer the quieter small canals. Watch your vaporetto driver curse the better-paid gondoliers.

Ahead 100 yards on the left, two palaces stand side by side (the city hall and the mayor's office). Their arched windows are similar and their stories are the same height, lining up to create the effect of one long balcony.

❽ San Silvestro

We now enter a long stretch of important **merchants' palaces,** each with proud and different facades. Because ships couldn't navigate beyond the Rialto Bridge, the biggest palaces—with the major shipping needs—line this last stretch of the navigable Grand Canal.

Palaces like these were multifunctional: ground floor for the warehouse, offices and showrooms upstairs, and the living quarters above the offices on the "noble floors" (with big windows designed to allow in maximum light). Servants lived and worked on the top floors (with the smallest windows). For fire safety reasons, the kitchens were also located on the top floors. Peek into the noble floors to catch a glimpse of their still-glorious chandeliers of Murano glass.

❾ Sant'Angelo

Notice how many buildings have a foundation of waterproof white stone *(pietra d'Istria)* upon which the bricks sit high and dry. Many canal-level floors are abandoned as the rising water level takes its toll. The **posts**—historically painted gaily with the equivalent of family coats of arms—don't rot under water. But the wood at the waterline, where it's exposed to oxygen, does. On the smallest canals, little blue gondola signs indicate that these docks are for gondolas only (no taxis or motor boats).

❿ San Tomà

Fifty yards ahead, on the right side (with twin obelisks on the rooftop) stands **Palazzo Balbi,** the palace of an early 17th-century captain general of the sea. These Venetian equivalents of five-star admirals were honored with twin obelisks decorating their palaces. This palace, like so many in the city, flies three flags: Italy (green-white-red), the European Union (blue with ring of stars), and Venice (red, gold, and with the lion). Today it houses the administrative headquarters of the regional government.

Look around the corner, behind the admiral's palace down a side canal. On the right of that canal, before the bridge, see the traffic light and the **fire station** (with four arches hiding fireboats parked and ready to go).

The impressive **Ca' Foscari,** with a classic Venetian facade (on the corner, across from the fire station), dominates the bend in the canal. This is the main building of the University of

Venice, which has about 25,000 students. Notice the elegant lamp on the corner.

The grand, heavy, white **Ca' Rezzonico,** just before the next stop (of the same name), houses the Museum of 18th-Century Venice (described on page 145). Across the canal (and a bit behind you) is the cleaner and leaner **Palazzo Grassi,** the last major palace built on the canal, erected in the late 1700s—and recently purchased by a French tycoon.

⓫ Ca' Rezzonico

Up ahead, the Accademia Bridge leads over the Grand Canal to the **Accademia Gallery** (right side), filled with the best Venetian paintings (described on page 145). The bridge was put up in 1934 as a temporary one. Locals liked it, so it stayed.

⓬ Accademia

From here look through the graceful bridge and way ahead to enjoy a classic view of the **La Salute Church,** topped by a crown-shaped dome supported by scrolls (probably will be scaffolded in 2008; church described on page 54). This Church of Saint Mary of Good Health was built to thank God for delivering Venetians from the devastating plague of 1630 (which had killed about a third of the city's population).

The low white building among greenery (100 yards ahead, on the right, between the Accademia Bridge and the church) is the **Peggy Guggenheim Collection.** The American heiress "retired" here, sprucing up the palace that had been abandoned in mid-construction. Peggy willed the city her fine collection of modern art (described on page 157).

As you approach the next stop, notice on the right how the fine line of higgledy-piggledy palaces evoke old-time Venice. Two doors past the Guggenheim, Palazzo Dario has a great set of characteristic **funnel-shaped chimneys.** These forced embers through a loop-the-loop channel until they were dead—required in the days when stone palaces were surrounded by humble, wooden buildings, and a live spark could make a merchant's workforce homeless.

Notice this early Renaissance building's flat-feeling facade with "pasted-on" Renaissance motifs. Three doors later is the **Salviati building** (with the fine mosaics), which was once a glass works.

⓭ Santa Maria del Giglio

Back on the left stands the fancy Gritti Palace hotel (Hemingway and Woody Allen both stayed here).

Take a deep whiff of Venice. What's all this nonsense about stinky canals? All I smell is my shirt. By the way, how's your captain? Smooth dockings? To get to know him, stand up in the bow and block his view.

⓮ Salute

The huge La Salute Church, towering overhead as if squirted from a can of Catholic Cool Whip, like Venice itself, rests upon pil-

ings. To build the foundation for the city, more than a million trees were piled together, reaching beneath the mud to the solid clay. Much of the surrounding countryside was deforested by Venice. Trees were exported and consumed locally to fuel the furnaces of Venice's booming glass industry, to build Europe's biggest merchant marine, and to prop up this city in the mud.

As the Grand Canal opens up into the lagoon, the last building on the right with the golden ball is the 17th-century **Customs House** (due to open to the public in 2009 as a contemporary art gallery). Its two bronze Atlases hold a statue of Fortune riding the ball. Arriving ships stopped here to pay their tolls.

(Note that the next stop—San Marco—is the second-to-last stop of this tour. If you plan to immediately follow up this cruise with my self-guided tour of St. Mark's Square, you can avoid having to backtrack by getting off the boat at the San Marco stop, heading up Calle Vallaresso, turning right onto Salizada San Moisè, then turning to the next chapter.)

⓯ San Marco

Look from left to right out over the lagoon. On the left, the green pointed tip of the Campanile marks **St. Mark's Square** (the political and religious center of Venice). A wide harborfront walk leads past elegant hotels to the green area in the distance. This is the public garden, the largest of Venice's few parks, which hosts the Biennale art show (next held in 2009). Farther in the distance is the **Lido,** the island with Venice's beach. It's tempting, with sand

and casinos, but its car traffic breaks into the medieval charm of Venice.

Opposite St. Mark's Square, across the water, the ghostly white church that seems to float is Andrea Palladio's **San Giorgio Maggiore.** Because your vaporetto ticket is good for an hour, consider staying on this boat for the free ride out to the church—it's worth a visit because its pointy bell tower is home to the best view in town (elevator, no lines—see San Giorgio Maggiore Tour, page 175). If you're interested in heading out there right now, check the time stamped on your ticket; it'll be tight. If you don't think you'll make it there within the hour, don't sweat it—the ride to San Giorgio Maggiore on boat #2 costs only €2 (leaves from the San Zaccaria–M.V.E. stop—two docks down from where this tour ends, across from the big equestrian statue).

Across the lagoon (to your right) is the residential island Giudecca, which stretches from close to San Giorgio Maggiore past the Venice youth hostel (with a nice view, directly across) to the new Hilton Hotel (no view, far right end of island).

Cruising on, you pass (with the towering Campanile gliding behind) the bold facade of the old mint (where Venice's golden ducat, the dollar of the Venetian Republic, was made) and the library facade. Then St. Theodore and St. Mark appear, standing atop their twin columns as they have since the 15th and 16th centuries, when they welcomed VIP guests who arrived by sea to the most important square in Europe: Piazza San Marco. In the distance you can see two giant figures standing on the **clock tower.** They've been whacking the hour regularly since 1499. The busy domed features of **St. Mark's Basilica** are eclipsed by the lacy yet powerful facade of the **Doge's Palace.** As you cruise, look to the back side of the Doge's Palace where the **Bridge of Sighs**—leading from the palace to the prison—comes into view. The bridge in front of it is generally packed with tourists sighing at that legendary sky walk. Beyond that, to the right, begins that grand harborside promenade, the **Riva.**

⑯ San Zaccaria

Okay, you're at your last stop. Quick—muscle your way off this boat!

This boat makes three more stops before crossing the lagoon to the Lido—stay on the boat if you want to head out to San Giorgio Maggiore.

ST. MARK'S SQUARE TOUR

Piazza San Marco

Venice was once Europe's richest city, and the Piazza San Marco was its center. As middleman in the trade between Asia and Europe, Venice reaped wealth from both sides. In 1450, Venice had 180,000 citizens (far more than London) and a gross "national" product that exceeded that of entire countries.

The rich Venetians taught the rest of Europe the good life—silks, spices, and jewels from the East, crafts from northern Europe, good food and wine, fine architecture, music, theater, and laughter. Venice was a vibrant city full of painted palaces, glittering canals, and impressed visitors. Five centuries after its power began to decline, Venice is all of these still, with the added charm of romantic decay. In this tour, we'll spend an hour in the heart of this Old World superpower.

ORIENTATION

Getting There: Signs all over town point to *San Marco*—meaning both the square and the basilica—located where the Grand Canal spills out into the lagoon. Vaporetto stops: San Marco or San Zaccaria.

Campanile: If you ascend the bell tower, it'll cost you €6 (daily July–Aug 9:00–21:00, Sept–June 9:00–19:00).

Clock Tower: After a lengthy restoration, the clock tower is open to the public, though you must reserve a visit in advance and take a tour. A guide takes you to close-ups of the clock's innards and out to a terrace with views of the square. English tours run Mon–Wed in the morning, and Thu–Sun in the afternoon. You can reserve in person at the Correr Museum, or call 041-520-9070, or book online at www.museiciviciveneziani.it (€12, includes Correr Museum, but not the Doge's Palace; not covered by Museum Pass or Card).

Information and WCs: There are two TIs. One is in the southwest corner of the square; the other is along the waterfront at the San Marco–Giardinetti vaporetto stop. Handy public **WCs** (€1) are behind the Correr Museum, and at the Giardinetti Reali park.

Cuisine Art: Cafés with live music provide an engaging soundtrack for St. Mark's Square; cheaper places are just off the square (see page 245). The Correr Museum (far end of the square, opposite the basilica) has a quiet coffee shop overlooking the crowded square. For a list of restaurants in the area, see page 244.

Starring: Byzantine domes, Gothic arches, Renaissance arches... and the wonderful, musical space they enclose.

THE TOUR BEGINS

• *For an overview of this grand square and the buildings that surround it, view it from the far end of the square (away from St. Mark's Basilica).*

The Piazza

St. Mark's Basilica dominates the square with its Byzantine-style onion domes and glowing mosaics. Mark Twain said it looked like

"a vast warty bug taking a meditative walk." (I say it looks like tiara-wearing ladybugs copulating.) To the right of the basilica is its 300-foot-tall Campanile. Between the basilica and the Campanile, you can catch a glimpse of the pale-pink Doge's Palace. Lining the square are the former government offices (procuratie) that administered the Venetian empire's vast network of trading outposts, which stretched all the way to Turkey.

The square is big, but it feels intimate with its cafés and dueling orchestras. By day, it's great for people-watching and pigeon-chasing. By night, under lantern light, it transports you to another century, complete with its own romantic soundtrack. The piazza draws Indians in saris, English nobles in blue blazers, and Nebraskans in shorts. Napoleon called the piazza "the most beautiful drawing room in Europe." Napoleon himself added to the intimacy by building the final wing, opposite the basilica, that encloses the square.

For architecture buffs, here are three centuries of styles, bam,

St. Mark's Square

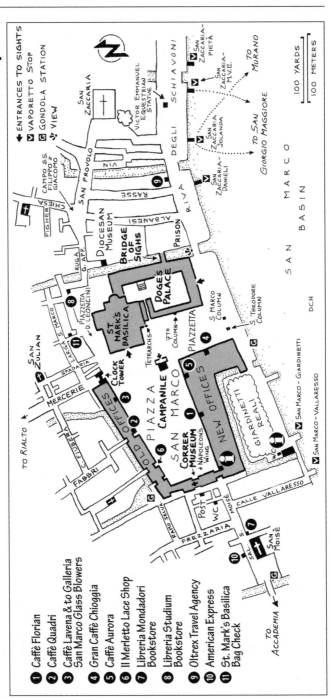

St. Mark's Sq.

ENTRANCES TO SIGHTS
VAPORETTO STOP
G GONDOLA STATION
VIEW

1 Caffè Florian
2 Caffè Quadri
3 Caffè Lavena & to Galleria San Marco Glass Blowers
4 Gran Caffè Chioggia
5 Caffè Aurora
6 Il Merletto Lace Shop
7 Libreria Mondadori Bookstore
8 Libreria Studium Bookstore
9 Oltrex Travel Agency
10 American Express
11 St. Mark's Basilica Bag Check

100 YARDS
100 METERS

side by side, *uno–due–tre,* for easy comparison:

1. On the left side (as you face the basilica) are the "Old" offices, built in about 1500 in solid, column-and-arch Renaissance style.

2. The "New" offices (on the right), in a High Renaissance style from a century later (c. 1600), are a little heavier and more ornate. This wing mixes arches, the three orders of columns from bottom to top—Doric, Ionic, and Corinthian—and statues in the Baroque style.

3. Napoleon's wing is Neoclassical (c. 1800)—a return to simpler, more austere classical columns and arches. Napoleon's architects tried to make his wing bridge the styles of the other two. But it turned out a little too high for one side and not enough for the other. Nice try.

Imagine this square full of water, with gondolas floating where people now sip cappuccinos. That happens every so often at very high tides *(acqua alta),* a reminder that Venice and the sea are intertwined. (Now that one's sinking and the other is rising, they are more intertwined than ever.)

Venice became Europe's richest city from its trade with northern Europeans, Turkish Muslims, and Byzantine Christians. Here in St. Mark's Square, the exact center of this East–West axis, we see both the luxury and the mix of Eastern and Western influences.

Watch out for pigeon speckle. The pigeons are not indigenous to Venice (they were imported by the Hapsburgs) nor loved by the locals. In fact, Venetians love seagulls because they eat pigeons. Vermin are a problem on this small island, where it's said that each Venetian has two pigeons and four rats. (The rats stay hidden, except when high tides flood their homes.)

• *The TI is nearby, in the corner of Napoleon's Wing. With Venice's inconsistent opening hours, it's wise to confirm your sightseeing plans here. Behind you (southwest of the piazza), you'll find the public WC (€1), a post office, and the American Express office.*

Now approach the basilica. If it's hot and you're tired, grab a shady seat at the foot of the Campanile.

St. Mark's Basilica—Exterior

The facade is a crazy mix of East and West. There are round, Roman-style arches over the doorways, golden Byzantine mosaics, a roofline ringed with pointed French Gothic pinnacles, and Muslim-shaped onion domes (wood, covered with lead) on the roof. The brick-structure building is blanketed in marble that came from everywhere—columns from Alexandria, capitals from Sicily, and carvings from Constantinople. The columns flanking the doorways show the facade's variety—purple, green, gray, white, yellow, some speckled, some striped horizontally, some vertically, some fluted, all topped with a variety of different capitals.

What's amazing isn't so much the variety as the fact that the whole thing comes together in a bizarre sort of harmony. St. Mark's remains simply the most interesting church in Europe, a church that (paraphrasing Goethe) "can only be compared with itself."

For more on the basilica, inside and out, see ✪ St. Mark's Basilica Tour, page 66.

• *Facing the basilica, turn 90 degrees to the left to see...*

The Clock Tower (Torre dell'Orologio)

Two bronze "Moors" (African Muslims) stand atop the Clock Tower (built originally to be giants, they only gained their ethnic-

ity when the metal darkened over the centuries). At the top of each hour they swing their giant clappers. The clock dial shows the 24 hours, the signs of the zodiac, and, in the blue center, the phases of the moon. Above the dial is the world's first digital clock, which changes every five minutes. The Clock Tower retains some of its original coloring of blue and gold, a reminder that, in centuries past, this city glowed with bright color.

An alert winged lion, the symbol of St. Mark and the city, looks down on the crowded square. He opens a book that reads *"Pax Tibi Marce,"* or "Peace to you, Mark." As legend goes, these were the comforting words that an angel spoke to the stressed evangelist, assuring him he would find serenity during a stormy night that the saint spent here on the island. Eventually, St. Mark's body found its final resting place inside the basilica, and now his lion symbol is everywhere. (Find four in 20 seconds. Go.)

Venice's many lions express the city's various mood swings through history—triumphant after a naval victory, sad when a favorite son has died, hollow-eyed after a plague, and smiling when the soccer team wins. The pair of lions squatting between the Clock Tower and basilica have probably been photographed being ridden by every Venetian child born since the dawn of cameras.

The Campanile

The original Campanile (cam-pah-NEE-lay), or bell tower, was a lighthouse and a marvel of 10th-century architecture until the 20th century (1902), when it toppled into the center of the piazza. It had groaned ominously the night before, sending people scurrying from the cafés. The next morning...crash! The golden angel on top landed right at the basilica's front door, standing up.

The Campanile was rebuilt 10 years later complete with its golden angel, which always faces the breeze. You can ride a lift to the top for the best view of Venice. It's crowded at peak times, but well worth it.

In 2008, you're likely to see construction work around the Campanile's base. Hoping to prevent a repeat of the 1902 collapse, they're wrapping the underground foundations with a titanium girdle to shore up a crack that appeared in 1939.

Notice the tide gauges on the side of the bell tower. Because St. Mark's Square is the first place in town to start flooding, it's an obvious place to take tidal measurements. Three factors cause high water: low pressure, a full moon, and a wind from the south (called a sirocco wind). When these come together, Venice floods. The puddles appear first around round, white pavement stones like the one next to the Campanile.

If the tide is mild (around 20 inches), the water merely seeps up through the drains. But when there's a strong tide (around 40 inches), it looks like someone's turned on a faucet down below. The water bubbles upward and flows like a river to the lowest points in the square, which can be covered with a few inches of water in an hour or so. Check out the stone plaque (at the exit door, about three feet above the pavement) showing the 196-centimeter (77-inch) high-water line from the disastrous floods of 1966, caused by three straight days of a strong sirocco.

• *The small square between the basilica and the water is...*

The Piazzetta

This "Little Square" is framed by the Doge's Palace on the left, the library on the right, and the waterfront of the lagoon. In former days, the Piazzetta was closed off to the public for a few hours a day so that government officials and bigwigs could gather in the sun to strike shady deals.

The pale-pink Doge's Palace is the epitome of the style known as Venetian Gothic. Columns

support traditional, pointed Gothic arches, but with a Venetian flair—they're curved to a point, ornamented with a trefoil (three-leaf clover), and topped with a round medallion of a quatrefoil (four-leaf clover). The pattern is found on buildings all over Venice, but nowhere else in the world (except Las Vegas).

Venetian Gothic

$$\bigwedge + \bigcap + \bigcap + \clubsuit = $$

The two large 12th-century columns near the water were looted from Constantinople. Mark's winged lion sits on top of one. The lion's body (nearly 15 feet long) predates the wings and is more than 2,000 years old. The other column holds St. Theodore (battling a crocodile), the former patron saint who was replaced by Mark. I guess stabbing crocs in the back isn't classy enough for an upwardly mobile world power. These columns were used to execute criminals in hopes that the public could learn its lessons vicariously.

Venice was the "Bride of the Sea" because she was dependent on sea trading for her livelihood. This "marriage" was celebrated annually by the people. The doge, in full regalia, boarded a ritual boat (his Air Force One equivalent) here at the edge of the Piazzetta and sailed out into the lagoon. There a vow was made, and he dropped a jeweled ring into the water to seal the marriage.

In the distance, on an island across the lagoon, is one of the grandest scenes in the city, the Church of San Giorgio Maggiore.

With its four tall columns as the entryway, the church, designed by the late-Renaissance architect Andrea Palladio, influenced future government and bank buildings around the world.

Speaking of architects, I will: Sansovino. Around 1530, Jacopo Sansovino designed the library (here in the Piazzetta) and the delicate Loggetta at the base of the Campanile (it was destroyed by the collapse of the tower in 1902 and was pieced back together as much as possible).

St. Mark's Sq.

Cafés on St. Mark's Square

Cafés line the square. All three café orchestras feature similar food, prices, and a three- or four-piece combo playing a selection of classical and pop hits, from Brahms to "Bésame Mucho." If you get just a drink, expect to pay about €15, including the cover charge. (A coffee is €3 at the bar, €6 at a table, and €12 outside when the orchestra plays.) It's perfectly acceptable to nurse a cappuccino for an hour—you're paying for the music with the cover charge.

Caffè Florian (on the right as you face the church—see map on page 58) is the most famous Venetian café and one

of the first places in Europe to serve coffee. It's been a popular spot for a discreet rendezvous in Venice since 1720. The orchestra plays a more classical repertoire than the other cafés. The outside tables are the main action, but do walk inside through the richly decorated, old-time rooms where Casanova, Lord Byron, Charles Dickens, and Woody Allen have all paid too much for a drink (reasonable prices at bar in back).

Caffè Quadri, opposite the Florian, has an equally illustrious history of famous clientele, including the writers Stendhal and Dumas, and composer Richard Wagner. Caffè Lavena, near the Clock Tower, is newer and less prestigious.

Gran Caffè Chioggia, on the Piazzetta facing the Doge's Palace, charges slightly less, with one or two musicians playing cocktail jazz.

Caffè Aurora, in the shadow of the Campanile, features nearly all the ambience at half the price. Enjoy coffee or gelato while listening to second-hand music from other establishments.

St. Mark's Sq.

The Tetrarchs and the Doge's Palace's Seventh Column

Where the basilica meets the Doge's Palace is the traditional entrance to the palace, decorated with four small Roman statues—the Tetrarchs. While no one knows for sure who they are, I like the legend that says they're the scared leaders of a divided Rome during its fall—holding their swords and each other as all hell breaks loose around them. Whatever the legend, these statues—made of precious purple porphyry marble—are symbols of power. They were looted from Constantinople, and then placed here proudly as spoils of war. How old are they? They've guarded the doge's entrance since the city first rose from the mud.

The Doge's Palace's seventh column (the seventh from the water) tells a story of love, romance, and tragedy in its carved capital: (1) In the first scene (the carving facing the Piazzetta), a woman on a balcony is wooed by her lover, who says, "Babe, I want *you!*" (2) She responds, "Why, little ol' *me?*" (3) They get married. (4) Kiss. (5) Hit the sack—pretty racy for 14th-century art. (6) Nine months later,  guess what? (7) The baby takes its first steps. (8) And as was all too common in the 1300s...the child dies.

The pillars along the Doge's Palace look short—a result of the square being built up over the centuries. It's happening again today. The stones are taken up, sand is added, and the stones are replaced, buying a little more time as the sea slowly swallows the city.

• *At the waterfront in the Piazzetta, turn left and walk (east) along the water. At the top of the first bridge, look inland at...*

The Bridge of Sighs

In the Doge's Palace (on your left), the government doled out justice. On your right are the prisons. (Don't let the palatial facade  fool you—see the bars on the windows?) Prisoners sentenced in the palace crossed to the prisons by way of the covered bridge in front of you. This was called the Prisons' Bridge until the Romantic poet Lord Byron renamed it in the 19th century. From this bridge (according to romantic—and false—legend), the convicted got their final view of sunny, joyous Venice before entering the black and dank prisons. They sighed.

Venice has been a major tourist center for four centuries. Anyone who's ever come here has stood on this very spot, looking at the Bridge of Sighs. Lean on the railing leaned on by everyone from Casanova to Byron to Hemingway.

Escape from St. Mark's Square

Crowds getting to you? Here are some relatively quiet areas near St. Mark's Square.

Correr Museum: Sip a cappuccino in the café of this uncrowded history museum in a building that overlooks St. Mark's Square (enter at the far end of the piazza). ✪ See Correr Museum Tour, page 100.

Giardinetti Reali: The small park is along the waterfront, west of the Piazzetta (facing the water, turn right—it's next to the TI and the only place for a legal picnic).

San Giorgio Maggiore: This is the fairy-tale island you see from the Piazzetta (catch vaporetto #2 from the San Zaccaria–M.V.E. stop, farthest away from the Bridge of Sighs). ✪ See San Giorgio Maggiore Tour, page 175.

Il Merletto: This lace shop is in a small chapel (daily 9:30–17:00, near the northwest corner of St. Mark's Square, on Sotoportego del Cavalletto). The history of local lace is explained in English (posted at the door).

La Salute Church: This cool church in a quiet neighborhood is a short €2 hop on vaporetto #1 from the San Marco–Vallaresso stop. ✪ See La Salute Church Tour, page 170.

Caffè Florian: The plush interior of this luxurious 18th-century café, located on St. Mark's Square, is generally quiet and nearly empty. An expensive coffee here can be a wonderful break (see "Cafés on St. Mark's Square," page 63).

St. Mark's Sq.

I stood in Venice, on the Bridge of Sighs,
a palace and a prison on each hand.
I saw, from out the wave, her structures rise,
as from the stroke of the enchanter's wand.
A thousand years their cloudy wings expand
around me, and a dying glory smiles
o'er the far times, when many a subject land
looked to the Winged Lion's marble piles,
where Venice sat in state, throned on her hundred isles!

—from Lord Byron's *Childe Harold's Pilgrimage*

• *Sigh.*

ST. MARK'S BASILICA TOUR

Basilica di San Marco

Among Europe's churches, St. Mark's is peerless. From the outside, it's a riot of domes, columns, and statues, completely unlike the towering Gothic churches of northern Europe or the heavy Baroque of Italy. Inside, the decor of mosaics, colored marbles, and oriental treasures is rarely seen elsewhere. Even the Christian symbolism is unfamiliar to Western eyes, done in the style of Byzantine icons and even Islamic designs. Older than most of Europe's churches, it feels like a remnant of a lost world.

This is your best chance (outside of Istanbul or Ravenna) to glimpse a forgotten and somewhat mysterious part of the human story—Byzantium.

ORIENTATION

Cost: While entering the church is free, I'd pay for each of its three separate admissions inside: the Treasury (€2, includes informative audioguide—free for the asking), Golden Altarpiece (€2), and San Marco Museum (€3, enter museum from atrium either before or after you tour the church). The San Marco Museum is the one most worth its entry fee.

Dress Code: To enter the church, modest dress is required even of kids (no shorts or bare shoulders). People who ignore the dress code hold up the line while they plead fruitlessly with the dress-code police.

Hours: The church (including the Treasury and Golden Altarpiece) is open Mon–Sat 9:45–17:00 (until 16:30 off-season), Sun 14:00–16:00. The San Marco Museum is open Mon–Sat 9:45–16:30, Sun 9:45–16:00. To enjoy the gilded, mosaic-covered church in all its medieval glory, see it when it's lit up (usually Mon–Sat 11:30–12:30).

Getting There: Signs throughout Venice point to *San Marco,* meaning the square and the church. It's on St. Mark's Square (Piazza San Marco), near the end of the Grand Canal. Vaporetto stops: San Marco or San Zaccaria.

Lines: There's almost always a long line to get into St. Mark's. To deal with the relentless crowds, the church interior is roped off. You just have to shuffle through on a one-way system. It's best to read this chapter before you go...or while standing in line (bring a small flashlight to illuminate the text). Those checking a bag can skip to the front of the line—see "Bag Check," below.

Bag Check: While small purses are allowed inside the church, larger bags and backpacks are not. Check them for free at the nearby Ateneo San Basso, a former church (open roughly Mon–Sat 9:30–17:30, Sun 14:00–16:30; head to the left of basilica, down narrow Calle San Basso, 30 yards to the second door on your right; see map on page 58 for location).

Those with a bag to check actually get to skip the line. Here's how it works: Drop by Ateneo San Basso. Leave your bag (for up to one hour) and pick up the claim tag. Two people per tag are allowed to go to the basilica's gatekeeper, present the tag, and scoot directly in, ahead of the line. After touring the church, come back and pick up your bag.

Theft Alert: St. Mark's Basilica is the most dangerous place in Venice for pickpocketing—inside, it's always a crowded jostle.

Information and WCs: Tel. 041-522-5205. Guidebooks are sold in the bookstand in the basilica's atrium. A free **WC** is inside the San Marco Museum. Other public WCs (€1) are near St. Mark's Square (one behind the Correr Museum, another at the Giardinetti Reali park).

Tours: In the atrium, see the schedule board that lists free English guided tours (schedules vary, but generally May–Oct Tue, Wed, and Thu at 11:00, one hour, meet guide just to the right of main doors).

Length of This Tour: Allow one hour.

Cuisine Art: Pricier cafés offering live music are on St. Mark's Square; less expensive sandwich bars are just off the square (see Eating, page 226).

Photography: Not allowed.

Starring: St. Mark, Byzantium, mosaics, and ancient bronze horses.

THE TOUR BEGINS

Start outside in the square, far enough back to take in the whole facade. Then zero in on the details. As you tour the interior, do your best to follow this tour. At busy times, your actual itinerary

St. Mark's Basilica

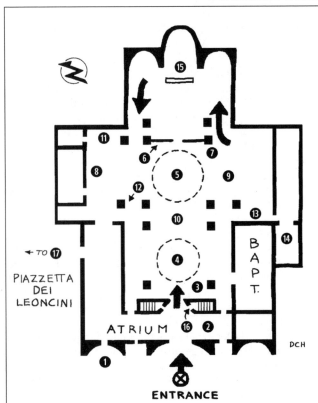

PIAZZETTA
DEI
LEONCINI

ATRIUM

B
A
P
T.

DCH

ENTRANCE

PIAZZA SAN MARCO

❶ Exterior – Mosaic of
Mark's Relics

❷ Atrium – Mosaic of Noah's
Ark and the Great Flood

❸ Nave – Mosaics and
Greek-Cross Floor Plan

❹ Pentecost Mosaic

❺ Central Dome –
Ascension Mosaic

❻ Rood Screen

❼ Doge's Pulpit

❽ Tree of Jesse Mosaic

❾ Last Supper Mosaic

❿ Crucifixion Mosaic

⓫ Nicopeia Icon

⓬ Rifle on Pillar

⓭ Discovery of Mark Mosaic

⓮ Treasury

⓯ Golden Altarpiece

⓰ Stairs up to Loggia:
San Marco Museum &
Bronze Horses

⓱ To Ateneo S. Basso
Bag Check across Square

Basilica Tour

and pace may be determined by the sheer flow of the masses.

❶ Exterior—Mosaic of Mark's Relics

St. Mark's Basilica is a treasure chest of booty looted during Venice's glory days. That's most appropriate for a church built on the bones of a stolen saint.

The **mosaic over the far left door** shows the theft that put Venice on the pilgrimage map. Two men (in the center, with crooked staffs) enter the church bearing a coffin with the body of St. Mark, who looks somewhat grumpy from the long voyage.

St. Mark was the author of one of the four Bible books telling the story of Jesus' life (Matthew, Mark, Luke, and John). Seven centuries after his death, his holy body was in Muslim-occupied Alexandria, Egypt. In 828, two visiting merchants of Venice "rescued" the body from the "infidels," hid it in a pork barrel (which was unclean to Muslims), and spirited it away to Venice.

The merchants presented the body—not to a pope or bishop—but to the doge (with white ermine collar, on the right) and his

wife, the dogaressa (with entourage, on the left), giving instant status to Venice's budding secular state. They built a church here over Mark's bones and made him the patron saint of the city. You'll see his symbol, the winged lion, all over Venice.

The original church burned down in 976. Today's structure was begun in 1063. The mosaic, from 1260, shows that the church hasn't changed much since then—you can see the onion domes and famous bronze horses on the balcony.

The St. Mark's you see today, mostly from the 11th century, was modeled after a sixth-century church in Constantinople. Venice needed roots. By building a retro church, the city could imply that it had been around for longer than it actually had been. (Throughout European history, upstarts loved to fake deep roots this way. Germany embraced mystic, medieval lore as it emerged as a modern nation in the 19th century, England cooked up the King Arthur legend, and so on.)

In subsequent centuries, the church was encrusted with materials looted from buildings throughout the Venetian empire. Their prize booty was the four bronze horses that adorn the balcony, stolen from Constantinople during the Fourth Crusades (these are

---

St. Mark's...Cathedral, Church, or Basilica?

All three are correct. The church is also a cathedral, because it's the home church of the local bishop. It's a basilica, because it's the home of a patriarch and because the meaning of "basilica" evolved into an honorary title conferred on select churches by the pope. Coincidentally, it's also a basilica in the architectural sense. Its floor plan (if you ignore the transepts) has a central nave with flanking side aisles, a layout patterned after the ancient Roman public buildings called "basilicas." The transepts turn the basilica plan into a cross—in this case, a Greek cross, as it has four equal arms.

---

copies, as the originals are housed inside the church museum). The architectural style of St. Mark's has been called "Early Ransack."

• *Enter the atrium (entrance hall) of the basilica, past the guard who makes sure all who enter have covered legs and shoulders. The door is a sixth-century, bronze-paneled, Byzantine job.*

Immediately after entering the first door (crowd flow permitting), peel off to the right, and look overhead into an archway (not a dome) decorated with fine mosaics.

❷ Atrium—Mosaic of Noah's Ark and the Great Flood

St. Mark's famous mosaics, with their picture symbols, were easily understood in medieval times, even by illiterate masses. Today's

literate masses have trouble reading them, so let's practice on these, some of the oldest (13th century), finest, and most accessible mosaics in the church.

Turn around and face the door you just came through. To your left you'll see (on top of the arch) scenes from the story of Noah's Ark. Venetians—who were great ship builders—related to the Ark. At its peak, Venice's Arsenale warship building plant employed several thousand. Nearby, the mosaic of the tower of Babel looks just like the Campanile tower outside.

Take a closer look at the Ark scenes. Noah and sons are sawing logs to build the boat. Below that are three scenes of Noah putting all species of animals into the Ark, two by two. (Who's at the head of the line? Lions.) Turning around and facing the church interior, you'll see the Flood in full force, drowning the wicked. Noah sends out a dove twice to see whether there's any dry land

Christ as Pantocrator

Most Eastern Orthodox churches have at least one mosaic or painting of Christ in a standard pose—as "Pantocrator," a Greek word meaning "Ruler of All." St. Mark's features several Pantocrators, including the central dome, over the altar, and over the entrance door. The image, so familiar to Orthodox Christians, is a bit foreign to Protestants, Catholics, and secularists.

As King of the Universe, Christ sits (usually on a throne) facing directly out, with penetrating eyes. He wears a halo divided with a cross, worn only by the Trinity. In his left hand is a Bible, while his right hand blesses, with the fingers forming the Greek letters chi and rho, the first two letters of "Christos." The thumb touches the fingers, symbolizing how Christ unites both his divinity and his humanity. On either side of Christ's head are the Greek letters "IC XC," short for "IesuC XristoC."

where he can dock. He finds it, leaves the Ark with a gorgeous rainbow overhead, and offers a sacrifice of thanks to God. Easy, huh?

• *Now that our medieval literacy rate has risen, rejoin the slow flow of people. As you inch along, remember you're stepping on marble mosaics that were "inherited" from Constantinople. Notice the entrance to the San Marco Museum (Loggia dei Cavalli), which you can visit later. Glance above the door at the golden mosaic of Mark, who opens his arms to say, "Welcome to my church." Now climb seven steps, pass through the doorway, and enter the nave. Loiter somewhere just inside the door (crowd flow permitting) and let your eyes adjust.*

❸ The Nave—Mosaics and Greek-Cross Floor Plan

The initial effect is dark and unimpressive (unless they've got the floodlights on). But as your pupils slowly unclench, you'll notice that

the entire upper part is decorated in mosaic—4,750 square yards (imagine paving a football field with contact lenses). These golden mosaics are in the Byzantine style, though many were designed by artists from the Italian Renaissance and later. The often-overlooked lower walls are covered with green-, yellow-, purple-,

Basilica Tour

and rose-colored marble slabs, cut to expose the grain, and laid out in geometric patterns. Even the floor is mosaic, mostly geometrical designs. It rolls like the sea. Venice is sinking and shifting, creating these cresting waves of stone.

The church is laid out with four equal arms, topped with domes, radiating out from the center to form a Greek Cross (+). Those familiar with Eastern Orthodox churches will find familiar elements in St. Mark's: a central floor plan, domes, mosaics, and iconic images of Mary and Christ as Pantocrator—ruler of all things. As your eyes adjust, the mosaics start to give off a "mystical, golden luminosity," the atmosphere of the Byzantine heaven. The air itself seems almost visible, like a cloud of incense. It's a subtle effect, one that grows on you as the filtered light changes. There are more beautiful, bigger, more overwhelming, and even holier churches, but none is as stately.

• *Find the chandelier near the entrance doorway (in the shape of a Greek Cross cathedral space station), and run your eyes up the support chain to the dome above.*

❹ Pentecost Mosaic

In a golden heaven, the dove of the Holy Spirit shoots out a pinwheel of spiritual lasers, igniting tongues of fire on the heads of the 12 apostles below, giving them the ability to speak other languages without a Rick Steves phrase book. You'd think they'd be amazed, but their expressions are as solemn as...icons. One of the oldest mosaics in the church (c. 1125), it has distinct "Byzantine" features: a gold background and apostles with halos, solemn faces, almond eyes, delicate blessing hands, and rumpled robes, all facing forward.

This is art from a society still touchy about the Bible's commandment against making "graven images" of holy things. Byzantium had recently emerged from two centuries of "Iconoclasm," in which statues and paintings were broken and burned as sinful "false gods." The Byzantine style emphasizes otherworldliness rather than literal human detail. The poet W. B. Yeats stood here and described what he saw: "O sages standing in God's holy fire as in the gold mosaic of a wall, come from the holy fire...and be the singing-masters of my soul."

• *Shuffle along with the crowds up to the central dome.*

Mosaics

St. Mark's mosaics are designs or pictures made with small cubes of colored stone or glass pressed into wet plaster. Ancient Romans paved floors, walls, and ceilings with them. When Rome "fell," the art form died out in the West but was carried on by Byzantine craftsmen. They perfected the gold background effect by baking gold leaf into tiny cubes  of glass called *tesserae* (tiles). The surfaces of the tiles are purposely cut unevenly to capture light and give off a shimmering effect. The reflecting gold mosaics helped to light thick-walled, small-windowed, lantern-lit Byzantine churches, creating a golden glow that symbolized the divine light of heaven.

St. Mark's mosaics tell the entire Christian history from end to beginning. Entering the church, you're greeted with scenes from the end of the world (Apocalypse) and the Pentecost. As you approach the altar, you walk backward in time to the source, experiencing Jesus' Passion and crucifixion, his miraculous life, and continuing back to his birth and Old Testament predecessors. Over the altar at the far end of the church (and over the entrance door at the near end) are images of Christ—the beginning and the end, the Alpha and Omega of the Christian universe.

❺ Central Dome—Ascension Mosaic

Gape upward to the very heart of the church. Christ—having lived his miraculous life and having been crucified for man's sins—ascends into the starry sky on a rainbow. He raises his right hand and blesses the universe. This isn't the dead, crucified, mortal Jesus featured in most churches, but a powerful, resurrected god, the ruler of all.

Christ's blessing radiates out, rippling down to the ring of white-robed apostles below. They stand amid the trees of the Mount of Olives, waving good-bye as Christ ascends. Mary is with them, wearing blue with golden Greek crosses on each shoulder and looking ready to play patty-cake. From these saints, goodness descends, creating the Virtues that ring the base of the dome between the windows. In Byzantine churches, the window-lit dome represented heaven, while the dark church below represented Earth—a microcosm of the hierarchical universe.

Beneath the dome at the four corners, the four Gospel writers ("Matev," "Marc," "Luca," and "Ioh") thoughtfully scribble down

Byzantium

The Byzantine Empire was the eastern half of the ancient Roman Empire that *didn't* "fall" in A.D. 476. It remained Christian, Greek-speaking, and enlightened for another thousand years.

In A.D. 330, Constantine, the first Christian emperor, moved the Roman Empire's capital to the newly expanded city of Byzantium, which he humbly renamed Constantinople (modern Istanbul). With him went Rome's best and brightest. When the city of Rome decayed and fell, plunging Western Europe into its "Dark Ages," Constantinople lived on as the greatest city in Europe.

Venice had strong ties with Byzantium from its earliest days. In the sixth century, Byzantine Emperor Justinian invaded northern Italy, briefly reuniting East and West, and making Ravenna his regional capital. In 800, Venetians asked the emperor in Constantinople to protect them from Charlemagne's marauding Franks.

Soon Venetian merchants were granted trading rights to Byzantine ports in the Adriatic and eastern Mediterranean. They traded raw materials from Western Europe for luxury goods from the East.

When Muslim Turks threatened the Christian Byzantine Empire, the Venetians joined the Crusades, the series of military expeditions that were designed to "save" Jerusalem and Constantinople. Venetians grew rich renting ships to the Crusaders in exchange for money, favors, and booty.

During the Fourth Crusade (1202–1204), which went horribly awry, the Crusaders—led by the Venetian doge Dandolo—

the heavenly events. This wisdom flows down like water from the symbolic Four Rivers below them, spreading through the church's four equal arms (the "four corners" of the world), and baptizing the congregation with God's love. The church building is a series of perfect circles within perfect squares—the cosmic order—with Christ in the center solemnly blessing us. God's in his heaven, saints are on Earth, and all's right with the world.

Under the Ascension Dome— The Church as Theater

Look around at the church's furniture and imagine a service here. The **rood screen ❻**, topped with 14 saints, separates the congregation from the high altar, heightening the "mystery" of the Mass. The **pulpit on the right** was reserved for the doge, who led prayers and made important announcements ❼. Mosaics were visual aids for the priest, telling the whole story of Jesus, from his ancestors

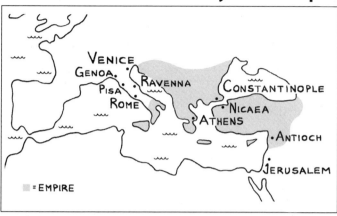

The Byzantine Empire

VENICE
GENOA
PISA
ROME
RAVENNA
CONSTANTINOPLE
NICAEA
ATHENS
ANTIOCH
JERUSALEM

= EMPIRE

sacked Constantinople, a fellow Christian city. This was, perhaps, the lowest point in Christian history, at least until the advent of TV evangelism. The Venetians carried home the bronze horses, the Pala d'Oro enamels, the Treasury's treasures, the Nicopeia icon, and much of the marble that now covers the (brick) church.

Venice rose while the Byzantine Empire faded. Then both civilizations nose-dived when Constantinople finally fell to the Turks in 1453.

Today, we find hints of the Byzantine Empire in the Eastern Orthodox Church, in mosaics and icons, and in the looted treasures shipped back to Venice.

Basilica Tour

perched in the **Tree of Jesse** ❽ (in the north transept; facing the altar, turn 90-degrees left, and it's on the far north wall), to the **Last Supper** ❾ (in the arch leading to the south transept), to the **Crucifixion** ❿ (in the west arch).

The Crucifixion mosaic features a stick-figure Christ, emphasizing the symbolic solemnity of the moment, not its Mel Gibson gruesomeness. In fact, there aren't very many crucifixes at all in the church, giving it an Eastern Orthodox flavor. While Western Christianity focuses on the death of Jesus, to Orthodox believers, Christ's death is just the tragic Act I. Other scenes in the arch show the rest of the story, Christ's triumphant Resurrection and post-death miracles, leading to the climax, his Ascension (in the central dome).

The Venetian church service is a theatrical multimedia spectacle, combining words (prayers, biblical passages, Latin and Greek phrases), music (chants, a choir, organ, horns, strings), costumes and props (priests' robes, golden reliquaries, candles, incense), set design (the mosaics, rood screen, Golden Altarpiece), and even stage direction (processionals through the crowd, priests' motions, standing, sitting, kneeling, crossing yourself). The symmetrical church is itself part of the set design. The Greek-cross floor plan symbolizes perfection, rather than the more common Latin cross of the crucifixion (emphasizing man's sinfulness). Coincidentally or not, the first modern opera—also a multimedia theatrical experience—was written by St. Mark's *maestro di cappella,* Claudio Monteverdi (1567–1643).

North Transept

In the north transept (the arm of the church to the left of the altar), today's Venetians pray to a painted wooden icon of Mary and baby Jesus known as **Nicopeia,** or "Our Lady of Victory" (on the east wall of the north transept) ⓫. Supposedly painted by the evangelist Luke, it was once enameled with bright paint and precious stones, and Mary was adorned with a crown and necklace of gold and jewels (now on display in the Treasury). This Madonna has helped Venice persevere through plagues, wars, and crucial soccer games. When Mary answers a prayer, grateful Venetians give her offerings, like the old **rifle** that hangs on a pillar (as you approach the north transept) ⓬. A wife prayed to the Madonna for her husband's safe return from war with Austria in 1848. When he came home alive, she gave his rifle to the Virgin in thanks.

• *In the south transept (to right of main altar), find the dim mosaic on the west wall.*

⓭ Discovery of Mark Mosaic

Not a biblical scene, this mosaic depicts the miraculous event that capped the construction of the present church.

It's 1094, the church is nearly complete (see the domes shown in cutaway fashion), and they're all set to re-inter Mark's bones under the new altar. There's just one problem: During the decades of construction, they forgot where they'd stored his body!

So (in the left half of the mosaic), all of Venice gathers inside the church to bow down and pray for help finding the bones. The doge (from the Latin "dux") leads them. Soon after (the right half), the patriarch (far right) is inspired to look inside a hollow column where he finds the relics. Everyone turns and applauds, including the womenfolk (left side of scene), who stream in from the upper-floor galleries. The relics were soon placed under the altar in a ceremony that inaugurated the current structure.

The south transept also features horseshoe arches atop slender columns, giving the transept the exotic flavor of a Muslim mosque. The door under the rose window leads directly from the Doge's Palace. On important occasions, the doge entered the church through here, ascended the steps of his pulpit, and addressed the people.

ST. MARK'S THREE MUSEUMS

Inside the church are three sights, each requiring a separate admission. The Treasury and Golden Altarpiece are viewable during the church's opening hours; the San Marco Museum is open Mon–Sat 9:45–16:30, Sun 9:45–16:00. None is a must-see, but they provide the easiest way (outside of Istanbul or Ravenna) to soak up Byzantine ambience—and admission to the San Marco Museum (the best of the bunch) gives you access to great views over the inside of the church, as well as to the square outside.

⓮ Treasury (Tesoro)

• *The tiny Treasury is in the south transept. Admission is €2 (includes audioguide when available—ask for it). The collection is crammed into two small rooms.*

You'll see Byzantine chalices, silver reliquaries, monstrous monstrances (for displaying the Communion wafer), and icons done in gold, silver, enamels, gems, and semiprecious stones. Some pieces represent the fruit of labor by different civilizations over a thousand-year period. For example, an ancient rock-crystal chalice made by the Romans might be decorated centuries later with Byzantine enamels, and then finished still later with gold filigree by Venetian goldsmiths. This is marvelous handiwork, but all the more marvelous for having been done when Western Europe was still rooting in the mud. Here are some highlights.

• *Enter the main room, to the right. Start with the large glass case in the center of the room.*

Main Room: This display case holds the most precious Byzantine objects. The hanging lamp with the protruding fish features fourth-century Roman rock-crystal framed in 11th-century Byzantine metalwork. Just behind it, a purple bucket, carved with scenes of satyrs chasing nymphs, epitomizes the pagan world that was fading as Christianity triumphed. Also in the case are blue-and-gold lapis lazuli icons of the Crucifixion and of the Archangel Michael featuring a Byzantine specialty—enamel work (more on that craft at the Golden Altarpiece). See various chalices (cups

The Legend (Mixed with a Little Truth) of Mark and Venice

Mark (died c. A.D. 68) was a Jewish-born Christian, and he might have actually met Jesus. (The Bible mentions a "Mark" and a "John Mark" who may have been him.) He traveled with fellow convert Paul, eventually settling in Alexandria as the city's first Christian bishop. On a trip to Rome, Peter—Jesus' right-hand man—asked him to write down the events of Jesus' life that became the Gospel of Mark.

During his travels, Mark stopped in the lagoon (in Aquileia on the north coast of the Adriatic), where he dreamed of a Latin-speaking angel who said, *"Pax tibi Marce, evangelista meus"* ("Peace to you, Mark, my evangelist"), promising him rest after death. Back in Alexandria, Mark was attacked by an anti-Christian mob. They tied him with ropes and dragged his body through the streets until he died.

Eight centuries later, his body lay in an Alexandrian church about to be vandalized by Muslim fanatics. Two Venetian traders on a business trip saved the relics from desecration by hiding them in a basket of pork—a meat considered unclean by Muslims—and quickly setting sail. The perilous voyage home was only completed after many more miracles. The doge received the body and, in 828, they built the first church of St. Mark's to house it. During construction of the current church (1094), Mark's relics were temporarily lost, and it took another miracle to find them, hidden inside a column. Today, Venetians celebrate Mark on the traditional date of his martyrdom, April 25.

The events of Mark's life are portrayed vividly in many mosaics throughout the Basilica. Unfortunately, most of them are either off-limits to tourists or in the dim reaches of the church. Enjoy them by buying a St. Mark's guidebook with photos.

used for the bread and wine during Mass) made of onyx, agate, and rock crystal, and an incense burner shaped like a domed church.

• *Along the walls, find the following displays (working counterclockwise around the room).*

The first three glass cases have bowls and urns made of glass or rock crystal, gold and silver, and precious stones. The styles blend elements from the three medieval cultures that cross-pollinated in the Eastern Mediterranean: Venetian, Byzantine, and Islamic. Next comes the Urn of Artaxerxes I (middle of the right wall), an Egyptian-made object that once held the ashes of the great Persian king who ruled 2,500 years ago (r. 465–425 B.C.). The next cases hold religious paraphernalia used for High Mass—chalices, reliquaries, candlesticks, bishops' robes, and a 600-year-old crosier (ceremonial shepherd staff) still used today by the chief priest on holy days.

Next is the Ciborio di Anastasia (far left corner), a small marble canopy that once arched over the blessed communion wafer during Mass. The object may be a gift from "Anastasia," the name carved on it in Greek. She was a lady-in-waiting in the court of the emperor Justinian (483–565). Christian legend has it that she was so beautiful that Justinian (a married man) pursued her amorously, so she had to dress like a monk and flee to a desert monastery.

Near the Ciborio, you'll see the first of two large golden candlesticks. What detail! The smiling angels at the top, the literary lion, the man with the weight on his shoulders, the row of queens... all the way down to the roots. Continuing counter-clockwise, see a photo of a Madonna adorned with jewels, gold, and enamel. If you like this, it's just a taste of what the Pala d'Oro offers.

Next to the Madonna, notice the granite column that extends below current floor level—you can see how the floor has risen as things have settled in the last 1,000 years.

Relics/Sanctuary Room: Straight ahead, the glass case over the glowing alabaster altar contains elaborate gold-and-glass reliquaries holding relics of Jesus' Passion—his torture and execution. The reliquary showing Christ being whipped (from 1125) holds a stone from the column he was tied to. You may scoff, but of all of Europe's "Pieces of the True Cross" and "Crown of Thorns," these have at least some claim of authenticity. Legend has it that Christ's possessions were gathered up in the fourth century by Constantine's mother and taken to Constantinople. During the Crusade heist of 1204, Venetians brought them here. They've been paraded through the city every Good Friday for 800 years.

Back by the room's entrance is a glass reliquary with the bones of Doge Orseolo (r. 976–978), who built the church that preceded the current structure, and one with the bones of St. George, legendary dragon slayer.

⓯ Golden Altarpiece (Pala d'Oro)

• *The Golden Altarpiece is located behind the main altar. Admission is €2.*

Under the stone canopy sits the high altar. Inside the altar is an urn (not visible) with the mortal remains of Mark, the Gospel writer. (Look through the grate of the altar to read *Corpus Divi Marci Evangelistae*, or "Body of the Evangelist Mark.") He rests in peace, as an angel had promised him. Shh.

As you shuffle along, notice the marble canopy's support columns carved with New Testament scenes in the 13th century. (On the right-hand pillar closest to the altarpiece, fourth row from the bottom: Is that a genie escaping from a bottle while someone tries to stuff him back in?)

The Golden Altarpiece is a stunning golden wall made of 250 blue-backed enamels with religious scenes, all set in a gold frame and studded with 15 hefty rubies, 300 emeralds, 1,500 pearls, and assorted sapphires, amethysts, and topaz. The Byzantine-made enamels (c. 1100) were part of the Venetians' plunder of 1204, subsequently pieced together  by Byzantine craftsmen specifically for St. Mark's high altar. It's a bit much to take in all at once, but get up close and find several details you might recognize:

In the center, Jesus as Ruler of the Cosmos sits on a golden throne, with a halo of pearls and jewels. Like a good Byzantine Pantocrator, he dutifully faces forward and gives his blessing while stealing a glance offstage at Mark ("Marcus") and the other saints.

Along the bottom row, Old Testament prophets show off the Bible's books they've written. With halos, solemn faces, and elaborately creased robes, they epitomize the Byzantine icon style.

Follow Mark's story in the panels along the sides. In the bottom-left panel, Mark meets Peter (seated) at the gates of Rome. It was Peter (legend has it) who gave Mark the eyewitness account of Jesus' life that Mark wrote down in his Gospel. Mark's story ends in the bottom-right panel with the two Venetian merchants returning by ship, carrying his coffin here to be laid to rest.

Byzantium excelled in the art of *cloisonné* enameling. A piece of gold leaf is stamped with a design, then filled in with pools of enamel paint, which are baked on. Look at a single saint to see the detail work: The gold background around the saint is the gold-leaf medallion that gets stamped. The golden folds in the robe are the raised edges of the impression. The different colors of the robe are different-colored paints in the recessed areas, each color baked on in a separate firing. Some saints even have pearl crowns or jewel collars pinned on. This kind of craftsmanship—and the social infrastructure that could afford it—made Byzantium seem like an enchanted world during Europe's dim Middle Ages.

After you've looked at some individual scenes, back up as far as this small room will let you and just let yourself be dazzled by the whole picture—this "mosaic" of Byzantine greatness. This magnificent altarpiece sits on a swivel (notice the mechanism at its

Basilica Tour

base) and is swung around on festival Sundays so the entire congregation can enjoy it.

⑯ San Marco Museum (Museo di San Marco)— Mosaics, Bronze Horses, View of the Piazza, and More

• *This is the one sight certainly worth the €3 admission price, if only for the views of St. Mark's Square, the Piazzetta, and the interior of the church from above. The staircase up to the museum is in the atrium near the main entrance. The sign says* Loggia dei Cavalli, Museo. *When you're upstairs, you'll spill out by the Museum's three highlights: view of the interior (right), view of the square (out the door to the left), and bronze horses (directly ahead). Belly up to the center of the stone balustrade to survey the interior.*

View of Church Interior

Take a closer look at the Pentecost Mosaic (first dome above you, described earlier). The unique design at the very top signifies the Trinity: throne (God), Gospels (Christ), and dove (Holy Spirit). The couples below the ring of apostles are the people of the world (I can find Asia, Judaea, and Cappadocia), who, despite their different languages, still understood the Spirit's message.

If you were a woman in medieval Venice, you'd enjoy this same close-up view, because in the Middle Ages, women did not worship on the floor level. They climbed the same stairs you just did and found a spot along the balconies at your feet. The church was divided into three realms—the balcony for women, the nave for men, and the altar for the priests. Back then the rood screen (the fence with the 15 figures on it) separated the priest from the public, and he officiated with his back to the people.

From up here you can appreciate the patterns of the mosaic floor—one of the finest in Italy—that covers the floor like a Persian carpet.

• *From here, the museum loops you to the far (altar) end of the church, then back to the bronze horses. Along the way, you'll see...*

Mosaic Fragments (Cassine)

These mosaics once hung in the church, but when they became damaged or aesthetically old-fashioned, they were replaced by new and more fashionable mosaics. These few fragments avoided the garbage can. You'll see mosaics from the church's earliest days (and most "Byzantine" style, c. 1070) to the more recent (1700s) with realistic Renaissance detail.

The mosaics—made from small cubes of stone or colored glass pressed into wet clay—were assembled on the ground, then cemented onto the walls. Artists draw the pattern on paper, lay it on the wet clay, and slowly cut the paper away as they replace it with cubes. The first mosaic on your left as you enter shows a reproduction of a paper "cast" of a mosaic.

• *Continuing on, you'll see other artwork and catch glimpses of the interior of the church from the north transept. Here you get a close-up view of the Tree of Jesse mosaic. Continue on to the Sala dei Banchetti (WCs near the room's entrance).*

Sala dei Banchetti

This large, ornate room—once the doge's banquet hall—is filled with religious objects, tapestries, carpets that once carpeted the church, Burano lace vestments, illuminated music manuscripts, a doge's throne, and much more.

Try reading some music. The manuscripts date from the 16th century—before the age of treble and bass clefs. You'll see a C clef along the left margin (which could slide along the staff to locate middle C). From this, you could chant notes in proper relationship to each other according to the rhythm indicated.

In the center of the hall stands the most prestigious artwork here, the basilica's workaday altarpiece, the Pala Feriale, by Paolo Veneziano (1345). On ordinary workdays, these 14 scenes painted on wood covered the golden Pala d'Oro—seven saints above (including crucified Christ) and seven episodes in Mark's life below. The panel of the sailboat tells the story of the Venetian merchants' trip home with Mark's relics. A storm at sea billows their sails, ripples the flag, churns the waves, and scares the crew as the ship heads toward the rocks. But then Mark himself appears miraculously at the stern and calms the storm, bringing the ship (and his own body) safely to Venice. Paolo proudly signed his name (along the bottom) and the names of his two assistants, his sons Luca and Giovanni. The second half of the altarpiece (nearer to the exit of the room) is done in later Renaissance style by Maffeo Verona (1614).

• *Now double back through displays of stone fragments from the church, finally arriving at...*

The Bronze Horses (La Quadriga)

Stepping lively in pairs and with smiles on their faces, they exude energy and exuberance. Art historians don't know how old they are—they could be from ancient Greece (fourth century B.C.) or ancient Rome during its Fall (fourth century A.D.). They look Greek Hellenistic (second century B.C.) to me, and Professor Carbon Fourteen says they're from

around 175 B.C. Originally, the horses pulled a chariot *Ben-Hur* style. These bronze statues were not hammered and bent into shape by metalsmiths, but were cast from clay molds by using the lost-wax technique. The bronze is high quality, with 97 percent copper. Originally gilded, they still have some streaks of gold. Long gone are the ruby pupils that gave the horses the original case of "red eye."

Megalomaniacs through the ages have coveted these horses not only for their artistic value, but because they symbolize Apollo, the Greco-Roman god of the sun...and of secular power. The doge spoke to his people standing between the horses when they graced the balcony atop the church's facade (where the copies—which you'll see next—stand today).

Their expressive faces seem to say, "Oh boy, Wilbur, have we done some travelin'." Legend says they were made in the time of Alexander the Great, then taken by Nero to Rome. Constantine took them to his new capital in Constantinople to adorn the chariot racecourse. The Venetians then stole them from their fellow Christians during the looting of noble Constantinople and brought them to St. Mark's.

What goes around comes around, and Napoleon came around and took the horses when he conquered Venice in 1797. They stood atop a triumphal arch in Paris until Napoleon's empire was "blown-aparte" and they were returned to their "rightful" home.

The horses were again removed from their spot when they were attacked by their most dangerous enemy yet—modern man. The threat of oxidation from pollution sent them galloping for cover inside the church.

• *The visit ends outside on the balcony overlooking St. Mark's Square.*

The Loggia and View of St. Mark's Square

You'll be drawn repeatedly to the viewpoint of the square, but remember to look at the facade to see how cleverly all the looted

architectural elements blend together. Ramble among the statues of water-bearing slaves that serve as drain spouts. The horses are modern copies (note the 1978 date on their hoofs).

Be a doge, and stand between the bronze horses overlooking St. Mark's Square. Under the gilded lion of St. Mark, in front of the four great Evangelists (who once stood atop the columns), and flanked—like Apollo—by the four glorious horses, he inspired the Venetians in

Basilica Tour

the square below to great things.

Admire the mesmerizing, commanding view of the center of this city, which so long ago was Europe's only superpower for centuries, and today is just a small town with a big history that's filled with tourists.

DOGE'S PALACE TOUR

Palazzo Ducale

Venice is a city of beautiful facades—palaces, churches, carnival masks—that can cover darker interiors of intrigue and decay. The Doge's Palace, with its frilly pink exterior, hides the fact that the "Most Serene Republic" (as it called itself—"serene" meaning stable) was far from serene in its heyday.

The Doge's Palace housed the fascinating government of this rich and powerful empire. It also served as the home for the Venetian ruler known as the doge (dohzh), or duke. For four centuries (about 1150–1550), this was the most powerful half-acre in Europe. The rest of Europe marveled at the way Venice could govern itself without a dominant king, bishop, or tyrant. The doges wanted their palace to reflect the wealth and secular values of the Republic, impressing visitors and serving as a reminder that the Venetians were Number One in Europe.

ORIENTATION

Cost: €13; this buys you the "Museum Card," which also includes admission to the Correr Museum and two other, lesser museums (you can't just buy a ticket for the Doge's Palace). For details on the Museum Card and the pricier Museum Pass, see page 18.

Hours: Daily April–Oct 9:00–19:00, Nov–March 9:00–17:00, last entry 1 hour before closing.

Getting There: The palace is next to St. Mark's Basilica, on the lagoon waterfront, and just off St. Mark's Square. Vaporetto stops: San Marco or San Zaccaria.

Crowd Control: To avoid the long peak-season line at the Doge's Palace, you have several options (the first is best):

    1. Buy your ticket ("Museum Card") at the Correr

Doge's Palace

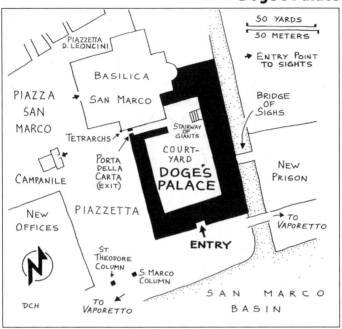

50 YARDS

50 METERS

➤ ENTRY POINT
TO SIGHTS

PIAZZETTA
D. LEONCINI

BASILICA

SAN MARCO

PIAZZA
SAN
MARCO

BRIDGE
OF
SIGHS

STAIRWAY
OF
GIANTS

TETRARCHS

PORTA
DELLA
CARTA
(EXIT)

COURT-
YARD
DOGE'S
PALACE

NEW
PRISON

CAMPANILE

NEW
OFFICES

PIAZZETTA

TO
VAPORETTO

(N)

ST.
THEODORE
COLUMN

S. MARCO
COLUMN

ENTRY

DCH

TO
VAPORETTO

S A N   M A R C O
B A S I N

Museum (at the far end of St. Mark's Square), then go directly to the turnstile of the Doge's Palace, skirting along to the right of the long ticket-buying line at the palace entrance.

2. Visit the palace at about 17:00, when the line disappears (but note that in the off-season, the museum closes two hours earlier).

3. Book a guided Secret Itineraries Tour (see "Tours," below). The only (minor) drawback is that your palace entry fee does not include the Correr Museum.

Information: There are some English descriptions, and guidebooks are on sale in the bookshop. Tel. 041-271-5911, www .museiciviciveneziani.it.

Services: Some WCs are in the courtyard; more are halfway up the stairs to the balcony level. The elevator (inside the ground-floor cafeteria) is available only to those with difficulty climbing the stairs. Free baggage check is available in the courtyard.

Tours: The high-tech Palm Pilot **audioguide tour** is dry but informative (€5, 90 min, need ID or credit card for deposit). Pick it up after you pass through the turnstile after the ticket counter.

The fine **Secret Itineraries Tour,** which follows the doge's footsteps through rooms not included in the general admission price, must be booked in advance—it's best to book at least two days early in peak season (€16; includes admission only to the Doge's Palace, not the Correr Museum, too; in English at 9:55, 10:45 and 11:35; 75 min). You can reserve online (www.museicivicineziani.it), by phone (tel. 041-520-9070 for advance reservations; tel. 041-291-5911 for same-day or day before), or by just showing up at the information desk and hoping for a free spot (unlikely at peak times). With your booking, arrive 20 minutes early to check in at the information desk in the room before the ticket counter—just *"scusi"* your way past the ticket-buying line. While the tour skips the main halls inside, it finishes inside the palace, and you're welcome to visit the halls on your own before you leave.

Length of This Tour: Allow 90 minutes.

Cuisine Art: There's a cafeteria in the palace courtyard, expensive cafés on St. Mark's Square, and several good sandwich bars on Calle della Rasse (two blocks behind the palace—see page 245 of Eating chapter).

Photography: Not allowed.

Starring: Big rooms bare of furnishings but crammed with history, Tintoretto masterpieces, and the doges.

THE TOUR BEGINS

Exterior

"The Wedding Cake," "The Table Cloth," or "The Pink House" is also sometimes known as the Doge's Palace. The style is called

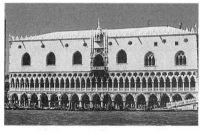

Venetian Gothic—a fusion of Italian Gothic with a delicate Islamic flair. The columns originally had bases on the bottoms, but these were covered over as the columns sank, and the square was built up over the centuries. If you compare this lacy, top-heavy structure with the massive fortress palaces of Florence, you realize the wisdom of building a city in the middle of the sea—you have no natural enemies except gravity. This unfortified palace in a city with no city wall was the doge's way of saying, "I am an elected and loved ruler. I do not fear my own people."

The palace was originally built in the 800s, but most of what we see came after 1300, as it was expanded to meet the needs of the empire. Each doge wanted to leave his mark on history with a new wing, but so much of the city's money was spent on the building that finally a law was passed levying an enormous fine on anyone who even mentioned any new building. That worked for a while, until one brave and wealthy doge proposed a new wing, paid his fine...and started building again.

• *Enter the Doge's Palace from along the waterfront. After you pass through the turnstile, ignore the signs and cross the square to stand at the foot of the grand staircase topped by two statues.*

The Courtyard and the Stairway of Giants (Scala dei Giganti)

Imagine yourself as a foreign dignitary on business to meet the doge. In the courtyard, you look up a grand staircase topped with

two nearly nude statues of, I think, Moses and Paul Newman (more likely, Neptune and Mars, representing Venice's prowess at sea and at war). The doge and his aides would be waiting for you at the top, between the two statues and beneath the Winged Lion. No matter who you were—king, pope, or emperor—you'd have to hoof it up. The powerful doge would descend the stairs for no one.

Many doges were crowned here, between the two statues. The doge was something like an elected king—which makes sense only in the dictatorial republic that was Venice. Technically, he was just a noble selected by other nobles to carry out their laws and decisions. Many doges tried to extend their powers and rule more as divine-right kings. Many others just put on their funny hats and accepted their role as figurehead and ceremonial ribbon-cutter. Most were geezers, elected in their seventies and committed to preserving the Venetian traditions.

The palace is attached to the church, symbolically welding together church and state. Both buildings have ugly brick behind a painted-lady veneer of marble. In this tour, we'll see the similarly harsh inner workings of an outwardly serene, polished republic.

You'll see a hodgepodge of architectural styles enclosing the courtyard, as the palace was refurbished over the centuries. There are classical statues in Renaissance niches, shaded by Baroque awnings, topped by Flamboyant Gothic spires, and crusted with the Byzantine onion domes of St. Mark's Basilica.

• *Cross back to near the entrance and follow the signs up the tourists' staircase to the first-floor balcony (loggias), where you can look back down on the courtyard (but not the backside of Paul Newman). From this point on, it's hard to get lost (though I've managed). It's a one-way system, so just follow the arrows.*

Doge's Palace

Midway along the balcony, you'll find a face in the wall, the...

Mouth of Truth

This fierce-looking androgyne opens his/her mouth, ready to swallow a piece of paper, hungry for gossip. Letterboxes like this (some with lions' heads) were scattered throughout the palace. Originally, anyone who had a complaint or suspicion about anyone else could accuse him anonymously *(denontie secrete)* by simply dropping a slip of paper in the mouth. This set the blades of justice turning inside the palace.

• *Toward Paul Newman is the entrance to the...*

Golden Staircase (Scala d'Oro)

The palace was propaganda, designed to impress visitors. This 24-karat gilded-ceiling staircase was something for them to write home about. As you ascend the stairs, look back at the floor below and marvel at its 3-D pattern.

• *Take the Golden Staircase to the first landing (Primo Piano Nobile), and turn right, which takes you up into the...*

Doge's Apartments (Appartamenti Ducale)

The dozen or so rooms on the first floor are where the doge actually lived. Wander around this once sumptuous, now sparse suite, and we'll meet up again in the big room with the maps and globes— Room 6, the Sala del Scudo (Shield Room). Along the way, admire elaborate ceilings (coffered, stuccoed, and gilded), chandeliers, big stone fireplaces, velvet-covered walls, and very little furniture, as doges were expected to bring their own. Despite his high office, the doge had to obey several rules that bound him to the city. He couldn't leave the palace unescorted, he couldn't open official mail in private, and he and his family had to leave their own home and live in the Doge's Palace.

In the large Sala del Scudo, which is ringed with maps, work clockwise around the room to trace the eye-opening trip across Asia—from Italy to Greece (quite accurate maps) to Palestine, Arabia, and "Irac"—of local boy Marco Polo (c. 1254–1325). Finally, he arrived at the other side of the world. This last map (shown "upside-down," with south on top) gives a glimpse of the Venetian worldview circa 1550. There's China, Taiwan (Formosa), and Japan (Giapan), while America is a nearby island with California and lots of Terre Incognite.

Doge's Palace

Just off the Sala del Scudo, midway down the Sala dei Filosofi (Philosophers' Hall), pop up the humble stairway and look back at a Titian quickie, painted in just three days. This fresco of St. Christopher carrying the Christ child across the lagoon was made for a doge who believed that if you looked at St. Christopher, you wouldn't die that day.

• *After browsing the dozen or so private rooms, continue up the Golden Staircase to the third floor, which was the "public" part of the palace. The first room at the top of the stairs is the...*

Square Room (Atrio Quadrato)

The ceiling painting, ***Justice Presenting the Sword and Scales to Doge Girolamo Priuli,*** is by Tintoretto. (Stand at the top of the painting for the full 3-D effect.) It's a late-Renaissance masterpiece. So what? As you'll soon see, this palace is wallpapered with Titians, Tintorettos, and Veroneses. Many have the same theme you see here: a doge, in his ermine cape, gold-brocaded robe, and funny one-horned hat with earflaps, kneeling in the presence of saints, gods, or mythological figures.

• *Enter the next room.*

Room of the Four Doors (Sala delle Quattro Porte)

This was the central clearinghouse for all the goings-on in the palace. Visitors presented themselves here and were directed to their destination—the courts, councils, or doge himself.

The room was designed by Andrea Palladio, the architect who did the impressive Church of San Giorgio Maggiore, across the Grand Canal from St. Mark's Square. On the intricate stucco ceiling, notice the feet of the women dangling down below the edge (above the windows), extending the illusion.

On the wall next to the door you entered is a painting by (ho-hum) Titian, showing a **doge kneeling** with great piety before a woman embodying Faith holding the Cross of Jesus. Notice old Venice in the misty distance under the cross. This is one of many paintings you'll see of doges in uncharacteristically humble poses—paid for, of course, by the doges themselves.

G. B. Tiepolo's well-known ***Venice Receiving Neptune*** is now displayed on an easel, but it was originally hung on the wall above the windows where they've put a copy (you'll get closer to the painting as you progress through the museum). The painting shows Venice as a woman—Venice is always a woman to artists—reclining in

Paintings by Titian, Veronese, and Tintoretto

The doge had only the top Venetian painters decorate his palace. While the palace was once rich in Titians, fires in the late 1500s destroyed nearly all the work by the greatest Venetian master. As the palace was hastily reconstructed, the Titians were replaced with works by Veronese and Tintoretto. (Most of these canvases were painted in workshops, and quickly patched in to fill empty spaces.)

Veronese used the best pigments available—from precious stones, sapphires, and emeralds—and his colors have survived vividly. These Veronese paintings are by his hand and are fine examples of his genius. Tintoretto, on the other hand, didn't really have his heart in these commissions, and the pieces here were done by his workshop.

The paintings of the Doge's Palace are a study of old Venice, with fine views of the old city and its inhabitants. The extravagant women's gowns in the paintings of Veronese show off a major local industry—textiles. While the paintings are not generally of masterpiece quality, they're historically interesting. They prove that in the old days, Venice had no pigeons.

---

luxury, dressed in the ermine cape and pearl necklace of a doge's wife *(dogaressa)*. Crude Neptune, enthralled by the First Lady's beauty, arrives bearing a seashell bulging with gold ducats. A bored Venice points and says, "Put it over there with the other stuff."

• *Enter the small room with the big fireplace and several paintings.*

Ante-Collegio Hall (Sala dell'Anticollegio)

It took a big title or bribe to get in to see the doge. Once accepted for a visit, you would wait here before you entered, combing your hair, adjusting your robe, popping a breath mint, and preparing the gifts you'd brought. While you cooled your heels and warmed your

hands at the elaborate fireplace, you might look at some of the paintings—among the finest in the palace, worthy of any museum in the world.

The Rape of Europa (on the wall opposite the fireplace), by Paolo Veronese, most likely shocked many small-town visitors with its risqué subject matter. Here Zeus, the king of the Greek gods, appears in the form of a bull with a foot fetish, seducing a beautiful earthling, while cupids spin playfully

Executive and Legislative Rooms

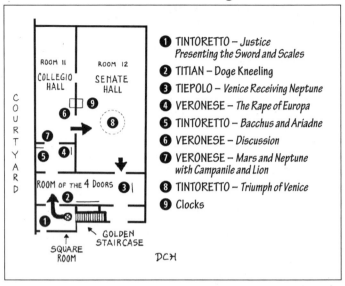

ROOM 11
COLLEGIO HALL

ROOM 12
SENATE HALL

COURTYARD

ROOM OF THE 4 DOORS

SQUARE ROOM

GOLDEN STAIRCASE

DCH

❶ TINTORETTO – *Justice Presenting the Sword and Scales*

❷ TITIAN – Doge Kneeling

❸ TIEPOLO – *Venice Receiving Neptune*

❹ VERONESE – *The Rape of Europa*

❺ TINTORETTO – *Bacchus and Ariadne*

❻ VERONESE – *Discussion*

❼ VERONESE – *Mars and Neptune with Campanile and Lion*

❽ TINTORETTO – *Triumph of Venice*

❾ Clocks

overhead. The Venetian Renaissance looked back to pagan Greek and Roman art, a big change from the saints and crucifixions of the Middle Ages. This painting doesn't portray the abduction in a medieval condemnation of sex and violence, but rather as a celebration in cheery pastel colors of the earthy, optimistic spirit of the Renaissance.

Tintoretto's **Bacchus and Ariadne** (to the left of the exit door) is another colorful display of Venice's sensual tastes. The God of Wine seeks a threesome, offering a ring to the mortal Ariadne, who's being crowned with stars by Venus, who turns slowly in zero gravity. The ring is the center of a spinning wheel of flesh, with the three arms like spokes.

But wait, the doge is ready for us. Let's go in.

• *Enter the next room and approach your imaginary doge.*

Collegio Hall (Sala del Collegio)

Flanked by his cabinet of six advisers—one for each Venetian neighborhood—the doge would sit on the wood-paneled platform at the far end to receive ambassadors, who laid their gifts at his feet and pleaded their countries' cases. All official ceremonies, such as the ratification of treaties, were held here.

Doge's Palace

At other times, it was the "Oval Office" where the doge and his cabinet (the executive branch) met privately to discuss proposals to give the legislature, pull files from the cabinets (along the right wall) regarding business with Byzantium, or rehearse a meeting with the pope. The wooden benches around the sides (where they sat) are original. The clock on the wall is a backward-running 24-hour clock with Roman numerals and a sword for hands.

The ceiling is 24-karat gold, with paintings by Veronese. These are not frescoes (painting on wet plaster), like in the Sistine Chapel, but actual canvases painted in Veronese's studio and then placed on the ceiling. Within years, Venice's humidity would have melted frescoes like mascara.

The T-shaped painting of the woman with the spider web (on the ceiling, opposite the big window) was the Venetian symbol of **Discussion.** You can imagine the webs of truth and lies woven in this room by the doge's nest of advisers.

In **Mars and Neptune with Campanile and Lion** (the ceiling painting near the entrance), Veronese presents four symbols of the Republic's strength—military, sea trade, city, and government (plus a cherub about to be circumcised by the Campanile).

• *Enter the large Senate Hall.*

Senate Hall (Sala del Senato)

While the doge presided from the stage, senators mounted the podium (middle of the wall with windows) to address their 120 colleagues. The legislators, chaired by the doge, debated and passed laws in this room.

Venice prided itself on its self-rule (independent of popes, kings, and tyrants) with most power placed in the hands of these annually elected men. Which branch of government really ruled? All of them. It was an elaborate system of checks and balances to make sure no one rocked the boat, no one got too powerful, and the ship of state sailed smoothly ahead.

Tintoretto's large **Triumph of Venice** on the ceiling (central painting, best viewed from the top) shows the city in all its glory. Lady Venice is up in heaven with the Greek gods, while barbaric lesser nations swirl up to give her gifts and tribute. Do you get the feeling the Venetian aristocracy was proud of its city?

On the wall are two large clocks, one of which has the signs of the zodiac and phases of the moon (pictured on page 93). And there's one final oddity in this room, in case you hadn't noticed it yet. In one of the wall paintings (above the entry door), there's actually a doge...not kneeling.

• *Pass again through the Room of the Four Doors, then around the corner into the large hall with a semicircular platform at the far end.*

Hall of the Council of Ten (Sala del Consiglio dei Dieci)

By the 1400s, Venice had a worldwide reputation for swift, harsh, and secret justice. The dreaded Council of Ten—10 judges, plus the doge and his six advisers—met here to dole out punishment to traitors, murderers, and "morals" violators. (Note the 17 wood panels where they presided.)

Slowly, they developed into a CIA-type unit with their own force of police officers, guards, spies, informers, and even assassins. They had their own budget and were accountable to no one, soon making them the de facto ruling body of the "Republic." It seemed no one was safe from the spying eye of the "Terrible Ten." You could be accused anonymously (by a letter dropped into a "Mouth of Truth"), swept off the streets, tried, judged, and thrown into the dark dungeons in the palace for the rest of your life without so much as a Miranda warning.

It was in this room that the Council decided who lived or died, and who was decapitated, tortured, or merely thrown in jail. The small, hard-to-find door leading off the platform (the fifth panel to the right of center) leads through secret passages to the prisons and torture chambers.

The large, central, oval ceiling painting by Veronese (a copy of the original stolen by Napoleon and still in the Louvre) shows ***Jupiter Descending from Heaven to Strike Down the Vices,*** redundantly informing the accused that justice in Venice was swift and harsh. To the left of that, Juno showers Lady Venice with coins, crowns, and peace.

Though the dreaded Council of Ten was eventually disbanded, today their descendants enforce the dress code at St. Mark's Basilica.

• *Pass through the next room, turn right and head up the stairs to the Armory Museum.*

Armory Museum

The aesthetic of killing is beyond me, but I must admit I've never seen a better collection of halberds, falchions, ranseurs, targes, morions,

Judicial Rooms

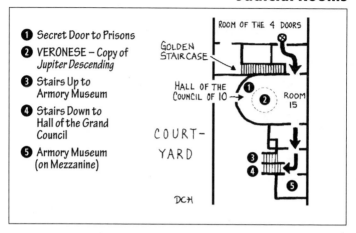

① Secret Door to Prisons

② VERONESE – Copy of Jupiter Descending

③ Stairs Up to Armory Museum

④ Stairs Down to Hall of the Grand Council

⑤ Armory Museum (on Mezzanine)

ROOM OF THE 4 DOORS

GOLDEN STAIRCASE

HALL OF THE COUNCIL OF 10 →

ROOM 15

COURT-YARD

DCH

and brigandines in my life. The weapons in these three rooms make you realize the important role the military played in keeping the East–West trade lines open.

Room 1: In the glass case on the right, you'll see the suit of armor worn by the great Venetian mercenary general, Gattamelata (far right, on horseback), as well as "baby's first armor" (how soon they grow up). A full suit of armor could weigh 66 pounds. Before gunpowder, crossbows (look up) were made still more lethal by turning a crank on the end to draw the bow with extra force.

Room 2: In the thick of battle, even horses needed helmets. The hefty broadswords were brandished two-handed by the strongest and bravest soldiers who waded into enemy lines. Suspended from the ceiling is a large banner captured from the Turks at the Battle of Lepanto (1571).

Room 3: At the far end is a very, very early (17th-century) attempt at a 20-barrel machine gun. On the walls and weapons, the "C-X" insignia means that this was the private stash of the "Council of Ten."

Room 4: Squint out the window to see Palladio's San Giorgio Maggiore and, to the left in the distance, the tiny green dome at Venice's Lido (beach). The glass case in the corner contains a tiny crossbow, some torture devices (including an effective-looking thumbscrew), the wooden "devil's box" (a clever item that could fire in four directions at once), and a nasty, two-holed chastity belt.

These "iron breeches" were worn by the devoted wife of the Lord of Padua.

• *Exit the Armory Museum (enjoy a closer look at that early machine gun). Go downstairs, turn left, and pass through the long hall with a wood-beam ceiling. Now turn right and open your eyes as wide as you can to see the...*

Hall of the Grand Council (Sala del Maggiore Consiglio)

It took a room this size to contain the grandeur of the Most Serene Republic. This huge room (175 by 80 feet) could accommodate up to 2,600 people at one time. The engineering is remarkable. The ceiling is like the deck of a ship—its hull is the rooftop, creating a huge attic above that.

The doge presided from the raised dais, while the nobles—the backbone of the empire—filled the center and lined the long walls. Nobles were generally wealthy men over 25, but the title had less to do with money than with long bloodlines. In theory, the doge, the Senate, and the Council of Ten were all subordinate to the Grand Council of nobles who elected them.

On the wall over the doge's throne is Tintoretto's monster-

piece, *Paradise,* the largest oil painting in the world. At 570 square feet, it could be sliced up to wallpaper an apartment with enough left over for placemats.

Christ and Mary are at the top of heaven, surrounded by 500 people. It's rush hour in heaven, and all the good Venetians made it. The painting leaves you feeling that you get to heaven not by being a good Christian, but by being a good Venetian. Tintoretto worked on this in the last years of his long life. On the day it was finished, his daughter died. He got his brush out again and painted her as saint number 501. She's dead center with the blue skirt, hands clasped, getting sucked up to heaven. (At least that's what an Italian tour guide told me.)

Veronese's *The Apotheosis of Venice* (on the ceiling at the Tintoretto end—view it from the top) is a typically unsubtle work showing Lady Venice being crowned a goddess by an angel.

Ringing the hall are portraits, in chronological order, of the first 76 doges. The one at the far end that's blacked out is the notorious **Doge Marin Falier,** who opposed the will of the Grand Council in 1355. He was tried for treason, beheaded, and airbrushed from history.

Hall of the Grand Council

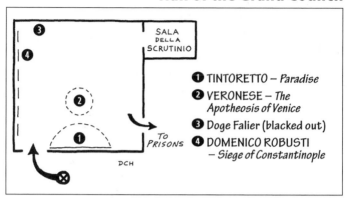

SALA
DELLA
SCRUTINIO

❶ TINTORETTO – *Paradise*
❷ VERONESE – *The Apotheosis of Venice*
❸ Doge Falier (blacked out)
❹ DOMENICO ROBUSTI – *Siege of Constantinople*

TO PRISONS

DCH

Along the entire wall to the right of Paradise, the ***Siege of Constantinople*** (by Tintoretto's son, Domenico Robusti) shows Venice's greatest military (if not moral) victory, the conquest

of the fellow-Christian city of Constantinople during the Fourth Crusade (1204). The mighty walls of Constantinople repelled every attack for nearly a thousand years. But the sneaky Venetians (in the fifth painting) circled around back and attacked where the walls rose straight up from the water's edge. Skillful Venetian oarsmen cozied their galleys right up to the dock, allowing soldiers to scoot along crossbeams attached to the masts, to the top of the city walls. In the foreground, an archer cranks up his crossbow. The gates are opened, the Byzantine emperor parades out to surrender, and tiny Doge Dandolo says, "Let's go in and steal some bronze horses."

But soon Venice would begin its long slide into historical oblivion. One by one, the Turks gobbled up Venice's trading outposts. In the West, the rest of Europe ganged up on Venice to reduce her power. By 1500, Portugal had broken Venice's East–West trade monopoly by finding a sea route to the East around the southern tip of Africa. To top it off, Venice suffered its greatest moral—if not military—victory in the draining Battle of Lepanto, 1571 (depicted in paintings in the adjoining Sala dello Scrutinio). Over the centuries, Venice remained a glorious city, but not the world power she once was. Finally, in 1797, the French general Napoleon marched into town shouting *"Liberté, Egalité, Fraternité."* The Most Serene Republic was finally conquered, and the last doge was deposed in the name of modern democracy.

Out the windows (if they're open) is a fine view of the domes of the basilica, the palace courtyard below, and Paul Newman.

A newly elected doge was presented to the people of Venice from the balcony of the nearby Sala dello Scrutinio room overlooking the Piazzetta. A noble would announce, "Here is your doge, if it pleases you." That was fine, until one time when the people weren't pleased. From then on they just said, "Here is your doge."

• *Consider reading about the prisons here in the Grand Council Hall, where there are more benches and fewer rats.*

Prisons

The palace had its own dungeons. In the privacy of his own home, a doge could oversee the sentencing, torturing, and jailing of political opponents. The most notorious cells were "the Wells" in the basement, so-called because they were deep, wet, and cramped.

By the 1500s, the Wells were full of political prisoners. New prisons were built across the canal to the east of the palace and connected with a covered bridge.

• *Exit the Grand Hall (squeezing through the door to the left of Tintoretto's monsterpiece) and pass through a series of rooms and once-secret passages, following signs for* Ponte dei Sospiri/Prigioni. *Room 31 contains four fascinating paintings by Hieronymus Bosch (once hung in the Hall of the Council of Ten), showing sinners tortured in hell by genetic mutants and* Wizard of Oz *monkeys. In a room adjoining Room 31, you'll find a narrow staircase down, following signs to the prisons. (Don't miss it, or you'll miss the prisons altogether and end up at the bookshop near the exit.) Then cross the covered Bridge of Sighs over the canal to the prisons. Start your visit in the cells to your left.*

Medieval justice was harsh. The cells consisted of cold stone with heavily barred windows, a wooden plank for a bed, a shelf, and a bucket. (My question: What did they put on the shelf?) You can feel the cold dampness.

Circle the cells. Notice the carvings made by prisoners—from olden days up until 1930—on some of the stone windowsills of the cells, especially in the far corner of the building.

Explore the rest of the prisons. One room displays the bored prisoners' moving and sometimes artistic graffiti. You may even be able to descend lower to the Wells.

• *Wherever you roam, you'll end up where you entered. Now re-cross...*

Doge's Palace

The Bridge of Sighs

According to romantic legend, criminals were tried and sentenced in the palace, then marched across the canal here to the dark prisons. On this bridge, they got their one last look at Venice. They gazed out at the sky, the water, and the beautiful buildings.

• *Cross back over the Bridge of Sighs, pausing to look through the marble-trellised windows at all of the tourists and the heavenly Church of San Giorgio Maggiore. Heave one last sigh and leave the palace.*

CORRER MUSEUM TOUR

Museo Civico Correr

A doge's hat, gleaming statues by Canova, and paintings by the illustrious Bellini family—for some people, that's a major museum; for others, it's a historical bore. But the Correr Museum has one more thing to offer, and that's a quiet refuge—a place to rise above St. Mark's Square when the piazza is too hot, too rainy, or too overrun with tourists. Besides, the museum is included if you've bought a ticket to the Doge's Palace. Those who enter are rewarded with an easy-to-manage overview of Venice's art and history.

ORIENTATION

Cost: €13 buys you the Museum Card, which includes two lesser museums within the Correr (National Archaeological Museum and the Monumental Rooms of the Marciana National Library—see tour info on page 108) and the Doge's Palace. For €12 you can get a ticket that covers the **Clock Tower** as well as the Correr, but nothing else (reserve ahead for the Clock Tower at the Correr Ticket desk—see map on page 102). You can avoid ticket lines at the crowded Doge's Palace by buying your Museum Card or Pass at the Correr Museum. For details on the Museum Card and pricier Museum Pass, which also covers the Correr Museum, see page 18.

Hours: Daily April–Oct 9:00–19:00, Nov–March 9:00–17:00, last entry 1 hour before closing.

Getting There: The entrance is on St. Mark's Square in Napoleon's Wing—the building at the far end of the square, opposite the basilica. Climb the staircase to the first-floor ticket office and bookstore.

Information: English descriptions are provided throughout. Tel. 041-240-5211, www.museiciviciveneziani.it.

Bag Check: Mandatory for larger bags, free.
Length of This Tour: Allow one hour.
Cuisine Art: The museum café has tables with a fine view of St. Mark's Square.
Starring: Canova statues, Venetian historical artifacts, three Bellinis, and a Carpaccio.

THE TOUR BEGINS

The Correr Museum gives you admission and access to three connected museums—the Correr proper (which we'll see), the National Archaeological Museum, and the Marciana National Library.

The Correr itself is on three long, skinny floors that parallel St. Mark's Square. This tour covers the first two floors: The first floor contains Canova statues and Venetian history; the second floor displays a chronological overview of Venetian paintings.

FIRST FLOOR

• *Buy your ticket. After entering you'll turn right into the long, skinny Room 3, the Loggia Napoleonica (though you may need to enter directly into the large Ballroom—Room 2, see below—depending on temporary exhibits). As you walk along the Loggia, admire the views of the piazza out the windows. At the end of the hall is a statue of the mythological hero, Paris.*

Room 3 (Loggia Napoleonica)
Canova—*Paris*
The guy with black measles is not a marble statue of Paris; it's a plaster of Paris, a life-size model that Venice's greatest sculptor, Antonio Canova, used in carving the real one in stone. The dots are sculptor's "points," which tell the sculptor how far into the block he should chisel to establish the figure's rough outline.

Nearby, find Canova's pyramid-shaped model of the **Monument to Titian (Monumento a Tiziano).** This was Canova's design (based on the pyramid of Gaius Cestius in Rome) for a tomb he intended for the painter Titian. The design was not used for Titian, but instead for a tomb for an Austrian princess in Vienna, as well as for Canova's own memorial in the Frari Church (for more on Titian's and Canova's monuments, see page 137).
• *From* Paris, *enter the large ballroom.*

Room 2 (Ballroom)
Canova—*Orpheus and Eurydice*
(*Orfeo*, 1775–1776; *Euridice*, 1775)
Orpheus is leading his beloved back from Hell when she is tugged

Correr Museum—First Floor

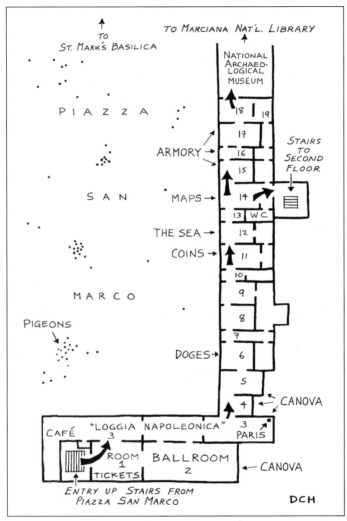

TO MARCIANA NAT'L. LIBRARY

TO ST. MARK'S BASILICA

P I A Z Z A

S A N

M A R C O

PIGEONS

NATIONAL ARCHAEOLOGICAL MUSEUM

18 19

17

ARMORY → 16

15

MAPS → 14

STAIRS TO SECOND FLOOR

13 WC

THE SEA → 12

COINS → 11

10

9

8

7

DOGES → 6

5

4 ← CANOVA

"LOGGIA NAPOLEONICA" 3

CAFÉ 3 PARIS

ROOM 1 BALLROOM 2 ← CANOVA

TICKETS

ENTRY UP STAIRS FROM PIAZZA SAN MARCO

DCH

from behind by the cloudy darkness. She calls for help. Orpheus looks back and smacks his forehead in horror...but he can do nothing to help, and he has to hurry on. In this youthful work, Canova already shows elements of his later style: high-polished, slender, beautiful figures; an ensemble

Correr Museum

Antonio Canova
(1757–1822)

Son of a Venetian stonemason, Canova grew up with a chisel in his hand in a studio along the Grand Canal, precociously mastering the sentimental, elegant Rococo style of the late 1700s. At 23, he went to Rome and beyond, studying ancient statues at then-recently discovered Pompeii. These new archaeological finds inspired a new Renaissance-style revival of the classical style. Canova's pure, understated elegance and "neo"-classical style soon became the rage all over Europe.

Called to Paris, Canova became Napoleon's court sculptor and carved perhaps his best-known work: Napoleon's sister as Venus, reclining on a couch (now in the Borghese Gallery, Rome). Canova combined Rococo sentiment and elegance with the cool, minimal lines of classicism.

---

arrangement, with more than one figure; open space between the figures that's almost as compelling as the figures themselves; and a statue group that's interesting from many angles.

Carved by a teenage Canova, this piece captures the Rococo spirit of Venice in the late 1700s—elegant and beautiful, but tinged with bittersweet loss. Even Canova's later works—which were more sober, minimalist, and emotionally restrained—always retained the elegance and romantic sentiment of the last days of the Venetian Republic.

• *Backtrack past* Paris *and into Room 4.*

Room 4

Canova—*Daedalus and Icarus* (*Dedalo e Icaro,* 1778–1779)

Serious Daedalus straps wings, which he's just invented, onto his son's shoulders. The boy is thrilled with the new toy, not knowing what we know—that they will soon melt in the sun and plunge him

to his death. Daedalus' middle-aged, sagging skin contrasts with Icarus' supple form. Canova, a stonemason's son, displays the tools of the family trade on the base.

Antonio Canova was only 20 when Venice's Procurator commissioned this work from the hometown prodigy. It was so realistic that it caused a stir—skeptics accused Canova of not really sculpting it, but making it from plaster casts of live humans.

Room 5

Canova—*Amor and Psyche*

Though not a great painting, this is Canova's 2-D version of a famous scene he set in stone (now in the Louvre). The two lovers spiral around each other in the never-ending circle of desire. The two bodies and Cupid's two wings form an X. But the center of the composition is the empty space that separates their hungry lips.

Other Canovas

The other large statues in the Canova rooms are either lesser works or more plaster ("gesso") studies for works later executed in marble. You'll also see small clay models, where Canova worked out ideas before chiseling into an expensive block of marble.

• *Enter the world of Venice's doges. On an easel in Room 6, find a doge portrait...*

Room 6: The Doge

Lazzaro Bastiani—*Portrait of Doge Francesco Foscari*

Doge Foscari, dressed in the traditional brocaded robe and cap with cloth earflaps, introduces us to the powerful, regal world of these "elected princes," who served as the ceremonial symbol of the glorious Republic.

Foscari (1373–1457, buried in the Frari Church) inherited Venice at its historical peak as a prosperous sea-trading empire

with peaceful ties to eastern Turks and mainland Europeans. He has a serene look of total confidence...that would slowly melt as he led Venice on a 31-year war of expansion that devastated northern Italy, embroiled Venice in messy European politics, and eventually drained the city's coffers. Meanwhile, the Turks captured Constantinople. By the time the Venetian Senate "impeached" Foscari, forcing his resignation, Venice was sapped, soon to be surpassed by the new sea-trading powers of Spain and Portugal.

In the glass case, find doge memorabilia, including the funny **doge cap** with a single horn at the back, often worn over a cloth cap with earflaps.

• *High on the wall opposite the room's entrance, find the large painting by...*

Andrea Michieli—*Arrival of Dogaressa Grimani* (*Lo Sbarco della Dogaressa Morosina Grimani*)

Although doges were men, several wives were crowned with ceremonial titles. This painting shows coronation ceremonies (1597) along the water by the Piazzetta. The lagoon is jammed with boats. Notice the Doge's Palace on the right, the Marciana National Library on the left (designed by Jacopo Sansovino), and the Campanile and Clock Tower in the distance. The dogess (left of center, in yellow, wearing her doge cap tilted back) arrives to receive the front-door key to the Doge's Palace.

The doge's private boat, the *Bucintoro* (docked at lower left, with red roof), has brought the First Lady and her entourage of red-robed officials, court dwarves, musicians, dancers, and ladies in formal wear. She walks toward the World Theater (on the right, in the water), a floating pavilion used for public ceremonies.

• *Find more doge memorabilia in the next room. Along the walls of Room 7 are two depictions of big parades.*

Room 7

Processions of the Doge in St. Mark's Square (a woodcut by Matteo Pagan, and a painting by Cesare Vecellio)

The woodcut shows the doge and his court parading around St. Mark's Square in the kind of traditional festivities that Venetians enjoy even today. At the head of the parade (to the right) come the

flag bearers and the trumpet players sounding the fanfare. Next are the bigwigs, the archbishop, the bearer of the doge cap, the doge's chair, and finally *Il Serenissimo* himself, under an umbrella. The ladies look on from the windows above.

Some doges were powerful dictators, but in general their power was severely restricted by the Venetian constitution and powerful senators. Many doges were simply ceremonial figureheads, expected to show up in their funny hats for ribbon-cutting ceremonies and state funerals. Doges even needed permission to leave the city.

The process of electing a new doge was as baffling as the American Electoral College: 30 nobles were chosen by casting lots, then 21 of them were eliminated by lots. The remaining nine elected 40 nobles, whose number was whittled down to 25 by lots...

and so on through several more steps, until, finally, 41 electors—chosen by their peers and by chance—selected the next doge.

In the painting, locate the very same windows of the room you're standing in (at far right of the painting). The square looks much like it does today (sans pigeons).

• *The displays in Rooms 8–10 change often. Browse the exhibits, but also admire the fact that these rooms were once government offices.*

Rooms 8–10: Government Offices

Some of the rich furnishings on display in these rooms—rare books in walnut bookcases, a Murano chandelier, wood-beamed ceiling, and paintings—are reminders that this wing once housed the administrative offices of a wealthy, sophisticated, trade-oriented republic.

• *Move to the next room to view Venetian coins. The collection runs chronologically clockwise around the room.*

Room 11: Coins and the Treasury

The Venetian ducat weighed only a bit more than a US penny but was mostly gold. (By decree, 99 percent pure gold, weighing 3.5 grams.) First minted around 1280  (find Giovanni Dandolo's *zecchino*, or "sequin," in the first glass case to the right of the door that leads into the next room), it became the strongest currency in all Europe for nearly 700 years, eventually replacing the Florentine florin. In Renaissance times, 100 ducats would be an average, middle-class salary for a year. The most common design shows Christ on the "heads" side, standing in an oval of stars. "Tails" features the current doge kneeling before St. Mark, with the inscription "sacred money of Venice."

Also in Room 11, find **Tintoretto's painting** of three red-robed treasury officials who handled ducats in these offices. The richness of their fur-lined robes suggests the almost religious devotion that officials were expected to have as caretakers of the "sacred money of Venice."

Room 12: Venice and the Sea

Venice's wealth came from its sea trade. Raw materials from Europe were exchanged for luxury goods from eastern lands controlled by Muslim Turks and Byzantine Christians.

Models of Galleys (Modello di Galera)

These fast oar- and wind-powered warships rode shotgun for

Venice's commercial fleets plying the Mediterranean. With up to 150 men (four per oar, some prisoners, mostly proud professionals) and three horizontal sails, they could cruise from here to Constantinople in about a month. In battle, they specialized in turning on a dime to aim cannons, or in quickly building up speed to ram and board other ships with their formidable prows. Also displayed are large lanterns from a galley's stern.

• *Find two similar paintings depicting...*

The Battle of Lepanto (Battaglia di Lepanto, 1571)

The two paintings capture the confusion of a famous battle fought in 1571 between Muslim Turks and a coalition of Christians off the coast of Greece. This battle ended Turkish dominance at sea. Sort it out by their flags. The turbaned Turks fought under the crescent moon. On the Christian side, Venetians had the winged lion, the pope's troops flew the cross, and Spain was marked with the Hapsburg eagle.

The fighting was fierce and hand-to-hand as they boarded each other's ships and cannons blasted away point-blank. Miguel de Cervantes fought in this battle; he lost his hand and had to pen *Don Quixote* one-handed.

The Christians won, sinking 113 Turkish ships and killing up to 30,000. It was a major psychological victory, as it finally put to rest the Muslim threat to Europe.

But for Venice, it marked the end of an era. The city lost 4,000 men and many ships, and never fully recovered its trading empire in Turkish lands. Moreover, Spain's cannon-laden sailing ships proved to be masters of the waves, making it a true seagoing power. Venice's shallow-hulled galleys, so swift in the placid Mediterranean, were no match on the high seas.

Room 13: The Arsenale

A painting by Antonio di Natale shows a bird's-eye view of the shipbuilding factory located near the tail of Venice. This rectangular, artificial harbor was surrounded by workshops where ships could be mass-produced as though on a modern assembly line (but it was the workers who moved). If needed, they could crank out a galley a day. The Arsenale's entrance (lower left of painting) is still guarded today by the two lions.

Room 14: The Map Room (Venezia Forma Urbis)

Old maps show a city relatively unchanged over the centuries, hemmed in by water. Find your hotel on Jacopo de' Barbari's big map from 1500. There's the Arsenale in the fish's tail. There's Piazza San Marco with a church standing where the Correr Museum entrance is today. The Accademia Bridge hadn't been built yet (nor had the modern train station). We'll see more about Barbari's impressive map upstairs.

Rooms 15–18: Armory

You'll find weapons from medieval times to the advent of gunpowder—maces, armor, swords, Turkish pikes, rifles, cannons, shields, and a teeny-tiny pistol hidden in a book (in a glass case in Room 17).

• *Those interested in visiting the National Archaeological Museum (Greek and Roman statues) and the impressive Marciana National Library can reach them from Rooms 18 and 19 (included with Correr Museum admission).*

The library displays antique globes, manuscripts, and tondi *(round) paintings of virtues and allegories of the liberal arts, such as mathematics, geometry, and music. The walls are richly decorated with portraits of renowned scholars and ancient philosophers who twist and turn in their niches in classical Baroque style. Tintoretto and Veronese, among other lesser artists, worked on these. The last room at the end of the hall features Roman copies of Greek statuary and an impressive trompe l'oeil ceiling (free guided tours of the library Sat–Sun at 10:00, 12:00, 14:00, and 15:00; meet at the entrance to the library a few minutes before the tour begins).*

Otherwise, to continue this tour, backtrack to Room 14 (WCs nearby), then head upstairs to the second floor, following signs to La Quadreria—Picture Gallery. *Enter Room 25.*

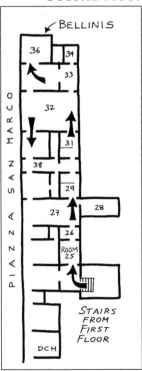

Correr Museum— Second Floor

SECOND FLOOR

Venetian Painting

The painting highlights (the Bellinis) are located at the far end of this wing, and you have permission to hurry there. But along the way, trace the development of

Venetian painting from golden Byzantine icons to Florentine-inspired 3-D to the natural beauty of Bellini and Carpaccio.

Room 25

Paolo Veneziano—*Six Saints* (c. 1310–1358)

Gold-backed saints combine traits from Venice's two cultural sources: Byzantine (serene, elongated, somber, and iconic, with gold background, like the mosaics in St. Mark's) and the Gothic of mainland Europe (curvy, expressive bodies posed at a three-quarters angle, colorful robes, and individualized faces).

Room 26

Lorenzo Veneziano—*Figures and Episodes of Saints (Figure e Storie di Santi,* c. 1356–1370)

Influence from the mainland puts icons in motion, adding drama to the telling of saints' lives (in the small scenes above the three saints). St. Nicholas grabs the executioner's sword and lifts him right off the ground before he even knows what's happening.

Room 27: Ornate (Flamboyant) Gothic

Architectural fragments of Gothic buildings remind us that Venice's distinctive architecture is Italian Gothic filtered through Eastern exoticism.

Room 29.II: International Gothic

Maestro dei Cassone Jarves— Two Painted Lids of a Hope Chest (c. 1425)

As humanism spread, so did art that was not exclusively religious. These scenes depict a story from Boccaccio's bawdy *Decameron*.

Done in the so-called International Gothic style, the painted lids emphasize decorative curves—curvy filigree patterns in clothes, curvy boats,

curvy sails, curvy waves, curvy horses' rumps—all enjoyed as a decorative pattern.

Room 31.I: Ferrarese Painters

Baldassare Estense—*Portrait of a Young Man* (*Ritratto di Gentiluomo*, c. 1442–1564)

The young man in red is not a saint, king, or pope, but an ordinary citizen painted, literally, wart and all. On the window ledge is a strongly foreshortened book. And behind the young man, the curtain opens to reveal a new world—a spacious 3-D vista courtesy of the Tuscan Renaissance.

Room 32

Jacopo de' Barbari—*Venetie MD* (1500)

How little Venice has changed in 500 years! Barbari's large, intricately detailed woodcut of the city put his contemporaries in a unique position—a mile up in the air, looking down on the rooftops. He chronicles nearly every church, alleyway, and gondola. Both the final product and the reverse-image woodcut are on display, a tribute to all of Barbari's painstaking labor.

Room 33: 15th-Century Flemish Artists

Pieter Brueghel the Younger—*Adoration* (*Adorazione dei Magi*)

Venetian artists were strongly influenced by the detailed, everyday landscapes of Northern masters. Lost in this snowy scene of the secular working world is baby Jesus in a stable (lower left), worshipped by the Magi. Venetians learned that landscape creates its own mood, and that humans don't have to be the center of every painting.

Room 34

Antonello da Messina— *Christ with Three Angels* (*Pietà con Tre Angeli,* c. 1475)

The Sicilian painter wowed Venice with this work when he visited in 1475, bringing a Renaissance style and new painting techniques. After a thousand years of standing rigidly on medieval crucifixes, Christ could finally let his body relax in a natural human posture. The scene is set in a realistic, distant landscape.

Remember this work, as I'll refer to it later.

Room 36: The Bellini Family (I Bellini)

One family single-handedly brought Venetian painting into the Renaissance—the Bellinis.

Jacopo Bellini—*Crucifixion (La Crocifissione)*

Father Jacopo (c. 1400–1470) had studied in Florence when Donatello and Brunelleschi were pioneering 3-D naturalism.

Daughter Cecilia (not a painter) married the painter Mantegna, whose precise lines and statuesque figures influenced his brothers-in-law.

Gentile Bellini— *Portrait of Doge Mocenigo*

Elder son Gentile (c. 1429–1507) took over the family business and established a reputation for documenting Venice's rulers and official ceremonies. His straightforward style and attention to detail capture the ordinary essence of this doge.

Giovanni Bellini—*Crucifixion (La Crocifissione)*

Younger son Giovanni (c. 1430–1516) became the most famous

Bellini, the man who pioneered new techniques and subject matter, trained Titian and Giorgione, and almost single-handedly invented the Venetian High Renaissance.

Compare this early Crucifixion (young Giovanni's earliest documented work) with his father's version. Young Giovanni weeds out all the crowded, medieval mourners, leaving only Mary and John. Behind, he paints a spacious (Mantegnesque) landscape, with a lake and mountains in the distance. Our eyes follow the winding road from Christ to the airy horizon, ascending like a soul to heaven.

Giovanni Bellini—*Christ Supported by Two Angels (Cristo Morto Sorreto da Due Angeli, 1453–1455)*

In another early work, Giovanni explores human anatomy, with exaggerated veins, a heaving diaphragm, and even a hint of pubic hair. Mentally compare this stiff, static work with Antonello da Messina's far more natural *Christ with Three Angels* done 20 years later to see how far Giovanni still had to go. In fact, Giovanni was greatly influenced by Antonello, appreciating the full potential of the new invention of oil-based paint. Armed with this more transparent paint, he could add subtler shades of color and rely less on the sharply outlined forms we see here.

Giovanni Bellini—*Madonna and Child (Madonna Frizzoni)*

Though the canvas is a bit wrinkled, it reminds us of the subject Giovanni would paint again and again—lovely, forever-young Mary (often shown from the waist up) holding rosy-cheeked baby Jesus. He portrayed their holiness with a natural-looking, pastel-colored, soft-focus beauty.

Room 38

Vittore Carpaccio—*Two Venetian Ladies (a.k.a. The Courtesans, c. 1500–1510)*

Two well-dressed Venetians look totally bored, despite being surrounded by a wealth of exotic pets and amusements. One lady absentmindedly plays with a dog, while the other stares into space. Romantics imagined them to be kept ladies awaiting lovers, but the recent discovery of the once-missing companion painting tells us they're waiting for their menfolk to return from hunting.

The colorful details and love of luxury are elements that would dominate the Venetian High Renaissance. Fascinating stuff, but my eyes—like theirs—are starting to glaze...

ACCADEMIA TOUR

Galleria dell'Accademia

The Accademia (ack-ah-DAY-mee-ah) is the greatest museum anywhere for Venetian Renaissance art, and a good overview of painters whose works you'll see all over town. Venetian art is underrated and, I think, misunderstood. It's nowhere near as famous today as the work of the florescent Florentines, but—with historical slices of Venice, ravishing nudes, and very human Madonnas—it's livelier, more colorful, and simply more fun.

ORIENTATION

Cost: €6.50, cash only.

Hours: Mon 8:15–14:00, Tue–Sun 8:15–19:15, last entry 30 min before closing.

Crowd Control: Visit early or late to miss crowds (300 people are allowed in at any one time). You can avoid the sometimes-crowded ticket line by making **reservations** for an entry time at least a day in advance: by phone (tel. 041-520-0345) or online (www.gallerieaccademia.org, click "Prenotazione").

Getting There: The museum faces the Grand Canal, just over the Accademia Bridge (15-min walk from St. Mark's Square—follow signs to *Accademia*). Vaporetto stop: Accademia.

Nearby: While you're in the Accademia neighborhood, consider visiting the Ca' Rezzonico, a five-minute walk west (❂ see tour on page 145); the Peggy Guggenheim Collection's excellent display of modern art, a five-minute walk east along the Grand Canal (❂ see tour on page 157); and the historic La Salute Church, just beyond the Guggenheim (❂ see tour on page 170).

Information: Some of the Accademia's rooms have sheets of information in English. The bookshop sells guidebooks for €8.20. Info tel. 041-522-2247.

Accademia

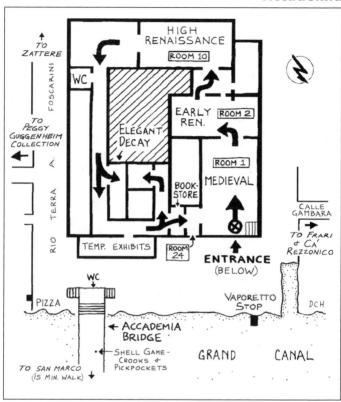

Tours: The **audioguide** costs €4 (€6/double set or Palm Pilot) and doesn't let you fast-forward to the works you want to hear about—you have to listen to the whole spiel for each room. One-hour **guided tours** in English are €5 (€7/2 people, Sat–Sun at 11:00).

Length of This Tour: Allow one hour.

Cuisine Art: Ristorante/Pizzeria Accademia Foscarini is a simple pizza joint with a great Grand Canal setting at the base of the Accademia Bridge (closed Tue).

Photography: Not allowed.

Starring: Titian, Veronese, Giorgione, Bellini, and Tintoretto.

THE TOUR BEGINS

Venice—Swimming in Luxury

The Venetian love of luxury shines through in Venetian painting. We'll see grand canvases of colorful, spacious settings peopled with happy locals in extravagant clothes having a great time. The museum proceeds chronologically from the Middle Ages to the 1700s. But before we start at the medieval beginning, let's sneak a peek at a work by the greatest Venetian Renaissance master, Titian.

• *Buy your ticket, check your bag, and head upstairs to a large hall filled with gold-leaf altarpieces. Immediately past the turnstile, turn left, enter the small Room 24, and take a seat.*

Titian (Tiziano Vecellio)—*Presentation of the Virgin*

A colorful crowd gathers at the foot of a stone staircase. A dog eats a bagel, a mother handles a squirming baby, an old lady sells eggs, and people lean out the windows. Suddenly the crowd turns and points at something. Your eye follows up the stairs to a larger-than-life high priest in a jeweled robe.

But wait! What's that along the way? In a pale blue dress that sets her apart from all the other colored robes, dwarfed by the enormous staircase and columns, the tiny, shiny figure of the child Mary almost floats up to the astonished priest. She's unnaturally small, easily overlooked at first glance. When we finally notice her, we realize all the more how delicate she is amid the bustling crowd, hard stone, and epic grandeur. Venetians love this painting and call it, appropriately enough, the "Little Mary."

The painting is a parade of colors. Titian (TEESH-un) leads your eyes from the massive buildings to the deep blue sky and mountains in the background to the bright red robe of the man in the crowd to glowing Little Mary. Titian painted the work especially for this room, fitting neatly around the door on the right. The door on the left was added later, cutting into Titian's masterpiece.

This work is typical of Venetian Renaissance art. Here and throughout this museum, you will find (1) bright, rich color; (2) big canvases; (3) Renaissance architectural backgrounds; (4) slice-of-life scenes of Venice; and (5) 3-D realism. It's a religious scene, yes, but it's really just an excuse to display secular splendor—Renaissance architecture, colorful robes, and human details.

Now that we've gotten a taste of Renaissance Venice at its peak, let's backtrack and see some of Titian's predecessors.

Accademia—Medieval Art

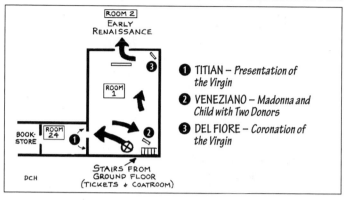

ROOM 2
EARLY RENAISSANCE

ROOM 1

BOOK-STORE

ROOM 24

STAIRS FROM GROUND FLOOR
(TICKETS + COATROOM)

DCH

❶ TITIAN – *Presentation of the Virgin*

❷ VENEZIANO – *Madonna and Child with Two Donors*

❸ DEL FIORE – *Coronation of the Virgin*

• *Return to Room 1, stopping at a painting (near the turnstile) of Mary and baby Jesus.*

Medieval Art—Pre-3-D

Paolo Veneziano—*Madonna and Child with Two Donors* (*Madonna col Bambino e Due Committenti*)

Mary sits in heaven. The child Jesus is a baby in a bubble, a symbol of his "aura" of holiness.

Notice how two-dimensional and unrealistic this painting is. The size of the figures reflects their religious importance—Mary is huge, being both the mother of Christ as well as "Holy Mother Church." Jesus is next, then the two angels who crown Mary. Finally, in the corner, are two mere mortals kneeling in devotion. The golden haloes let us know who is holy. Medieval Venetians, with their close ties to the East, bor-rowed techniques such as gold-leafing, frontal poses, and "iconic" faces from the religious icons of Byzantium (modern-day Istanbul).

Most of the paintings in Room 1 are altarpieces, intended to set in the center of a church for the faithful to meditate on during services. Many feature the Virgin Mary being crowned in triumph. Very impressive. But it took Renaissance artists to remove Mary from her golden never-never land, clothe her in human flesh, and bring her down to the real world we inhabit.

• *In the far right corner of the room, you'll find...*

Jacobello del Fiore—*Coronation of the Virgin* (*Incoronazione della Vergine*)

This swarming beehive of saints and angels is an attempt to cram as much religious information as possible into one space. The architectural setting is a clumsy try at three-dimensionality (the railings of the wedding-cake structure are literally glued on). The color-coordinated saints are simply stacked one on top of the other, rather than receding into the distance as they would in real life.

• *Enter Room 2 at the far end of this hall.*

Early Renaissance (1450–1500)

Only a few decades later, artists rediscovered the natural world and ways to capture it on canvas. With this Renaissance, or "rebirth" of the arts and attitudes of ancient Greece and Rome, painters took a giant leap forward. They weeded out the jumble of symbols, fleshed out cardboard characters into real people, and placed them in spacious 3-D settings.

Giovanni Bellini—*Madonna Enthroned with Child and Saints (Madonna in Trono col Bambino e Santi)*

Mary and the baby Jesus meet with saints in a sacred conversation *(sacra conversazione)* beneath an arched half dome. A trio of musician angels jam at her feet. In its original church setting, the painting's pillars and arches matched the real ones in the church (there may be a photo reconstruction nearby), as though Bellini had blown a hole in the wall and built another chapel, allowing us mortals to mingle with holies.

Giovanni Bellini (bell-EE-nee) takes only a few figures, places them in this spacious architectural setting, and balances them half on one side of Mary and half on the other. Left to right, you'll find St. Francis (medieval founder of an order of friars), John the Baptist, Job, St. Dominic (founder of another order of monks), St. Sebastian, and St. Louis.

The painting has a series of descending arches. At the top is a Roman arch. Hanging below that is a triangular canopy. Then comes a pyramid-shaped "arch" formed by the figures themselves, with Mary's head at the peak, echoed below by the pose of the three musicians. Subconsciously, this creates a mood of serenity, order, and balance, not the hubbub of the *Coronation*. Look at St. Sebastian— even arrows can't disturb his serenity.

Accademia—Early Renaissance

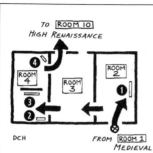

TO ROOM 10
HIGH RENAISSANCE

ROOM 4
ROOM 2
ROOM 3

DCH

FROM ROOM 1
MEDIEVAL

❶ GIOVANNI BELLINI – *Madonna Enthroned with Child and Saints*

❷ MANTEGNA – *St. George*

❸ GIO. BELLINI – *Madonna and Child between St. Catherine and Mary Magdalene*

❹ GIORGIONE – *The Tempest*

In Bellini's long career, he painted many altarpieces in the *sacra conversazione* formula: Mary and Child surrounded by saints "conversing" informally about holy matters while listening to some tunes. The formula, developed largely by Fra Angelico (1400–1455), became a common Renaissance theme—compare this painting with other *sacras* by Bellini in the Frari Church (on page 141) and the Church of San Zaccaria (on page 204).

• *Climb the small staircase and pass through Room 3 into the small Room 4.*

Andrea Mantegna—*St. George (San Giorgio)*

This Christian dragon slayer is essentially a Greek nude sculpture with armor painted on. He rests his weight on one leg *(contrapposto),* the same as a classical sculpture, Michelangelo's *David,* or an Italian guy on the street corner. The doorway he stands in resembles a niche designed for a classical statue.

Mantegna (mahn-TAYN-yah) was trained in the Tuscan tradition. There, painters were like sculptors, "carving" out figures (like this) with sharp outlines, filling them in with color, and setting them in distant backdrops like the winding road behind George. But when Mantegna married Giovanni Bellini's sister, he brought Florentine realism and draftsmanship to his in-laws.

St. George radiates Renaissance optimism—he's alert but relaxed, at rest but ready to spring into action, humble but confident. With the broken lance in his hand and the dragon at his feet, George is the strong Renaissance Man slaying the medieval dragon of superstition and oppression.

• *Find three women and a baby on a black background.*

Giovanni Bellini—*Madonna and Child between St. Catherine and Mary Magdalene*

In contrast to Mantegna's sharp-focus 3-D, this painting features three female heads on a flat plane with a black velvet backdrop.

Their features are soft, hazy, and atmospheric, glowing out of the darkness as though lit by soft candlelight. It's not sculptural line that's important here, but color—warm, golden, glowing flesh tones. The faces emerge from the canvas like cameos.

Bellini painted dozens of Madonna and Childs in his day. (Others are nearby.) This Virgin Mary's pretty, but she's upstaged by the sheer idealized beauty of Mary Magdalene (on the right). Mary Magdalene's hair is down like the prostitute that legend says she was, yet she has a childlike face, thoughtful and repentant. This is the perfect image of the innocent woman who sinned by loving too much.

Bellini was the teacher of two more Venetian greats, Titian and Giorgione, schooling them in the new medium of oil painting. Mantegna painted *St. George* using tempera paint (pigments dissolved in egg yolk), while Bellini pioneered oils (pigments in vegetable oil)—a more versatile medium. Applying layer upon transparent layer, Bellini made creamy complexions with soft outlines, bathed in an even light. His gift to the Venetian Renaissance was the "haze" he put over his scenes, giving them an idealized, glowing, serene—and much copied—atmosphere. (You can see more of Bellini's work at the Correr Museum, page 100; Frari Church, page 137; and the Church of San Zaccaria, page 204.)

• *Around the partition, you'll find...*

Giorgione—*The Tempest*

It's the calm before the storm. The atmosphere is heavy—luminous but ominous. There's a sense of mystery. Why is the woman nursing her baby in the middle of the countryside? And the soldier—is he ogling her or protecting her? Will lightning strike? Do they know that the serenity of this beautiful landscape is about to be shattered by an approaching storm?

The mystery is heightened by contrasting elements. The armed soldier contrasts with the naked lady with her baby. The austere, ruined columns contrast with the lusciousness of Nature. And, most important, the stillness of the foreground scene is in direct opposition to the threatening storm in the background. The landscape itself is the main subject, creating a mood, regardless of what the painting is "about."

Giorgione (jor-JONE-ay) was as mysterious as his few paintings, yet he left a lasting impression. A student of Bellini, he learned to use haziness to create a melancholy mood of beauty. But nothing beautiful lasts. Flowers fade, Mary Magdalenes grow old, Giorgione died at 33, and, in *The Tempest*, the fleeting stillness is about to be shattered by the slash of lightning—the true center of the composition.

• *Exit and browse through several rooms. Check out the bookstore (there's another one later), then continue up the five steps to the large Room 10.*

Venetian High Renaissance (1500–1600)— Titian, Veronese, and Tintoretto

Paolo Veronese—*Feast of the House of Levi*

Parrrrty!! Stand about 10 yards away from this enormous canvas, to where it just fills your field of vision...and hey, you're invited.

 Venice loves the good life, and the celebration is in full swing. You're in a huge room with a great view of Venice. Everyone's dressed to kill in colorful silk and velvet robes. Conversation roars and the servants bring on the food and drink.

This captures the Venetian attitude (more love, less attitude) as well as the style of Venetian Renaissance painting. Remember: (1) bright colors, (2) big canvases, (3) Renaissance architectural settings, (4) scenes of Venetian life, and (5) 3-D realism. Painters had mastered realism and now gloried in it.

The *Feast of the House of Levi* is, believe it or not, a religious work painted for a convent. The original title was *The Last Supper.* In the center of all the wild goings-on, there's Jesus, flanked by his disciples, sharing a final meal before his crucifixion.

This festive feast captures the optimistic spirit of Renaissance Venice. Life was a good thing and beauty was to be enjoyed. Renaissance men and women saw the divine in the beauties of Nature and glorified God by glorifying man.

Uh-uh, said the Church. In its eyes, the new humanism was

the same as the old hedonism. The false spring of the Renaissance froze quickly after the Reformation, when half of Europe left the Catholic Church and became Protestant.

Veronese (vayr-oh-NAY-zay) was hauled before the Inquisition. What did he mean by painting such a bawdy Last Supper? With dwarf jesters? And apostles picking their teeth (between the columns, left of center)? And dogs and cats? And a black man, God forbid? And worst of all, some German soldiers—maybe even Protestants!—at the far right!

Veronese argued that it was just artistic license, so they asked to see his—it had expired. But the solution was simple. Rather than change the painting, just fine-tune the title. *Sì, no problema.* Veronese got out his brush, and *The Last Supper* became the *Feast of the House of Levi,* written in Latin on the railing to the left: *"FECIT D. COVI..."*

Titian (Tiziano Vecellio)—*Pietà*

Jesus has just been executed, and his followers grieve over his body before burying it. Titian painted this to hang over his own tomb.

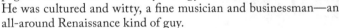

Titian was the most famous painter of his day—perhaps even more famous than Michelangelo. He excelled in every subject: portraits of dukes, kings, and popes; racy nudes for their bedrooms; solemn altarpieces for churches; and pagan scenes from Greek mythology.
He was cultured and witty, a fine musician and businessman—an all-around Renaissance kind of guy.

Titian was old when he painted this. He had seen the rise and decline of the Renaissance and had experienced much sadness in his own life. Unlike Titian's colorful and exuberant "Little Mary," done at the height of the Renaissance, this canvas is dark, the mood more somber.

Jesus is framed by a Renaissance arch like Bellini's *Sacred Conversation,* but here the massive stones overpower the figures, making them look puny and helpless. The lion statues are downright scary. Instead of the clear realism of Renaissance paintings, Titian uses rough, messy brush strokes, a technique that would be picked up by the Impressionists three centuries later. Titian adds a dramatic compositional element—starting with the lion at lower right, a line of motion sweeps up diagonally along the figures, culminating in the grief-stricken Mary Magdalene, who turns away, flinging her arm and howling out loud.

Finally, the kneeling figure of old, bald Nicodemus is a self-portrait of the aging Titian, tending to the corpse of Jesus, who

Accademia—High Renaissance

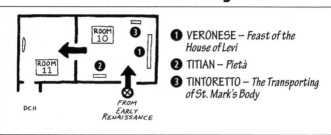

ROOM 10

ROOM 11

DCH

FROM
EARLY
RENAISSANCE

❶ VERONESE – *Feast of the House of Levi*

❷ TITIAN – *Pietà*

❸ TINTORETTO – *The Transporting of St. Mark's Body*

symbolizes the once powerful, now dead Renaissance Man. In the lower right, a painting-within-the-painting shows Titian and his son kneeling, asking the Virgin to spare them from the plague of 1576. Unfortunately, Titian's son died from it, and a heartbroken Titian died shortly after.

(To see more Titians, visit the Frari Church, which houses the painter's tomb, on page 137, and the Doge's Palace, on page 85.)
• *On the opposite wall, find...*

Tintoretto (Jacopo Robusti)—*The Transporting of St. Mark's Body (Trafugamento del Corpo di San Marco)*

The event that put Venice on the map is frozen at its most dramatic moment. Muslim fundamentalists in Alexandria are about to burn Mark's body (there's the smoke from the fire in the center), when suddenly a hurricane appears miraculously, sending them running for cover. (See the wisps of baby-angel faces in the storm, blowing on the infidels? Look hard, on the left-hand side.) Meanwhile, the Venetian merchants whisk away the body.

Tintoretto makes us part of the action. The square tiles in the courtyard run straight away from us, an extension of our real-

ity, as though we could step right into the scene—or the merchants could carry Mark into ours.

Tintoretto would have made a great black-velvet painter. His colors burn with a metallic sheen, and he does everything possible to make his subject popular with common people.

In fact, Tintoretto was a common man himself, self-taught, who apprenticed only briefly with Titian before striking out on his own. He sold paintings in the marketplace in his youth and insisted on living in the poor part of town even after he became famous.

Tintorettos abound here, in the next room, and throughout

Venice. Look for these characteristics, some of which became standard features of Mannerist and Baroque art that followed the Renaissance: (1) heightened drama, violent scenes, strong emotions; (2) elongated bodies in twisting poses; (3) strong contrasts between dark and light; (4) bright colors; and (5) diagonal compositions.

(Tintoretto fans will want to visit the Scuola San Rocco, Tintoretto's "Sistine Chapel"; see page 127.)

• *Spend some time in this room, the peak of the Venetian Renaissance and the climax of the museum. After browsing, enter Room 11 and find a large, round painting. Stand underneath it for the full effect.*

Elegant Decay (1600–1800)

G. B. Tiepolo—*Discovery of the True Cross*
(La Scoperta della Vera Croce)

Tiepolo blasts open a sunroof and we look up into heaven. We (the viewers) stand in the hole where they've just dug up Christ's cross, and look up dresses and nostrils as saints and angels cavort overhead.

Tiepolo was the last of the great colorful, theatrical Venetian painters. He took the colors, the grand settings, and the dramatic angles of previous Venetian masters and plastered them on the ceilings of Europe's Baroque palaces, such as the Royal Palace in Madrid, Spain; the Residenz in Würzburg, Germany; and the Ca' Rezzonico in Venice (❂ see Ca' Rezzonico Tour on page 145). This one is from a church ceiling.

Tiepolo's strongly "foreshortened" figures are masterpieces of technical skill, making us feel like the heavenly vision is taking place right overhead. Think back on those clumsy attempts at three-dimensionality we saw in the medieval room, and realize how far painting has come. The fresco fragments hanging around the corners of Room 11 were salvaged from a church bombed in World War I.

• *Works of the later Venetians are in rooms branching off the long corridor to your left. As you walk down the corridor, the first right leads to the WC. The first left is Room 17.*

Canaletto and Guardi: Views of Venice

By the 1700s, Venice had retired as a world power and become Europe's number-one tourist attraction. Wealthy offspring of the nobility traveled here to soak up its art and culture. They wanted souvenirs, and what better memento than a picture of the city itself?

Guardi and Canaletto painted "postcards" for visitors who lost their hearts to the romance of Venice. The city produced less art... as it became art itself. Here are some familiar views of a city that has aged gracefully.

Accademia—Elegant Decay

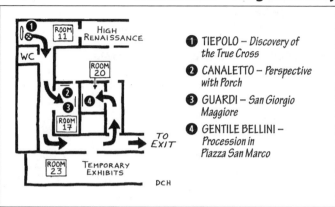

1. TIEPOLO – *Discovery of the True Cross*
2. CANALETTO – *Perspective with Porch*
3. GUARDI – *San Giorgio Maggiore*
4. GENTILE BELLINI – *Procession in Piazza San Marco*

DCH

Canaletto (Giovanni Antonio Canal, called Canaletto)— *Perspective with Porch (Prospettiva con Portico)*

Canaletto gives us a sharp-focus, wide-lens, camera's-eye perspective on the city. Although this view of a porch looks totally realistic, Canaletto has compressed the whole scene to allow us to see more than the human eye could realistically take in. We see the porch as though we were standing underneath it, yet we also see the whole porch at one glance. The pavement blocks, the lines of columns, and the slanting roof direct our eye to the far end, which looks very far away indeed. Canaletto even paints a coat of arms (at right) at a very odd angle, showing off his mastery of 3-D perspective.

Francesco Guardi—*San Giorgio Maggiore (Il Bacino di San Marco con San Giorgio Maggiore e Giudecca)*

Unlike Canaletto, with his sharp-focus detail, Guardi sweetens Venice up with a haze of messy brushwork. In this familiar view

across the water from St. Mark's Square, he builds a boatman with a few sloppy smudges of paint. Guardi catches the play of light at twilight, the shadows on the buildings, the green of the water and sky, the pink light off the distant buildings, the Venice that exists in the hearts of lovers—an

Impressionist work a century ahead of its time.

• *Follow the corridor, turn left at the end, then take another left, and then left again. Are you in Room 20? If so, find...*

Gentile Bellini—*Procession in Piazza San Marco (Processione in Piazza San Marco)*

A fitting end to our tour is a look back at Venice in its heyday. This wide-angle view by Giovanni's big brother—more than any human eye could take in at once—reminds  us how little Venice has changed over the centuries. There is St. Mark's gleaming gold with mosaics, the four bronze horses, the three flagpoles out front, the old Campanile on the right, and the Doge's Palace. There's the guy selling 10 postcards for a dollar. (But there's no Clock Tower with the two bronze Moors yet, the pavement's different, the church is covered with gold, and there are no café orchestras playing "New York, New York.") Every detail is in perfect focus regardless of its distance from us, presented for our inspection. Take some time to linger over this and the other views of old Venice in this room. Then get outta here and enjoy the real thing.

• *To exit, backtrack to the main corridor and turn left past the bookstore. There are often temporary exhibits in the large former chapel branching off the corridor. Say ciao to Titian's "Little Mary" on the way out.*

SCUOLA SAN ROCCO TOUR

Scuola Grande di San Rocco

The 50-plus paintings in the Scuola Grande di San Rocco—often called "Tintoretto's Sistine Chapel"—present one man's very personal vision of Christian history. Tintoretto (1518–1594) spent the last 20 years of his life working practically for free, driven by the spirit of charity that the Scuola, a Christian organization, promoted. For Tintoretto fans, this is the ultimate. Even for the art-weary, his large, colorful canvases, framed in gold on the walls and ceilings of a grand upper hall, are an impressive sight.

ORIENTATION

Cost: €7, includes fine audioguide. (If you see an evening concert here, you can enjoy the art as a bonus; see page 259.)

Hours: Daily April–Oct 9:00–17:30, Nov–March 10:00–17:00, last entry 30 min before closing.

Getting There: It's next to the Frari Church (❂ see Frari Church Tour on page 137). Vaporetto: San Tomà. To walk here from the Rialto Bridge, take my recommended St. Mark's to Rialto Walk, page 192.

Information and WCs: Tel. 041-523-4864, www.scuolagrandesanrocco.it. WCs are located to the left behind the ticket booth; get the key from the ticket clerk.

Mirrors: Use the mirrors scattered about the museum's first floor (some are set in rolling tables, others are handheld), because much of this art is on the ceiling and a pain in the neck.

Length of This Tour: Allow one hour.

Starring: Tintoretto, Tintoretto, and Tintoretto.

THE TOUR BEGINS

The art of the Scuola is contained in three rooms—the Ground Floor Hall (where you enter) and two rooms upstairs. We'll start upstairs, seeing the art roughly in the order that Tintoretto painted it:

1. Albergo Hall (a small room on the upper floor), with Passion scenes.
2. Great Upper Floor Hall, with the biggest canvases.
3. Ground Floor Hall, with the life of Mary.

• *Enter on the ground floor. When you buy your ticket, you find yourself in the Ground Floor Hall, which is lined with big, colorful Tintoretto canvases. Before heading upstairs, begin in the left corner with...*

❶ *The Annunciation*

An angel swoops through the doorway, dragging a trail of naked baby angels with him, to tell a startled Mary she'll give birth to Jesus. This canvas has many of Tintoretto's typical characteristics:

- **The miraculous and the everyday mingle side by side.** Glorious angels are in a broken-down house with stacks of lumber and a frayed chair.

- **Bright light and dark shadows.** A bright light strikes the brick column, highlighting Mary's face and the angel's shoulder, but casting dark shadows across the room.
- **Strong 3-D sucks you into the scene.** Tintoretto literally tears down Mary's wall to let us in. The floor tiles recede sharply into the distance, making Mary's room an extension of our real space.
- **Colors that are bright, almost harsh,** with a metallic "black-velvet" sheen, especially when contrasted with the soft-focus haze of Bellini, Giorgione, Veronese, and (sometimes) Titian.
- **Twisting, muscular poses.** The angel turns one way, Mary turns the other, and the baby angels turn every which way.
- **Diagonal composition.** Shadows run diagonally on the floor as Mary leans back diagonally.
- **Rough brushwork.** The sketchy pattern on Mary's ceiling contrasts with the precise photo-realism of the brick column.

And finally, *The Annunciation* exemplifies the general theme of the San Rocco paintings—God intervenes miraculously into our everyday lives in order to save us.

Scuola San Rocco

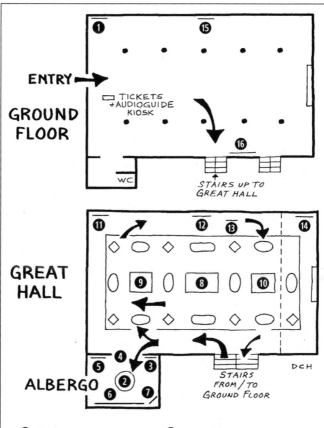

ENTRY →

GROUND FLOOR

TICKETS + AUDIOGUIDE KIOSK

WC

STAIRS UP TO GREAT HALL

GREAT HALL

ALBERGO

STAIRS FROM / TO GROUND FLOOR

DCH

❶ The Annunciation

❷ St. Roch in Glory

❸ Christ Before Pilate

❹ Christ Crowned with Thorns

❺ The Way to Calvary

❻ The Crucifixion

❼ Three Apples

❽ Moses and the Brass Serpent

❾ Moses Bringing Water from a Rock

❿ Manna from Heaven

⓫ The Adoration of the Shepherds

⓬ The Resurrection

⓭ Tintoretto's Carved Face

⓮ The Last Supper

⓯ The Flight into Egypt

⓰ The Circumcision

Jacopo Tintoretto
(1518–1594)

The son of a silk dyer ("Tintoretto" is a nickname meaning "little dyer"), Tintoretto applied a blue-collar work ethic to painting, becoming one of the most prolific artists ever. He trained briefly under Titian, but their egos clashed. He was influenced more by Michelangelo's recently completed *Last Judgment*, with its muscular, twisting, hovering nudes and epic scale.

By age 30, Tintoretto was famous, astounding Venice with the innovative *St. Mark Freeing the Slave* (now in the Accademia). He married, had eight children (three of whom became his assistants), and dedicated himself to work and family, shunning publicity and living his whole life in his old Venice neighborhood.

The last 20 years of his life were spent decorating the Scuola San Rocco. It was a labor of love, showing his religious faith, his compassion for the poor, and his artistic passion.

• *We'll return to the ground floor later, but let's start where Tintoretto did. Climb the staircase (admire the plague scenes that are not by Tintoretto) and enter the impressive Great Hall.*

Wow! Before we tackle these big canvases in this huge room, let's start where Tintoretto did, in the Albergo Hall—the small room in the left corner of the Great Hall. On the ceiling of the Albergo Hall is an oval painting of St. Roch, best viewed from the doorway.

Albergo Hall (Sala d'Albergo)—Christ's Passion

❷ *St. Roch in Glory* (1564)

Start at the feet of St. Roch (San Rocco), a French med student in the 1300s who dedicated his short life to treating plague victims. The Scuola San Rocco was a kind of Venetian "Elks Club" whose favorite charity was poor plague victims.

This is the first of Tintoretto's 50-plus paintings in the Scuola. It's also the one that got him the job, beating entries by Veronese and others.

Tintoretto amazed the judges by showing the saint from beneath, as though he hovered above in a circle of glory. This Venetian taste for dramatic angles and illusion would later become standard in Baroque ceilings. Tintoretto trained by dangling wax models from the ceiling and lighting them from odd angles.

• *On the walls are scenes of Christ's trial, torture, and execution. Work counterclockwise around the room, starting by the door with...*

❸ Christ Before Pilate (Ecce Homo)

Jesus has been arrested and brought before the Roman authorities in a cavernous hall. Although he says nothing in his own defense, he stands head and shoulders above the crowd, literally "rising above" the slanders. Tintoretto shines a bright light on his white robe, making Christ radiate innocence.

At Christ's feet, an old, bearded man in white stoops over to record the events on paper—it's Tintoretto himself.

❹ Christ Crowned with Thorns

Jesus was beaten, whipped, then mocked by the soldiers who dressed him as a king "crowned" with thorns. Seeing the bloodstains on the cloth must have touched the hearts of Scuola members, generating compassion for those who suffer.

❺ The Way to Calvary

Silhouetted against a stormy sky, Jesus and two other prisoners trudge up a steep hill, carrying their own crosses to the execution site. The cycle culminates with...

❻ The Crucifixion

The crucified Christ is the calm center of this huge and chaotic scene that fills the wall. Workers struggle to hoist

crosses, mourners swoon, riffraff gamble for Christ's clothes, and soldiers mill about aimlessly. Scarcely anyone pays any attention to the Son of God...except us, because Tintoretto directs our eye there.

All the lines of sight point to Christ at the center: the ladder on the ground, the cross being raised, the cross still on the ground, the horses on the right, and the hillsides that slope in. In a trick of multiple perspectives, the cross being raised seems to suck us in toward the center, while the cross still on the ground seems to cause the figures to be sucked toward us.

Above the chaos stands Christ, high above the horizon, higher than everyone, glowing against the dark sky. Tintoretto lets us appreciate the quiet irony lost on the frenetic participants—that this minor criminal suffering such apparent degradation is, in fact, triumphant.

• *Displayed on an easel to the left of and beneath* The Crucifixion *is a small fragment of...*

❼ *Three Apples*

This fragment, from the frieze around the upper reaches of the Albergo Hall, was discovered folded under the frieze in 1905. Because it was never exposed to light, it still retains Tintoretto's original bright colors. All of his paintings are darker today, despite cleaning, due to the irreversible chemical alteration of the pigments.

• *Now step back out into the Great Upper Hall...*

Great Upper Hall—Old Testament and New Testament

Thirty-four enormous oil canvases, set into gold frames on the ceiling and along the walls of this impressive room, tell biblical history from Adam and Eve to the Ascension of Christ. Tintoretto's storytelling style is straightforward, and anyone with knowledge of the Bible can quickly get the gist. Tintoretto's success in the Albergo Hall won him the job of the enormous Great Upper Hall.

Understanding What You're Standing Under

The ceiling has Old Testament scenes; the walls have New Testament scenes. The three large rectangles on the ceiling are stories of Moses.

Beyond that, it's difficult to say what overall program Tintoretto had in mind. It's not chronological. There's no consistent symbolism. Theologically, a few panels seem to belong together, matching, say, the *Fall of Man* with Christ's redemption. And some clusters of panels have similar motifs, such as water (at the Albergo end of the hall), plagues and death (middle of the hall), and nourishment (altar end).

But ultimately, Tintoretto's vision is a very personal one, open to many interpretations. The art was inspired by the charitable spirit of the Scuola—just as God has helped those who suffer, so should we.

• *Start with the large, central rectangle on the ceiling. View it from the top (the Albergo end), not directly underneath.*

Scuola S. Rocco

❽ *Moses and the Brass Serpent*

The tangle of half-naked bodies (at the bottom of the painting) represents the children of Israel, wrestling with poisonous snakes and writhing in pain. At the top of the pile, a young woman gestures toward Moses (in pink), who points to a pole carrying a brass serpent sent by God. Those who looked at the statue were miraculously healed. His work all done, God (above in the clouds) high-fives an angel.

This was the first of the Great Hall panels Tintoretto painted in response to a terrible plague that hit Venice in 1576. One in four died. Four hundred a day were buried. (They say that Titian, Tintoretto's colleague, died of heartbreak soon after his son died of the plague.) Like today's Red Cross, the Scuola sprang into action, raising funds, sending doctors, and giving beds to the sick and aid to their families. Tintoretto saw the dead and dying firsthand. While capturing their suffering, he gave a ray of hope that help is on the way: Turn to the cross, and be saved by your faith.

There are dozens of figures in the painting, shown from every conceivable angle. Tintoretto was well aware of where it would hang and how it would be viewed. Walk around beneath it and see the different angles come alive. The painting becomes a movie, and the children of Israel writhe like snakes.

• *The rectangular panel at the Albergo end of the hall is…*

❾ *Moses Bringing Water from a Rock*

Moses (in pink, in the center) hits a rock in the desert with his staff, and it miraculously spouts water, which the thirsty Israelites

catch in jars. The water spurts like a ray of light. Moses is a strong, calm center to a spinning wheel of activity.

Tintoretto worked fast and, if nothing else, his art is exuberant. He trained in fresco painting, where you have to finish before the plaster dries. With these paintings, he sketched an outline right onto the canvas, then improvised details as he went.

The sheer magnitude of the San Rocco project is staggering. This canvas alone is 300 square feet—like painting a bathroom with an artist's tiny brush. The whole project, counting the Albergo Hall, Great Upper Hall, and the Ground Floor Hall together, totals some 8,500 square feet—more than enough to cover a typical house, inside and out. (The Sistine Chapel ceiling, by comparison, is 5,700 square feet.)

• *The rectangular panel at the altar end of the hall is...*

⑩ Manna from Heaven

It's snowing bread, as God feeds the hungry Israelites with a miraculous storm. They stretch a blanket to catch it and gather it up in baskets. Up in the center of the dark  cloud is a radiant, almost transparent God painted with sketchy brush strokes that suggest he's an unseen presence.

Tintoretto tells these Bible stories with a literalness that was very popular with the poor, uneducated sick who sought help from the Scuola. He was the Spielberg of his day, with the technical know-how to bring imagination to life, to make the miraculous tangible.

• *You could grow old studying all the art here, so we'll select just a couple of the New Testament paintings on the walls. Start at the Albergo end with...*

⑪ The Adoration of the Shepherds

Christ's glorious life begins in a straw-filled stable with cows, chickens, and peasants who pass plates of food up to the new  parents. It's night, with just a few details lit by phosphorescent moonlight: the kneeling shepherd's forehead and leggings, the serving girl's shoulders, the faces of Mary and Joseph...and little baby Jesus, a smudge of light.

Notice the different points of view. Tintoretto clearly has placed us on the lower floor, about eye level with the cow, looking up through the roof beams at the night sky. But we also see Mary and Joseph in the loft above as though they were at eye level. By using multiple perspectives (and ignoring the laws of physics), Tintoretto could portray every detail at its perfect angle.

• *In the middle of the long wall, find...*

⓬ *The Resurrection*

Angels lift the sepulchre lid, and Jesus springs forth in a blaze of light. The contrast between dark and light is extreme, with great dramatic effect.

• *On your way to* The Last Supper, *look on the wall for a (⓭) wood carving of Tintoretto (third statue from altar, directly opposite entry staircase). The artist's craggy, wrinkled face squints out from under a black cap and behind a scraggly beard.*

⓮ *The Last Supper*

A dog, a beggar, and a serving girl dominate the foreground of Christ's final Passover meal with his followers. More servants

work in the background. The disciples themselves are dining in the dark, some with their backs to us, with only a few stray highlights to show us what's going on. Tintoretto emphasizes the human, everyday element of that gathering, in contrast to, say, Leonardo da Vinci's statelier version. And he sets the scene at a diagonal for dramatic effect.

The table stretches across a tiled floor, a commonly used device to create 3-D space. But Tintoretto makes the more distant tiles unnaturally small to exaggerate the distance. Similarly, the table and the people get proportionally smaller and lower until, at the far end of the table, tiny Jesus (with glowing head) is only half the size of the disciple at the near end.

Theatrically, Tintoretto leaves it to us to piece together the familiar narrative. The disciples are asking each other, "Is it I who will betray the Lord?" Jesus, meanwhile, unconcerned, hands out Communion bread.

• *Browse the Great Upper Hall and notice the various easel paintings by other artists. Contrast Titian's placid, evenly lit, aristocratic* Annunciation *(displayed on an easel by the altar) with the blue-collar Tintoretto version downstairs. After you've gotten your fill of the Great Upper Hall, head back downstairs for Tintoretto's last works.*

Ground Floor Hall—The Life of Mary

⓯ The Flight into Egypt

There's Mary, Joseph, and the baby, but they're dwarfed by palm trees. Tintoretto, in his old age,

returned to composing a Venetian specialty—landscapes—after years as champion of the Michelangelesque style of painting beefy, twisting nudes. The leafy greenery, the still water, the supernatural sunset, and the hut whose inhabitants go about their work tell us better than any human action that the holy family has found a safe haven.

⓰ The Circumcision

This painting, bringing the circumcision of the baby Jesus into

sharp focus, is the final canvas that Tintoretto did for the Scuola. He collaborated on this work with his son Domenico, who carried on the family business.

In his long and prolific career, Tintoretto saw fame and many high-paying jobs. But at the Scuola, the commission became an obsession. It stands as one man's very personal contribution to the poor, to the Christian faith, and to art.

FRARI CHURCH TOUR

Chiesa dei Frari

For many travelers, this church offers the best art-appreciation experience in Venice, because so much of its great art is *in situ* (right where it was designed to be seen, rather than hanging in museums). And it's about the only Gothic church you'll tour here. Because Venice's spongy ground could never support a real stone Gothic church (like you'd find in France), the Frari Church is made of light and flexible brick. The white limestone foundation insulates the building from the wet soil.

The church was built by the Franciscan order, which arrived in Venice around 1230 (the present building was consecrated in 1492). Franciscan men and women were inspired by St. Francis of Assisi (c. 1182–1226), who dedicated himself to a non-materialist lifestyle—part of a reform movement that spread across Europe in the early 1200s. The Roman Church felt distant and corrupt, and there was a hunger for religious teaching that connected with everyday people. While some of these movements were dubbed heretical (like the Cathars in southern France), the Franciscans (and Dominicans) eventually earned the Church's blessing.

The spirit of St. Francis of Assisi warms both the church of his "brothers" *(frari)* and the art that decorates it. The Franciscan love of all of creation—Nature and Man—later inspired Renaissance painters to capture the beauty of the physical world and human emotions, showing worshippers the glory of God in human terms.

ORIENTATION

Cost: €2.50.
Dress Code: Modest dress is recommended.
Hours: Mon–Sat 10:00–18:00, Sun 13:00–18:00 (closed Sun in Aug), last entry 15 min before closing, no visits during services.

Getting There: It's on the Campo dei Frari, near the San Tomà vaporetto and traghetto stops. (❂ See the St. Mark's to Rialto Walk on page 192 for an easy-to-follow route on foot from the Rialto Bridge.)

Nearby: For efficient sightseeing, combine your visit with the Scuola San Rocco (❂ see tour on page 127), located behind the Frari Church. The Ca' Rezzonico (❂ see tour on page 145) is a seven-minute walk away. To get from the Frari Church to Ca' Rezzonico: From the back end of the church, go through alleyway Sotoportego S. Rocco, turn left at the first T intersection, then right. The rest is easy.

Information: Audioguides are available (€1.60/person, €2.60/ double set). The church often hosts evening **concerts** (€15, tickets sold at the church; for concert details, look for fliers, call 041-272-8611, or check www.basilicadeifrari.it). Church info tel. 041-272-8618.

Length of This Tour: Allow one hour.

Photography: The use of flash is prohibited.

Starring: Titian, Giovanni Bellini, Paolo Veneziano, and Donatello.

THE TOUR BEGINS

• *Enter the church and turn right, finding a spot at the far end with a good view down the long nave toward the altar.*

❶ Church Interior and Choir (1250–1443)

The simple, spacious (110-yard-long), well-lit Gothic church—with rough wood crossbeams and a red-and-white color scheme—is truly a remarkable sight in a city otherwise crammed with exotic froufrou. Traditionally, churches in Venice were cross-shaped, but because the Franciscans were an international order, they weren't limited to Venetian tastes. This new T-shaped footprint featured a long, lofty nave—flooded with light and suited to large gatherings—where common people heard sermons.

The wooden choir area in the center of the nave allowed friars to hold smaller, more intimate services. As worshippers enter the church and look down the long nave to the altar, the sight that greets them—framed by the arch of the choir entrance—is Titian's altarpiece.

Walk prayerfully toward the Titian, stopping in the finely carved 1480s choir. Notice the fine inlay above the chairs, showing the Renaissance enthusiasm for Florentine-style 3-D. Surviving choirs such as this are rare. (In response to Luther's challenge, Counter-Reformation churches discarded the idea of the choirs and altar screens in order to get priests closer to their flocks.)

Frari Church

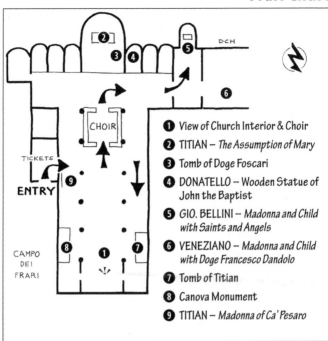

❶ View of Church Interior & Choir

❷ TITIAN – *The Assumption of Mary*

❸ Tomb of Doge Foscari

❹ DONATELLO – Wooden Statue of John the Baptist

❺ GIO. BELLINI – *Madonna and Child with Saints and Angels*

❻ VENEZIANO – *Madonna and Child with Doge Francesco Dandolo*

❼ Tomb of Titian

❽ Canova Monument

❾ TITIAN – *Madonna of Ca' Pesaro*

• *Approach Titian's heavenly vision.*

❷ Titian—*The Assumption of Mary* (1518)

Glowing red and gold like a stained-glass window, this altarpiece sets the tone of exuberant beauty found in this church. Mary, at the end of her life (though looking 17), was miraculously "assumed" into heaven. As cherubs lift her up to meet a Jupiter-like God, the stunned apostles on Earth reach up to touch the floating bubble of light.

Look around. The church is littered with chapels and tombs "made possible by the generous financial support" of rich people who donated to the Franciscans for the good of their souls (and usually for tomb-topping statues of themselves, as well). But the Franciscans didn't sell their main altar, instead hiring new wiz artist, Titian, to create a dramatic altar painting.

Unveiled in 1518, the work scandal-ized a Venice accustomed to simpler, more

subdued church art. The rich colors, twisting poses, and mix of saccharine angels with blue-collar apostles were unheard of. Most striking, this Virgin is fully human, not a stiff icon on a throne. The Franciscans thought this Mary aroused excitement rather than spirituality. They agreed to pay Titian only after the Holy Roman Emperor offered to buy the altar if they refused.

In a burst of youthful innovation, Titian (1488–1576) had rewritten the formula for church art, hinting at changes to come with the Mannerist and Baroque styles. He energized the scene with a complex composition, overlapping a circle (Mary's bubble) and a triangle (draw a line from the apostle reaching up to Mary's face and down the other side) on three horizontal levels (God in heaven, Man on Earth, Mary in between). Together, these elements draw our eyes from the swirl of arms and legs to the painting's focus—the radiant face of a triumphant Mary, "assumed body and soul into heaven."

• *Also in the apse (behind the main altar) are marble tombs lining the walls. On the wall to the right of the altar is the...*

❸ Tomb of Doge Foscari

In contrast to the poverty of the Franciscans, this heavy, ornate tomb marks the peak of Venice's worldly power. Doge Francesco Foscari (1373–1457) assumed control of Venice's powerful seafaring empire and then tried to expand it farther onto the mainland, battling Milan in a 31-year war of attrition that swept through northern Italy. Meanwhile, on the unprotected eastern front, the Turks took Constantinople (1453) and scuttled Venice's trade. Venice's long slide into historical oblivion had begun. Financially drained city fathers forced Foscari to resign, turn in his funny hat, and hand over the keys to the Doge's Palace.

• *In the first chapel to the right of the altar, you'll find...*

❹ Donatello—Wooden Statue of John the Baptist

Emaciated from his breakfast of bugs 'n' honey and dressed in animal skins, the cockeyed prophet of the desert freezes mid-rant when he spies something in the distance. His jaw goes slack, he twists his face and raises his hand to announce the coming of...the Renaissance.

The Renaissance began in the Florence of the 1400s, where Donatello (1386–1466) created realistic statues with a full range

of human emotions. This warts-and-all John the Baptist contrasts greatly with, say, Titian's sweet Mary. Florentine art (including painting) was sculptural, strongly outlined, and harshly realistic, with muted colors. Venetian art was painterly, soft-focus, and beautiful, with bright colors.

Florentine expatriates living in Venice commissioned Donatello to make this statue for their local chapel.

• *Enter the sacristy through the door at the far end of the right transept. You'll bump into an elaborate reliquary altar. Opposite that (near the entrance door) is a clock, intricately carved from a single piece of wood. At the far end of the room, you'll find...*

❺ Giovanni Bellini—*Madonna and Child with Saints and Angels* (1488)

The Pesaro family, who negotiated an acceptable price and place for their family tomb, funded this delightful chapel dominated by a Bellini masterpiece.

Mary sits on a throne under a half dome, propping up baby Jesus (who's just learning to stand), flanked by saints and serenaded by musician angels. Giovanni Bellini (c. 1430–1516), the father of the Venetian Renaissance, painted fake columns and a dome to match the real ones in the gold frame, making the painting seem to be an extension of the room. He completes the illusion with glimpses of open sky in the background. Next, he fills the artificial niches with symmetrically posed, thoughtful saints—left to right, find Saints Nicholas, Peter, Mark, and Sean Connery (Benedict).

Bellini combined the meditative poses of the Venetian Byzantine tradition with Renaissance improvements in modern art. He pioneered painting in oil (pigments dissolved in vegetable oil) rather than medieval tempera (egg yolk–based). It allowed subtler treatment of colors, made with successive layers of paint. And because darker colors aren't so muddy when painted in oil, they "pop," effectively giving the artist a broader palette.

Bellini virtually invented the formula (later to be broken by his precocious pupil, Titian) for Venetian altarpieces. This type of "holy conversation" *(sacra conversazione)* between saints and Mary can also be seen in Venice's Accademia (page 114) and Church of

San Zaccaria (page 204).

Renaissance humanism demanded Madonnas and saints that were accessible and human. Bellini delivers, but places them in a physical setting so beautiful that it creates its own mood of serene holiness. The scene is lit from the left, but no one casts a harsh shadow—Mary and the babe are enveloped in a glowing aura of reflected light from the golden dome. The beauty is in the details, from the writing in the dome to the red brocade backdrop to the swirls in the marble steps to the angels' dimpled legs.

• *In the adjoining room, find a Gothic-arch-shaped painting.*

❻ Paolo Veneziano—*Madonna and Child with Doge Francesco Dandolo* (c. 1339)

Bellini's Byzantine roots can be traced to Paolo Veneziano (literally, "the Venetian"), the first "name" artist in Venice, who helped shape the distinct Venetian style. In turn, Veneziano was inspired by Byzantine artists who came to Venice in search of more freedom of expression. They had chafed under strict societies (both Byzantine and, in some locales, Islamic) that frowned on painting figurative images. In Venice, these expats found an eager community of rich patrons who indulged their love of deeper color, sentiment, movement, and decoration. (Venice clung to this style to the point that it eventually lagged behind Western Europe.)

In this altarpiece, Veneziano paints Byzantine icons, then sets them in motion. Baby Jesus turns to greet a kneeling Doge Dandolo, while Mary turns to acknowledge the doge's wife. None other than St. Francis presents "Francis" (Francesco) Dandolo to the Madonna. Both he and St. Elizabeth (on the right) bend at the waist and gesture as naturally as 14th-century icons can.

• *Return to the nave and head toward the far end. Turn around and face the altar. The Tomb of Titian is in the second bay on your right.*

❼ Tomb of Titian (Titiano Ferdinandus MDCCCLII)

The tomb celebrates both the man (see a carved statue of Titian in the center with beard and crown of laurels) and his famous paintings (depicted in relief).

Titian (1488?–1576) was the greatest Venetian painter, excelling equally in inspirational altarpieces, realistic portraits, joyous mythological scenes, and erotic female nudes.

He moved to Venice as a child, studied first as a mosaic-maker and then under Giovanni Bellini, before establishing his own bold style starring teenage Madonnas (see a relief of *The Assumption* behind Titian). He became wealthy and famous, traveling Europe to paint stately portraits of kings and nobles, and colorful, sexy works for their bedrooms. Titian resisted the temptation of big money that drew so many of his contemporary Venetian artists to Rome. Instead he always returned to his beloved Venice (see winged lion on top)...and favorite Frari Church.

In his old age, Titian painted dark, tragic masterpieces, including the *Pietà* (see relief in upper left) that was intended for his tomb but ended up in the Accademia (see page 114). Nearing 90, he labored to finish the *Pietà* as the plague enveloped Venice. One in four people died, including Titian's son and assistant, Orazio. Heartbroken, Titian died soon afterward of natural causes. His tomb was built three centuries later to remember and honor this great Venetian.

• *On the opposite side of the nave is the pyramid-shaped...*

❽ Canova Monument

Antonio Canova (1757–1822, see his portrait above the door) was Venice's greatest sculptor, creating gleaming, white, highly polished statues of beautiful Greek gods and goddesses in the Neoclassical style. (See several of his works at the Correr Museum, page 100.)

The pyramid shape is timeless, suggesting pharaohs' tombs and the Christian Trinity. Mourners, bent over with grief, shuffle

up to pay homage to the master artist. Even the winged lion is choked up.

Follow me here. Canova himself designed this pyramid-shaped tomb, not for his own use, but as the tomb of an artist he greatly admired: Titian. But the Frari Church used another design for Titian's tomb, so Canova used the pyramid for an Austrian princess...in Vienna. After his death, Canova's pupils reused the design here to honor their master. In fact, Canova isn't buried here—instead, he lies in southern Italy. But inside the tomb's open door, you can (barely) see an urn, which contains his heart.

• *Head back toward the altar. Halfway up the left wall is...*

❾ Titian—*Madonna of Ca' Pesaro* (1526)

Titian's second altarpiece for the Frari Church displays all of his many skills. Following his teacher, Bellini, he puts Mary (seated) and baby (standing) on a throne, surrounded by saints having a holy conversation. And, like Bellini, he paints fake columns that echo the church's real ones.

But wait. Mary is off-center, Titian's idealized saints mingle with Venetians sporting five o'clock shadows, and the stairs run diagonally away from us. Mary sits not on a throne, but on a pedestal. Baby Jesus is restless. The precious keys of St. Peter seem to dangle unnoticed. These things upset traditional Renaissance symmetry, but they turn a group of figures into a true scene. St. Peter (center, in blue and gold, with book) looks down at Jacopo Pesaro, who kneels to thank the Virgin for his recent naval victory over the Turks (1502). A flag-carrying lieutenant drags in a turbaned captive. Meanwhile, St. Francis talks to baby Jesus while gesturing down to more members of the Pesaro family. The little guy looking out at us (lower right) is the Pesaro descendant who administered the trust fund to keep prayers coming for his dead uncle.

Titian combines opposites: a soft-focus Madonna with photo-realist portraits, chubby winged angels with a Muslim prisoner, and a Christian cross with a battle flag. In keeping with the spirit of St. Francis' humanism, Titian lets mere mortals mingle with saints. And we're right there with them.

Frari Church

CA' REZZONICO TOUR

Museum of 18th-Century Venice
(Museo del Settecento Veneziano)

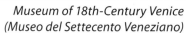

"Endowed by nature with a pleasing physical appearance, a confirmed gambler, a great talker, far from modest, always running after pretty women...I was certain to be disliked. But, as I was always willing to take responsibility for my actions, I decided I had a right to do anything I pleased."
—from *The Memoirs of Giacomo Casanova* (1725–1798)

Venice in the 1700s was the playground for Europe's aristocrats, including the wealthy Rezzonico family, who owned this palace. Today, the Ca' Rezzonico (ret-ZON-ee-koh) contains furniture, decoration, and artwork from the period. This grand home on the Grand Canal is the best place in town to capture the luxurious, decadent spirit of Venice in the Settecento (the 1700s).

ORIENTATION

Cost: €6.50.

Hours: April–Oct Wed–Mon 10:00–18:00, Nov–March Wed–Mon 10:00–17:00, closed Tue. Last entry 1 hour before closing.

Getting There: The museum is located on the west bank of the Grand Canal, right where the canal makes its hairpin turn. There are a number of ways to reach the museum: If you're on vaporetto #1, simply get off at the Ca' Rezzonico stop (between Rialto and Accademia). If you're on the east side of the Grand Canal at San Samuele (near the entrance to Palazzo Grassi), take a quick *traghetto* ride across the canal. If you're coming from the Accademia, it's a 10-minute walk heading northwest: When you reach Campo San Barnaba, cross the bridge in the far-right corner and turn right immediately on Fondamenta Rezzonico. If you're coming on foot from the

Rialto Bridge, it's a 20-minute walk heading southwest (en route, you could visit the Frari Church and the neighboring Scuola San Rocco).

Information and Services: The Ca' Rezzonico is also known as the Museo del Settecento Veneziano (tel. 041-241-0100). Audioguides cost €4 per person (€6/double set) and last 90 minutes. On the ground floor you'll find a free, mandatory baggage check (for anything larger than 8" × 12"), a bookstore, and WCs.

Length of This Tour: Allow 90 minutes.

Cuisine Art: The museum's café has simple fare and a few scenic tables facing the Grand Canal.

Photography: Prohibited.

Starring: A beautiful palace with 18th-century furnishings and paintings by G. B. Tiepolo, Canaletto, and Guardi.

THE TOUR BEGINS

Our Ca' Rezzonico tour covers two floors. The first floor has rooms decorated with period furniture and ceiling frescoes by G. B. Tiepolo. The second floor displays paintings by Canaletto, Guardi, G. D. Tiepolo, Longhi, and others. (The third floor painting gallery—which we won't visit—shows lots of flesh in lots of rooms.)

First, step onto the dock on the Grand Canal and admire Ca'

Rezzonico's heavy stone facade. This dock was, of course, the main entrance back in the 1700s. Next, admire the 1700s-era covered gondola in the courtyard. Picture this arriving at the Ca's dock for a party during Carnevale. A charcoal heater inside kept the masked and caped passengers warm, as they sipped Prosecco and chatted in French, enjoying their winter holiday away from home....

FIRST FLOOR

• *Buy tickets on the ground floor, then ascend the grand staircase to the first floor (where you show your ticket), entering the ballroom.*

Room 1: Ballroom

A great place for a wedding reception. At 5,600 square feet, it's the biggest private venue in the city. Stand in the center, and the room gets even bigger, with a ceiling painting that opens up to the

Ca' Rezzonico—First Floor

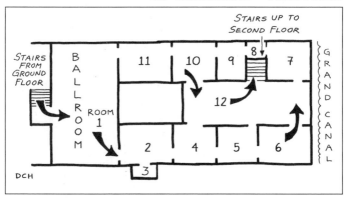

heavens and painted, trompe l'oeil (optical illusion) columns and arches that open onto fake alcoves.

Imagine dancing under candlelit chandeliers to Vivaldi's *Four Seasons*. Servants glide by with drinks and finger foods. The gentlemen wear powdered wigs, silk shirts with lacy sleeves, tight velvet coats and breeches, striped stockings, and shoes with big buckles. They carry snuffboxes with dirty pictures inside the lids. The ladies powder their hair, pile it high, and weave in stuff—pictures of their children or locks of a lover's hair. And everyone carries a mask on a stick to change identity in a second.

The chandeliers of gold-covered wood are original. But most of the furniture we'll see, while it is from the 1700s, is not from the Rezzonico family collection.

• *Promenade across the floor into the next room.*

Room 2: Nuptial Allegory Room

In fact, there *was* a wedding here—see the happy couple on the ceiling, arriving in a chariot pulled by four white horses and serenaded by angels, cupids, and Virtues. In 1757, Ludovico Rezzonico exchanged vows with Faustina Savorgnan in this room, under the bellies of the horses painted for the occasion by Giovanni Battista ("John the Baptist") Tiepolo. G. B. Tiepolo (1696–1770), the best-known decorator of Europe's palaces, was at the height of his fame and technique. He knocked this off in 12 days. His bright colors, mastery of painting figures from every possible angle, wide knowledge of classical literary subjects, and sheer, unbridled imagination made his frescoes blend seamlessly with ornate Baroque and Rococo furniture.

The Rezzonicos were a family of *nouveaux riches* who bought their way into the exclusive club of Venetian patrician families. The **Portrait of Clement XIII** (on easel), pink-cheeked and well-fed, shows the most famous Rezzonico. As pope (elected 1758), Clement spent his reign defending the Jesuit society from anti-Catholic European nobles. A prayer kneeler (in the tiny adjoining chapel, Room 3) looks heavily used, dating from the sin-and-repent, sin-and-repent era of Settecento Venice.

Room 4: Pastel Room

Europe's most celebrated painter of portraits in pastels was a Venetian, Rosalba Carriera (1675–1757). Wealthy French and English tourists on holiday wanted a souvenir of Venice, and Carriera obliged, with miniature portraits on ivory rather than the traditional vellum (soft animal skin). She progressed to portraits in pastel, a medium that caught the luminous,

pale-skin, white-haired, heavy-makeup look that was considered so desirable. Still, her **Portrait (Ritratto) of Sister Maria Caterina** has a warts-and-all realism that doesn't hide the nun's heavy eyebrows, long nose, and forehead vein, which only intensifies the spirituality she radiates.

At age 45, Carriera was invited by tourists whom she'd befriended to visit them in Paris. There she became the toast of the town. Returning triumphantly to Venice, she settled into her home on the Grand Canal and painted until her eyesight failed.

Also in the room is the portrait of Cecilia Guardi Tiepolo: wife of famous painter Giovanni Battista Tiepolo, sister of famous painter Francesco Guardi, and mother of not-very-famous painter Lorenzo Tiepolo, who painted this when he was 21.

Room 5: Tapestry Room

Tapestries, furniture, a mirror, and a door with Asian themes that shows an opium smoker on his own little island paradise (lower panel) give a sense of the Rococo luxury of the wealthy. In a century dominated by the French court at Versailles, Venice was one of the few cities that could hold its own. The fur-niture ensemble of gilded wood chairs, tables, and chests hints at the Louis XIV (claw-foot) style, but the pieces were made in a Venetian workshop.

Despite Venice's mask of gaiety, in the 1700s it was a poor, politically bankrupt, dirty city. Garbage floated in the canals, the streets were either unpaved or slippery with slime, and tourists could hardly stand visiting St. Mark's Basilica or the Doge's Palace because of the stench of mildew. But its reputation for decay and sleaze was actually romanticized into a metaphor for adventures into shady morality. With licensed casinos and a reputed "20,000 courtesans" (prostitutes), it was a fun city for foreigners freed from hometown blinders.

Room 6: Throne Room

"Nowhere in Europe are there so many and such splendid fêtes, ceremonies, and public entertainments of all kinds as there are

in Venice," wrote a visitor from France. As you check out the view of the Grand Canal, imagine once again that you're attending a party here. You could watch the *Forze d'Ercole* (Force of Hercules) acrobats, who stood in boats and kept building a human pyramid—of up to 50 bodies—until they tumbled laughing into the Grand Canal. At midnight the hosts would dim the mirrored candleholders on the walls, so you could look out on a fireworks display over the water.

Carnevale, Venice's prime party time, stretched from the day after Christmas to Lent. Everyone wore masks. Frenchmen, dressed as turbaned Turks, mingled with Turkish traders dressed as harlequins. Fake Barbary pirates fought playfully with skin-blackened "Moors."

Famous 18th-Century Venetians

Canaletto (Giovanni Antonio Canal): Painter of Venice views

Antonio Canova: Neoclassical sculptor

Giacomo Casanova: Gambler, womanizer, revolutionary

Carlo Goldoni: Playwright of realistic comedies

Francesco Guardi: Painter of romantic Enlightened ideas

Giovanni Battista (G. B.) Tiepolo: Painter of Rococo ceilings

Giovanni Domenico (G. D.) Tiepolo: Painter son of famous Tiepolo

And long-nosed Pulcinella clowns were everywhere, reveling in the time when all social classes partied as one because "the mask levels all distinctions." (For information on this year's Carnevale celebration, see page 346).

The **ceiling fresco,** again by Giovanni Battista Tiepolo, certainly trompes my oeil. (It's best viewed from the center.) Tiepolo opens the room's sunroof, allowing angels to descend to Earth to pick up the Rezzonico clan's patriarch. The old, bald, bearded fellow is crowned with laurels and begins to rise on a cloud up to the translucent temple of glory. The angels hold Venice's Golden Book, where the names of the city's nobles were listed. In 1687, the Rezzonico family bought their way into the exclusive club. Tiepolo captures the moment just as the gang is exiting out the "hole" in the ceiling. The leg of the lady in blue hangs over the "edge" of the fake oval. Tiepolo creates a zero-gravity universe that must have astounded visitors. Walk in circles under the fresco, and watch the bugling angel spin.

• Pass through the large next room and into...

Room 7: Tiepolo Room

The ceiling painting by G. B. Tiepolo depicts Nobility and Virtue as a kind of bare-breasted Xena and Gabriela defeating Treachery, who tumbles down. The painting—which is on canvas, not a fresco like the others—was moved here from another palazzo.

Portraits around the room are by Tiepolo and his sons, Lorenzo and Giovanni Domenico. The paintings are sober and down-to-earth, demonstrating the

artistic range of this exceptional family. Giovanni Battista ("G. B.") was known for his flamboyance, but he passed to his sons his penchant for painting wrinkled, wizened old men in the Rembrandt style. In later years, G. B. had the pleasure of traveling with his sons to distant capitals, meeting royalty, and working on palace ceilings. Giovanni Domenico ("G. D.") contributed some of the minor figures in the Ca' Rezzonico ceilings and went on to carve his own niche. (We'll see his work upstairs.)

This room was the Rezzonicos' game room, and you can see a card table in the center. The big walnut cabinet along the wall is one of the few original pieces of furniture from the Rezzonicos' collection.

Room 8: Passage
This narrow corridor displays vessels for serving three foreign stimulants that became popular beverages in 1700s Venice—coffee, tea, and hot chocolate.

Room 9: Library
Ca' Rezzonico was the home of the English poet Robert Browning (1812–1889) in his later years. Imagine him here in this study, in a melancholy mood after a long winter, reading a book and thinking of words from a poem of his: "Oh to be in England, now that April's there...." Antonio Corradini's marvelous bust of the *Veiled Woman* adds to the somber mood.

Room 10: Lazzarini Room
The big, colorful paintings are by Gregorio Lazzarini (1655–1730), Tiepolo's teacher. Tiepolo took Lazzarini's color, motion, and twisted poses and suspended them overhead.

Room 11: Brustolon Room
Andrea Brustolon (1662–1732) carved Baroque fantasies into the custom-made tables, chairs, and vase stand that he crafted in his Venice workshop. In black ebony, reddish boxwood, and brown walnut, they overwhelm with the sheer number of figures, yet each carving is a gem worth admiring. The big vase stand is a harmony of different colors: a white vase supported by ebony slaves in chains

Giacomo Casanova
(1725–1798)

"I began to lead a life of complete freedom, caring for nothing except what pleased me."
—from *The Memoirs of Giacomo Casanova*

Casanova, a real person who wrote an exaggerated autobiography, typifies the Venice that so entranced the rest of Europe. In his life, he adopted many personae, worked in a number of professions, and always took the adventurous path.

Casanova was born just across the Grand Canal from the Ca' Rezzonico. The son of an actor, Casanova trained to be a priest, but was expelled for seducing nuns. To Venetians he was first known as a fiery violinist at fancy parties in palaces such as the Ca' Rezzonico. He would later serve time in the Doge's Palace prison, accused of being a magician.

As a professional gambler and charmer, he roamed Europe's capitals seducing noblewomen, dueling with fellow men of honor, and impressing nobles with his knowledge of Greek literature, religion, politics, and the female sex. His memoirs, published after his death, cemented his reputation as a genial but cunning rake, rogue, and rapscallion.

and a brown boxwood Hercules. The slaves' chains are carved from a single piece of wood—a racist sentiment, but an impressive artistic feat.

The room's flowery Murano glass chandelier—of pastel pinks, blues, and turquoise—is original.

• *Backtrack to Room 10, then turn right into the large, sparsely decorated room called the...*

Room 12: Portego

That funny little cabin in the room is a sedan chair, a servant-powered taxi for Venice's nobles. Four strong-shouldered men ran poles through the iron brackets on either side, then carried it on their shoulders, while the rich rode in red-velvet luxury above the slimy streets.

• *The staircase to the second floor is here in Room 12, in the middle of the long wall. On the second floor, you emerge into Room 13.*

SECOND FLOOR

The first floor showed the rooms and furniture of the 1700s. The second-floor paintings depict the people who sat in those chairs.

Ca' Rezzonico—Second Floor

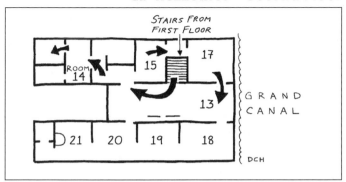

Room 13: Painting Portego

Rich tourists wanting to remember their stay in Venice sought out Canaletto (1697–1768) for a "postcard" view. The ***Grand Canal from Palazzo Balbi to Rialto*** (by Giovanni Antonio Canal, called il Canaletto) captures the view you'd see from the palazzo two doors down. With photographic clarity, Canaletto depicts buildings, boats, and shadows on the water, leading the eye to the tiny, half-hidden Rialto Bridge on the distant horizon.

The ***View of Rio dei Mendicante*** chronicles every chimney, every open shutter, every pair of underwear hanging out to dry.

Canaletto was a young theater-set painter working on Scarlatti operas in Rome when he decided his true calling was painting

reality, not Baroque fantasy. He moved home to Venice, set up his easel outside, and painted scenes like these two, directly from nature. It was considered a very odd thing to do in his day.

Despite the seeming photorealism and crystal clarity, these wide-angle views are more than any human eye could take in without turning side to side. Canaletto, who meticulously studied the mathematics of perspective, was not above tweaking those rules to compress more of Venice into the frame. In the *Grand Canal from Palazzo Balbi to Rialto,* notice there are shadows along both sides of the canal—physically impossible, but more pictur-esque. His paintings still have a theater-set look to them, but here, the Venice backdrop is the star.

To meet the demand for postcard scenes of Venice, Canaletto resorted in later years to painting from engravings or following formulas. But these two early works reflect his pure vision to accu-rately paint the city he loved.

• *From here, we'll move roughly clockwise around the second floor. Head for the door behind your right shoulder. Room 14 is actually a maze of several rooms displaying...*

Room 14: G. D. Tiepolo's Frescoes from the Villa in Zianigo

The son of G. B. Tiepolo decorated the family villa with frescoes for his own enjoyment. They're far more down-to-earth than G. B.'s high-flying fantasies. **New**  **World** features butts, as ordinary folk crowd around a building with a peep-show window. The only faces we see are the two men in profile—Giovanni Domenico Tiepolo (far right, with eyeglass) and his father, G. B. Tiepolo (arms folded)—and baby brother Lorenzo (center). The **Pulcinella Room** (far right corner) has sev-

eral scenes (including one overhead) of the hook-nosed, white-clothed, hunchbacked clown who, at Carnevale time, represented the lovable country bumpkin. But here, he and his similarly dressed companions seem tired, lecher-ous, and stupid. The decadent gaiety of Settecento Venice was at odds with the *Liberté, Egalité,* and *Fraternité* erupting in France.

• *Traveling through the maze of Room 14, wind your way into a room with a harpsichord, cleverly named the...*

Room 15: Harpsichord Room

The 1700s saw the development of new keyboard instruments that would culminate by century's end in the modern piano. This par-ticular specimen has strings that are not hammered (like a piano) but plucked (like a mechanical guitar). The spacing of "white" keys and "black" keys is chromatic like a modern piano. This newly invented "tempered" scale of evenly spaced notes let you play in all keys without retuning.

Room 17: Parlor Room

Francesco Guardi (1712–1793), like Canaletto, supplied foreigners with scenes of Venice. But Guardi uses rougher brushwork that casts a romantic haze over the decaying city.

The Parlor (Il Parlatorio delle Monache di S. Zaccaria) is an interior landscape featuring visiting day at a convent school. The

girls, secluded behind grills, chat and have tea with family members, friends, ladies with their pets, and potential suitors. Convents were like finishing schools for aristocratic girls, where they got an education and learned manners before reentering the world. Note the puppet show (starring spouse-abusing Pulcinella).

Guardi's *Il Ridotto di Palazzo Dandolo* shows party-goers in masks at a Venetian palace licensed for gambling. Casanova and others claimed that these casino houses had back rooms for the private use of patrons and courtesans. The men wear the traditional *bautta*—a three-piece outfit consisting of a face mask, three-cornered hat, and cowl. This get-up was actually required by law in certain seedy establishments to ensure that every sinner was equally anonymous. The women wear Lone Ranger masks, and parade a hint of cleavage to potential customers.

• *Continuing along, you'll pass back through the Painting Portego and into...*

Room 18: Longhi Room

There is no better look at 1700s Venice than these genre scenes by Pietro Longhi (1702–1785), depicting everyday life among the upper classes. See

ladies and gentlemen going to the hairdresser or to the dentist, dressed in the finery that was standard in every public situation.

Contrast these straightforward scenes with G. B. Tiepolo's sumptuous ceiling painting of nude gods and goddesses. The Rococo fantasy world of aristocrats was slipping increasingly into the more prosaic era of the bourgeoisie.

• *Pass through several rooms to the far corner.*

Room 21: The Alcove

Casanova daydreamed of fancy boudoirs like this one, complete with a large bed (topped with a Madonna by Rosalba Carriera), a walnut dresser, Neoclassical wallpaper, and silver toiletries. Even the presence of the baby cradle would not have dimmed his ardour.

PEGGY GUGGENHEIM COLLECTION TOUR

Peggy Guggenheim (1898–1979)—an American-born heiress to the Guggenheim fortune, and niece of Solomon Guggenheim (who built New York's modern-art museum of the same name)—made her mark as a friend, lover, and patron of modern artists.

As a gallery owner, she introduced Europe's avant-garde to a skeptical America. As a collector, she gave instant status to modern art that was too radical for serious museums. As a patron, she fed starving artists such as Jackson Pollock. And as a person, she lived larger than life, unconventional and original, with a succession of lovers that enhanced her reputation as a female Casanova.

In 1948, Peggy "retired" to Venice, moving into a small, unfinished palazzo on the Grand Canal. Today it's a museum, decorated much as it was during her lifetime, with one of the best collections anywhere of 20th-century art. It's the only museum I can think of where the owner is buried in the garden.

ORIENTATION

Cost: €10, generally includes temporary exhibits (displayed near the café and museum shop).

Hours: Wed–Mon 10:00–18:00, closed Tue, last entry 15 min before closing.

Getting There: The museum, overlooking the Grand Canal, is at Dorsoduro 704, a five-minute walk from the Accademia Bridge (vaporetto: Accademia) or from La Salute Church (vaporetto: Salute).

Information: The museum shop sells an excellent €5 mini-guidebook. Tel. 041-240-5440, www.guggenheim-venice.it.

Tours: Audioguide tours cost €7. You can book a guided 60- to

90-min tour (€60) by calling the museum. Art interns guarding the works are happy to tell you about particular pieces if you ask.

Length of This Tour: Allow one hour.

Baggage Check: Free and required.

Cuisine Art: Pricey café on site.

Photography: Permitted only in garden and terrace.

Starring: Picasso, Kandinsky, Mondrian, Dalí, Pollock...and Peggy herself.

THE TOUR BEGINS

After passing through a garden courtyard sprinkled with statues, you enter the palazzo. There's a wing to the left and a wing to the right, plus a modern annex. The collection is (very) roughly chronological, starting to the left with Cubism and ending to the right with young, postwar artists.

The collection's strength is its Abstract, Surrealist, and Abstract-Surrealist art. The placement of the paintings may change, so use this chapter as an overview, not a painting-by-painting tour.

• *Walk through Peggy's collection...and through her life, which is mirrored in the art on the walls. From the sculpture garden, you walk into the...*

Entrance Hall: Meet Peggy Guggenheim

Picture Peggy Guggenheim greeting guests here—standing under the **trembling-leaf mobile by Alexander Calder,** surrounded by her yapping dogs and wearing her Calder-designed earrings, Mondrian-print dress, and "Catwoman" sunglasses.

During the 1950s and 1960s, this old palazzo on the Grand Canal was a mecca for "Moderns," from composer Igor Stravinsky to actor Marlon Brando, from painter Mark Rothko to writer Truman Capote, from choreographer George Balanchine to Beatle John Lennon and performance artist Yoko Ono. They came to sip cocktails, tour the great art, talk about ideas, and meet the woman who had become a living legend.

Pablo Picasso—*On the Beach* (1937)

Curious, balloon-animal women play with a sailboat while their friend across the water looks on. Of all Peggy's many paintings, this was her favorite.

By the time Peggy Guggenheim first became serious about modern art (about the time this was painted), Pablo Picasso—the most famous and

Peggy Guggenheim Collection

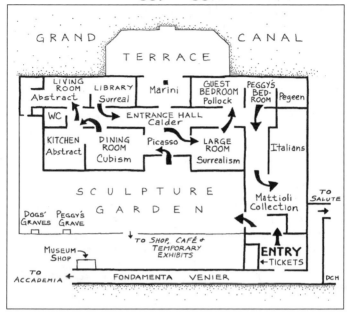

versatile modern artist—had already been through his Blue, Rose, Fauve, Cubist, Synthetic Cubist, Classical, Abstract, and Surrealist phases, finally arriving at a synthesis of these styles. Peggy had some catching up to do.

• *Enter the first room to the left, and you'll see a dining-room table in the center.*

1900–1920: Cubists in the Dining Room

Peggy's dining-room table reminds us that this museum was, indeed, Peggy's home for the last 30 years of her life. (Scattered through the museum are a few small black-and-white photos of Peggy taken here.) Most of the furniture is now gone, but the walls are decorated much as they were when she lived here, with paintings and statues by her friends, colleagues, and mentors. Here, she entertained countless artists and celebrities (more name-dropping), from actor Paul Newman to poet Allen Ginsberg, from sculptor Henry Moore to playwright Tennessee Williams, from James Bond creator Ian Fleming to glass sculptor Dale Chihuly.

The art in the dining room dates from Peggy's childhood, when she was raised in the lap of luxury in New York, oblivious to the artistic upheavals going on in Europe.

In 1912, the *Titanic* went down, taking Peggy's playboy tycoon father with it...and leaving his 14-year-old daughter with a small but comfortable trust fund and a man-sized hole in her life.

Approaching adulthood, Peggy rejected her traditional American upbringing, hanging out at a radical bookstore, getting a nose job (a botched operation, leaving her with a rather bulbous schnozz)...and planning a trip to Europe.

In 1920, 21-year-old Peggy arrived in Paris, where a revolution in art was taking place.

• *Find the following early-20th-century art (or similar pieces) in the Dining Room and rooms nearby—the Kitchen, the Living Room, the Entrance Hall, and the Library.*

Pablo Picasso—*The Poet* (1911)

Picasso, a Spaniard living in Paris, shattered the Old World into brown shards ("cubes") and reassembled it in Cubist style. It's a vaguely recognizable portrait of a man from the waist up—tapering to a head at the top, smoking a pipe (?), and cradling the traditional lyre of a poet. While the newfangled motion-picture camera could capture a moving image, Picasso suggests motion with a collage of stills.

Marcel Duchamp—*Nude (Study), Sad Young Man on a Train* (1911–1912)

In a self-portrait, Duchamp poses gracefully with a cane, but the

moving train jiggles the image into a blur of brown. Duchamp is best known, not for paintings like this, but for his outrageous conceptual pieces: his urinal-as-statue *(Fountain)* and his moustache on the *Mona Lisa* (titled *L.H.O.O.Q.*, which—when spoken aloud in French— is a pun that translates loosely as "she has a hot ass"). In a 2004 poll of British artists, Duchamp's urinal was named the most influential modern artwork of all time.

Umberto Boccioni—*Dynamism of a Speeding Horse + Houses* (assemblage, 1915)

This statue captures the blurred motion of the modern world— accelerated by technology, then shattered by World War I, which left nine million Europeans dead and everyone's moral compass spinning. (In fact, this statue was shattered by the destructive force of Boccioni's own kids, who scattered the cardboard "houses" while using it as a rocking horse.)

Constantin Brancusi—*Maiastra* (bronze statue, c. 1912)

For the generation born before air travel, flying was magical. This high-polished bird is the first of many by Brancusi, who dreamed of flight. But this bird just sits there. For centuries, a good sculptor was one who could capture movement in stone. Brancusi reverts to the style of "primitive" African art, where even the simplest statues radiate mojo.

Marc Chagall—*Rain* (1911)

The rain clouds gather over a farmhouse, the wind blows the trees and people, and everyone pre-

pares for the storm. Quick, put the horse in the barn, grab an umbrella, take a leak, and round up the goats in the clouds.

Marc Chagall, a Russian living in France, found the romantic, weightless, child-like joy of topsy-turvy Paris.

1920s: Abstraction and Various "-Isms"

In the Roaring Twenties, Peggy spent *her* twenties right in the center of avant-garde craziness: Paris. For the rest of her life, Europe—not America—would be her permanent address.

In Paris, trust-funded Peggy lived the bohemian life. Post–WWI Paris was cheap and, after the bitter war years, ready to party. Days were spent drinking coffee in cafés, talking ideas with the likes of activist Emma Goldman, writer Djuna *(Nightwood)* Barnes, and photographer Man Ray. Nights were spent abusing the drug forbidden in America (alcohol), dancing to jazz music into the wee hours, and talking about Freud and s-e-x.

One night, on top of the Eiffel Tower, a dashing artist and intellectual nicknamed "The King of Bohemia" popped the question. Peggy and Laurence Vail soon married and had two children, but the partying only slowed somewhat. This thoroughly modern couple dug the wild life and the wild art it produced.

Wassily Kandinsky—*White Cross* (1922)

I see white, I see crosses, but where's the white cross? Oh, there it is on the right, camouflaged among black squares.

Like a jazz musician improvising from a set scale, Kandinsky plays with new patterns of related colors and lines, creating something that's simply beautiful, even if it doesn't "mean" anything. As Kandinsky himself would say, his art was like "visual music—just open your eyes and look."

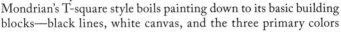

Piet Mondrian—
Composition with Red (1938–1939)

Like a blueprint for Modernism, Mondrian's T-square style boils painting down to its basic building blocks—black lines, white canvas, and the three primary colors

(red, yellow, and blue) arranged in orderly patterns. This stripped-down canvas even omits yellow and blue.

Mondrian started out painting realistic landscapes of the orderly fields in his native Holland. Increasingly, he simplified things into horizontal and vertical patterns, creating rectangles of different proportions. This one has horizontal lines to the left, vertical ones to the right. The horizontals appear to dominate, until we see that they're balanced by the tiny patch of red.

For Mondrian, who was heavily into Eastern mysticism, up vs. down and left vs. right were metaphors for life's ever-shifting dualities—good vs. evil, man vs. woman, fascism vs. communism. The canvas is a bird's-eye view of Mondrian's personal landscape.

1930s: Abstract Surrealists

In 1928, Peggy's marriage to Laurence Vail ended, and she entered into a series of romantic attachments—some loving and stable, others sexual and impersonal. Though not stunningly attractive, she was easy to be with, and she truly admired artistic men.

In 1937, she began an on-again, off-again (so to speak) sexual relationship with playwright Samuel *(Waiting for Godot)* Beckett. Beckett steered her toward Modern painting and sculpture—things she'd never paid much attention to.

She started hanging out with the French Surrealists, from artist Marcel Duchamp to writer André Breton to filmmaker/artist Jean *(Beauty and the Beast)* Cocteau. Duchamp, in particular, mentored her in modern art, encouraging her to use her money to collect and promote it. Nearing 40, she moved to London and launched a new career.

Guggenheim

Abstract Art

Abstract art simplifies. A man becomes a stick figure. A squiggle is a wave. A streak of red expresses anger. Arches make you want a cheeseburger. These are universal symbols that everyone from a caveman to a banker understands. Abstract artists capture the essence of reality in a few lines and colors, even things a camera can't—emotions, abstract concepts, musical rhythms, and spiritual states of mind.

Most 20th-century paintings are a mix of the real world ("representation") and the colorful patterns of "abstract" art. Artists purposely distort camera-eye reality to make the resulting canvas more decorative.

Yves Tanguy—*The Sun in Its Jewel Case* (1937)

In May 1938, this painting was featured at Guggenheim Jeune, the art gallery Peggy opened in London. Tanguy's painting sums up the turbulent art that shocked a sleepy London during that first season.

Weird, phallic, tissue-and-bone protuberances cast long shadows across a moody, dream-like landscape—the landscape of the mind. (Peggy said the picture "frightened" her, but added, "I got over my fear... and now I own it.") The figures are Abstract (unrecognizable), and the mood is Surreal, producing the style cleverly dubbed Abstract Surrealism.

Peggy was drawn to Yves Tanguy and had a short but intense affair with the married man. Tanguy, like his art, was wacky and spontaneous, occasionally shocking friends by suddenly catching and gobbling up a spider and washing it down with white wine. The Surrealists saw themselves as spokesmen for Freud's "id," the untamed part of the personality that thinks dirty thoughts when the "ego" goes to sleep.

The Guggenheim Jeune gallery exhibited many of the artists we see in this museum, including Kandinsky, Mondrian, and Calder. Guggenheim Jeune closed as a financial failure after just two years, but its shocking paintings certainly created a buzz in the art world, and over the years the gallery's failure gained a rosy glow of success.

1939–1940: Peggy's Shopping Spree in Paris

Peggy moved back to Paris and rented an apartment on the Ile St. Louis. In September, Nazi Germany invaded Poland, sparking World War II. All of France waited...and waited...and waited for the inevitable Nazi attack on Paris.

Meanwhile, Peggy spent her days shopping for masterpieces. Using a list compiled by Duchamp and others, she personally visited artists in their studios—from Brancusi to Dalí to Giacometti—often negotiating directly with them. (Picasso initially turned Peggy down, thinking of her as a gauche, bargain-hunting housewife. When she entered his studio he said, "Madame, you'll find the lingerie department on the second floor.") In a few short months, she bought 37 of the paintings now in the collection, perhaps saving them from a Nazi regime that labeled such art "decadent."

In 1941, with the Nazis occupying Paris and most of Europe, Peggy fled her adopted homeland. With her stash of paintings and a new companion—Max Ernst—she sailed from Lisbon to safety in New York.

• *Pass back through the Entrance Hall—where Peggy welcomed celebrity guests, from writer Somerset Maugham to actor Rex Harrison to painter Marc Chagall—and into the east wing. The right entryway leads to a room (called the Large Room) filled with Surrealist canvases.*

1941–1945: Surrealists Invade New York

Trees become women, women become horses, and day becomes night. Balls dangle, caves melt, and things cast long shadows across film-noir landscapes—Surrealism. The world was moving fast, and Surrealists caught the jumble of images. They scattered seemingly unrelated things on the canvas, leaving us to trace the connections in a kind of connect-the-dots game without numbers.

Peggy spent the war years in America. She married the painter Max Ernst, and their house in New York City became a gathering place for exiled French Surrealists and young American artists.

In 1942, she opened a gallery/museum in New York called Art of This Century that featured, well, essentially the collection we see here in Venice. But patriotic, gung-ho America was not quite ready for the non-conformist, intellectual art of Europe.

Max Ernst—*The Antipope* (c. 1942)

The horse-headed nude in red is a portrait of Peggy—at least, that's what she thought when she saw it. She loved the painting and insisted that Max give it to her as a wedding

(sidebar) Guggenheim

present, renamed *The Mystic Marriage.*

Others read more into it. Is the horse-headed warrior (at right) Ernst himself? Is he being wooed by one of his art students? Is that Peggy's daughter, Pegeen (center), watching the scene, sadly, from a distance? And is Peggy turning toward her beloved Max, subconsciously suspicious of the young student...who would (in fact) soon steal Max from her? Ernst uses his considerable painting skill to bring to light the tangle of hidden urges, desires, and

fears—hidden like the grotesque animal faces in the reef they stand on.

Paul Delvaux—
The Break of Day (1937)
Full-breasted ladies with roots cast long shadows and awaken to a mysterious dawn. If you're counting boobs, don't forget the one reflected in the nightstand mirror.

René Magritte—*Empire of Light* (1953–1954)
Magritte found that, even under a sunny blue sky, suburbia has its dark side.

Salvador Dalí—*The Birth of Liquid Desires* (1931–1932)
Salvador Dalí could draw exceptionally well. He painted "unreal" scenes with photographic realism, making us believe they could really happen. This creates an air of mystery—the feeling that anything is possible—that's

both exciting and unsettling. His men explore the caves of the dream world and morph into something else before our eyes.

Personally, Peggy didn't like Dalí or his work, but she dutifully bought this canvas (through his wife, Gala) to complete her collection.
• *Across the hall is the Guest Bedroom, with a fireplace and works by Pollock.*

1945–1948, The Postwar Years: Pollock in the Guest Bedroom
Certain young American painters—from Mark Rothko to Robert Motherwell to Robert De Niro, Sr. (the actor's father)—were

strongly influenced by Peggy's collection. Adopting the Abstract style of Kandinsky and Mondrian, they practiced Surrealist spontaneity to "express" their personal insights. The resulting style (duh): Abstract Expressionism.

Jackson Pollock—*Enchanted Forest* (1947)

"Jack the Dripper" attacked America's postwar conformity with a can of paint, dripping and splashing a dense web onto the canvas. Picture Pollock in his studio, jiving to the hi-fi, bouncing off the walls, throwing paint in a moment of alcohol-fueled enlightenment.

Peggy helped make Pollock a celebrity. She bought his earliest works (which show Abstract-Surrealist roots), exhibited his work at her gallery, and even paid him a monthly stipend to keep experimenting.

By the way, if you haven't yet tried the Venetian specialty *spaghetti al nero di seppia* (spaghetti with squid in its own ink), it looks something like this.

In 1946, Peggy published her memoirs, titled *Out of This Century: The Informal Memoirs of Peggy Guggenheim*. The front cover was designed by Max Ernst, the back by Pollock. Peggy herself was now a celebrity.

• *The room on the other side of the fireplace was Peggy's Room.*

1950s: Peggy in the Bedroom

As America's postwar factories turned swords into kitchen appliances, Peggy longed to return "home" to Europe. The one place that kept calling to her was Venice, ever since a visit with Laurence Vail in the 1920s. "I decided Venice would be my future home," she wrote. "I felt I would be happy alone there."

In 1947, after a grand finale exhibition by Pollock, she closed the Art of This Century gallery, crated up her collection, and moved to Venice. In 1948, she bought this palazzo and moved in.

This was Peggy's bedroom. She painted it turquoise. She commissioned the **silver headboard by Alexander Calder** for her canopy bed, using its silver frame to hang her collection of earrings, handmade by the likes of Calder and Tanguy. Venetian mirrors hung on the walls, along with a sentimental portrait of herself and her sister as children. Ex-husband Laurence Vail's collage-decorated bottles sat on the nightstand.

In 1951, Peggy met the last great love of her life, an easygoing, blue-collar Italian with absolutely no interest in art. She was 53, Raoul was 30, and their relationship, though rather odd, was tender and mutually satisfying. When Raoul died in 1954 in a car accident, Peggy comforted herself with her pets.

• *The tiny corner room adjoining the bedroom displays paintings by Pegeen.*

Pegeen

Peggy's daughter, named Pegeen, inherited some of Laurence Vail's artistic talent, painting childlike scenes of Venice, populated by skinny Barbie dolls with antennae.

The guest bedroom (where the Pollocks are) was a busy place. Pegeen and her brother, Sinbad, visited their mother, as did Peggy's ex-husbands and their new loves. Other overnight guests ranged from sculptor Alberto Giacometti (who honeymooned here) to author and cultural explorer Paul Bowles to artist Jean Arp.

• *Cross the hall and go down a few steps into the wing perpendicular to the palazzo, the Mattioli Annex.*

Italians in the Annex

You'll find a few paintings by famous Italians (**Modigliani, Boccioni**) and a lot by the postwar generation of young Italians who were strongly influenced by Peggy's collection. In 1948, Peggy showed her collection in its own pavilion at the Biennale, Venice's "world's fair of art," and it was the hit of the show. Europeans were astounded and a bit dumbfounded, finally seeing the kind of "degenerate" art forbidden during the fascist years, plus the radical new stuff coming out of New York City.

Peggy sponsored young artists, including **Tancredi**—just one name, back when that was odd—who was given a studio in the palazzo's basement. Tancredi had a relationship with daughter Pegeen, with her mother's blessing. (Pegeen died in 1967 of an overdose of barbiturates.)

• *Return to the Entrance Hall, then go out onto the Terrace, overlooking the Grand Canal.*

Exhibitionists on the Terrace

"You fall in love with the city itself. There is nothing left over in your heart for anyone else."

—Peggy Guggenheim

Marino Marini's equestrian statue, *The Angel of the City* (1948), faces the Grand Canal, spreads his arms wide, and tosses his head back in sheer joy, with an eternal hard-on for the city of Venice. Every morning, Peggy must have felt a similar exhilaration as she sipped coffee with this unbelievable view.

Marini originally designed his bronze rider with a screw-off penis (which sounds dirtier than it is) that could be removed for prudish guests or by curious ones. Someone stole it for some unknown purpose, so the current organ is permanently welded on.

The palazzo—called Palazzo Venier dei Leoni—looks modern but is old. Begun in 1748, only its ground floor was built before construction was halted. Legend has it that members of the rival family across the canal in Palazzo Corner squelched the plans for the upper stories to prevent their home from being upstaged. The palazzo remained unfinished until Peggy bought it in 1948 and spruced it up. She added the annex in 1958. The **lions** *(leoni)* of the original palace still guard the waterfront entrance.

Peggy's outlandish and rather foreign presence in Venice—drinking, dressing up outrageously, and sunbathing on her rooftop for all to see—was not immediately embraced by the Venetians. But for artists in the 1950s and 1960s, Peggy's palazzo was *the* place to be, especially when the Biennale brought the jet set. Everyone from actor Alec Guinness to political satirist Art Buchwald to gossip columnist Hedda Hopper signed her guest book. Picture Peggy and guests, decked out in evening clothes, hopping into Peggy's custom-built gondola (nicknamed *La Barchessa*, after the doge's private boat) to ride slowly down the canal for a martini and a Bellini at Harry's Bar.

• *Pass back through the Entrance Hall, then outside to the...*

Sculpture Garden

Peggy opened her impressive collection of sculpture to the Venetian public for free. It features first-rate works by all the greats, from Brancusi to Giacometti. After so much art already, you might find the trees—so rare in urban Venice—more interesting.

If, after your visit here, you still don't like modern art, think of what Peggy used to tell puzzled visitors: "Come back again in fifty years."

• *In the southwest corner of the garden (along the brick wall), find...*

Peggy's Grave and Her Dogs' Graves

"Here Lie My Beloved Babies," marks the grave of her many dogs that were her steady companions as she grew old. Note the names of some of these small, long-haired Lhasa apsos. Along with "Cappuccino" and "Baby," you'll see "Pegeen," after her daughter, and "Sir Herbert," for Herbert Read, the art critic who helped Peggy select her collection.

Peggy's ashes are buried alongside, marked with a simple plaque: "Here Rests Peggy Guggenheim 1898–1979."

Over your right shoulder, the stumpy olive tree is a gift from one of Peggy's old traveling buddies—Yoko Ono.

In the nonconformist 1960s, Peggy's once shocking art and unconventional lifestyle became more acceptable, even commonplace. By the 1970s, she was universally recognized as a major force in early modern art and was finally even honored by the Venetians with a nickname—"The Last Dogaressa" *(L'Ultima Dogaressa)*. When she died in a Padua hospital in 1979, she was mourned by the art world, from composer Virgil Thomson to choreographer Jerome Robbins to writer George Plimpton to composer John Cage to...

Guggenheim

LA SALUTE CHURCH TOUR

Santa Maria della Salute

Where the Grand Canal opens up into the lagoon stands one of Venice's most distinctive landmarks, the church dedicated to Santa Maria della Salute (Our Lady of Health). The architect, Baldassare Longhena—who also did St. Mark's Square's "New" Wing and the Ca' Rezzonico—remade Venice in the Baroque style. Crown-shaped La Salute was his crowning achievement, and the last grand Venetian structure built before Venice's decline began.

ORIENTATION

Cost and Hours: Church—free, daily 9:00–12:15 & 14:30–17:30. Sacristy—€1.50, Mon–Sat 10:00–12:00 & 15:00–17:00, Sun 15:00–17:00. Tel. 041-274-3928.

Getting There: The church is on the Grand Canal, near the point where the canal spills into the lagoon. It's a 10-minute walk from the Accademia Bridge (past the Peggy Guggenheim Collection). The Salute vaporetto stop is at its doorstep (for example, catching the vaporetto from the San Marco–Vallaresso stop across the Grand Canal to the Salute stop costs €2). If it's November 21, you can walk directly to the church across the Grand Canal on a floating, pontoon-like bridge.

Length of This Tour: Allow 30 minutes.

Starring: Baldassare Longhena's church and minor works by Titian and Giordano.

THE TOUR BEGINS

Exterior

The white stone church has a steep dome (likely to be covered in scaffolding in 2008) that rises above a circular structure. It's

La Salute Church

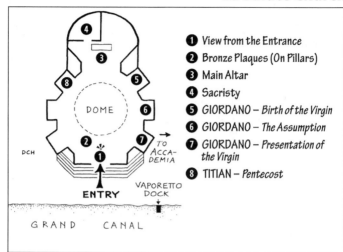

① View from the Entrance
② Bronze Plaques (On Pillars)
③ Main Altar
④ Sacristy
⑤ GIORDANO – *Birth of the Virgin*
⑥ GIORDANO – *The Assumption*
⑦ GIORDANO – *Presentation of the Virgin*
⑧ TITIAN – *Pentecost*

encrusted with Baroque scrolls, leafy Corinthian columns, and 125 statues, including the lovely ladies lounging over the central doorway. The architect conceived of the church "in the shape of a crown."

During the bitter plague of 1630, the Virgin Mary took pity on the city of Venice, miraculously allowing only one in three Venetians (46,000 souls) to die. During this terrible time, Venetians built this church in honor of Our Lady of Health. Her statue tops the lantern, and she's dressed as an admiral, hand on a rudder, welcoming ships to the Grand Canal.

Even today, Mary's intercession is celebrated every November 21, when a floating bridge is erected across the Grand Canal and Venetians can walk from San Marco across the water and right up the seaweed-covered steps to the front door.

At age 32, architect Baldassare Longhena (1598–1682) supported the city's heaviest dome by sinking countless pilings (locals claim over a million) into the sandy soil to provide an adequate foundation. The 12 Baroque scrolls at the base function as buttresses to help support the mammoth dome.

Interior

① View from the Entrance

The church has a bright, healthy glow, with white stone (turned gray because of a fungus) illuminated by light filtering through the dome's windows. The church is circular, surrounded by chapels. In contrast with the ornate Baroque exterior, the inside is simple, with only some Corinthian columns and two useless balcony railings up in the dome. The red, white, and yellow marble of the floor adds a cheerful note.

Longhena focuses our immediate attention on the main altar. Every other view is blocked by heavy pillars. Longhena, a master of "theatrical architecture," only reveals the side chapels one by one as we walk around and explore.

The church is an octagon surrounding a circular nave that's topped by the dome. Viewed from the center of the church, the altar and side chapels are framed by arches.

Some of the "marble" is brick covered with marble dust. The windows are the simple shape that a drop of molten glass makes, to bring in maximum light.

• *Look at the pillars in the rear of the church, opposite the altar, to find the...*

❷ Bronze Plaques

The church is dedicated not just to physical health but to spiritual health as well. The plaques tell us that on September 16, 1972, the future Pope John Paul I—the predecessor of John Paul II—visited here and paid homage to the Virgin of Health (six years later, he fell sick and died after only 30 days in office).

❸ Main Altar

The marble statues on the top tell the church's story: Mary and Child (center) are approached for help by a kneeling, humble Lady Venice (left). Mary takes compassion and sends an angel baby (right) to drive away Old Lady Plague.

The icon of a black, sad-eyed Madonna with a black baby (12th-century Byzantine) is not meant to be racially accurate. Here, a "black" Madonna means an otherworldly one.

• *Through the door to the left of the altar is the...*

❹ Sacristy

If it's open, you can see several great paintings in the sacristy. The three Titians on the ceiling were made by the artist during his "Mannerist crisis." After visiting Rome and seeing the work of Michelangelo in the Sistine Chapel, Titian left his standard, sweet, and tested style (such as the smaller painting over the Sacristy altar) and painted big, statuesque, and dramatic works in the Mannerist style.

In Tintoretto's equally dramatic *Marriage at Cana*, the 12 apostles actually portray leading Venetian artists of his day.

While it costs €1.50 to get in, cheapskates can get a glimpse of the paintings for free at the entry.

• *Back in the circular nave, there are six side chapels—three to the left, three to the right. Start near the altar, on the right side (to your right as you face the altar).*

Side Chapel Paintings
Luca Giordano (1632–1705) celebrates the Virgin in three paintings with a similar composition—heaven and angels above, dark earth below.

Giordano, a prolific artist from Naples, was known as "Luca fa presto" (Fast Luke) for his ambidextrous painting abilities.

• *In the chapel to the right of the altar is...*

❺ Giordano—*Birth of the Virgin* (1674)
Little baby Mary in her mom's arms seems like nothing special. But God the Father looks down from above and sends the dove of the Spirit.

• *In the middle chapel...*

❻ Giordano—*The Assumption*
Mary, at the end of her life, is being taken gloriously by winged babies, up from the dark earth to the golden light of heaven. The apostles cringe in amazement. A later artist thought his statue was better and planted it right in our way.

• *In the chapel closest to the entrance...*

❼ Giordano—*Presentation of the Virgin*
Notice how the painting fits the surrounding architecture. It's great to enjoy art *in situ*. The child Mary (in blue, with wispy halo) ascends a staircase that goes diagonally "into" the canvas. Giordano places us viewers at the foot of the stairs. The lady in the lower left asks her kids, "Why can't you be more like her?!"

• *From here, look directly across to the other side of the nave, to the chapel closest to the main altar. At this distance and angle, Titian's painting looks its best.*

❽ Titian (Tiziano Vecellio)— *Pentecost* (1546)

The dove of the Holy Spirit sends spiritual rays that fan out to the apostles below, giving them tongues of fire above their heads. They gyrate in amazement, each

one in a different direction. Using floor tiles and ceiling panels, Titian has created the 3-D illusion of a barrel-arched chapel, with the dove coming right into the church through a fake window. But the painting was not designed for this location and, up close, the whole fake niche looks...fake.

SAN GIORGIO MAGGIORE TOUR

This dreamy church-topped island is a five-minute vaporetto ride away from St. Mark's Square. Even if you're not interested in Palladio's influential architecture, Tintoretto's famous *Last Supper*, or the stunning bell-tower views of Venice and the lagoon, it's worth a trip just to escape from tourist-mobbed St. Mark's Square.

ORIENTATION

Cost: Admission to the church is free. It costs €3 to go up the bell tower.

Hours: Church open daily May–Sept 9:00–12:00 & 14:30–18:30, Oct–April 9:30–12:45 & 14:30–17:00, but closed to sightseers on Sun during Mass (11:00–12:00, and possibly other times as well). The bells ring (loudly) at 12:00. The elevator up the bell tower closes 30 minutes before the church does.

Getting There: San Giorgio Maggiore is the impressive church you see across the lagoon from St. Mark's Square; the only way to reach it is by vaporetto. Take the five-minute ride on vaporetto #2 (€2, 6/hr) from the San Zaccaria–M.V.E. stop (the San Zaccaria dock farthest from the Bridge of Sighs, 50 yards past the large equestrian statue).

WC: There's a WC at the base of the elevator, inside the church.

Gregorian Mass: A Gregorian Mass is sung Mon–Sat at 8:00 and Sun at 11:00 (confirm times at TI). On Sunday, ring the bell at the door to the right of the main entrance for admission to the Mass, held in the Conclave. If you plan to attend the 8:00 Gregorian Mass, it's better to reach the church from the nearby San Zaccaria–Jolanda vaporetto stop.

Cuisine Art: A fine little harborside café/bar, rarely used by tourists, is about 100 yards around the left of the church. Its terrace is peaceful—except at lunchtime, when it's mobbed by librarians (€6 pastas, salads, daily 10:00–20:00, off-season 11:00–15:00).

Length of This Tour: Allow one hour, more with a trip to the café.

Starring: Palladio, Tintoretto, and views of Venice.

THE TOUR BEGINS

Exterior

The facade looks like a Greek temple, a style well-known today because of its architect, Andrea Palladio (1508–1580). Palladio's hugely influential treatise on architecture inspired centuries of architects in England and America with his expert application of Greco-Roman styles. Countless villas, palaces, and churches look like this. They are "Palladian."

Palladio's facade is similar to two temple fronts overlapping. The four tall columns topped by a triangular pediment resemble a Greek porch, marking the entryway to the tall, central nave. This is superimposed over the facade of the lower side aisles. Behind the facade rises a dome topped with a statue of St. George (the Christian slayer of medieval dragons) holding a flag. The whole complex is completed by the bell tower, which echoes the Campanile in St. Mark's Square across the water.

This church feels so striking because it just doesn't fit with old-school Venice. Palladio makes no concession to the Byzantine legacy of Venice that you see across the water at the Doge's Palace.
• *Walk into the interior of the church…*

❶ View Down the Nave, then Up the Nave

The interior matches the outer facade, with a high nave flanked by lower side aisles. The walls are white; the windows have clear, rather than stained, glass; and the well-lit church has a clarity, orderliness, and mathematical perfection that exudes the classical world. In keeping with Palladio's classical sensitivity, all decor is in order (compared to the relative chaos of the Frari Church). Walk to the high altar in front and look back down the

nave (towards the entry). Oh, the stout, stony symmetry and mathematical purity—with light spilling in from the canal—it's enough to give a Renaissance architect a…never mind.

San Giorgio Maggiore

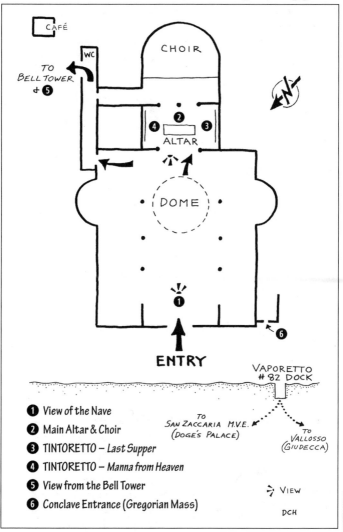

1 View of the Nave

2 Main Altar & Choir

3 TINTORETTO – *Last Supper*

4 TINTORETTO – *Manna from Heaven*

5 View from the Bell Tower

6 Conclave Entrance (Gregorian Mass)

❷ Main Altar and Choir

The altar is topped with a bronze globe of the world. The monks who once lived on this island congregated in the choir area behind the main altar. The choir is designed with acoustics in mind, and the barrel-vault ceiling is backed up with a woofer-shaped apse— all to amplify the Gregorian chants that still fill this church daily.

• *On the wall to the right of the altar is...*

❸ Tintoretto—*Last Supper*

This is the last of several versions of the *Last Supper* by Tintoretto (1518–1594) that decorate Venice, each one different and inventive.

Here, the table stretches diagonally away from us on a tiled floor. The convincing 3-D effect is theatrical, engaging the viewer. The scene is crowded—servants and cats mingle with wispy, unseen angels. A blazing lamp radiating supernatural light illuminates the otherwise dark interior. At the far left, a beggar is fed, illustrating Christ's concern for the poor. The devilish guy on the right turns away from a simple meal (basket of communion wafers), choosing a hedonistic banquet. Your eyes go right to a well-lit Christ, serving his faithful with both hands—wholeheartedly.

San Giorgio was the church for a Benedictine monastery, an order that stressed a simple lifestyle and concern for the poor. They hired Tintoretto (a common-man's painter) and worked closely with him to hone the message that all are welcome—saints, servants, beggars, sinners—into the Christian faith. The monks appreciated Tintoretto's jumble of the spiritual with the mundane, proclaiming that God works miraculously with us on an everyday level.

This canvas works together theologically with the other canvas flanking the altar.

• *On the wall to the left of the altar is...*

❹ Tintoretto—Manna from Heaven

This painting illustrates the Benedictine motto: work and pray. Here we see the sunny morning after the storm when God

rained bread down on the hungry Israelites. Some work (oblivious to the manna), others relax prayerfully, and others gather the heavenly meal in baskets, basking in the glow of the miracle. The message: work and pray and God will take care of you.

• *You'll find the lift to the top of the bell tower in the far left corner of* the church. Be kind to the attendant: He travels six miles a day up and down, day after day, and goes nowhere.

View from San Giorgio Maggiore

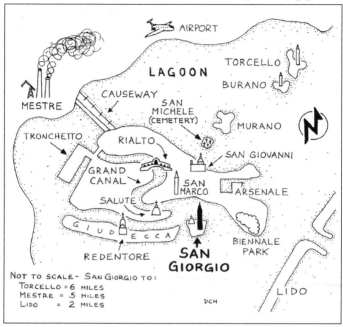

AIRPORT

LAGOON

TORCELLO

BURANO

MESTRE

CAUSEWAY

SAN MICHELE (CEMETERY)

MURANO

TRONCHETTO

RIALTO

SAN GIOVANNI

GRAND CANAL

SAN MARCO

ARSENALE

SALUTE

G I U D E C C A

SAN GIORGIO

BIENNALE PARK

REDENTORE

LIDO

NOT TO SCALE - SAN GIORGIO TO:
    TORCELLO = 6 MILES
    MESTRE = 5 MILES
    LIDO = 2 MILES

DCH

❺ View from the Bell Tower

The bell tower has no grill (unlike the Campanile at St. Mark's, which has one to keep suicidal people from jumping) and gives a grand view in all directions. Start by looking at the city (to the north), and go clockwise:

Facing North (toward the city): This is the famous view of Venice's skyline, with St. Mark's Campanile dominating. The big, long, brick church farther inland is Santi Giovanni e Paolo. Farther to the right (east) is the barely visible basin of the Arsenale, the former ship factory, which in its medieval heyday bragged that it was capable of producing a ship a day. Farther still is the green parkland where the Biennale

International Art Exhibition is held (next in 2009). North of Venice, in the hazy distance, you can glimpse several islands: tiny San Michele (with cypress trees and cemetery; from here, the island looks connected to Venice), Murano (the next-closest, beyond the forested cemetery), Burano (to the distant right, with its leaning bell tower), and Torcello (trust me, just beyond Burano).

Facing East and South: Look out at the lagoon, which leads to the open Adriatic. This tower was once used to spot approaching enemy boats. The lagoon is too shallow for serious shipping; posts mark the channels dredged to let boats pass through. There's a strict speed limit: 5 kph on the small canals, 7 kph on the Grand Canal, and 11 kph around the perimeter of the island city.

The long, narrow Lido island in the distance is six miles long and only a half-mile wide (with cars and ferry service to the

mainland). The green dome on the island marks the Lido's town center, home to modern hotels and beaches. The Lido serves as a natural breakwater against the wind and waves of the Adriatic Sea, helping create the placid waters of the Venetian lagoon. At the right end of the Lido is the narrow opening to the Adriatic, where the proposed, long-delayed, underwater flood barriers are to be built—the 10-year, $3.5 billion "Moses Project"—to block the *acqua alta* flooding. A series of hinged barriers would rise up to block high tides threatening the lagoon.

Once a year, the mayor of Venice sails to the opening of the Adriatic to celebrate the ritual marriage of Venice and the sea—the same ritual performed centuries ago by the doges in their gold-leaf boat.

Between the Lido and San Giorgio are several smaller islands, which have been home over the centuries to monasteries and hospitals. The plain, rectangular white building on San Servolo, the little island just before the Lido, was an 18th-century hospital for the insane that now houses a university.

At your feet are the green gardens and the cloisters of the Abbey of San Giorgio.

Facing West: Below is the church, with its dome topped by a green St. George carrying a flag. You can see the white statues atop

the back of Palladio's false-front facade. Stretching to the left is the island of Giudecca, which is oh-so-close to the island you're on, but must be reached by a short swim or vaporetto #2. The Giudecca, which has always been isolated from the rest of the city, was a popular place to build villas

in Venice's heyday. The island's separation also made it a perfect place for exiles such as Michelangelo, who found refuge and peace here between commissions. Today, except for a few churches, a youth hostel, and a couple of luxury hotels, the Giudecca is home to locals going about their quiet lives, oblivious to the tourism that dominates the rest of Venice. You can see the swimming pool of the jet-setty Ciprani Hotel, the domes of three Palladian churches (the only sights on this otherwise residential island), and, at the far end, the Mulino Stucky, an old, industrial flour mill that opened in 2007 as the Hilton Hotel.

To the right, across the water on the point that marks the opening of the Grand Canal, is the golden globe of the old Customs House and the nearby grand dome (likely swathed in scaffolding) of La Salute Church. And in the far distance, through the smog, are the burning smokestacks and cranes of lovely Mestre on the mainland.

VENICE'S LAGOON TOUR

Cimitero, Murano, Burano, and Torcello

Several interesting islands (including San Giorgio Maggiore, see previous chapter) hide out in Venice's lagoon, a calm section of the Adriatic protected from wind and waves by the natural breakwater of the Lido. The brackish marsh—a mix of fresh water and silt from the mainland's rivers, plus the tide-driven saltwater of the Adriatic—is set among a maze of sandbars. The lagoon is big (212 square miles) and so shallow that you could walk across most of it without getting your hair wet. The shallow water and treacherous sandbars made the Isle of Venice safe from attack by land or sea. It's the only great medieval city that never needed a wall.

Cradled by the lagoon are three islands easily laced together in a side trip, a nice escape from the hubbub of Venice. Murano is known for glass, Burano for lace and photogenic pastel houses, and tranquil Torcello for its church.

ORIENTATION

Cost: Transportation to and between the islands can be free (if you sit through a sales pitch), or it can cost €15, depending on how and where you go (see "Getting There," below). Murano's Glass Museum costs €5.50, Burano's Lace Museum is €4, and all of Torcello's sights cost €8 (cheaper per individual sight).

When to Go: The best days to visit sights on all three islands are Thu–Sun. Murano's Glass Museum is closed Wed, Burano's Lace Museum is closed Tue, and Torcello's church museum is closed Mon (though the island's other sights are open).

Getting There: The islands are reached easily, cheaply, and slowly by vaporetto. (All boats, even speedboats, must obey strict speed limits designed to reduce boat wakes.) Pick up a free map of the islands from any TI.

Venice's Lagoon

Here's the best **vaporetto plan:** Catch vaporetto #41 or #42 from the Fondamenta Nuove vaporetto stop on the north shore of Venice for the 10-minute ride to the Colonna stop on Murano (note that if you catch vaporetto #41 from the San Zaccaria–Jolanda stop on the other side of town, it takes 45 minutes to reach Murano). On Murano, leave from the Faro stop (not Colonna) for the 40-minute cruise to Burano on Line LN (or take #41 to return to Venice). Line T shuttles between Burano and Torcello in five minutes. If you plan to visit even two of these islands, get a 24-hour €15 vaporetto pass.

Speedboat tours of these three lagoon destinations take 3–5 hours, and leave twice a day from the dock past the Doge's Palace. Look for the signs and booth (€25, April–Oct usually at 9:30 and 14:30, Nov–March 14:30 only, tel. 041-523-8835). The tours are speedy indeed—live guides race through the commentary in up to five languages, stopping for roughly 40 minutes at each island (for glassblowing and lacemaking demonstrations followed by sales pitches, leaving no time left to explore the islands).

Many tourists are almost kidnapped from St. Mark's Square by sales reps who bundle people onto a **free speedboat**

shuttle to Murano Island, with no obligation other than to check out their factory/salesroom. It's a free and handy way to get to Murano. You must watch the 20-minute glassmaking show (and sales pitch), but then you're free to escape and see the rest of the island, and then find your own way back to Venice (note that the sales-rep speedboats don't take you back to Venice).

Length of This Tour: Allow five hours to see all four islands.

Starring: World-famous Venetian glass and lace, and the mosaics of the oldest Venetian church.

THE TOUR BEGINS

Cimitero

Boats connecting Venice and Murano stop at San Michele, the **cemetery** island. Consider a quick stopover, since boats come every 10 minutes. Provided you are continuing on, rather than returning to the Venice mainland, you can hop off and back on using the same ticket. If you enjoy wandering through old cemeteries, you'll dig this one.

The island, which is dedicated to St. Michael and holds a Renaissance church, became Venice's cemetery in 1806 when Napoleon decreed that it was unhygienic to bury bodies within a city. As a result, Venice's coffins were shipped out to San Michele, and since then, locals have been buried here. Foreign Romantics and artists who made Venice their adopted hometown (including the Russian-born composer Igor Stravinsky and the American-born poet Ezra Pound) also chose this spot as their final resting place. Here you'll find the dearly departed sorted into sections of priests *(preti)*, nuns *(suore)*, monks *(frati)*, civilian victims of war, soldiers and sailors *(marinai)* of war, and so on.

Murano

Approaching the island of Murano, you'll see its ghostly **light-house** *(faro)*. In centuries past, the *faro* guided boats from the open sea into town.

Murano is famous for its **glass factories.** A 1292 law restricted glass production (and its dangerous furnaces) to the isle of Murano to prevent fires on the main island... and to protect the secrets of Venetian glassmaking. Originally, glassmakers made mosaic tiles, later branching

Lagoon Tour

Legend:
- ☑ VAPORETTO STOP
- ⌒ BRIDGE
- ••• BOAT
- --- ON FOOT

NOT TO SCALE

CHURCH COMPLEX

TORCELLO

10 MIN. WALK

LAGOON

5 MIN.

MAZZORBO

LACE MUSEUM

40 MIN.

MURANO

GLASS MUSEUM

BURANO

COLONNA

FARO

5 MIN.

CIMITERO

LAGOON

5 MIN.

FONDAMENTA NUOVE

FONDAMENTA NUOVE

#41 & #42
(CATCH BOAT FROM LEFT SIDE OF DOCK)

VENICE

DCH

1. Cemetery
2. Trattoria Busa alla Torre
3. Church of San Pietro Martire
4. Glass Museum
5. Bell Tower
6. Merletti d'Arte dalla Lidia
7. Lace Museum
8. Ristorante al Vecio Pipa
9. Locanda Cipriani
10. Santa Maria Assunta Complex

Lagoon Tour

Boating in Venice

Italian law stipulates that a luxury tax is levied on all boats—except in Venice, where they're considered a necessity. Locals go everywhere by boat. Calling a taxi? A boat comes. Going to the hospital to have a baby? Just hop the vaporetto. Garbage day? You put your bag on the canal edge and a garbage boat mashes it and takes it away.

Many locals own a boat, though it's not always practical for everyday activities. If you want to cruise to the grocery store, you first have to check the tide table to make sure your boat can fit beneath certain bridges. And parking is always a huge problem everywhere—either you know a friend nearby with a grandfathered parking space or your partner has to "circle the block" while you shop.

Locals rely more on the public *vaporetti* and *traghetti*. While tourists pay plenty for these boats, locals ride cheap and easy. An all-year pass costs less than €1 a day.

Gondolas are strictly for tourists these days, but in earlier times, these flat-bottomed boats were the only way to negotiate the tricky, shallow lagoon. The oarsman had to stand up in the back of the boat to see oncoming sandbars. Today, boats ply confidently between the shifting sandbanks of the lagoon, thanks to thoroughfares defined by modern pilings.

While many Venetians own a car for driving on the isle of Lido or the mainland, they admit, "We're not very much beloved on the road."

out to produce the ornate vases, beaded necklaces, glass sculptures, and wine decanters you'll see here today.

Upon arrival (at the Colonna vaporetto stop), wander up Via Fondamenta Vetrai (along the canal of the glassmakers) and check out the various factories *(fabricca* or *fornace)*. They each offer a free 20-minute glassblowing demonstration of an artisan in action firing up something in a furnace, followed by an almost comically high-pressure sales pitch. (The spiel is brief, and there's absolutely no obligation to buy anything.) If you buy something, remember that shipping is very expensive—you're likely to pay as much or more for the shipping as you are for the item(s). Make sure the shop insures their merchandise *(assicurazione)*, or you're out of luck if it breaks. If your item arrives broken and it has been insured, take a photo of the pieces, send it to the shop, and they'll replace it for free.

Continue up Via Fondamenta Vetrai. The many 19th-century factories give the city a brick, Industrial Age look and feel. For lunch, consider **Trattoria Busa alla Torre,** located at the end of the canal under a cute little tower (which was built as a fire lookout); it has pleasant seating on Campo Santo Stefano (open daily, €10 pizza and pastas, €15 *secondi,* €1.50 cover, tel. 041-739-662). At the Grand Canal of Murano, cross the big, green metal bridge and head right 150 yards for the Glass Museum (following signs for *Museo Vetrario*).

On the way you'll see the **Church of San Pietro Martire** at the far (north) end of the main drag. It features Giovanni Bellini's *Virgin Enthroned with Mark and a Kneeling Doge* (right wall of the nave in the center), Tintoretto's *Baptism of Jesus* (closer to the altar on the right wall), and Veronese's *Saints Agatha and Jerome* (near the postcard-shop door). The sacristy is worth the €1.50 entry fee for its ornately carved caryatids representing mythological, philosophical historical figures and allegories (each identified by faded labels on the base of their pedestals). The high-relief carved panels in-between recount scenes from the life of John the Baptist (Mon–Sat 9:00–18:00 and Sun 12:00–17:00).

The **Glass Museum** displays the very best of 700 years of Venetian glassmaking, as well as exhibits on ancient and modern glass art. While the display is pretty old-school musty, it's well-described in English (€5.50, April–Oct Thu–Tue 10:00–18:00, Nov–March Thu–Tue 10:00–17:00, closed Wed, tel. 041-739-586, www.museiciviciveneziani.it).

See more than glass while on Murano. Get off the beaten path by taking the back streets behind the Duomo on Calle di Conterie for a look at village Venezia. In this old shell, there's a new vibrancy, as high prices of real estate and apartments in Venice drive locals to outlying islands such as these. Murano is a workaday community of 6,000 residents. It has real neighborhoods, with moms shopping at markets, schools filled with noisy children, and benches warmed by Venetian old-timers. They give Murano a "Venice without the tourism" charm.

When you're ready to go, head to the Faro vaporetto stop and take Line LN to Burano (from left side of dock) or the #41 back to Venice (right side of dock).

Burano

Famous for its lace and picturesque pastel houses, Burano is a sleepy island with a sleepy community (pop. 2,700)—village Venice without the glitz. Its colorfully painted homes look like Venice before the plaster peeled off. Each adjoining townhouse is painted its own color. While Venice is a showy city of merchants, Burano is a humble town of fishermen. At night it's almost entirely

Burano

MAZZORBO

TO TORCELLO

100 YARDS

100 METERS

VAPORETTO STOP

SAN MAURO

MARCELLO

TO MURANO

2

VIA GALUPPI

PITONA

LACE MUSEUM

1

VIGNA

POST

N

LAGOON

FISH MKT

WC

PARK

PIAZZA GALUPPI
S. MARTINO CHURCH & LEANING BELL TOWER

DCH

1 Merletti d'Arte dalla Lidia Lace Shop & Museum

2 Ristorante al Vecio Pipa

tourist-free. Laundry hangs over alleyways, and sunshades (typical of the area) cover the doors of residents' homes. The church's bell tower leans at a five-degree angle... the same as Pisa's.

This town's history is ancient, explained in part by its name. "Burano" comes from the local word for "breeze"—and a breeze meant survival on the lagoon. It kept away the malaria-carrying mosquitoes that made other places (like Torcello) less habitable.

The island can be covered in a five-minute stroll. From the vaporetto dock, follow the crowds into the center. Turn left at the canal. A bridge leads to Piazza Galuppi, and beyond that—on the far side of the little island—is Burano's famous leaning church **bell tower.** The church has a fine, restored Tiepolo painting of the Crucifixion.

The main drag from the vaporetto stop into town is packed with tourists and lined with shops, some of which sell Burano's locally produced white wine. Wander to the far side of the island,

and the mood shifts. Explore to the right of the leaning tower for a peaceful yet intensely pastel, small-town lagoon world. Benches lining a little promenade at the water's edge make another pretty picnic spot.

Most tourists visit Burano for its lace, and they're not disap-pointed. Lace is cheaper in Burano than in Venice, and serious shoppers should com-parison-shop in Venice before visiting Burano. Of the many lace shops, **Merletti d'Arte dalla Lidia** has a fine private museum. Ask for a magni-fying glass to marvel at the intricate knots, and be sure to go upstairs (daily 9:30–19:00, just off the big square opposite the leaning tower at Via Galuppi 215, tel. 041-730-052).

The **Lace Museum,** currently closed for renovation, will reopen in the fall of 2008 (*Museo del Merletto di Burano,* €4, April-Oct Wed-Mon 10:00-17:00, Nov-March Wed-Mon 10:00-16:00, closed Tue, some English descriptions, tel. 041-730-034).

You'll find plenty of touristy eateries on Burano, all enthusi-astic about their fish. The **Ristorante al Vecio Pipa** serves lovingly prepared local specialties at affordable prices, with both indoor and outdoor seating (€10 pastas, fixed-price meals, great fish splurges, daily 12:00–15:30—lunch only, on the main drag near the vaporetto dock at San Sauro 397, tel. 041-730-045).

For a picnic, the park next to Burano's only vaporetto dock is hard to beat.

On Burano, there's only one dock with boats to and from the Venice mainland. From that dock, a shuttle boat (Line T) runs back and forth at :00 and :30 past the hour to and from Torcello, located just five minutes away. Confirm the times upon arrival to avoid needless waiting.

Torcello

This is the birthplace of Venice, where the first mainland refugees settled, escaping the barbarian hordes. Yet today, it's the least-developed island (pop. 20) in its most natural state, marshy and shrub-covered. There's little for the tourist to see except the church (a 10-min walk from the dock), which claims to be the oldest in Venice and has impressive mosaics.

From the vaporetto dock, walk through a salty landscape and think of the original inhabitants. Romanized farmers came here, escaping the Germanic barbarians that started streaming through the mainland in the 5th century. By the 11th century, the

Lagoon Tour

teeny island had 11 churches. But one look around tells you that this place was inhospitable—the farming was poor, there was no fresh water, and mosquitoes and malaria were big problems. Even though residents diverted the flow of mainland rivers, the lagoon silted up around them anyway, and the island was slowly abandoned.

Approaching the church, you'll pass by the remote yet fancy **Locanda Cipriani Hotel** next door, with its five rooms, which has hosted Thomas Mann, Queen Elizabeth II, and Princess Diana.

The **church complex** consists of four sights: the church itself (Santa Maria Assunta), the bell tower (behind the church, climb

a ramped stairway for great lagoon views), a sacristy, and a small museum (facing the church, in two separate buildings) that displays Roman sculpture and medieval sculpture and manuscripts. Tickets cost €3 for any one sight, €5.50 for any two sights, or €8 for all sights, including an audioguide (most open daily March–Oct 10:30–18:00, Nov–Feb 10:00–16:30, museum closed Mon; museum tel. 041-730-761; church/bell tower tel. 041-730-119). There's a pay WC between the museum's two buildings.

The ruins in front of the church used to be a baptistery from the sixth century, the days when you couldn't enter a church until you were baptized.

Inside the **church,** the brick walls and wood-beam ceiling are classic Venetian building materials—that is, flexible—to accommodate the ever-shifting sands underneath. The altar has the relics of St. Heliodorus (d. 390), a local-born bishop who was the travel partner of the famed St. Jerome on a trip to the Holy Land. The columns of the rood screen (separating the altar area from the congregation) were obviously scavenged from elsewhere—note the variety of capitals. You can see a bit of the church's original black-and-white mosaic floor (ninth century) under a small glassed-over section on the right side of the nave. In the 12th century, flooding forced them to rebuild 12 inches higher. The apse mosaic (over the altar) shows Mary and baby Jesus above and the 12 apostles below. In the right apse, find Christ Pantocrater, ruler of all, flanked by archangels Michael and Gabriel floating regally above the four evangelists. On the ceiling, Christ is represented by the sacrificial lamb.

The mosaic on the back wall is famous. Six horizontal bands depict the Last Judgment (and other scenes). From top to bottom, see:

1. The Crucifixion.

2. A striding Christ pulling a soul out from Limbo while stepping on a devil.

3. Christ, in an almond-shaped bubble, as the Creator, flanked by souls in Paradise. From the bottom of the bubble pours a river of fire, which runs down the wall to Hell.

4. Angels preparing the Throne of Judgment—empty except for a book.

5 and 6. Archangel Michael (over the door) weighing souls in a scale, while mischievous devils try to tip the scales in their favor. On the right are the fires of hell, where sinners—many of them turbaned Muslims—are tormented by black-skinned demons. A crude display of the seven deadly sins on the lower right: pride (crowned heads in flames), lust (bodies in flames), gluttony (guys eating even their hands), envy (skulls with worms eating out their coveting eyes), greed (fancy earrings), laziness (useless hands and cut-off feet), and anger.

Avoid the eighth deadly sin—missing your vaporetto—by allowing at least 10 minutes to get from the church back to the boat dock. Boats generally depart at :15 and :45 past the hour.

ST. MARK'S TO RIALTO WALK

Two rights and a left (simple!) can get you from St. Mark's Square to the Rialto Bridge via a completely different route from the one most tourists take. Along the way, take in some lesser sights in the area west of St. Mark's Square. You finish where many fish do—at the market.

As an alternative, you could end this walk where many art-lovers do—at the Frari Church. Beyond the Rialto Bridge and market, extend your walk into the less-touristy San Polo neighborhood, ending at the Frari Church.

ORIENTATION

Length of This Walk: Allow one hour for a leisurely walk (30 min with no stops).

La Fenice Opera House: €7, includes 45-minute audioguide (generally open daily 10:00–16:00 depending on practice and performance schedules, www.teatrolafenice.it).

Scala Contarini del Bovolo: €3.50 to enter and climb tower (April–Oct daily 10:00–18:00, Nov–March open Sat–Sun only). It's viewable for free any time from the outside.

Rialto Market: The souvenir stalls are open daily; the produce market is closed on Sunday; and the fish market is closed on Sunday and Monday. The market is lively only in the morning.

The Route

There are actually three easy routes from St. Mark's Square to Rialto: (1) along the crowded Mercerie (follow the tourists underneath the Clock Tower), (2) a straight shot on Calle dei Fabbri (exit St. Mark's Square next to Quadri Café), and (3) the slightly longer but more interesting route described in this chapter. To follow this walk:

• From the waterfront at St. Mark's Square, head 100 yards west along the water, jogging inland at Harry's Bar, then continuing west on Calle Larga XXII Marzo.

• Turn right on Calle del Sartor da Veste; head north 200 yards.

• Turn right at the T intersection on Calle de la Mandola and head east 50 yards.

• After a brief detour south to see Scala Contarini del Bovolo, continue east 50 yards to Campo San Luca.

• Turn left on Calle del Forno and work your way north to the Grand Canal.

Confused? Just start the walk and follow the directions as you go.

THE WALK BEGINS

Start at St. Mark's Square

• *From the square, walk to the waterfront and turn right. You're walking on newly raised Venice—in 2006, the stones were taken up and six inches of extra sand laid to minimize flooding. Continue along the water, past the gardens to the top of the bridge in front of the TI pavilion.*

Along the waterfront, you'll see the various boats that ply Venice's waters. The gondolas here are often more expensive than elsewhere. Water taxis, in classic wooden motorboats, are pricey (about €60 from here to the train station), but they are a classy splurge if you can split the fare with four others. Hotel shuttle boats bring guests from distant, $700-a-night hotels.

The Giardinetti Reali (Royal Gardens) offer some precious greenery in a city built of stone on mud. Nearby are €1 WCs, a TI in a cute, 18th-century, former coffeehouse pavilion, and public pay phones where you can call home just to tell everyone where you are right now. Look across the mouth of the Grand Canal to view the big (and likely covered in scaffolding) dome of La Salute Church, and the guy balancing a bronze ball on one foot—the old Customs House.

• *Twelve steps down and 20 yards ahead on the right is...*

❶ Harry's American Bar

Hemingway put this bar on the map by making it his hangout in the late 1940s. If Dennis Hopper or Henry Winkler are in town (I've seen both), this is where they'll be. If they're not, you'll see

St. Mark's to Rialto Walk

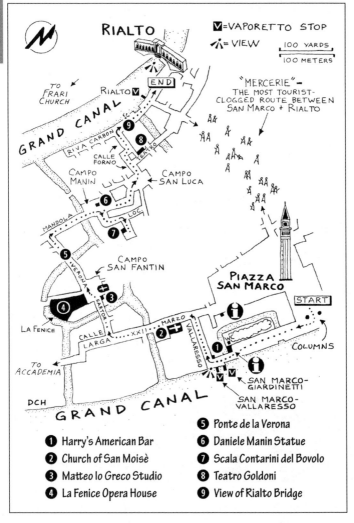

① Harry's American Bar
② Church of San Moisè
③ Matteo lo Greco Studio
④ La Fenice Opera House
⑤ Ponte de la Verona
⑥ Daniele Manin Statue
⑦ Scala Contarini del Bovolo
⑧ Teatro Goldoni
⑨ View of Rialto Bridge

plenty of dressed-up Americans looking around for celebrities. In practice, the street-level bar is for gawkers...the discreet restaurant upstairs is where the glitterati hang out. If you wear something a bit fancy (or artsy bohemian), you can pull up a stool at the tiny bar by the entrance and enjoy a decent martini or a Bellini (Prosecco and peach juice)—which was invented right here.

• *Head inland down Calle Vallaresso, one of Venice's most exclusive streets, past fancy boutiques such as Pucci, Gucci, and Roberto Cavalli. At the T intersection, turn left and head west on (what becomes) Calle*

Larga XXII Marzo. You'll pass the fine Mondadori Bookstore (left), American Express (right), then continue to the first bridge and a square dominated by the fancy facade of a church. Climb the bridge, and against a soundtrack of tourists negotiating with hustling gondoliers, look back at the ornate...

❷ Church of San Moisè

This is the parish church for St Mark's; because of tourist crowds at the basilica, this is where the community actually worships. While it's one of Venice's oldest churches, dating from the 10th century (note the old tower on the right), its busy facade is only Baroque (17th century). This was an age when big shots who funded such projects expected to see their faces featured (see the bust of Mr. Fini in the center). Moses *(Moisè)* caps the facade.

The ugly modern building on the right marks the former Venice headquarters of the Nazis during World War II. Its fascist facade still gives locals the Mussolini-creeps. Now a five-star hotel, it's one of the few modern buildings in town.

• *Continue past the bridge, down Calle Larga XXII Marzo, a big street that seems too wide and large for Venice. It was created during the 19th century by filling in a canal. You can still see the sidewalks that once flanked the now-gone canal. The 19th-century buildings (including the stock exchange, on right) were designed to face the new, wide street.*

Halfway down the street, turn right on tiny Calle del Sartor da Veste. Go straight, crossing a bridge, and passing the Matteo lo Greco Studio (#3 on map), with his plump people in bronze celebrating life with a lighter-than-air joy. Then, at the next square, you'll find...

❹ La Fenice Opera House (Gran Teatro alla Fenice)

Venice's famed opera house, built in 1792, was reduced to a hollowed-out shell by a disastrous fire in 1996. After a vigorous restoration campaign, "The Phoenix"—true to its name—has risen again from the ashes. La Fenice resumed opera productions in 2004, opening with *La Traviata*. The theater is usually open daily to the public (for information, see page 192).

Venice is one of the cradles of the art form known as opera. An opera is a sung play and a multimedia event, blending music, words, story, costume, and set design. Some of the great operas were first performed here in this luxurious setting. Verdi's *Rigoletto*

(1851) and *La Traviata* (1853) were actually commissioned by La Fenice. The man who put words to Mozart's tunes was a Venetian who drew inspiration from the city's libertine ways and joie de vivre. In recent years, La Fenice's musical reputation was overshadowed by its reputation as a place for the wealthy to parade in furs and jewels.

• *Continue north along the same street (though its name is now Calle de La Verona), to a small bridge over a quiet canal.*

❺ Ponte de la Verona

Pause atop this bridge, with reflections that can make you wonder which end is up. Looking above you, see bridges of stone propping up leaning buildings, and there's a view of the "Leaning Tower" of Santo Stefano.

People actually live in Venice. See their rooftop gardens, their laundry, electricity lines snaking into their apartments, and the rusted iron bars and bolts that hold their crumbling homes together. On one building, find centuries-old relief carvings—a bearded face and a panel of an eagle with its prey.

While many Venetians own (and love) their own boat, parking a boat is a huge problem. Getting a spot is tough, and when you finally find one, it's very expensive and rarely near your apartment. For more on boating in Venice, see page 186. People once swam freely in the canals. Find the sign that reads *Divieto di Nuoto* (literally, "swimming not allowed").

• *Continue north. At the T intersection, you reach a main thoroughfare connecting the Accademia (left) and St. Mark's Square (right). Turn right on Calle de la Mandola. You'll cross over a bridge into a spacious square dominated by a statue and an out-of-place modern building.*

❻ Campo Manin

The centerpiece of the square is **a statue of Daniele Manin** (1804–1857), Venice's fiery leader in the battle for freedom from Austria and eventually a united Italy (the Risorgimento). The statue faces the red house he lived in. Chafing under Austrian rule, the Venetians rose up. The Austrians laid siege to the city (1849) and bombed it into surrender. Manin was banished and spent his final years in Paris, still proudly drumming up support for modern Italy. In a rare honor, he's buried in St. Mark's Basilica.

• *Scala Contarini del Bovolo is well-signposted a block south of here. Facing the Manin statue, turn right and exit the square down an alley. Follow yellow signs to the left, then right, into a courtyard with one of Venice's hidden treasures...*

❼ Scala Contarini del Bovolo

The Scala is a cylindrical brick tower with five floors of spiral staircase faced with white marble banisters. Built in 1499, it was the external staircase of a palace (external stairs saved interior space for rooms). Architecture buffs admire the successful blend of Gothic, Byzantine, and Renaissance styles.

For €3.50, you can wind your way up the "snail shell" (*bovolo* in the local dialect). It's 113 steps to the top, where you're rewarded with views of the Venetian skyline.

• *Unwind and return to the Manin statue. Continue east, circling around the big, modern Cassa di Risparmio bank, into Campo San Luca. At Campo San Luca, turn left (north) on Calle del Forno. Note the 24-hour pharmacy vending machine that dispenses shower gel, Band-Aids, bug repellant, condoms, toothbrushes, toothpaste, and other necessities. Heading north, glance 20 yards down the street to the right at the flag-bedecked...*

❽ Teatro Goldoni

Though this theater looks modern, it dates from the 1500s, when Venice was at the forefront of secular entertainment. Many of Carlo Goldoni's (1707–1793) groundbreaking comedies got their first performance here, and the theater was renamed in his honor. It's still a working theater of mainly Italian productions.

• *Continue north on Calle del Forno. You're very close to the Grand Canal. Keep going north, jogging to the right, then left down a teeny-tiny alleyway. Pop! You emerge on the Grand Canal, about 150 yards "downstream" from the...*

❾ Rialto Bridge

Of Venice's more than 400 bridges, only four cross the Grand Canal. Of these four, the Rialto was the first.

The original Rialto Bridge, dating from 1180, was a platform supported by boats tied together. It linked the political side (Palazzo Ducale) of Venice with the economic center (Rialto). Rialto, which takes its name from *riva alto* (high bank), was one of the earliest Venetian settlements. When Venice was Europe's economic superpower, this was where bankers, brokers, and merchants conducted their daily business.

Rialto Bridge II was a 13th-century wooden drawbridge. It was replaced in 1588 by the current structure, with its bold single arch spanning 160 feet and arcades on top designed to strengthen the stone bridge. Its immense foundations stretch 650 feet on either side. Heavy buildings were then built atop the foundations to hold everything in place. The Rialto remained the only bridge crossing the Grand Canal until 1854.

Reliefs of the Venetian Republic's main mascots, St. Mark and St. Theodore, crown the arch. Barges and *vaporetti* run the busy waterways below, and merchants vie for tourists' attention on top.

The Rialto has long been a symbol of Venice. Aristocratic inhabitants built magnificent palaces just to be near it. The poetic Lord Byron swam to it all the way from Lido Island. And thousands of marriage proposals have been sealed right here, with a kiss, as the moon floated over *La Serenissima*.

• *Your St. Mark's Square to the Rialto walk finishes here.*

OPTIONAL EXTENSION:
RIALTO TO FRARI CHURCH

If you have the energy (and are heading for the Frari Church anyway), follow this extension, which carries on down the engaging street, the Ruga, and stops by Campo San Polo en route to the Frari. The area west of the Grand Canal is less touristy—the place where "real" Venetians live. This 20-minute walk is the most direct route from the Rialto Bridge to the Frari Church and Scuola San Rocco.

• *Cross the Rialto Bridge, and dive headlong into Venice's thriving market area.*

❿ Market (Erberia)

The street west of the Rialto Bridge (nicknamed "tourist lane") is lined with stalls selling cheese, arugula, dripping coconut slices, glass beads, postcards, masks, leather purses, and T-shirts. To relieve the congestion on this pedestrian street, the latest vision is to move all the stalls to an empty area adjacent to the market.

• *Beyond "tourist lane," look left down the street called the Ruga. Then turn right, toward the Grand Canal, to the bustling...*

⓫ Fish Market (Pescheria)

This is especially vibrant and colorful in the morning (but closed Sun–Mon). The open-air stalls have the catch of the day—Venice's culinary specialty. Find eels, scallops, and crustaceans with five-inch antennae. This is the Venice that has existed for centuries: Workers toss boxes of fish from delivery boats while shoppers step from the *traghetto* (gondola shuttle) into the action. It's a good peek at workaday Venice.

• *From the fish market, return to the end of "tourist lane," and head down Ruga Vecchia San Giovanni (roughly paralleling the Grand Canal).*

⓬ The Ruga

This busy street is lined with shops that get progressively less touristy. You'll see fewer trinkets and more clothes, bread, shoes, watches, shampoo, and underwear.

⓭ Campo San Polo

One of the largest squares in Venice, Campo San Polo is shaped like an amphitheater, with its church tucked away in the corner (just ahead of you). Antica Birraria la Corte, a fine and family-friendly pizzeria/ristorante, is located at the far side (see the "Eating" chapter on page 226). The square's amphitheater shape was determined by a curved canal at the base of the buildings. Today, the former canal is now a *rio terra*—a street made of landfill. There are a few rare trees in the square, and rare benches occupied by grateful locals. In the summer, bleachers and

Rialto to Frari Church Walk

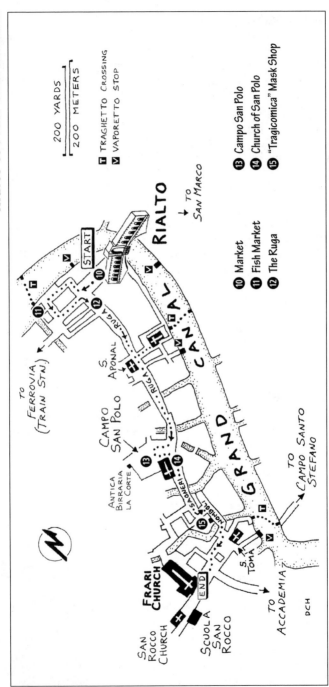

200 YARDS
200 METERS

🅣 TRAGHETTO CROSSING
🆅 VAPORETTO STOP

RIALTO

→ TO SAN MARCO

⑩ Market
⑪ Fish Market
⑫ The Ruga

⑬ Campo San Polo
⑭ Church of San Polo
⑮ "Tragicomica" Mask Shop

START

TO FERROVIA (TRAIN STN.)

S. APONAL

RUGA

CANAL

GRAND

CAMPO SAN POLO

ANTICA BIRRARIA LA CORTE

⑬ ⑭

⑮

SAONERI

TOLETTA

TO CAMPO SANTO STEFANO

S. TOMA

TO ACCADEMIA

FRARI CHURCH   END

SAN ROCCO CHURCH

SCUOLA SAN ROCCO

DCH

a screen are erected for open-air movies, a true *Cinema Paradiso* experience.

• *On the square is the...*

⓮ Church of San Polo (S. Paolo Apostolo)

This church is one of the oldest in Venice, dating from the ninth century (€2.50, English description at ticket desk). The wooden boat-shaped ceiling recalls the earliest basilicas built after Rome's fall. Art enthusiasts visit to see Tintoretto's *Last Supper,* G. B. Tiepolo's *Virgin Appearing to St. John of Nepomuk* and *Stations of the Cross,* and Veronese's *Betrothal of the Virgin with Angels.*

• *From the Church of San Polo, continue about 200 yards (following signs to* Ferrovia*). Jog left when you have to, then right, onto Calle dei Nomboli. On the right, just before a small bridge, you'll see the...*

⓯ "Tragicomica" Mask Shop

One of Venice's best mask stores (daily 10:00–19:00, tel. 041-721-102), it's also a workshop that offers a glimpse into the process of mask-making. Venice's masks have always been a central feature of the celebration of Carnevale—the local pre-Lent, Mardi Gras–like blowout. (The translation of Carnevale is "goodbye to meat," referring to the lean days of Lent.) You'll see Walter and Alessandra hard at work.

Many masks are patterned after standard characters of the theater style known as Commedia dell'Arte: the famous trickster Harlequin, the beautiful and cunning Columbina, the country bumpkin Pulcinella (who later evolved into the wife-beating "Punch" of marionette shows), and the solemn, long-nosed Doctor *(dottore).*

• *Continuing along, cross the bridge, and veer right. You'll see purple signs directing you to* Scuola Grande di San Rocco. *Follow these until you bump into the back end of the Frari Church, with Scuola San Rocco next door.*

✪ See Frari Church Tour on page 137; also see Scuola San Rocco Tour on page 127.

ST. MARK'S TO SAN ZACCARIA WALK

San Zaccaria, one of the oldest churches in Venice, with a Bellini altarpiece and a submerged crypt (the oldest place in Venice?), is just a few minutes on foot from St. Mark's Square. Along the way, there's a great view of the Bridge of Sighs.

ORIENTATION

Length of This Walk: Allow about an hour for a leisurely walk (though the actual distance is shorter).

Church of San Zaccaria: Free, Mon–Sat 10:00–12:00 & 16:00–18:00, Sun 16:00–18:00 only. Admission to the crypt costs €1. A €0.50 coin illuminates Bellini's altarpiece.

The Route

You can make a square circuit from St. Mark's Square to the Church of San Zaccaria to the waterfront, and back to St. Mark's Square. Along the way, you'll pass a variety of lace and mask shops.

- From St. Mark's Square, walk behind St. Mark's Basilica to the Church of San Zaccaria.
- Turn right at San Zaccaria, and walk a block to the waterfront.
- Turn right and walk along the Riva, returning to St. Mark's Square.

THE WALK BEGINS

❶ Start at St. Mark's—Piazzetta dei Leoncini

Facing St. Mark's Basilica, start in the small square to the left of the church (the Piazzetta dei Leoncini), with the 18th-century

St. Mark's to San Zaccaria Walk

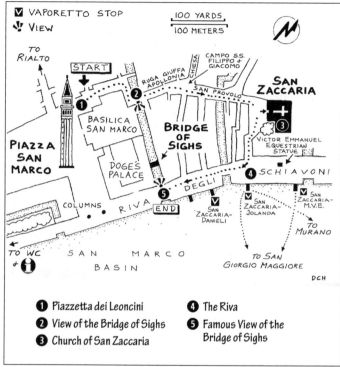

St. Mark's/Zacc

- ☑ VAPORETTO STOP
- ⚘ VIEW

100 YARDS
100 METERS

TO RIALTO

START

PIAZZA SAN MARCO

BASILICA SAN MARCO

DOGE'S PALACE

1 — **2**

RUGA GIUFFA APOLLONIA

CHIESA

CAMPO S.S. FILIPPO & GIACOMO

SAN PROVOLO

SAN ZACCARIA

✝ **3**

VICTOR EMMANUEL EQUESTRIAN STATUE

BRIDGE OF SIGHS

DEGLI **4** SCHIAVONI

COLUMNS

RIVA **5** END

SAN ZACCARIA-DANIELI

SAN ZACCARIA-JOLANDA

SAN ZACCARIA-M.V.E.

TO MURANO

TO WC ⓘ

S A N   M A R C O   B A S I N

TO SAN GIORGIO MAGGIORE

DCH

- **1** Piazzetta dei Leoncini
- **2** View of the Bridge of Sighs
- **3** Church of San Zaccaria
- **4** The Riva
- **5** Famous View of the Bridge of Sighs

stone lions that kids love to sit on. The white building at the east end of the square houses the offices of Venice's "patriarch," the special title given to the local bishop (see the yellow Vatican flag). In the 1950s, this is where the future Pope John XXIII presided as Venice's patriarch and cardinal. The popular, warm-hearted bishop went on to become the "Sixties pope," who oversaw major reforms in the Catholic Church.

• *Head east along Calle de la Canonica, circling behind the basilica. You'll reach a bridge with a...*

❷ View of the Bridge of Sighs

This lesser-known view of the Bridge of Sighs also lets you see the white facade of the Church of San Giorgio Maggiore in the distance, framed by the arch of the Bridge of Sighs.

• *Continue east, crossing the bridge. You'll pass the Diocesan Museum (with the art of various local churches on display—see page 35). Continuing east, you'll cross another bridge with a view of a "Modern Bridge of Sighs," which connects two wings of the exclusive Danieli Hotel. Continue east another 50 yards, through the former gate of a cloistered Benedictine convent, until you run into the...*

❸ Church of San Zaccaria

Back in the ninth century, when Venice was just a collection of wooden houses and before there was a St. Mark's Basilica, a stone church and convent stood here. This is where the doges worshipped, public spectacles occurred, and sacred relics were kept. Today's structure dates mostly from the 15th century.

The tall facade by Mauro Codussi (who also did the Clock Tower in St. Mark's Square) is early Renaissance. The "vertical" effect produced by the four support pillars that rise up to an arched crown is tempered by the horizontal, many-layered stories and curved shoulders.

In the northwest corner of Campo San Zaccaria (near where you entered) is a plaque from 1620 listing all the things that were prohibited "in this square" *(in questo campo)*, including games, obscenities, dishonesty, and robbery, all "under grave penalty" *(sotto gravis pene)*.

• *Enter the church. The second chapel on the right holds the...*

Body of Zechariah (S. Zaccaria, Patris S. Jo: Baptista)

Of the two bodies in the chapel, the upper one in the glass case

(supported by stone angels) is the reputed body of Zechariah, the father of John the Baptist. Back when mortal remains were venerated and thought to bring miracles to the faithful, Venice was proud to own the bones of St. Zechariah ("San Zaccaria," also known as Zacharias).

• *The church is virtually wallpapered with art. On the opposite side of the nave (second chapel on the left), you'll find...*

Giovanni Bellini's *Madonna and Child with Saints* (*Sacra Conversazione*, 1505)

Mary and the baby, under a pavilion, are surrounded by various saints engaged in a so-called "holy conversation," which in this painting is more like a quiet meditation. The saints' mood is melancholy, with lidded eyes and downturned faces. A violinist angel plays a sad solo at Mary's feet.

This is one of the last of Bellini's paintings in the *sacra conversazione* formula (see his others in the Accademia and Frari Church). The life-size saints stand in an imaginary extension of the church—the pavilion's columns match the real church columns. We see a glimpse of trees and a cloudy sky beyond. He establishes a 3-D effect using floor tiles. The four saints pose symmetrically, and there's a harmony of big blocks of rich-colored robes—blue, green, red, white, and yellow. A cool white light envelops the whole scene, casting no dark shadows.

The 75-year-old Bellini was innovative and productive until the end of his long life. The German artist Albrecht Dürer said of him: "He is very old, and still he is the best painter of them all."

• *On the right-hand side of the nave is the entrance (€1 entry fee) to...*

The Crypt

Before you descend into the crypt, the first room (Chapel of the Choir) contains **Tintoretto's *Birth of John the Baptist*** (on the altar). Mother Elizabeth lies in bed in the background, while nurses hold and coo over little John. The father, Zechariah—the star of this church—is on the far right, witnessing the heavens opening up.

The five **gold chairs** were once seats for doges. Every Easter, the current doge would walk from St. Mark's Square to this religious center and thank the nuns of San Zaccaria for giving the land that would become Piazza San Marco. In the small next room, with religious objects, there's an engraving of the doge parading into Campo San Zaccaria.

The Chapel of Gold (to the left of the room with the religious objects) is dominated by an impressive 15th-century prickly gold altarpiece by Vivarini. Look down through glass in the floor to see the 12th-century mosaic floor from the original church. In fact,

these rooms were parts of the earlier churches.

Finally, go downstairs into the **crypt**—the foundation of a church built in the 10th century. The crypt is low and the water table high, so the room is often flooded. It's a weird experience, calling up echoes of the Dark Ages.

• *Emerge from the Church of San Zaccaria into the small* campo *in front, and turn left (south). Exit the* campo *past the pink ex-convent (now the Carabinieri station), and pop out at the waterfront.*

❹ The Riva

The waterfront promenade known as the "Riva" gives a great view of the Church of San Giorgio Maggiore. To get there, catch vaporetto #2 (to the left, not in front of you) from the San Zaccaria–M.V.E. stop on the far side of the equestrian statue. ✪ See San Giorgio Maggiore Tour, page 175.

This big equestrian monument is of Victor Emmanuel II—the "M.V.E" on the vaporetto stop stands for "Monumento Vittorio Emanuele." He helped lead Italy to unification, becoming the country's first king in 1861. Beyond that (over the bridge) is the four-columned La Pietà Church, where Antonio Vivaldi once directed the music. A bit beyond that (not visible from here) is the Arsenale.

The Riva is lined with many of Venice's most famous luxury hotels. For a peek at the most famous and luxurious, turn right, cross over one bridge, and nip into the Danieli Hotel. Tuck in your shirt, stand tall and aristocratic, and (with all the confidence of a guest) be swept by the revolving door into the sumptuous interior of what was once the Gothic Palazzo Dandolo. Since 1820, this has been Venice's most exclusive hotel. Exquisite as all this is, it still gets flooded routinely in the winter.

• *Facing the water, turn right and head west toward St. Mark's Square. The commotion atop a little bridge marks the...*

❺ Famous View of the Bridge of Sighs

From this bridge (according to romantic legend), prisoners took one last look at Venice before entering the dark and dank pris-

ons. And sighed. While that rogue Casanova wrote of the bridge in his memoirs, he was actually imprisoned in the Doges' Palace (high up on your left). Lord Byron picked up on the legend in the early 1800s and gave it the famous nickname, and this sad bridge became a big stop on the Grand Tour. While the bridge is a human traffic jam of gawking tourists and clever pickpockets during the day, it's breathtakingly romantic in the lonely late-night hours.

From here, you can take one last look at the lagoon before returning to the crowded and sweaty St. Mark's Square...and sigh.

SLEEPING

For hassle-free efficiency and the sheer magic of being close to the action, I favor hotels that are handy to sightseeing activities. I've listed rooms in three neighborhoods: the Rialto action, St. Mark's bustle, and the quiet Dorsoduro area behind the Accademia art museum. Hotel websites are particularly valuable in Venice, because they often come with a map.

I try to list accommodations that are clean, small enough to have a hands-on owner, central yet not in the tourist flood zone, relatively quiet at night (except for the song of gondoliers), reasonably priced, friendly, and run with a respect for Venetian traditions.

Reserve ahead if you're traveling on major holidays—Carnevale (Jan 25–Feb 5 in 2008), Easter and Easter Monday (March 23–24), April 25 (St. Mark's Day), May 1 (Labor Day), November 1 (All Saints' Day)—and on Fridays and Saturdays year-round. Also see "Holidays and Festivals" on page 346 of the appendix.

Outside of holidays and weekends, it's possible to visit Venice without booking ahead, but it's smart, simple, and less stressful to have a reservation in place (see "Making Reservations," below). Book a room as soon as you know when you'll be in town. Contact the hotel directly, not through any tourist information room-finding service (they can't give opinions on quality). If everything's full, don't despair. Call a day or two in advance and fill in a cancellation.

TYPES OF ACCOMMODATIONS

Hotels

My listings range in price from €21 bunks to plush €250 doubles with Grand Canal views. Double rooms run as low as about €90 (very simple), with most clustered around €140–170 (with private bathrooms). Three or four people can economize by sharing larger rooms. Solo travelers find that the cost of a *camera singola* (single room) is often only 25 percent less than a *camera doppia* (double room). Most listed hotels have rooms for anywhere from one to five people. If there's room for an extra cot, they'll cram it in for you.

Double beds are called *matrimoniale,* even though hotels aren't interested in your marital status. Twins are *due letti singoli.* Even if a single or triple room isn't listed, ask—they can accommodate you.

Many hotel rooms have a TV and phone. Rooms in fancier hotels usually come with a small safe; a stocked mini-fridge called a *frigo bar* (FREE-goh bar) where you pay for what you use; and air-conditioning (sometimes with an extra per-day charge). The government stipulates that air-conditioning can only be used mid-May through September, unless conditions are extreme. The same goes for heat from October through April.

If you arrive on an overnight train, your room might not be ready. Drop your bag at the hotel and dive right into Venice.

When you check in, usually the receptionist will ask for your passport and keep it for a couple of hours. Italian hotels are legally required to register each guest with the local police. Relax. Americans are notorious for making this chore more difficult than it needs to be.

Rooms are safe. Still, zip cameras and keep money out of sight. More pillows and blankets are usually in the closet or available on request. In Italy, towels and linens aren't always replaced every day. Hang your towel up to dry.

Your hotelier, a good source of advice, can direct you to the nearest launderette and Internet café.

Apartment Rentals

Those staying a minimum of four nights (the longer the stay, the lower the rate) can book an apartment with **Venice Rentals.** This may make sense for families who want a bit more space and a kitchen. Doubles start at €100 per night, a bigger place for a family of four to five rents for around €200, and a palazzo for eight is €600/night. An American representative will meet you upon arrival and get you oriented (US tel. 617-472-5392, www.venicerentals.com, owner Denise—a Bostonian).

PRACTICALITIES

Pricing and Discounts

The major advantages of this book are its extensive listing of good-value hotels and the special prices promised to my readers (often much below the "rack rates"—the highest rates a hotel charges).

Venetian hoteliers are hard to pin down. They're experts at perfect price discrimination: They list a huge range of rates for the same room (e.g., €90–160) and refuse to give a firm price, enabling them to judge the demand and charge accordingly. As soon as they know what the market will bear, they max it out. Also, hotels are being squeezed by the very popular online-booking services (which take about a 20 percent commission). Between wanting to keep their gouging options open for high-season weekends and trying to recover these online commissions, hoteliers set their rack rates sky-high.

My listings are more likely to give a straight price. I've assured hoteliers that my readers will book direct, so they'll get 100 percent of what you pay; therefore, you'll get the fair net rate. I've listed only prices for peak season: April, May, June, September, and October. Prices will be higher during festivals, and almost all places drop prices from November through March (except during Carnevale and Christmas) and in July and August.

Booking direct (not through a Web service) is your ticket to better rates. Prices can be soft if you do any of the following: offer to pay cash, stay at least three nights, or mention this book. You can also try asking for a cheaper room or a discount, or offer to skip breakfast. To save money during a relatively slow time, consider arriving without a reservation and dropping in at the last minute. Big, fancy hotels put empty rooms on an aggressive push list, offering great prices.

If you book through a Web service, I wash my hands of your problems. Help me enforce honest business practices by reporting any hotel charging more than the listed rates in 2008 to those who book direct. Email me at rick@ricksteves.com. Thanks.

Phoning

Italy's country code is 39. If you're phoning Italy from the US or Canada, dial 011-39—followed by the 10-digit local number (in Venice that starts with 041). If calling Italy from another European country, dial 00-39—then the local number. To call a Venice hotel from anywhere in Italy (including Venice), simply dial the 10-digit local number. Land lines start with 0, mobile lines start with 3. For more information on telephoning, see page 340 in the appendix.

Making Reservations

Given the quality of the gems I've found for this book, I'd recommend that you reserve your rooms in advance, particularly if you'll be traveling during peak season. Book several weeks ahead, or as soon as you've pinned down your travel dates. Note that some national holidays jam things up and merit your making reservations

Sleep Code

(€1 = about $1.30)

To help you easily sort through these listings, I've divided the rooms into three categories based on the price for a standard double room with bath:

$$$ **Higher Priced**—Most rooms €180 or more.
 $$ **Moderately Priced**—Most rooms between €130–180.
  $ **Lower Priced**—Most rooms €130 or less.

To give you maximum information in a minimum of space, I use the following code to describe the accommodations. Prices listed are per room, not per person. Unless I note otherwise, the staff speaks English and breakfast is included. You can assume a hotel takes credit cards unless you see "cash only" in the listing. While most places have Internet access for a fee, I only list Internet access when it is available to guests for free.

S = Single room (or price for one person in a double).
D = Double or Twin room. "Double beds" are often two twins sheeted together, and are usually big enough for nonromantic couples.
T = Triple (generally a double bed with a single).
Q = Quad (usually a double bed and 2 small singles).
b = Private bathroom with toilet and shower or tub.
s = Private shower or tub only (the toilet is down the hall).

According to this code, a couple staying at a "Db-€140" hotel would pay a total of €140 (about $170) for a double room with a private bathroom.

far in advance (see list on page 207). To make a reservation, contact hotels directly by email, phone, or fax.

The recommended hotels are accustomed to English-only travelers. Email is the clearest and most economical way to make a reservation. If phoning from the US, be mindful of time zones (see page 8). To ensure you have all the information you need for your reservation, use the form in this book's appendix (also at www.ricksteves.com/reservation). If you don't get a reply to your email or fax, it usually means the hotel is already fully booked.

When you request a room for a certain time period, use the European style for writing dates: day/month/year. Hoteliers need to know your arrival and departure dates. For example, a two-night stay in July would be "2 nights, 16/07/08 to 18/07/08." Consider in advance how long you'll stay; don't just assume you can extend your reservation for extra days after you arrive.

If the response from the hotel gives its room availability and rates, it's not a confirmation. You must tell them that you want that room at the given rate.

The hotelier will sometimes request your credit-card number for a one-night deposit. While you can email your credit-card information (I do), it's safer to share that personal info via phone call, fax, or secure online reservation form (if the hotel has one on its website).

If you must cancel your reservation, it's courteous to do so with as much advance notice as possible (simply make a quick phone call or send an email). Hotels, which are often family-run, lose money if they turn away customers while holding a room for someone who doesn't show up. Understandably, some hotels bill no-shows for one night. Hotels in larger cities sometimes have strict cancellation policies (for example, you might lose a deposit if you cancel within two weeks of your reserved stay, or you might be billed for the entire visit if you leave early); ask about cancellation policies before you book.

Always reconfirm your room reservation a few days in advance from the road. If you'll be arriving after 17:00, let them know. Don't have the tourist office reconfirm rooms for you; they'll take a commission.

On the small chance that a hotel loses track of your reservation, bring along a hard copy of their emailed or faxed confirmation.

ACCOMMODATIONS IN VENICE

Hotels in Venice can be tricky to locate. While I've tried to give clear directions, you'll do best by following the arrival instructions provided on your hotel's website. Most sites have a good map. (If yours does, print it out.) Remember that Venice has six districts: San Marco, Castello, Cannaregio, San Polo, Santa Croce, and Dorsoduro. Each district has about 6,000 address numbers.

Near St. Mark's Square
East of St. Mark's Square
Located near the Bridge of Sighs, just off the Riva degli Schiavoni waterfront promenade, these places rub drainpipes with Venice's most palatial five-star hotels. Ride the vaporetto to San Zaccaria (#51 from train station, #2 from Tronchetto parking lot).

$$$ Hotel Campiello, lacy and bright, was once part of a 19th-century convent. Ideally located 50 yards off the waterfront, on a tiny little namesake square, its 16 rooms offer a tranquil, friendly refuge for travelers who appreciate comfort and professional service (Sb-€130, Db-€200, 10 percent discount with cash and this book in 2008, strict cancellation penalties enforced,

Sleeping

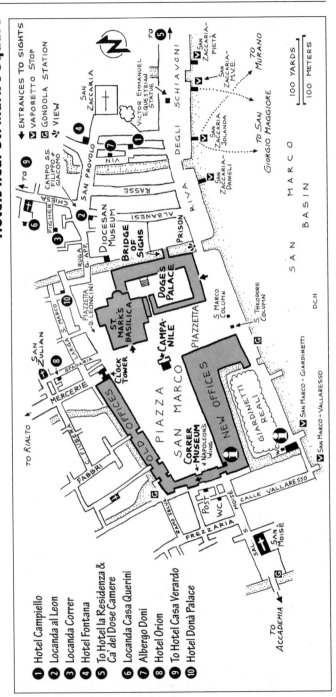

Hotels near St. Mark's Square

1. Hotel Campiello
2. Locanda al Leon
3. Locanda Correr
4. Hotel Fontana
5. To Hotel la Residenza & Ca' del Dose Camere
6. Locanda Casa Querini
7. Albergo Doni
8. Hotel Orion
9. To Hotel Casa Verardo
10. Hotel Donà Palace

← ENTRANCES TO SIGHTS
▼ VAPORETTO STOP
ⓖ GONDOLA STATION
✤ VIEW

air-con, Internet access, elevator; from the waterfront street—Riva degli Schiavoni—take Calle del Vin, between pink Hotel Danieli and Hotel Savoia e Jolanda, to #4647, Castello; tel. 041-520-5764, fax 041-520-5798, www.hcampiello.it, campiello@hcampiello.it; family-run for four generations, currently by Thomas and sisters Monica and Nicoletta). They also rent three modern, plush, and quiet family apartments, under rustic timbers just steps away (up to €380/night).

$$ Locanda al Leon rents 14 rooms outfitted in 18th-century Venetian style just off Campo S.S. Filippo e Giacomo (Db-€145, bigger Db-€165, these prices with cash and this book in 2008, air-con, Campo S.S. Filippo e Giacomo 4270, Castello, tel. 041-277-0393, fax 041-521-0348, www.hotelalleon.com, leon@hotelalleon .com, Giuliano and Marcella). From the San Zaccaria vaporetto stop, take Calle dei Albanesi (two streets left of pink Hotel Danieli). The hotel is at the far end of the street on the left.

$$ Locanda Correr offers five elegant rooms with silk wallpaper and gilded furniture, decorated in classic 17th-century Venetian style with all the amenities on a quiet street a few blocks from St. Mark's Square and Campo S.S. Filippo e Giacomo (Db-€145 with cash and this book in 2008, air-con, Calle Figher 4370, Castello, tel. 041-277-7847, fax 041-277-5939, www.locandacorrer .com, info@locandacorrer.com). From the San Zaccaria vaporetto stop, take the street to the right of the Bridge of Sighs to Campo S.S. Filippo e Giacomo, continue on Calle drio la Chiesa, then go left down Calle Figher, past Hotel Castello.

$$ Hotel Fontana is a two-star, family-run place with 14 rooms and lots of stairs on a touristy square two bridges behind St. Mark's Square (Sb-€110, Db-€160, family rooms, 10 percent discount with cash, quieter rooms on garden side, 2 rooms have terraces for €10 extra, air-con, Campo San Provolo 4701, Castello, tel. 041-522-0579, fax 041-523-1040, www.hotelfontana.it, info @hotelfontana.it, Diego and Gabriele). Take vaporetto #1 or #51 to San Zaccaria, then take Calle delle Rasse—to the left of pink Hotel Danieli—turn right at the end, and continue to the first square.

$$ Hotel la Residenza is a grand, old palace facing a peaceful square. Its 15 great rooms ring a huge, luxurious, and heavily frosted lounge. You'll feel like you're in the Doge's Palace after hours. This is a great value for romantics. Mention Rick Steves when you book to get the following discounted rates (Sb-€100, Db-€165, air-con, Internet access, Campo Bandiera e Moro 3608, Castello, tel. 041-528-5315, fax 041-523-8859, www.venicelaresidenza.com, info @venicelaresidenza.com, Gianni). From the Bridge of Sighs, walk east along Riva degli Schiavoni, cross three bridges, and take the first left up Calle del Dose to Campo Bandiera e Moro. Find the hotel across the square.

\$\$ Locanda Casa Querini rents six plush rooms on a quiet square tucked away behind St. Mark's. You can enjoy your breakfast or a sunny picnic/happy hour sitting right on the sleepy little square (Db-€150 with cash and this book in 2008, €5 more for view rooms, air-con, gazebo, halfway between San Zaccaria vaporetto stop and Campo Santa Maria Formosa at Campo San Giovanni in Oleo 4388, Castello, tel. 041-241-1294, fax 041-241-4231, www .locandaquerini.com, casaquerini@hotmail.com, Patrizia and Silvia). From the San Zaccaria vaporetto stop, take the street to the right of the Bridge of Sighs to Campo S.S. Filippo e Giacomo, continue on Calle drio la Chiesa, take the second left, and curl around to the left into the little square.

\$ Albergo Doni is dark, hardwood, clean, and quiet—a bit of a time-warp—with 13 dim but classy rooms run by a likable smart aleck named Gina and her son, an Italian stallion named Nikos (D-€90, Db-€115, T-€120, Tb-€155, reserve with credit card but pay in cash for these special prices, ceiling fans, Fondamenta del Vin, 4656 Castello, tel. & fax 041-522-4267, www.albergodoni .it, albergodoni@libero.it). From the San Zaccaria vaporetto stop, cross one bridge to the right, take the first left past the pink Hotel Danieli, turn left at the little square named Ramo del Vin, jog left, and find the hotel ahead on Fondamenta del Vin.

\$ Ca' del Dose Camere is a rough and funky little six-room guesthouse where high-energy Anna scrambles to keep her guests happy (Db-€100, Tb-€120, 10 percent discount with cash and this book in 2008, air-con, Castello 3801, tel. & fax 041-520-9887, www.cadeldose.com, info@cadeldose.com). It's located four bridges past the Doge's Palace, about 100 yards off the high-rent Riva degli Schiavoni on Calle del Dose, and a few steps before the wonderfully homey square called Campo Bandiera e Moro. Anna also runs the slicker Palazzo Soderini nearby (three Db-€150 rooms with breakfast, on Campo Bandiera e Moro).

North of St. Mark's Square

\$\$ Hotel Orion has 18 neat-as-a-pin, relaxing, and spacious rooms. Just off St. Mark's Square, it's a tranquil escape from the bustling streets (Db-€165 with this book in 2008, 5 percent discount with cash, air-con, Spadaria 700a, San Marco 30100, tel. 041-522-3053, fax 041-523-8866, www.hotelorion.it, info @hotelorion.it, cheery Massimiliano and Matteo). From St. Mark's Square, walk to the left of the basilica's facade. Turn left on Calle S. Basso (which changes to Spadari). The hotel is just before the timbered overpass.

West of St. Mark's Square

$$$ Hotel Flora sits buried in a sea of fancy designer boutiques and elegant hotels almost on the Grand Canal. It's formal, with uniformed staff and grand public spaces, yet the 43 rooms have a homey warmth and the garden oasis is a sanctuary for foot-weary guests (generally Db-€240, but check their website for deals and email Sr. Romanelli to ask about a Rick Steves discount, air-con, San Marco 2283/A, tel. 041-520-5844, fax 041-522-8217, www.hotelflora.it, info@hotelflora.it). It's at the end of Calle dei Bergamaschi, a long, skinny dead-end lane just off Calle Larga XXII Marzo on the Grand Canal side.

West of the Rialto Bridge

$$ Albergo Guerrato, above a handy and colorful produce market two minutes from the Rialto action, is run by friendly, creative, and hardworking Roberto and Piero. (Piero's the Venetian Tom Jones—a request to sing brings him great joy.) Giorgio takes the afternoon shift, and it's Monica in the evening. Their 800-year-old building—with 24 spacious, air-conditioned, and charming rooms—is simple, airy, and wonderfully characteristic (D-€90, Db-€130, Tb-€150, Qb-€170, Quint/b-€185, prices promised through 2008 with this book and cash, during slow times—Nov–Feb and Aug—you'll do better with their Web deals, Rick Steves readers can ask for €5 per night discount below off-season Web specials, Calle drio la Scimia 240a, San Polo, tel. & fax 041-528-5927, www.pensioneguerrato.it, hguerrat@tin.it). Walk over the Rialto Bridge away from St. Mark's Square, go straight about three blocks, turn right on Calle drio la Scimia (not simply Scimia, the block before), and you'll see the hotel sign. My tour groups book this place for 50 nights each year. Sorry. The Guerrato also rents family apartments in the old center (great for groups of 4–8) for around €55 per person.

$$ Hotel al Ponte Mocenigo is off the beaten path—a 10-minute walk northwest of the Rialto Bridge—but it's a great value. This 16th-century Venetian palazzo has a garden terrace and 10 comfy, beautifully appointed, and tranquil rooms (Sb-€100, Db-€140–160 depending on view and amenities, 8 percent discount with cash and this book in 2008, air-con, Internet access, Santa Croce 2063, tel. 041-524-4797, fax 041-275-9420, www.alpontemocenigo.com, info@alpontemocengio.com, Sandro and Walter). Take vaporetto #1 to the San Stae stop, head inland along the right side of the church, and take the first left down tiny Calle della Campanile.

Hotels near the Rialto Bridge

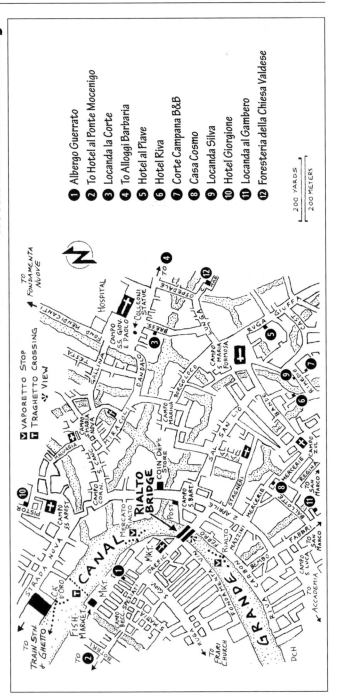

1. Albergo Guerrato
2. To Hotel al Ponte Mocenigo
3. Locanda la Corte
4. To Alloggi Barbaria
5. Hotel al Piave
6. Hotel Riva
7. Corte Campana B&B
8. Casa Cosmo
9. Locanda Silva
10. Hotel Giorgione
11. Locanda al Gambero
12. Foresteria della Chiesa Valdese

East of the Rialto Bridge

$$ Locanda la Corte, a three-star hotel, is perfumed with elegance. Its 16 attractive, high-ceilinged, wood-beamed rooms—done in pastels—circle a small, quiet courtyard (Sb-€120, standard Db-€150, superior Db-€170, 10 percent discount with cash, ask for Rick Steves rates to get these prices, Web deals may be better, suites available, air-con, Castello 6317, tel. 041-241-1300, fax 041-241-5982, www.locandalacorte.it, info@locandalacorte .it, Marco and Raffaela). Take vaporetto #52 from the train station to Fondamenta Nuove, exit the boat to your left, follow the waterfront, and turn right after the second bridge to get to S.S. Giovanni e Paolo square. Facing the Rosa Salva bar, take the street to the left (Calle Bressana); the hotel is a short block away at #6317 before the bridge.

$ Alloggi Barbaria rents eight quiet, spacious, backpacker-type rooms. Beyond Campo S.S. Giovanni e Paolo, this Ikea-style place is a long walk from the action but still a good value (Db-€110 with cash and this book in 2008, extra bed-€30, family deals, air-con, tel. 041-522-2750, fax 041-277-5540, www.alloggibarbaria.it, info@alloggibarbaria.it, Giorgio and Fausto). Take vaporetto #52 to Ospedale stop, turn left as you get off the boat, then right down Calle de le Capucine to #6573 (Castello). From the airport, take the Alilaguna speedboat to Fondamenta Nuove, turn left, then go right down Calle de le Capucine.

Southeast of the Rialto Bridge

$$ Hotel al Piave, with 27 fine air-conditioned rooms above a bright and classy lobby, is fresh, modern, and comfortable. You'll enjoy the neighborhood and always get a cheery welcome (Db-€160, Tb-€220, family suites-€270 for 4, €300 for 5, or €330 for 6, prices good through 2008 with this book, cash discount, Internet access, Ruga Giuffa 4838/40, Castello, tel. 041-528-5174, fax 041-523-8512, www.hotelalpiave.com, info@hotelalpiave.com, Mirella, Paolo, and Ilaria speak English, faithful Molly doesn't). From the San Zaccaria vaporetto stop, take the street to the right of the Bridge of Sighs to Campo S.S. Filippo e Giacomo, and continue on Calle drio la Chiesa. Cross the bridge, continue forward, then turn left onto Ruga Giuffa until you find the Piave on your left at #4838/40.

$ Hotel Riva, with gleaming marble hallways, big exposed beams, fine antique furnishings, and bright rooms, is romantically situated on a canal along the gondola serenade route. You could actually dunk your breakfast rolls in the canal (but don't). Sandro might hold a corner *(angolo)* room if you ask, and there are also a few rooms overlooking the canal. Ten of the 32 rooms come with air-conditioning for the same price—request one when you reserve

---

Flexible Floors

All over town, from palaces to cheap, old hotels, you'll find speckled floors (pavimento alla Veneziana). While they might look like cheap linoleum, these are historic—protected by the government and a pain for local landlords to maintain. As Venice was built, it needed flexible flooring to absorb the inevitable settling of the buildings. Through an expensive and laborious process, several layers of material were built up and finished with a broken marble top that was shaved and polished to what you see today. While patterns were sometimes designed into the flooring, it's often just a speckled hodgepodge. Keep an eye open for this. Once a year, the floor is rubbed with natural oil to maintain its flexibility. Craftspeople still give landlords fits when repairs are needed.

(S-€70, Sb-€90, two D with adjacent showers-€100, Db-€120, Tb-€170, €10 extra for view, reserve with credit card but pay with cash only, Ponte dell'Angelo, tel. 041-522-7034, fax 041-528-5551, www.hotelriva.it, info@hotelriva.it). Facing St. Mark's Basilica, walk behind it on the left along Calle de la Canonica, take the first left (at blue *Pauly & C* mosaic in street), continue straight, go over the bridge, and angle right to the hotel at Ponte dell'Anzolo.

$ Corte Campana B&B, run by enthusiastic and helpful Riccardo, rents three quiet and characteristic rooms just behind St. Mark's Square, plus two apartments just around the corner (Db-€125, Tb or Tb apartment-€165, Qb or Qb apartment-€190, prices are soft, cash only, 2-night minimum stay, Internet access, Calle del Remedio 4410, Castello, tel. & fax 041-523-3603, mobile 389-272-6500, www.cortecampana.com, info@cortecampana.com). Facing St. Mark's Basilica, take Calle de la Canonica (left of church) and turn left before the canal on Calle dell'Anzolo. Take the second right (onto Calle del Remedio), cross the bridge, and follow signs. Ring the bell at the black gate; the door is across the courtyard on the left wall, and the B&B is up three flights of stairs.

$ Casa Cosmo is a humble little five-room place run by Davide and his parents. While it comes with minimal services and no public spaces, it's air-conditioned, very central, inexpensive, and quiet, with a tiny terrace (Db-€110, ask for possible Rick Steves cash discount when you book, no breakfast, Calle di Mezo 4976, San Marco, tel. & fax 041-296-0710, www.casacosmo.com, info@casacosmo.com). Take vaporetto #2 to Rialto and head inland on Larga Mazzini (which becomes Merceria after passing a square and a church). Turn right onto San Salvador, then immediately left onto tiny Calle di Mezo to find the hotel ahead on your right at #4976.

$ Locanda Silva is a big, basic, beautifully located place renting 23 decent old-school rooms (S-€55, Sb-€80, D-€85, Db-€120, substantially less during slow times, Fondamenta del Remedio 4423, tel. 041-522-7643, fax 041-528-6817, www.locandasilva.it, fino@locandasilva.it). From San Marco, head north toward Campo Santa Maria Formosa, go down Calle del Remedio, and turn left at the canal to Fondamenta del Remedio.

Near the Accademia Bridge

When you step over the Accademia Bridge, the commotion of touristy Venice is replaced by a sleepy village laced with canals. You'll pay a premium to sleep here but, for many, the location is worth the price. This quiet area, next to the best painting gallery in town, is a 15-minute walk from the Rialto or St. Mark's Square. The fast vaporetto #2 connects the Accademia Bridge with both the train station (15 min) and St. Mark's Square (5 min).

South of the Accademia Bridge

To reach these hotels from the train station, you can take a vaporetto to the Accademia stop (more scenic, down Grand Canal) or the Zattere stop (less scenic, around outskirts of Venice, but faster). Or, from the airport, take the Alilaguna speedboat to the Zattere stop.

$$$ Hotel Belle Arti has a grand entry and a formal, stern staff. With the ambience and comforts of a modern American hotel, it feels a bit out of place in musty Old World Venice. It has plush public areas and 65 newly renovated rooms (Sb-€130, Db-€230, Tb-€265, air-con, elevator; 100 yards behind Accademia art museum: facing museum, take left, then forced right, to Via Dorsoduro 912, Dorsoduro; tel. 041-522-6230, fax 041-528-0043, www.hotelbellearti.com, info@hotelbellearti.com).

$$$ Pensione Accademia fills the 17th-century Villa Maravege. Its 27 rooms are comfortable, elegant, and air-conditioned. You'll feel aristocratic gliding through its grand public spaces and lounging in its wistful, breezy gardens (Sb-€140, standard Db-€220, bigger "superior" Db-€265, Qb-€340, 5 percent cash discount promised to readers during high season, 10 percent discount the rest of the year, ask for Rick Steves discount when you book; facing Accademia art museum, take first right, cross first bridge, go right to Dorsoduro 1058; tel. 041-523-7846, fax 041-523-9152, www.pensioneaccademia.it, info@pensioneaccademia.it).

$$$ Hotel agli Alboretti is a cozy, family-run, 23-room place in a quiet neighborhood a block behind the Accademia art museum. With red carpeting and wood-beamed ceilings, it feels classy (Sb-€110, Db-€200, Tb-€225, Qb-€250, air-con, elevator, 100 yards from the Accademia vaporetto stop on Rio Terra

Hotels near the Accademia Bridge

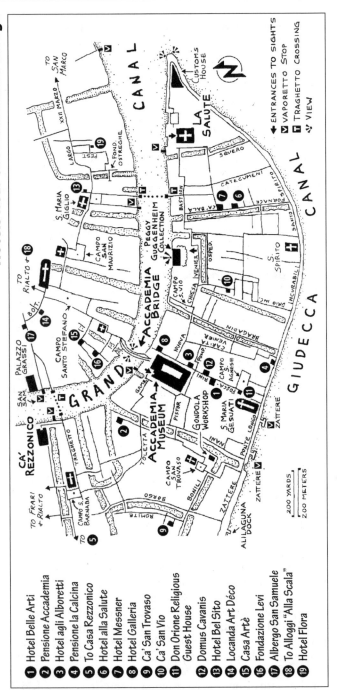

1 Hotel Belle Arti
2 Pensione Accademia
3 Hotel agli Alboretti
4 Pensione la Calcina
5 To Casa Rezzonico
6 Hotel alla Salute
7 Hotel Messner
8 Ca' San Trovaso
9 Ca' San Vio
10 Don Orione Religious Guest House
11 Domus Cavanis
12 Hotel Bel Sito
13 Locanda Art Déco
14 Casa Artè
15 Fondazione Levi
16 Albergo San Samuele
17 To Alloggi "Alla Scala"
18 Hotel Flora

A. Foscarini at #884, Dorsoduro, tel. 041-523-0058, fax 041-521-0158, www.aglialboretti.com, info@aglialboretti.com). Facing the Accademia art museum, go left, then forced right; or from the Zattere Alilaguna stop, head inland on Rio Terra A. Foscarini 100 yards to the hotel. They run a nearby gourmet restaurant that's a local favorite.

$$ Pensione la Calcina, the home of English writer John Ruskin in 1876, maintains a 19th-century formality. It comes with all the three-star comforts in a professional yet intimate package. Its 33 rooms are squeaky clean, with good wood furniture, hardwood floors, and a peaceful canal-side setting facing Giudecca Island (Sb-€100, Sb with view-€110, Db-€150–225 depending on size of room and view, air-con, rooftop terrace, killer sundeck on canal and canal-side buffet-breakfast terrace, Dorsoduro 780, at south end of Rio di San Vio, tel. 041-520-6466, fax 041-522-7045, www.lacalcina.com, la.calcina@libero.it). From the Tronchetto parking lot, take vaporetto #2, or from the train station take #51 or #61, to Zattere (at vaporetto stop, exit right and walk along canal to hotel). Guests get a discounted dinner at their La Piscina restaurant and are welcome to use the terrace outside of meal times without buying anything.

$$ Casa Rezzonico is a silent getaway far from the madding crowds. Its private garden terrace has perhaps the lushest grass in Italy, and its seven spacious rooms have garden/canal views (Sb-€120, Db-€160, Tb-€180, Qb-€220, ask for Rick Steves discount when you book, air-con, Fondamenta Gherardini 2813, Dorsoduro, tel. 041-277-0653, fax 041-277-5435, www.casarezzonico.it, info @casarezzonico.it). Take vaporetto #1 to the Ca' Rezzonico stop, head up Calle del Traghetto, cross Campo San Barnaba to the canal, and continue forward on Fondamenta Gherardini to #2813.

$$ Hotel alla Salute, a basic and impersonal retreat buried deep in Dorsoduro with 50 rooms, works for those wanting a quiet Venice residence (Db-€150, cheaper with cash, a few annex rooms have air-con, facing the Rio delle Fornace Canal near La Salute church, Salute 222, Dorsoduro, tel. 041-523-5404, fax 041-522-2271, www.hotelsalute.com, info@hotelsalute.com).

$$ Hotel Messner, a sprawling place popular with groups, rents 38 bright, newly refurbished rooms (half in main building, half in nearby, simpler annex), in a peaceful canal-side neighborhood near La Salute Church (Sb-€110, Db with air-con-€145, Db without air-con in annex-€115, Tb-€145, Qb-€160, 5 percent discount with cash if you book direct, peaceful garden, midway between lagoon and Grand Canal on Rio delle Fornace canal, Dorsoduro 216, tel. 041-522-7443, fax 041-522-7266, www .hotelmessner.it, messnerinfo@tin.it).

$ Hotel Galleria has nine tight, velvety rooms, most with views of the Grand Canal. Some rooms are quite narrow (S-€80, D-€110, Db-€130, big canal-view Db #8 and #10-€165, includes scant breakfast in room, fans, near Accademia art museum, and next to recommended Foscarini pizzeria, Dorsoduro 878a, tel. 041-523-2489, fax 041-520-4172, www.hotelgalleria.it, galleria @tin.it).

$ Ca' San Trovaso rents nine classy, spacious rooms split between the main hotel and a nearby annex. The location is peaceful, on a small canal (Sb-€90, Db-€115, bigger canal-view with air-con Db-€130, Tb-€145, these prices promised with cash and this book in 2008, breakfast in your room, fans, small roof terrace, Dorsoduro 1350/51, tel. 041-277-1146, fax 041-277-7190, www .casantrovaso.com, s.trovaso@tin.it, Mark and his son Alessandro). Take vaporetto #2 from the Tronchetto parking lot (or #51 from Piazzale Roma or the train station), get off at Zattere, exit left, and cross a bridge. Turn right at tiny Calle Trevisan (just past the white building with all the flags), cross another bridge, cross the adjacent bridge, take an immediate right, and then the first left.

$ Ca' San Vio is a tiny place run by the Ca' San Trovaso folks on a quiet canal with five fine air-conditioned rooms (small French bed Db-€110, bigger Db-€130, Tb-€150, cash only, breakfast in room, no public spaces, Calle delle Mende 531, Dorsoduro, tel. 041-241-3513, fax 041-241-3953, www.casanvio.com, info @casanvio.com, Roberto, Alessandro, and Marco).

$ Don Orione Religious Guest House is a big cultural center dedicated to the work of a local man who became a saint in modern times. Filling an old monastery, it feels like a modern retreat center—clean, peaceful, and strictly run, with 80 rooms. It's beautifully located, comfortable, and a fine value (Sb-€75, Db-€130, Tb-€165, profits go to mission work in the developing world, groups welcome, air-con, on the Giudecca Canal directly across from the Accademia Bridge facing Campo Sant'Agnese, Zattere 909a, Dorsoduro, tel. 041-522-4077, fax 041-528-6214, www .donorione-venezia.it, info@donorione-venezia.it).

$ Domus Cavanis, across the street from—and run by— Hotel Belle Arti (described on page 219), is a big, dim, stark place, renting 30 basic, dingy rooms for a good price (Sb-€75, Db-€120, Tb-€160, family rooms, includes breakfast at Hotel Belle Arti, air-con, hounds of hell bathroom fans, elevator, Dorsoduro 895, tel. 041-528-7374, fax 041-528-0043, info@hotelbellearti.com).

North of the Accademia Bridge

$$ Hotel Bel Sito offers pleasing yet well-worn Old World character, 38 rooms, a peaceful courtyard, and a picturesque location— facing a church on a small square between St. Mark's Square and the Accademia (Sb-€105, Db-€170, these special Rick Steves prices with this book in 2008, air-con, elevator; catch vaporetto #1 to Santa Maria del Giglio stop, take street inland to square, hotel is at far end to your right at Santa Maria del Giglio 2517, San Marco; tel. 041-522-3365, fax 041-520-4083, www.hotelbelsito .info, info@hotelbelsito.info, manager Rosella).

$$ Locanda Art Déco is a charming little place. While the Art Deco theme is scant, a wrought-iron staircase leads from the inviting lobby to seven thoughtfully decorated rooms (Db-€170, 3-night minimum on weekends, 5 percent discount with cash, 2 family rooms, air-con, just north of the Accademia Bridge off Campo Santo Stefano at Calle delle Botteghe 2966, San Marco, tel. 041-277-0558, fax 041-270-2891, www.locandaartdeco.com, info@locandaartdeco.com).

$ Casa Artè has eight homey rooms with high ceilings, old-style Venetian furnishings, air-con, and thoughtful touches in a red-velvet ambience. An annex contains eight peaceful, simpler rooms (Sb-€100, Db-€140, 10 percent discount with cash, family room sleeps up to 6, just north of Accademia Bridge, 100 yards west of Campo Santo Stefano on Calle de Frutariol 2900/01, San Marco, tel. 041-520-0882, fax 041-277-8395, www.casaarte.info, info@casaarte.info, Nicole).

$ Fondazione Levi, run by a foundation that promotes research on Venetian music, offers 18 quiet, institutional, yet comfortable and spacious rooms (Sb-€64, Db-€105, Tb-€120, Qb-€140, twin beds only, elevator, San Vidal 2893, San Marco, tel. 041-786-711, fax 041-786-766, foresterialevi@libero.it). It's 80 yards from the base of the Accademia Bridge on the St. Mark's side. From the Accademia vaporetto stop, cross the Accademia Bridge and take an immediate left, crossing the bridge Ponte Giustinian and going down Calle Giustinian directly to the Fondazione. Buzz the *Foresteria* door to the right.

$ Albergo San Samuele's 12 basic budget rooms are located in a crumbling historic palazzo just a few blocks from Campo Santo Stefano (S-€60, D-€90, Db-€125, cash only, no breakfast, Salizzada San Samuele 3358, San Marco, tel. 041-522-8045, fax 041-520-5165, www.albergosansamuele.it, info@albergosansamuele.it).

$ Alloggi "Alla Scala" is a basic, grandmotherly retreat with six homey rooms located next to the Bovolo staircase just off Campo Manin (Sb-€50, Db-€90, 6 percent cash discount, breakfast-€5, Corte Contarini del Bovolo 4306, San Marco, tel. 041-521-0629, fax 041-522-6451, www.alloggiallascala.com, info @alloggiallascala.com). At Campo Manin ask for (or follow signs to) Corte Contarini del Bovolo—100 yards away.

Near the Train Station

I don't recommend the train station area. It's crawling with noisy, disoriented tourists with too much baggage and people whose life's calling is to scam visitors out of their money. It's so easy just to hop a vaporetto upon arrival and get into the Venice of your dreams. Still, some like to park their bags near the station, and these places work well. The nearest self-service laundry is Speedy Wash (daily 8:00–22:00, Rio Terra S. Leonardo 5120 just east of the Guglie bridge, tel. 041-524-4188).

$$ **Locanda Herion,** a shiny little inn, has 17 fine rooms and a pretty little garden courtyard perfect for dinner picnics or a glass of wine (Db-€150, €10–20 discount for cash, air-con, Rio Terà San Leonardo 1704, Cannaregio, between Guglie and S. Marcuola vaporetto stops, tel. 041-275-9426, fax 041-275-6647, www .locandaherion.com, info@locandaherion.com).

$ **Albergo Marin** and its friendly, helpful staff offer 17 good-value, quiet, and immaculate rooms handy to the train station (Sb-€85, Db-€110, these are the maximum prices with this book in 2008, 5 percent discount with cash, fans on request, Ramo delle Chioverete #670B, Santa Croce, tel. 041-718-022, fax 041-721-485, www.albergomarin.it, info@albergomarin.it). From the station, cross the Grand Canal and turn immediately right. Take the first left, then the first right, then right again to Ramo delle Chioverete.

$ **Hotel S. Lucia,** just 150 yards from the station down a quiet alley, is a peaceful family-owned hotel offering budget travelers a haven from Venice's hustle and bustle. Its 15 rooms are simple, clean, and cheery, and guests can enjoy their sunny garden terrace (S-€55, Db-€100, discounts for longer stays and cash, breakfast-€5, air-con, Calle della Misericordia 358, Cannaregio, tel. 041-715-180, fax 041-710-610, www.hotelslucia.com, info@hotelslucia .com). Exit the station toward the Grand Canal and head left, then take the second left onto Calle della Misericordia. The hotel is 100 yards ahead on the right.

$ **Alloggi Henry,** a homey little family-owned hotel, rents eight ramshackle rooms with dated comforters in a quiet neighborhood a five-minute walk from the train station (D-€80, Db-€90–100 with cash and this book in 2008, no breakfast, air-con, Calle Ormesini 1506e, Cannaregio, tel. 041-523-6675, fax 041-715-680, www.alloggihenry.com, info@alloggihenry.com). From the station, follow Lista di Spagna, Rio Terra San Leonardo, and Rio Terra Farsetti, then take the second left on Calle Ormesini. The hotel's at #1506.

Big, Fancy Hotels

Here are four big, plush, four-star places with greedy, sky-high rack rates (around Db-€300) that often have great discounts (as low as Db-€100) for drop-ins, off-season travelers, or online booking through their websites. If you want a sliding-glass-door, uniformed-receptionist kind of comfort and formality in the old center, these are worth considering: **$$$ Hotel Giorgione** (big, garish, shiny, near Rialto Bridge, www.hotelgiorgione.com—see map on page 216); **$$$ Hotel Casa Verardo** (elegant and quietly parked on a canal behind St. Mark's, more stately, www.casaverardo.it—see map on page 212); **$$$ Hotel Donà Palace** (sitting like Las Vegas in the touristy zone just northeast of St. Mark's, www.donapalace .it—see map on page 212); and **$$$ Locanda al Gambero,** with 30 comfortable rooms near San Marco (www.locandaalgambero .com—see map on page 216).

Cheap Dormitory Accommodations

$ Foresteria della Chiesa Valdese, warmly run by the Methodist Church, offers 60 beds in doubles and 3- to 8-bed dorms, half-way between St. Mark's Square and the Rialto Bridge. This run-down but charming old place has elegant ceiling paintings (dorm bed-€23, D-€60, Db-€76, includes breakfast, sheets, towels, and lockers; must check in and out when office is open—9:00–13:00 & 18:00–20:00, Fondamenta Cavagnis 5170, Castello, tel. 041-528-6797, fax 041-241-6238, foresteriavenezia@diaconiavaldese.org). From Campo Santa Maria Formosa, walk past Bar all'Orologio to the end of Calle Lunga and cross the bridge onto Fondamenta Cavagnis.

    $ Venice's youth hostel, on Giudecca Island with grand views across the Bay of San Marco, is a godsend for backpackers shell-shocked by Venetian prices (€21 beds with sheets and break-fast in 12- to 16-bed dorms, cheaper for hostel members, office open daily 7:00–9:30 & 13:30–24:30, catch vaporetto #2 from station to Zittele, tel. 041-523-8211, can reserve online at www .hostelbooking.com). The budget cafeteria also welcomes non-hostelers (nightly 18:00–23:00).

EATING

The Italians are masters at the art of fine living. That means eating...long and well. Lengthy, multicourse lunches and dinners and endless hours sitting in outdoor cafés are the norm. Americans eat on their way to an evening event and complain if the check is slow in coming. For Italians, dining is an end in itself, and only rude waiters rush you. When you want the bill, mime-scribble on your raised palm or ask for it: *"Il conto?"*

Even those of us who liked dorm food will find that the local cafés, cuisine, and wines become a highlight of our Italian adventure. Trust me: This is sightseeing for your palate, and even if the rest of you is sleeping in cheap hotels, your taste buds will relish an occasional first-class splurge. You can eat well without going broke. But be careful: You're just as likely to blow a small fortune on a disappointing meal as you are to dine wonderfully for €20.

Restaurants

Looking for an "untouristy restaurant" in Venice is like looking for one at Disneyland. Venice restaurants exist to feed tourists. Still, some cater to groups and sloppy big spenders, while others respect their clientele—both locals and travelers. High-rent restaurants parked on famous squares or canals must pass on their costs, and generally serve tourists bad food at high prices. Locals eat better at low-rent, holes-in-the-wall, which need to be good to be known. While Venetians still eat out and have their favorites, a local restaurateur recently confided in me that no restaurant in Venice can be truly untouristy: They all want and need the tourist euro.

The words *trattoria* and *osteria* (which historically meant a simple, local-style restaurant) can now mean that a place is just as elegant and pricey as a *ristorante*. While set-price meals can be cheap and easy, galloping gourmets order à la carte with the help

Eating with the Seasons

Italian cooks love to serve you fresh produce and seafood at its tastiest. If you must have porcini mushrooms outside of October and November, they'll be frozen. Each region in Italy has its own specialties, which you'll see displayed in local markets. To get the freshest veggies at a fine restaurant, request *"Un piatto di verdure della stagione, per favore"* (A plate of seasonal vegetables, please).

Here are a few examples of what's fresh when:

April–May:	Squid, green beans, asparagus, artichokes, and zucchini flowers
April, May, Sept, Oct:	Black truffles
May–June:	Asparagus, zucchini, cantaloupe, and strawberries
May–Aug:	Eggplant
Oct–Nov:	Mushrooms, white truffles, and chestnuts
Nov–Feb:	Radicchio
Fresh year-round:	Clams, meats

Eating

of a menu translator. (*The Marling Italian Menu-Master* is excellent. *Rick Steves' Italian Phrase Book & Dictionary* has a menu decoder with enough phrases for intermediate eaters.)

A full meal consists of an appetizer (*antipasto*, €3–6), a first course (*primo piatto*, pasta, rice, or soup, €5–12), and a second course (*secondo piatto*, expensive meat and fish dishes, €10–20). Vegetables *(contorni, verdure)* may come with the *secondo* or cost extra (€3–5) as a side dish. The euros can add up in a hurry. Light and budget eaters get a *primo piatto* each and share an antipasto. Or they indulge in bar snacks called *cicchetti* (explained on page 231).

Note that seafood and steak may be sold by weight; if you see "100 g" or *"l'etto"* by the price on the menu, you'll pay that price per 100 grams—about a quarter pound. Similarly, *"s.q."* means according to quantity. Fish is usually served whole with the head and tail; you can't just get half a fish or a filet unless it already comes prepared as just a filet (*filetto*, sometimes *trancio*—slice, as in tuna or swordfish). However, you can ask your waiter to select a smaller fish for you.

Some special dishes come in large quantities meant for two people; the shorthand way of showing this on a menu is "x2" (meaning "times two"), and the price listed generally indicates the cost per person.

Restaurants normally pad the bill with a cover charge (*pane e coperto*—"bread and cover charge," of around €2, which is not negotiable, even if you don't eat the bread) and occasionally a service charge (*servizio*, 15 percent, see "Tipping," below); these charges are listed on the menu.

Tipping

Tipping is an issue only at restaurants that have waiters and wait-resses. If you order your food at a counter, don't tip. (Many Italians never tip.)

If the menu states that service is included *(servizio incluso)*, there's no need to tip beyond that, but if you like to tip and you're pleased with the service, throw in €1–2 per person.

If service is not included, tip 5–10 percent by rounding up or leaving the change from your bill. Leave the tip on the table or hand it to your server. It's best to tip in cash even if you pay with your credit card—otherwise, the tip might never reach your waiter.

Cheap Meals

The keys to cheap eating in Venice are pizza, bars/cafés, and picnics. *Panini* and *tramezzini* (sandwiches, described on page 232) are sold fast and cheap at bars everywhere and can stave off mid-morning hunger. For speed, value, and ambience, you can get a filling plate of local appetizers at nearly any bar. For budget eating, I like small, stand-up mini-meals at *cicchetti* **bars** best (see page 239).

Pizzerias

Pizza is cheap and readily available. Key pizza vocabulary: *capricciosa* (generally ham, mushrooms, olives, and artichokes), *funghi* (mushrooms), *marinara* (tomato sauce, oregano, garlic, no cheese), *quattro formaggi* (four different cheeses), and *quattro stagioni* (different toppings on each of the pizza's four quarters, for those who can't choose just one menu item). If you ask for pepperoni on your pizza, you'll get *peperoni* (green or red peppers, not sausage). Kids like *diavola*, which is the closest thing in Italy to American pepperoni, and *margherita*—the classic mozzarella, tomato sauce, and basil pizza named for Queen Margherita in 1889.

Bars/Cafés

Italian "bars" are not taverns, but cafés. These local hangouts serve coffee, mini-pizzas, sandwiches, and drinks from the cooler. Many dish up plates of fried cheese and vegetables from under the glass counter, ready to reheat. This budget choice is the Italian equivalent of English pub grub—but usually much tastier. Unique to Venice, *cicchetti* bars specialize in finger foods and appetizers that can combine to make a quick and tasty meal. See "The Stand-Up Progressive Venetian Pub-Crawl Dinner," page 238.

For quick meals, bars usually have trays of cheap, ready-made sandwiches *(panini* or *tramezzini)*—some are delightful grilled. (Others are lots of mayo between crustless slices of Wonder Bread.) To save time for sightseeing and room for dinner, consider a ham-and-cheese *panino* at a bar (called *toast,* have it grilled twice if you want it really hot) for lunch.

To get food "for the road," say, *"Da portar via"* (or *"da portar canale"*...for the canal). Many bars are small—if you can't find a table, you'll need to stand up. Most charge extra for table service. All bars have a WC *(toilette, bagno)* in the back, and customers (and the discreet public) may use it.

Bars serve drinks—hot, cold, sweet, or alcoholic. Chilled bottled water *(natural* or *frizzante)* is sold cheap to-go. Fresh-squeezed orange and grapefruit juice *(una spremuta)* are common. *Cioccolato* is hot chocolate. *Tè* is hot tea. *Tè freddo* (iced tea) is usually from a can—sweetened and flavored with lemon or peach.

Coffee: Take some time to learn Italian coffee lingo—the names and the rituals are a little different than at your hometown java joint. If you ask for *"un caffè,"* you'll get espresso. If you ask for a latte, you'll get just that—a glass of hot milk. Starbucks-style mochas aren't on the menu at all. Cappuccino is served to locals before noon and to tourists at any time of day. (To an Italian, cappuccino is a breakfast drink and a travesty after anything with tomatoes.) Italians like their coffee only warm—to get it hot, request *"Molto caldo"* (very hot) or *"Più caldo, per favore"* (hotter, please; pew KAHL-doh, pehr fah-VOH-ray).

Experiment with a few of the options...
- *Caffè:* Espresso
- *Macchiato:* Espresso with just a little milk (*macchiato* means "marked" or "stained")
- *Cappuccino:* Coffee with hot milk, topped with foam (sometimes referred to as a *cappucio)*
- *Caffè latte:* Coffee with lots of hot milk, no foam
- *Latte macchiato:* Hot milk with a shot of espresso
- *Caffè americano:* Espresso diluted with water
- *Caffè freddo:* Sweet and iced espresso
- *Cappuccino freddo:* Iced cappuccino
- *Caffè hag:* Instant decaf (you can order decaffeinated versions of any coffee drink—just ask for it *decaffeinato;* day-kah-fay-ee-NAH-toh)
- *Caffè corretto:* Espresso with a shot of liqueur, usually *grappa* or Sambuca, but amaretto is also good

Beer: Beer on tap is *"alla spina."* Get it *piccola* (33 centiliters or 1.4 cups), *media* (50 cl, about a pint), or *grande* (a liter, about 2 pints). Italians drink mainly lager beers. You'll find local brews (Peroni or Moretti) and imports such as Heineken as well. A *lattina* is a can and a *bottiglia* (boh-TEEL-yah) is a bottle.

Wine: To order a glass (*bicchiere;* bee-kee-AY-ree) of red *(rosso)* or white *(bianco)* wine, say, "*Un bicchiere di vino rosso/bianco.*" *Secco* is dry, *corposo* means full-bodied, and *frizzante* is fizzy. House wine comes in a carafe: quarter-liter *(un quarto),* half-liter *(un mezzo),* or liter *(un litro).* An *ombra* is the smallest glass.

Prices: You'll notice a two-tiered pricing system. Drinking a cup of coffee while standing at the bar is cheaper than drinking it at a table. There's often a *listino prezzi* (price list) with two columns—*al bar* and *al tavolo*—posted somewhere by the bar or cash register. If you're on a budget, don't sit without first checking out the financial consequences. Ask, "Same price if I sit or stand?" by saying, "*Costa uguale al tavolo o al banco?*" (KOH-stah oo-GWAH-lay ahl TAH-voh-loh oh ahl BAHN-koh?).

If the bar isn't busy, you'll often just order and pay when you leave. Otherwise: (1) decide what you want; (2) find out the price by checking the price list on the wall, the prices posted near the food, or by asking the barman; (3) pay the cashier; and (4) give the receipt to the barman (whose clean fingers handle no dirty euros) and tell him what you want.

Picnics

Picnicking saves lots of euros and is a great way to sample local specialties. Note that the only legal place to picnic in Venice is Giardinetti Reali, the waterfront park near St. Mark's Square.

A local *alimentari* is your one-stop corner grocery store (most will slice and stuff your sandwich for you if you buy the ingredients there).

Juice-lovers can get a liter of O.J. for the price of a Coke or coffee. Look for "100% *succo*" (juice) on the label or be surprised by something diluted and sugary sweet. Hang onto the half-liter plastic mineral-water bottles (sold everywhere for about €1). Buy juice in cheap liter boxes, drink some, and store the extra in your water bottle. You'll also save money by buying water in big bottles (a third the price of small bottles—even cheaper in supermarkets) to keep in your hotel room and use to refill your smaller, more portable bottle. (I drink the tap water—*acqua del rubinetto.*)

Picnics can be adventures in high cuisine. Be daring. Try the fresh mozzarella, presto pesto, shriveled olives, marinated eggplant or artichokes, sundried tomatoes, and any UFOs the locals are excited about. Shopkeepers are happy to sell small quantities of produce. Rather than pick your own produce, it is customary to say when you plan to eat it. If you plan to eat it today, say, "*Per oggi*" (pehr OH-jee), and let her grab the pieces that are best for you. If you suspect you're being overcharged, know the cost per kilo and study the weighing procedure as if you're doing the arithmetic.

A typical picnic for two might be fresh rolls, 100 grams of cheese, 100 grams of meat (about a quarter pound, called *un etto* in Italy), two tomatoes, three carrots, two apples, yogurt, and a liter box of juice. Total cost—about €10.

Picnic Supplies near the Rialto: The **produce market** that sprawls for a few blocks just past the Rialto Bridge is a great place to assemble a picnic (best Mon–Sat 8:00–13:00, closed Sun). The adjacent fish market is wonderfully slimy (closed Sun–Mon). Side lanes in this area are speckled with fine little hole-in-the-wall munchie bars, bakeries, and cheese shops.

A tiny *alimentari* just around the corner from the Rialto market has *salumi,* cheese, bread, and an intriguing (and spicy!) concoction of cheese, kalamata olives, sundried tomatoes, olive oil, and hot peppers. It goes great with a fresh roll. To get there from the market, walk to the end of Ruga degli Orefici, turn left onto Ruga Vecchia S. Giovanni, and then right under Sotoportego dei do' Mori—it's just on your left (open daily).

Picnic Supplies near the Accademia Bridge: A small deli hides along the main route between the Accademia and St. Mark's Square (on the zigzag bridge near the church of Santa Maria del Giglio).

Supermarkets: A handy **SuVe** supermarket, between St. Mark's and Campo Santa Maria Formosa, is on the corner of Salizada San Lio and Calle del Mondo Novo (Mon–Sat 8:45–19:30, closed Sun). **Billa** supermarket is at the far west end of Dorsoduro, on the corner of Zattere al Ponte Longo and Calle della Massena (Mon–Sat 8:00–20:00, Sun 9:00–20:00, tel. 041-522-6187). Assemble your picnic, and then dine in style overlooking Giudecca Canal.

VENETIAN CUISINE

Venetian cuisine relies more heavily on fish, shellfish, risotto, and polenta than the rest of Italy. Along with the usual pizza and pasta fare, here are some typical foods you'll encounter:

Bar Snacks

Venetians often eat a snack—*cicchetti* or *panini*—while standing at a bar. (Remember, you'll usually pay more if you sit, rather than stand.)

Cicchetti: Generic name for various small finger foods served in some pubs—like appetizers or tapas, Venetian-style. Designed as a quick meal for working people, the selection and ambience are best on workdays (Mon–Sat lunch and early dinner). See "The Stand-Up Progressive Venetian Pub-Crawl Dinner," page 238.

Panini: Sandwiches made with rustic bread, filled with meat, vegetables, and cheese, served cold or toasted—*riscaldato* (ree-skahl-DAH-toh). You can eat your sandwich at the bar or take it with you.

Tramezzini: Crustless, white bread sandwiches served cold and stuffed with a variety of fillings (e.g., egg, tuna, or shrimp), mixed with a mayonnaise dressing. The selection is best in the morning and skimpy by afternoon.

Appetizers *(Antipasti)*

Antipasto di mare: A marinated mix of fish and shellfish served chilled.

Asiago cheese: The Veneto region's specialty, a cow's-milk cheese that's either *mezzano*—young, firm, and creamy; or *stravecchio*—aged, pungent, and granular.

Sarde in saor: Sardines marinated with onions.

Rice *(Riso)*, Pasta, and Polenta

Risotto: Short-grain rice, simmered in broth and often flavored with fish and seafood. For example, *risotto nero* is risotto made with squid and its ink, and *risotto ai porcini* contains porcini mushrooms.

Risi e bisi: Rice and peas.

Pasta e fagioli: Bean and pasta soup.

Bigoli in salsa: A long, fat, whole-wheat noodle (one of the few traditional pastas) with anchovy sauce.

Polenta: Cornmeal boiled into a mush and served soft or cut into firm slabs and grilled. Polenta is a standard accompaniment with cod *(baccalà),* or calf liver and onions *(fegato alla veneziana).*

Seafood *(Frutti di Mare)*

Some sea creatures found in the Adriatic are slightly different from their American cousins. Generally, Venetian fish are smaller than American salmon and trout (think sardines and anchovies). The shellfish are more exotic. The weirder the animal (eel, octopus, frogfish), the more local it is. Remember that seafood can be sold by weight rather than a set price (if you see "100 g" or *"l'etto"* by a too-good-to-be-true price on the menu, that's the cost per 100 grams—about a quarter pound). The abbreviation *s.q.* is similar, meaning according to quantity (you pay for the weight of the particular piece).

Baccalà: Reconstituted dried salt cod served with polenta, or chopped up and mixed with mayonnaise as a topping for *cicchetti* (appetizers).

Branzino: Sea bass, grilled and served whole (with head and tail).

Calamari: Squid, usually cut into rings and either deep-fried or marinated.

Cozze: Mussels, often steamed in an herb broth with tomato.

Gamberi: The generic name for shrimp. *Gamberetti* are small shrimp, and *gamberoni* are large shrimp. (Language tip: *-etti* signifies little, and *-oni* indicates big.)

Moleche col pien: Fried soft-shell crabs.

Orata: Sea bream, a common European game fish.

Pesce fritto misto: Assorted deep-fried seafood (often calamari and prawns).

Pesce spada: Swordfish.

Rombo: Delicately flavored flat fish.

Rospo: Frogfish, a small marine fish.

Seppia: Cuttlefish, a squid-like creature that sprays black ink when threatened. *Seppia al nero* is the squid in its own ink, often served over spaghetti. Sweet and tender when grilled—either *grigliata* or *alla griglia* (without its ink).

Sogliola: Sole, served poached or oven-roasted.

Vitello di mare: "Sea veal," like swordfish—firm, pink, mild, and grilled.

Vongole: Small clams steamed with fresh herbs and wine, or served as a first course, such as *spaghetti alle vongole*.

Zuppa di pesce: Seafood stew.

Dessert (Dolci)

Tiramisù: Spongy ladyfingers soaked in coffee and marsala, layered with mascarpone cheese and bitter chocolate. Arguably Venetian in origin, the literal meaning of the word is "pick-me-up."

Venetian cookies: There are numerous varieties, due perhaps to Venice's position in trade (spices) and the Venetians' love of celebrations. Many treats were created for certain feast days and religious holidays. *Pinza,* a sweet made with corn, wheat flour, and raisins (and sometimes figs, almonds, and lemon), is made for Epiphany, January 6. *Fritole* are tiny doughnuts associated with Carnevale (Mardi Gras). *Bussola* rings are made for Easter. Other popular treats are *bisse* (seahorse-shaped cookies) and *croccante* (made with toasted corn and almonds, similar in texture to peanut brittle).

Cocktails *(Aperitivos)*

Spritz: The dominant aperitivo among Venetians is the spritz. This refreshing pre-dinner drink *(aperitivo)* mixes white wine, soda, and ice with a liquor of your choice and is garnished with an olive or skewer of fruit. Most popular with locals are *uno spritz con Campari* (bitter—traditionally the man's choice) or *con Aperol* (sweeter, a feminine choice). Between 18:00 and 20:00, this happy pink drink seems to dominate Venice's watering holes.

Bellini: A cocktail of Prosecco and white-peach puree; invented (and drunk by Hemingway) at the pricey Harry's Bar (near San Marco–Vallaresso vaporetto stop).

Tiziano: Grape juice and Prosecco.

Top Local Wines

Prosecco: Sparkling wine, usually a pre-dinner drink, but can be ordered any time. It's neutral-tasting, making it easy to drink too much.

Soave: Crisp white (great with seafood) from near Verona. *Soave Classico* designates a higher quality.

Valpolicella: Light, dry, fruity red from the hills north of Verona. It's likely what you're drinking if you ordered the house wine *(vino della casa)*.

Bardolino: Also made from Valpolicella grapes, it's a similar wine but grown near Lake Garda.

Amarone: Rich, intense red, with alcohol content at about 16 percent, made from Valpolicella grapes.

Fragolino: A sweet, slightly fizzy dessert wine made from a strawberry-flavored grape.

Grappa: Distilled *vinacce* (grape skins and stems left over from winemaking) make this powerful local firewater. A *stravecchio* is an aged *grappa*, making it somewhat mellower.

RESTAURANTS

While touristy restaurants are the scourge of Venice, these places are still popular with locals and respect the tourists who happen in. First trick: Walk away from triple-language menus. Second trick: Order the daily special. Third trick: For freshness, eat fish. Most seafood dishes are the local catch-of-the-day. Remember that a place may feel really touristy at 7:00, but come back at 9:00 and it will be filled with locals. Tourists eat barbarically early, which is fine with the restaurants because they fill tables that would otherwise be used only once in an evening.

Eating

Near the Rialto Bridge
North of the Bridge

These restaurants are located between Campo S.S. Apostoli and Campo S.S. Giovanni e Paolo.

Trattoria da Bepi is bright, alpine-paneled, and family run. Owner Loris scours the market for just the best ingredients—especially seafood—and takes good care of the hungry clientele. There's good seating inside and out (€10 pastas, €15 *secondi*, Fri–Wed 12:00–14:30 & 19:00–22:00, closed Thu, near Rialto, half a block north of Campo Santi Apostoli on Salizada Pistor, tel. 041-528-5031).

Trattoria Ca' d'Oro, while a little less accessible and inviting to the tourist, is a venerable favorite with a small, appealing menu and an enthusiastic local following. Just to sip a wine and enjoy *cicchetti* at the bar is a treat. It's also fine for a meal (€9 pastas, €10 *secondi*, lunch from 11:00, dinner from 18:30, closed Thu, reservations a must, from the Ca' d'Oro boat dock walk 100 yards directly away from the canal, cross Strada Nuova, and you'll hit it, tel. 041-528-5324).

Osteria da Alberto, with excellent €20 seafood dinners, €8 pastas, a good house wine, and a woody and characteristic interior, is one of my standbys (Mon–Sat 12:00–15:00 & 19:00–23:00, closed Sun, midway between Campo S.S. Apostoli and Campo S.S. Giovanni e Paolo, next to Ponte de la Panada on Calle Larga Giacinto Gallina, tel. 041-523-8153, run by Graziano and Giovanni).

Cicchetti, plus Pasta: **Osteria al Bomba** is a *cicchetti* bar with a female touch. It's unusual (clean, no toothpicks, no cursing) and quite good, with lots of veggies. You can stand and eat at the bar—try a little €2 plate of polenta and cod—or oversee the construction of the house *"antipasto misto di cicchetti"* plate (€22, enough fish and vegetables for 2). Then grab a seat at the long table to complete your pub crawl with a plate of pasta (daily 18:00–23:00, near Campo S.S. Apostoli, a block off Strada Nuova on Calle dell'Oca, tel. 041-520-5175). You'll find more pubs nearby, in the side streets opposite Campo Santa Sofia, across Strada Nuova.

East of the Rialto Bridge, near Campo San Bartolomeo

Osteria di Santa Marina, on the wonderful Campo Marina, serves pricey, near-gourmet food that's made with only the best seasonal ingredients. The quality food and classy ambience make this a good splurge. Cheap eating tricks are frowned on in this elegant, border-line stuffy restaurant (enticing menu with €15 pastas and €25 *secondi*, Sun–Mon 19:30–21:30, Tue–Sat 12:30–14:30 & 19:30–22:00, reservations smart for dinner, eat indoors or outdoors on pleasant little square, midway between Rialto Bridge and Campo

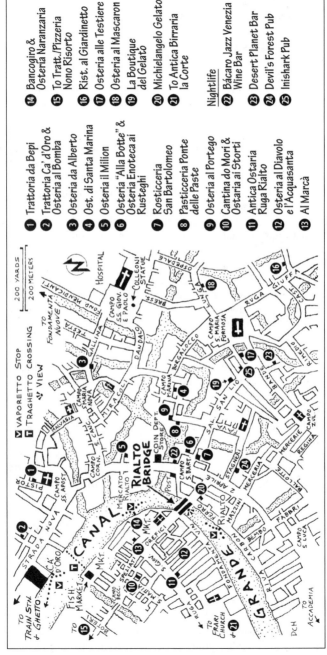

Eating

Restaurants near the Rialto Bridge

1. Trattoria da Bepi
2. Trattoria Ca' d'Oro & Osteria al Bomba
3. Osteria da Alberto
4. Ost. di Santa Marina
5. Osteria il Milion
6. Osteria "Alla Botte" & Osteria Enoteca ai Rusteghi
7. Rosticceria San Bartolomeo
8. Pasticceria Ponte delle Paste
9. Osteria al Portego
10. Cantina do Mori & Ostaria ai Storti
11. Antica Ostaria Ruga Rialto
12. Osteria al Diavolo e l'Acquasanta
13. Al Marcà
14. Bancogiro & Osteria Naranzaria
15. To Tratt./Pizzeria Nono Risorto
16. Rist. al Giardinetto
17. Osteria alle Testiere
18. Osteria al Mascaron
19. La Boutique del Gelato
20. Michielangelo Gelato
21. To Antica Birraria la Corte

Nightlife
22. Bácaro Jazz Venezia Wine Bar
23. Desert Planet Bar
24. Devil's Forest Pub
25. Inishark Pub

Santa Maria Formosa on Campo Marina, tel. 041-528-5239).

Osteria il Milion, with bow-tied waiters and dressy, candle-lit tables indoors and out, is quietly situated next to Marco Polo's home. It's touristy but tasty (€9 pastas, €13 *secondi,* Thu–Tue 12:00–15:00 & 18:30–23:00, closed Wed; near Rialto Bridge, head north from Campo San Bartolomeo, over one bridge, take first right off San Giovanni Grisostomo before the church, walk under the sign *Corte Prima del Milion o del forno,* it's at #5841; tel. 041-522-9302).

Cicchetti: **Osteria "Alla Botte" Cicchetteria** is packed with a young, local, bohemian-jazz clientele. It's good for a *cicchetti* snack with wine at the bar, or for a light meal in the small back room—find the posted menus (Mon–Wed & Fri–Sat 10:00–15:00 & 17:30–23:00, Sun 10:00–15:00, closed Thu, two short blocks off Campo San Bartolomeo in the corner behind the statue—down Calle de la Bissa, notice the "day after" photo showing a debris-covered Venice after the notorious 1989 Pink Floyd open-air concert, tel. 041-520-9775). Just around the corner from "Alla Botte" Cicchetteria is their wine shop *(enoteca),* which sells quality bulk wine *(vino sfuso)* for about €2 per liter. Bring an empty water bottle or pick one up there, and select among several local wines such as pinot grigio, tocai, cabernet, or merlot to take on a picnic (Mon–Sat 10:00–13:00 & 16:00–20:00, closed Sun, Calle della Bissa 5529, San Marco, tel. 041-296-0596).

Osteria Enoteca ai Rusteghi proudly serves fine wines by the affordable glass and tasty miniature *panini* in a peaceful courtyard with alfresco tables, just a few steps from the hubbub on Campo San Bartolomeo and the Rialto Bridge (Mon–Sat 10:00–15:00 & 18:00–21:30, closed Sun, Corte del Tentor 5513, San Marco, tel. 041-523-2205). From Campo San Bartolomeo, with your back to the statue's back, head forward down the tiny alleyway on your right and turn right, then left under the overpass into the Corte del Tentor.

Rosticceria San Bartolomeo is a cheap—if confusing—self-service restaurant with a likeably surly staff. Take out, grab a table, or munch at the bar (good €6–7 pasta, great fried *mozzarella al prosciutto* for €1.30, daily 9:00–21:30, delightful fruit salad, €1 glasses of wine, prices listed on wall behind counter, no cover or service charge, tel. 041-522-3569). To find this venerable budget eatery, imagine the statue on the Campo San Bartolomeo walking backwards 20 yards, turning left, and going under a passageway—now, follow him.

If pub crawling from Rosticceria San Bartolomeo, continue over a bridge to Campo San Lio. Here, turn left, passing Hotel Canada on your right and following Calle Carminati straight about 50 yards over another bridge. On the left is the pastry shop *(pasticceria),* and straight ahead is Osteria Al Portego (at #6015).

The Stand-Up Progressive Venetian Pub-Crawl Dinner

My favorite Venetian dinner is a pub crawl *(giro d'ombra)*—a tradition unique to Venice, where no cars means easy crawling. (*Giro* means stroll, and *ombra*—slang for a glass of wine—means shade, from the old days when a portable wine bar scooted with the shadow of the Campanile bell tower across St. Mark's Square.)

Venice's residential back streets hide plenty of characteristic bars *(baccari)* with countless trays of interesting toothpick munchies *(cicchetti)* and blackboards listing the wines that are uncorked and served by the glass. This is a great way to mingle and have fun with the Venetians. Bars don't stay open very late, and the *cicchetti* selection is best early, so start your evening by 18:00. Most bars are closed on Sunday.

Cicchetti bars have a social stand-up zone and a cozy gaggle of tables where you can generally sit down with your *cicchetti* or order from a simple menu. In some of the more popular places, the local crowds happily spill out into the street. Food generally costs the same price whether you stand or sit.

I've listed plenty of pubs in walking order for a quick or extended crawl. If you've crawled enough, most of these bars make a fine one-stop, sit-down dinner.

While you can order a plate, Venetians prefer going one-by-one…sipping their wine and trying this…then give me one of those…and so on. Try deep-fried mozzarella cheese, gorgonzola, calamari, artichoke hearts, and anything ugly on a toothpick. *Crostini* (small toasted bread with something on it) are popular, as

Both are listed below.

Pasticceria Ponte delle Paste is a feminine and pastel *salon de tè*, popular for its homemade pastries and pre-dinner drinks. Italians love taking 15-minute breaks to sip a *spritz* with friends before heading home after a long day's work. Ask sprightly Monica for a *spritz al bitter* (white wine, *amaro*, and soda water, €1.80; or choose from the menu on the wall) and munch some of the free goodies at the bar around 18:00 (daily 7:00–20:30, Ponte delle Paste).

Osteria al Portego is a friendly, local-style bar—one of the best in town. Sebastian, Ricardo, and Carlo serve great *cicchetti* (best around 18:00, picked over by 21:00) and good meals (€10 pastas, Mon–Sat 10:30–15:00 & 18:00–21:30, closed Sun, Calle Malvasia 6015, Castello, tel. 041-522-9038). The *cicchetti* here can make a great meal, but you should also consider sitting down for an actual dinner. They have a fine menu. Prices for food and wine are posted clearly on the wall.

are marinated seafood, olives, and prosciutto with melon. Meat and fish (*pesce;* PESH-ay) munchies can be expensive; veggies

(*verdure*) are cheap, at about €3 for a meal-sized plate. In many places, there's a set price per food item (e.g., €1.50). To get a plate of assorted appetizers for €8 (or more, depending on how hungry you are), ask for: *"Un piatto classico di cicchetti misti da €8"* (oon pee-AH-toh KLAH-see-koh dee cheh-KET-tee MEE-stee da OH-toh ay-OO-roh). Bread sticks (*grissini*) are free for the asking.

Bar-hopping Venetians enjoy an *aperitivo,* a before-dinner drink. Boldly order a Bellini—a *spritz con Aperol*—or a Prosecco, and draw approving looks from the locals.

Drink the house wines. A small glass of house red or white wine (*ombra rosso* or *ombra bianco*) or a small beer (*birrino*) costs about €1. The house keg wine is cheap—€1 per glass, about €4 per liter. *Vin bon,* Venetian for fine wine, may run you from €1.50 to €6 per little glass. There are usually several fine wines uncorked and available by the glass. A good last drink is *fragolino,* the local sweet wine—*bianco* or *rosso.* It often comes with a little cookie (*biscotti*) for dipping.

Cicchetterie and Light Meals West of the Rialto Bridge

All of these places (except the last one, Nono Risorto) are within 200 yards of each other, in the neighborhood around the Rialto market. This area is very crowded by day, nearly empty early in the evening, and crowded with young locals later.

Cantina do Mori has been famous with locals (since 1462) and savvy travelers (since 1982) as a classy place for fine wine and *francobolli* (a spicy selection of 20 tiny, mayo-soaked sandwiches nicknamed "stamps"). Choose from the featured wines. Go here to be abused in a fine atmosphere—the frowns are part of the shtick (Mon–Sat 12:00–20:30, closed Sun, stand-up only, arrive early before the *cicchetti* are gone, San Polo 429, tel. 041-522-5401). From Rialto Bridge, walk 200 yards down Ruga degli Orefici, away from St. Mark's Square—then turn left on Ruga Vecchia S. Giovanni, then right at Sotoportego do Mori.

Ostaria ai Storti offers lots of veggies, great prices, a homey feel, and a wonderful, fun place to congregate outdoors. Check out the photo of the market in 1909, below the bar. Prices are the same whether you stand or sit (Mon–Sat 12:00–15:00 & 18:00–22:30, closed Sun, 20 yards from Cantina do Mori on Calle do Spade 819, tel. 041-214-2255).

Antica Ostaria Ruga Rialto, a.k.a. "the Ruga," is a local fixture where Giorgio and Marco serve great bar snacks and wine to a devoted clientele. Bar or table, no problem—they are happy to make a €3, €5, or €7 mixed plate (daily 11:00–14:30 & 19:00–24:00, easy to find, just past the Chinese restaurant on Ruga Vecchia S. Giovanni 692, tel. 041-521-1243).

Osteria al Diavolo e l'Acquasanta, three blocks west of the Rialto Bridge, serves good—if pricey—Venetian-style pasta and makes a handy lunch stop for sightseers and gondola riders. While they list *cicchetti* and wine by the glass on the wall, I'd come here for a light meal rather than for appetizers (Mon 12:00–14:30, Wed–Sun 12:00–14:30 & 19:00–21:30, closed Tue, hiding on a quiet street just off Ruga Vecchia S. Giovanni, on Calle della Madonna, tel. 041-277-0307).

Al Marcà, on Campo Cesare Battisti, is a fancy little hole-in-the-wall where young locals gather to grab drinks and little snacks. They clearly list the prices for wine and sandwiches (Mon–Sat 9:00–15:00 & 18:00–21:00, closed Sun, located on empty part of square just below courthouse).

Bancogiro (Osteria da Andrea), a simple bar behind the Rialto market, has stark outdoor seating overlooking the Grand Canal. Peruse their wine list and menu of creative pastas and entrées at the bar, or ask for a recommendation on a few strong local cheeses to go with your wine. Order and grab a table—worth the small cover charge (Tue–Sun 10:30–24:00, closed Mon, cash only, less than 200 yards from Rialto Bridge on Campo San Giacometto, San Polo 122, tel. 041-523-2061). Consider their €15 fish and vegetable plate.

Osteria Naranzaria, which shares a prime piece of Grand Canal real estate with Bancogiro a few doors towards the Rialto Bridge, is a great stop (described under "Romantic Canalside Settings," page 244).

Trattoria Pizzeria Nono Risorto is unpretentious, inexpensive, youthful, and famous for some of the best pizza in town. You'll sit in a gravelly garden, under a leafy canopy, surrounded by a young, enthusiastic waitstaff and Italians enjoying huge €8 salads, €9 pastas, and delicious €8 pizzas. Reserve on weekends (Thu 19:00–22:30, Fri–Tue 12:00–14:30 & 19:00–22:30, closed Wed, a 3-min walk from the Rialto fish market, find Campo San Cassiano and it's just over the bridge on Sotoportego de Siora Bettina, tel. 041-524-1169).

Near Campo Santa Maria Formosa

These eateries can be found on the map on page 236.

Ristorante al Giardinetto has white tablecloths, a formal-but-fun waitstaff, and a spacious, shady garden under a grapevine canopy. While it used to be set up for big tour groups—and still feels it—groups no longer come here, and the dining experience has improved. This is a good, solid, no-stress restaurant option (€9 pastas, €15 main courses, €2 *coperto,* closed Thu, at intersection of Ruga Giuffa and Calle Corona, tel. 041-528-5332).

Osteria alle Testiere is my most gourmet recommendation in Venice. Hugely respected, they are passionate about quality, serving up creative, artfully presented market-fresh seafood (there's no meat on the menu) and fine wine in what the chef calls a "Venetian Nouvel" style. Reservations are required for their three daily seatings: 12:30, 19:00, and 21:15. With only 22 seats, it's tight and homey yet elegant (€15 pastas, €24 *secondi,* plan on spending €50 for dinner, closed Sun–Mon, Calle del Mondo Novo 5801, tel. 041-522-7220).

Osteria al Mascaron is where I've gone for years to watch Gigi and his food-loving band of ruffians dish up rustic-yet-sumptuous pastas with steamy seafood to salivating local foodies. The pastas, while pricey, are for two (it's okay to ask for single portions). The €16 *antipasto misto* plate—have fun pointing—and two glasses of wine make a wonderful light meal (Mon–Sat 12:00–15:00 & 19:00–22:30, closed Sun, a block past Campo Santa Maria Formosa at Calle Longa Santa Maria Formosa 5225, tel. 041-522-5995).

In Dorsoduro

Near the Accademia Bridge

For locations, see the map on page 242.

Ristorante/Pizzeria Accademia Foscarini, next to the Accademia Bridge and Galleria, offers decent €8–10 pizzas in a great canalside setting. While the food may be forgettable, this place is both scenic and practical—I grab a quick lunch here on each visit to Venice (Wed–Mon 9:00–23:00 in summer, until 20:00 in winter, closed Tue, Dorsoduro 878C, tel. 041-522-7281).

Enoteca Cantine del Vino Già Schiavi is much loved for its €1 *cicchetti.* It's also a good place for a €2 glass of wine and appetizers (Mon–Sat 8:00–20:30, closed Sun, 100 yards from Accademia art museum on San Trovaso canal; facing Accademia, take a right and then a forced left at the canal to the second bridge—S. Trovaso 992, tel. 041-523-0034). You're welcome to enjoy your wine and finger food hanging out at the bar, sitting on the bridge out front, or in the nearby square—which actually has grass. This is primarily a wine shop with great prices for bottles to go—and plastic glasses for picnickers.

Eating

Eating

Restaurants near the Accademia Bridge

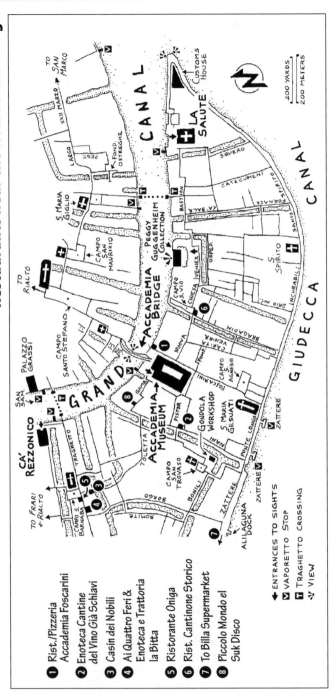

1. Rist./Pizzeria Accademia Foscarini

2. Enoteca Cantine del Vino Già Schiavi

3. Casin dei Nobili

4. Ai Quattro Feri & Enoteca e Trattoria la Bitta

5. Ristorante Oniga

6. Rist. Cantinone Storico

7. To Billa Supermarket

8. Piccolo Mondo el Suk Disco

→ ENTRANCES TO SIGHTS

◪ VAPORETTO STOP

⊡ TRAGHETTO CROSSING

⚓ VIEW

Near Campo San Barnaba

A number of restaurants are worth the hike to this small square. From the Accademia, head northwest, following the curve of the Grand Canal. In five minutes, you'll spill out onto Campo San Barnaba (and the nearby Campo Santa Margherita). Follow the straight and narrow path (Calle Lunga San Barnaba) west of the square for more restaurants. With so many places within about 100 yards of each other, it would be fun to survey and choose, but reservations are often necessary.

Casin dei Nobili (Pleasure Palace of Nobles) has a diverse, reasonably priced menu in a high-energy, informal, modern setting. The patio is filled with simple tables, happy tourists, and inviting €10 daily specials (€13 pastas, €20 *secondi,* good pizzas, and "fantasy salads," Tue–Sun 12:00–15:00 & 19:00–23:00, closed Mon, a half-block south of Campo San Barnaba, Calle delle Casin 2765, tel. 041-241-1841). The ambience is dark and subdued, yet family-friendly.

Ai Quattro Feri is a noisy, bustling, trattoria-style eatery, best for its catch-of-the-day seafood, especially the excellent grilled fish (€10 pastas, €12 *secondi,* Mon–Sat 12:00–15:00 & 19:00–23:00, closed Sun, just off the square on Calle Lunga San Barnaba 2754, tel. 041-520-6978, reservations required).

Enoteca e Trattoria la Bitta is dark and woody with a soft jazz, bistro feel and a small, forgettable back patio. They serve beautifully presented, traditional Venetian food with—proudly— no fish. Their helpful wait staff and small menu is clearly focused on quality cooking. Reservations are required (€9 pastas, €15 *secondi,* dinner only, Mon–Sat 18:30–23:00, closed Sun, cash only, next to Quattro Feri on Calle Lunga San Barnaba 2753, tel. 041-523-0531).

Ristorante Oniga, right on Campo San Barnaba, is a wine bar/ restaurant serving up Italian cuisine with a modern twist (Wed– Mon 12:00–14:00 & 19:00–22:00, closed Tue, tel. 041-522-4410).

On or near Campo San Polo

Antica Birraria la Corte is an everyday eatery on the very special Campo San Polo. Enjoy a pizza or simple meal on the far side of this great, homey, family-filled square. While the interior is a sprawling beer hall, the square is a joy, where metal tables teeter on the cobbles, the wind plays with the paper mats, and children run free (daily 12:00–14:30 & 19:00–22:30, on the way to Frari Church, Campo San Polo 2168, San Polo, tel. 041-275-0570).

Romantic Canalside Settings

Of course, if you want a meal with a canal view, it generally comes with lower quality or a higher price. But if you're aiming for a canal-side dining memory, these places can be great. I've listed the better-value places below, along with advice for coping with the tourist traps.

Near the Rialto Bridge: **Osteria Naranzaria** is one of two wonderful eateries on the Grand Canal between the market and the Rialto Bridge (the other is **Bancogiro,** a few doors down away from the Rialto, listed on page 240). Somehow they've taken a stretch of unbeatable but overlooked canal-front property and filled it with trendy candlelit tables. Foodies appreciate Stefano Monti's Nouveau Italian cuisine. He loves sushi, and because Venice was the gateway to the Orient (remember Marco Polo), he includes sushi on his menu, along with cold cuts, inventive entrées, and fine wine. Peasants may take their glasses to the steps along the canal for bar prices, but the romantic table service doesn't cost that much extra. This is the best-value Grand Canal eatery I have found (€10 pastas, €15 *secondi*, Tue–Sun 12:00–24:00, closed Mon, tel. 041-724-1035).

Rialto Bridge Tourist Traps: Locals are embarrassed by the lousy food and aggressive "service" at the string of joints dominating the best romantic, Grand Canal–fringing real estate in town. Still, if you want to linger over dinner with a view of the most famous bridge and the songs of gondoliers oaring by (and don't mind eating with other tourists), this can be enjoyable. Don't trust the waiter's recommendations for special meals. The budget ideal would be to get a simple pizza or pasta and a drink for €15, and savor the ambience without getting ripped off. But few restaurants will allow you to get off that easy. To avoid a dispute over the bill, ask if there's a minimum charge—before you sit down (most places have one).

Near St. Mark's Square: At **Trattoria da Giorgio ai Greci,** a few blocks behind St. Mark's, Giorgio and sons Roberto and Davide serve homemade pastas and fresh seafood. While they have inside seating, you come here for the canal-side dining—it's the best I've found anywhere in town. Call to reserve a canal-side table (€17–21 fixed-price meals, daily 12:00–22:30, two canals east of St. Mark's on Ponte dei Greci 4988, tel. 041-528-9780).

Ristorante Alla Conchiglia (Trattoria da Giorgio ai Greci's low-key neighbor) has wonderful pink tableclothed tables lining the sleepy canal. They specialize in fish and have a reasonable-for-the-romantic-setting menu. Call to reserve a canal-side table (€9 pizzas, €12 big salads, €17–22 fixed-price meals, daily specials,

Thu–Tue 11:30–22:15, closed Wed, Fondamenta dei Greci, tel. 041-528-9095).

Near the Accademia Bridge: **Ristorante Cantinone Storico** sits on a peaceful canal in Dorsoduro between the Accademia Bridge and the Guggenheim. It's dressy, touristy, specializes in fish and traditional Venetian dishes, has a half-dozen tables on the canal, and is worth the splurge. Reservations are smart (€15 pastas, €20 *secondi,* €3 cover, Mon–Sat 12:30–14:30 & 19:30–21:30, later in summer, closed Sun, on the canal Rio de S. Vio, tel. 041-523-9577).

On Fondamenta Nuove with a View of the Open Lagoon: **Algiubagio's** is a good opportunity to eat well overlooking the lagoon. The name is a combination of the owners' four names—Alberto, Giulio, Barbara, and Giovanna—who strive to impress visitors with quality, creative Venetian cuisine made using the best ingredients. Reserve a table on the lagoon facing San Michele Island or in their classy cantina dining room (€16 pastas, €25 *secondi,* €2.50 cover, Wed–Mon 12:00–15:00 & 19:00–22:30, closed Tue, to the left of the vaporetto dock as you face the water at Fondamenta Nuove 5039, Cannaregio, tel. 041-523-6084).

Eating Inexpensively near St. Mark's Square

For locations, see the map on page 246.

Sandwich Row (Calle delle Rasse): This street, just steps away from the tourist intensity at St. Mark's Square, is the closest place to get a decent sandwich at a decent price with a decent place to sit down (from the Bridge of Sighs, head down the Riva and take the second lane left). The entire street is lined with sandwich bars (most open daily 7:00–24:00, €1 extra to sit). **Birreria Forst** is best, with a selection of meaty €2.50 sandwiches with tasty sauce on wheat bread, or made-to-order sandwiches for around €3 (air-con, rustic wood tables, Calle delle Rasse 4540, tel. 041-523-0557). Also good is **Osteria da Bacco,** with great osteria-type seating, an honest menu, and tasty wine by the glass (Calle delle Rasse 4620, tel. 041-522-2887). **Bar Verde** is a more modern sandwich bar with big €4 sandwiches and splittable €8 salads (facing Campo S.S. Filippo e Giacomo at the end of Calle delle Rasse).

At **Salad and Juice Bar Oasi 2000,** Alessandro and Giorgia serve big salads, sandwiches, a few hot pasta dishes, and fresh-squeezed juice in a small student-cantina atmosphere (daily 8:30–20:30, just behind St. Mark's Basilica off Calle San Provolo at Calle di Albanesi 4263, tel. 041-528-9937).

Chat Qui Rit Self Service is a big, fresh, modern oasis of efficiency, tucked away three blocks from the back of Piazza San Marco on Calle Frezzaria. They have a long cafeteria line of appealing dishes and reasonable prices. Sit at a table on the sidewalk, in a peaceful garden, or in an air-conditioned room behind the garden

Restaurants and Nightlife on and near St. Mark's Square

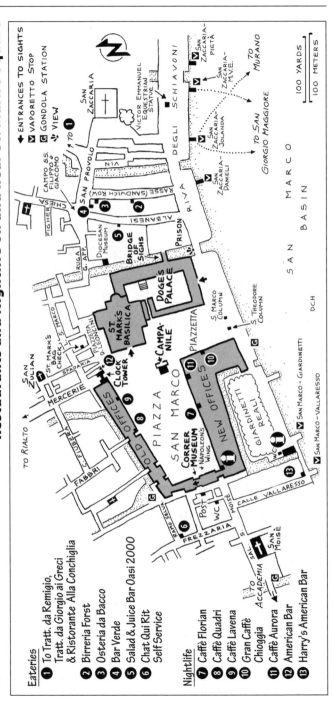

Eateries

1. To Tratt. da Remigio, Tratt. da Giorgio ai Greci & Ristorante Alla Conchiglia
2. Birreria Forst
3. Osteria da Bacco
4. Bar Verde
5. Salad & Juice Bar Oasi 2000
6. Chat Qui Rit Self Service

Nightlife

7. Caffè Florian
8. Caffè Quadri
9. Caffè Lavena
10. Gran Caffè Chioggia
11. Caffè Aurora
12. American Bar
13. Harry's American Bar

(€5 pastas, €8 *secondi,* daily 11:00–21:30; exit St. Mark's Square through middle arches, turn right, left, then right again, follow Calle Frezzaria 100 yards—it's on the right at Angolo Frezzeria; tel. 041-522-9086).

Dining near St. Mark's Square

Trattoria da Remigio is well-known for high-quality, serious Venetian cuisine. Its indoors-only setting is a bit dressy, with a mix of tourists and locals, and lots of commotion (Wed–Sun lunch from 12:30, dinner from 19:30, closed Mon–Tue, just past Rio dei Greci on a tiny square at the end of Calle Madonna, tel. 041-523-0089).

The **cafés on St. Mark's Square** offer music, inflated prices, and an unbeatable setting for a drink or light meal (for a description, see page 63).

Near the Train Station

For fast, cheap food near the station, consider **Brek,** a popular self-service cafeteria (after serving breakfast, it's open daily 11:30–22:00, with back to station, facing canal, go left on Rio Terra—it becomes Lista di Spagna in two short blocks, Lista di Spagna 124, tel. 041-244-0158).

Gelato

La Boutique del Gelato is considered the best *gelateria* in Venice, with the most generous €1 scoops you'll find (daily 10:00–20:30,

closed Dec–Jan, located on map on page 236, two blocks off Campo Santa Maria Formosa on corner of Salizada San Lio and Calle Paradiso, next to Hotel Bruno, at #5727—just look for the crowd).

Late-Night Gelato: At the Rialto, try **Michielangelo,** just off Campo San Bartolomeo, on the St. Mark's side of the Rialto Bridge on Salizada Pio X (daily 10:00–23:00). At St. Mark's Square, get your scoop late at **Grand Café Lavena** (daily until 24:00, first café to left of the Clock Tower, behind the first orchestra).

VENICE
WITH
CHILDREN

Some of the best kid fun I've had with my family has been in Venice. The city doesn't need an amusement park...it is one big fantasy world. It's safe and like nothing else your kids have ever seen. While there's lots of pavement and few parks or playgrounds, just being there—and free to wander—can be delightful. Consider these tips:

• Don't overdo it. Tackle just one or two key sights each day and mix in a healthy dose of enjoyable activities. A vaporetto ride is a great way to start your visit. If your child is old enough, he or she can be the tour guide and read this book's self-guided tours. (Standard tip for good guides: a two-scoop gelato.)

• Follow this book's crowd-beating tips. Kids dislike long lines even more than you do.

• Eat dinner early (19:00 at restaurants), and skip the romantic places. Try self-service cafeterias, out-of-the-way bars (kids are welcome), or fast-food restaurants, where kids can move around without bothering others. For pizza, kids' favorite choices are usually *margherita* (tomato and cheese) and spicy *diavola,* which is the closest thing on the menu to sliced pepperoni sausage (if you ask for *peperoni,* you'll get bell peppers). Picnic lunches and dinners work well. For ready-made picnics, drop by the *rosticcerie* (delis).

• Give your kid a cheap camera. Venice turns anyone into a photographer.

• Keep in mind that there are rarely any fences or walls between the sidewalk and the water, so keep toddlers safely in hand. You won't have much use for strollers. With hundreds of bridges (many with steps), Venice is an obstacle course. Try carrying a small tot in a child backpack or snuggly instead.

• While Venice is short on parks, its many small squares have served as playgrounds for local children for centuries. Let your kids run around while you take a seat at a café or bench.

• Turn the city into a scavenger hunt. Look on buildings for a winged lion, search the shop windows for a mask with a long nose, scour the canal for a fire boat—and extra points for a (yuck) dead pigeon! Wait for the world's first digital clock (on the Clock Tower in St. Mark's Square) to flip over. Find pickpockets in action at the viewing point for the Bridge of Sighs. Wave at romantics in gondolas from bridges over popular gondola routes.

• In Venice, pick up a copy of *VivaVenice: A Guide to Exploring, Learning, and Having Fun* by Paola Zoffoli. It's full of interesting facts, and it's available at many bookstores in the city. *Venice for Kids,* by Elisabetta Pasqualin, is a great guidebook for tweens and up, available at many museum bookshops.

• Involve your children in the trip. Let them lead you through the maze of Venice's back streets. Get lost together.

SIGHTS AND ACTIVITIES

Feed the pigeons on St. Mark's Square. (A packet of seed can be €1 very well spent.) If you yell, the birds will just ignore you, but

tossing a sweater into the air kicks off a pigeon evacuation. And anyone of any age enjoys the magic of St. Mark's Square at night.

Ride the elevator to the top of the **Campanile** bell tower to enjoy the grand view, and be there as the huge bells whip into ear-shattering action at the top of each hour (daily July–Aug 9:00–21:00, Sept–June 9:00–19:00, see page 61).

Take in a **glassblowing demonstration** (just off St. Mark's Square, see page 56). Part of the **Doge's Palace** tour includes the dark, dank prison and a creative armory (see page 85).

Ride lots of **boats** (vaporetto, gondola, *traghetto,* or speedboat tours of the lagoon). Sit in the front seat of a vaporetto for the Grand Canal Cruise (see page 44). See how many kinds of service boats you can spot during your time on the canal (UPS, police, fire, and so on).

The Rialto **fish market** is as fishy as they get (closed Sun–Mon, on the canal 2 blocks west of Rialto Bridge). Watch the people unload the boats at the market. You can leave by *traghetto* and cross the Grand Canal (*traghetto* dock at market).

Be choosy when taking kids to museums. The venerable and fascinating (to adults) Accademia will probably bore children. But don't skip art entirely. Kids like holding mirrors to see the ceiling paintings at the **Scuola San Rocco.** The **Peggy Guggenheim**

Children

Collection has colorful modern art, by Picasso and others, that interests kids.

A **children's park** is near the train station (facing the canal with your back to station, walk down the stairs and a block left past the shops to a small opening in wall on left—you'll see the playground inside). The bigger **Public Gardens** (Giardini Pubblici) have swings and playground equipment (on the far end of town—in Venice's "fishtail," near Giardini vaporetto stop). The **Lido** (beach) island sounds more intriguing than it is, though it can be a kid-friendly place to visit or stay, given the beaches.

If your kids are likely to enjoy a **soccer game,** consider a trip to the stadium located in the Sant'Elena district. Venice's team is currently in the second division (the equivalent of our minor league), but even though their team hasn't won a league championship since World War II, the fans are passionate nevertheless. Matches take place on Sundays from August to June (ask at the TI). Buy a scarf with the team colors—black, orange, and green—and join the fun. Goal!

Make a point to include some **Venetian history.** Taking advantage of the information in this book, explain St. Mark (look for winged lions, page 60), the birth of the city (page 322), how and why the city floods (page 26), and the story of the gondolas (page 256).

For fast and kid-friendly **meals** in the center, you'll find a couple of American hamburger joints between the Rialto Bridge and St. Mark's Square, great pizzerias on squares everywhere, and plenty of gelato.

Children

SHOPPING

Long a city of aristocrats, luxury goods, and merchants, Venice was built to entice. While no one claims it's great for bargains, it has a shopping charm that makes paying too much strangely enjoyable. Carnevale masks, lace, glass, antique paper products, designer clothing, fancy accessories, and paintings are all popular with tourists visiting Venice.

Shops are generally open from 9:00 to 13:00 and from 15:00 to 19:30. In touristy Venice, more shops are open on Sunday than the Italian norm. If you're buying a substantial amount from nearly any shop, bargain—it's accepted and almost expected. Offer less and offer to pay cash; merchants are very conscious of the bite taken by credit-card companies. Anything not made locally is pricey to bring in and therefore generally more expensive than elsewhere in Italy. The shops near St. Mark's Square charge the most.

For ordinary items (not high-priced tourist baubles), the best all-purpose department store is the Coin store on the St. Mark's Square side of the Rialto Bridge. (From the bridge, head north toward Ferrovia, the train station.)

For information on VAT refunds and customs regulations, see page 345 in the appendix.

Shopping Streets

Here's the best route to kick off your Venetian shopping spree:

St. Mark's Square: Walk the entire colonnaded square past pricey jewelry, glass, lace, and clothing stores. A half-block detour out the far end leads to several high-fashion shops along Calle de Vallaresso.

Mercerie: This is the main street between St. Mark's Square (leave the square under the Clock Tower) and the Rialto, noted for its high rent, high prices, fancy windows, and designer labels.

Mask Making

In the 1700s, when Venice was Europe's party town, masks were popular—sometimes even mandatory—to preserve the anonymity of nobles doing things forbidden back home. At Carnevale (the weeks-long Mardi Gras leading up to Lent), everyone wore masks. The most popular were based on characters from the low-brow comedic theater called *Commedia dell'Arte*. We all know Harlequin (simple, Lone Ranger–type masks), but there were also long-nosed masks for the hypocritical plague doctor, pretty Columbina masks, and so on.

Masks are made with the simple technique of papier-mâché. You make a mold of clay, smear it with Vaseline (to make it easy to remove the finished mask), then create the mask by draping layers of paper and glue atop the clay mold.

You'll see mask shops all over town. Just behind St. Mark's Square, on a quiet canal just inland from the Church of San Zaccaria (on Fondamenta dell'Osmarin), is a corner with two fascinating mask and costume shops. The **Ca' del Sol** mask and costume shop (two showrooms connected by a little bridge) and **Atelier Marega** are both worth a look. After you cross the bridge to the second Ca' del Sol shop, head to the next door farther on, the wood-carving shop of **Paolo Brandolisio** (Mon–Fri 9:30–13:00 & 15:30–19:00, tel. 041-522-4155). You can pop in to watch him carving the traditional *forcola* (the oarlock of the gondola, a symbol of Venetian life and a popular art piece).

Out near the Frari Church, the **Tragicomica** mask shop is highly respected, and likely to have artisans at work (daily 10:00–19:00, 200 yards past Church of San Polo on Calle dei Nomboli, tel. 041-721-102).

Then, go over the...

Rialto Bridge: The streets at either side are a cancan of shopping temptations. Continue down the street to...

Ruga Vecchia San Giovanni (a.k.a. Ruga): Away from the intensity of the tourist center, you'll enter the San Polo neighborhood (west side of Rialto Bridge) with plenty of inviting shops, but fewer crowds and better prices.

Elsewhere in Venice: Art-lovers browse the **art galleries** between the Accademia and the Peggy Guggenheim Collection.

Venetian Glass

Popular Venetian glass is available in many forms: vases, tea sets, decanters, glasses, jewelry, lamps, mod sculptures (such as solid-

glass aquariums), and on and on. Shops will ship it home for you (snap a photo of it before it's packed up). For a cheap, packable souvenir, consider the glass-bead necklaces sold at vendors' stalls throughout Venice.

If you're serious about glass, visit the small shops on **Murano Island.** Murano's glassblowing demonstrations are fun; you'll usually see a vase and a "leetle 'orse" made from molten glass. Prices, however, are usually no better on Murano than what you'll find in Venice.

Around St. Mark's Square, various companies offer glassblowing demos for tour groups. **Galleria San Marco,** a tour-group staple, offers great demos just off St. Mark's Square every few minutes. They have agreed to let individual travelers flashing this book sneak in with tour groups to see the show (and sales pitch). And, if you buy anything, show this book and they'll take 20 percent off the listed price. The gallery faces the square behind the orchestra nearest the church; at #139, go through the shop and climb the stairs (daily 9:00–18:00, tel. 041-271-8650, manager Roberto).

Souvenir Ideas

The most popular souvenirs and gifts are Murano glass (see above), Burano lace (fun lace umbrellas for little girls), Carnevale masks (fine shops and artisans all over town), art reproductions (posters, postcards, and books), prints of Venetian scenes, traditional stationery (pens and marbled paper products of all kinds), calendars with Venetian scenes, silk ties, scarves, and plenty of goofy knickknacks (Titian mousepads, gondolier T-shirts, and little plastic gondola condom holders).

Along Venice's many shopping streets, you'll notice fly-by-night street vendors selling knockoffs of famous-maker handbags (Louis Vuitton, Gucci). These vendors are willing to bargain. But buyer beware: Legitimate manufacturers are raising a stink about these street

merchants, and the government is trying to rid the city of them. As authorities are frustrated in attempts to actually arrest the merchants, they have made it illegal to buy items from them. Their hope: The threat of a huge fine will scare potential customers away from them—so unlicensed merchants will be driven out of business and off the streets.

NIGHTLIFE

You must experience Venice after dark. The city is quiet at night, as tour groups stay in the cheaper hotels of Mestre on the mainland, and the masses of day-trippers return to their beach resorts and cruise ships.

Do what you must to reserve energy for evening: Take a nap, or skip a few sights during the day. When the sun goes down, a cool breeze blows in from the lagoon, the lanterns come on, the peeling plaster glows in the moonlight, and Venice resumes its position as Europe's most romantic city.

Though Venice comes alive after dark, it does not party into the wee hours. By 22:00, restaurants are winding down; by 23:00, many bars are closing; and by midnight, the city is shut tight. Evenings are made for wandering—even Venice's dark and distant back lanes are considered very safe after nightfall. Enjoy the orchestras on St. Mark's Square. Pop into small bars for an appetizer and a drink. Lick gelato. As during the day, it's the city itself that is the star. But Venice under a cloak of darkness has an extra dose of magic and mystery—the ambience that has attracted visitors since the days of Casanova.

Schedule of Events

Venice has a busy schedule of events, festivals, and entertainment. Check at the TI for listings in publications such as the free *Un Ospite di Venezia* magazine (monthly, bilingual, available at top-end hotels, www.aguestinvenice.com).

Sightseeing

You can stretch your sightseeing day at the Doge's Palace (daily until 19:00 April–Oct), Accademia (Tue–Sun until 19:15), and the

Gondolas

Two hundred years ago, there were 10,000 gondolas in Venice. Although the aristocracy preferred horses to boats through the early Middle Ages, beginning in the 14th century, when horses were outlawed from the streets of Venice, the noble class embraced gondolas as a respectable form of transportation.

The boats became *the* way to get around the lagoon's islands. To navigate over the countless shifting sandbars, the boats were flat (no keel or rudder) and the captains stood up to see.

Today, there are only 500 gondolas, used only by tourists. The boats are prettier, but they work the same way they always have. Single oars are used both to propel and to steer the boats, which are built curved a bit on one side so that an oar thrusting from that side sends the gondola in a straight line.

These sleek yet ornate boats typically are about 35 feet long and 5 feet wide, and weigh about 1,100 pounds. They travel about three miles an hour (same as walking) and take the same energy to row as it does to walk. They're always painted black (six coats)—the result of a 17th-century law a doge enacted to

Campanile (the bell tower on St. Mark's Square, daily until 21:00 July–Aug).

Gondola Rides

Gondolas cost lots more after 20:00 but are also more romantic and relaxing under the moon. A rip-off for some, this is a traditional must for romantics. Gondoliers charge about €75–80 for a 40-minute ride during the day; from 19:30 on, figure on €95–105 (for *musica*—singer and accordionist—it's an additional €35). You can divide the cost—and the romance—among up to six people per boat, but you'll need to save two seats for the musicians if you choose to be serenaded. Note that only two seats (the ones in back) are next to each other. If you want to haggle, you'll find softer prices on back lanes where single gondoliers hang out, rather than at the bigger departure points. Establish the price and duration before boarding, enjoy your ride, and pay only when you're finished.

If you've hired musicians and want to hear a Venetian song (*un canto Veneziano*), try requesting *"Venezia La Luna e Tu."* Asking eliminate competition between nobles for the fanciest rig. But each has unique upholstery, trim, and detailing, such as the squiggly shaped, carved-wood oarlock *(forcula)* and metal "hood ornament" *(ferro)*. The six horizontal lines and curved top of the *ferro* represent Venice's six *sestieri* (districts) and the doge's funny cap. All in all, it takes about two months to build a gondola.

The boats run about €35,000–50,000, depending on your options (air-con, cup holders, etc.). Every 40 days, the boat's hull must be treated with a new coat of varnish to protect against a lagoon-dwelling creature that eats into wood. A gondola lasts about 15 years, after which it can be refinished (once) to last another 10 years.

You can see Venice's most picturesque gondola workshop (from the outside; it's not open to the public) in the Accademia neighborhood (walk down the Accademia side of the canal called Rio San Trovaso; as you approach Giudecca Canal you'll see the beached gondolas on your right across the canal). The workmen, traditionally from Italy's mountainous Dolomite region (because they need to be good with wood), maintain this refreshingly alpine-feeling little corner of Venice.

There are about 400 licensed gondoliers. When one dies, the license passes to his widow. And do the gondoliers sing, as the popular image has it? My mom asked our gondolier that very question, and he replied, "Madame, there are the lovers and there are the singers. I do not sing."

to hear *"O Sole Mio"* (which comes from Naples) is like asking a bartender in Cleveland to sing "The Eyes of Texas."

Glide through nighttime Venice with your head on someone's shoulder. Follow the moon as it sails past otherwise unseen buildings. Silhouettes gaze down from bridges while window glitter spills onto the black water. You're anonymous in the city of masks, as the rhythmic thrust of your striped-shirted gondolier turns old crows into songbirds. This is extremely relaxing (and, I think, worth the extra cost to experience at night). Because you might get a nar-

ration plus conversation with your gondolier, talk with several and choose one you like who speaks English well. Women, beware... while gondoliers can be extremely charming, local women say that anyone who falls for one of these Romeos "has slices of ham over her eyes."

For cheap gondola thrills during the day, stick to the €0.50 one-minute ferry ride on a Grand Canal *traghetto*. At night, vaporetti are nearly empty, and it's a great time to cruise the Grand Canal on the slow boat #1. Or hang out on a bridge along the gondola route and wave at—or drop leftover pigeon feed on—romantics.

Dining

Locals and those spending the night in Venice fill the piazzas, restaurants, and bars. *The* local way to spend an evening is to enjoy a slow and late dinner in a romantic canalside or piazza setting (see Eating chapter, page 226). Another option is a fast-paced, stand-up dinner of *cicchetti* in a local pub (see "The Stand-Up Progressive Venetian Pub-Crawl Dinner" sidebar, page 238).

St. Mark's Square

For tourists, St. Mark's Square is the highlight, with lantern light and live music echoing from the cafés. Just being here after dark is a thrill, as **dueling café orchestras** entertain (see "Cafés on St. Mark's Square" on page 63). Every night, enthusiastic musicians play the same songs, creating the same irresistible magic. Hang out for free behind the tables (which allows you to move easily on to the next orchestra when the musicians take a break), or spring for a seat and enjoy a fun and gorgeously

set concert. If you sit a while, it can be €15 well spent (for a drink and the cover charge for music). Dancing on the square is free (and encouraged).

Streetlamp halos, live music, floodlit history, and a ceiling of stars make St. Mark's magic at midnight. You're not a tourist, you're a living part of a soft Venetian night...an alley cat with money. In the misty light, the moon has a golden hue. Shine with the old lanterns on the gondola piers, where the sloppy lagoon splashes at the Doge's Palace...reminiscing.

More Music

Baroque Concerts: Take your pick of traditional Vivaldi concerts in churches throughout town. Homegrown Vivaldi is as trendy here as Strauss is in Vienna and Mozart is in Salzburg. In fact, you'll find frilly young Vivaldis all over town hawking concert tickets. The TI has a list of this week's Baroque concerts (tickets from €18, shows start at 21:00 and generally last 90 min). You'll find posters in hotels all over town. There's music most nights at **Scuola San Teodoro** (east side of Rialto Bridge) and **San Vitale Church** (north end of Accademia Bridge), among others. Consider the venue carefully. The general rule of thumb: Musicians  in wigs and tights offer better spectacle; musicians in black-and-white suits are better performers. For the latest on church concerts, check any TI or visit www.turismovenezia.it.

If you're attending a concert at **Scuola San Rocco** (tickets €15–30), arrive 30 minutes early to enjoy the art (which you'd have to pay €7 to see during the day).

Another unique music experience is a Rondo Veneziano concert—classically inspired music with a modern electronic sound.

Movies

Venetian cinema is rarely in the original language; expect to hear it in Italian. **Outdoor cinema** on Campo San Polo is a fun scene (July–Aug). Every September, Venice's **film festival** (with some English-language films) doubles the viewing choices and brings out the stars.

Theater

Venice's two most famous theaters are **La Fenice** (grand old opera house, see page 35) and **Teatro Goldoni** (mostly Italian live theater). Opera performances take place in Venice from late November through the end of June. For the latest, see *Un Ospite di Venezia* magazine (free at higher-end hotels), pick up a list of events and exhibits from the TI, or visit www.teatrolafenice.it.

Pubs, Clubs, and Late-Night Spots

While a pub-crawl dinner (see page 238) is fun and colorful, most serious eating is finished early to make way for drinking.

Campo Santa Margherita, the university student zone, is likely to be lively late. This popular-with-locals square has a good restaurant, café, and bar scene—especially May through September (Bar Rosso is particularly popular).

Paradiso Perduto, on Fondamenta della Sensa (on Rio della Sensa) in Cannaregio, is notorious for being noisy late at night. When locals complain, night owls say there's got to be someplace in Venice that stays open late. It's a restaurant and bar with a huge following for its good casual food, ambience, and open mic (tel. 041-720-581).

Other places likely to be open after 23:00 include the touristy **American Bar** (under the Clock Tower on St. Mark's Square). To locate the following places, see the map on page 246. **Bácaro Jazz Venezia wine bar** is open late (food served until 3:00 in the morning, closed Wed, on St. Mark's side of Rialto Bridge in front of the central post office just north of Campo San Bartolomeo). **Desert Planet** serves up pizzas and pastas until 1:00 in the morning, and drinks until 2:30 (3 blocks north of St. Mark's at Calle Casselleria 5281). I like the little no-name portable wooden **wine bar** tucked on a street corner along the Grand Canal (on the fish market side of the Rialto, several blocks south of the bridge). Take your glass for a canalside walk and return it later.

Also open late are Irish pubs, such as the **Devil's Forest Pub** (fine prices, daily 11:00–24:00, meals served 12:00–15:00, bar snacks all the time, closed Sun in Aug, no cover or service charge, a block off Campo San Bartolomeo on Calle dei Stagneri, tel. 041-520-0623) and **Inishark Pub** (until 1:30 in the morning, closed Mon, just west of Campo Santa Maria Formosa on Calle Mondo Nuovo, see map on page 236). While Irish pubs are popular with locals rather than tourists, the venerable **Harry's American Bar** (serving expensive food and American cocktails to dressy tourists at the San Marco vaporetto stop—see the map on page 246) is just the opposite.

Venice doesn't have a good dance scene. The close proximity of apartments means loud music isn't tolerated late at night. The few *discoteche* are overpriced with expensive drinks and little actual dancing. Still, for a cultural experience and a throbbing techno beat, check out the incredibly soundproofed disco piano bar **Piccolo Mondo el Suk** near the Accademia art museum (daily 22:00–4:00 in the morning, Nov–March closed Mon, €10 cover charge includes one cocktail, drinks after that are all €10, *Advanced Booking Only* sign on the door really only means that drunks and rowdies won't be admitted, locals won't show up until at least 23:30 or midnight, Calle Corfù 1056A, Dorsoduro, tel. 041-520-0371).

TRANSPORTATION CONNECTIONS

A two-mile-long causeway (with highway and train lines) connects Venice to the mainland. Mestre, the sprawling mainland transportation hub, has fewer crowds, cheaper hotels, and plenty of cheap parking lots, but zero charm. Don't stop in Mestre unless you're parking your car or transferring trains.

Santa Lucia Train Station

Trains to Venice stop at either Venezia Mestre (on the mainland) or at the Santa Lucia station on the island of Venice itself. If your train only stops at Mestre, worry not. Shuttle trains regularly connect Mestre's station with Venice's Santa Lucia station (6/hr, 10 min).

Venice's **Santa Lucia train station** plops you right into the old town on the Grand Canal, an easy vaporetto ride or fascinating 40-minute walk to St. Mark's Square. Upon arrival, skip the station's crowded TI, because the two TIs at St. Mark's Square are better, and it's not worth a long wait for a minimal map (buy a good one from a newsstand or pick up a free one at your hotel). Confirm your departure plan (stop by train info desk or just study the *partenze*—departure—posters on walls).

Consider storing unnecessary heavy bags, although lines for **baggage check** may be very long (at head of platform 14, €8/12 hours, €11/24 hours, daily 6:00–24:00, no lockers, 45-pound weight limit on bags).

To avoid the long lines for buying train tickets and making seat and *cuccetta* reservations, many travelers use the automatic ticket machines at the station. These gray-and-yellow touch-screen *Biglietto Veloce* (Fast Ticket) machines have an English option, display train schedules, issue train tickets and reservations, and accept payment in cash or by credit/debit card. Or you could take

Italy's Public Transportation

RAIL   PRIVATE RAIL   •••• SHIP   --- BUS

✈ AIRPORTS (NOT ALL SHOWN)

NOT TO SCALE

care of these tasks at downtown travel agencies (see page 22). The cost is about the same (some agencies charge a small fee); it can be more convenient (if you find yourself near a travel agency while sightseeing); and the staff is likely to speak some English.

To get from the train station to downtown Venice, walk straight out of the station to the canal. On your left is the dock for **vaporetto** #2 (fast boat down Grand Canal, catch from right side of dock). To your right is the dock for vaporetto #1 (slow boat down Grand Canal, catch from far right dock) and #51 (goes counterclockwise around Venice, handy for Dorsoduro hotels). See the hotel listings in the "Sleeping" chapter to find out which boat to catch to get to your hotel.

Buy a €6 ticket at the ticket window (a few shorter runs are only €2) and hop on a boat. You can also buy a pass for unlimited use of *vaporetti* and ACTV buses (sold in 12-hour increments—€13/12 hrs, €15/24 hrs, and so on up to €30/72 hrs). If you're taking #2 or #1, confirm that it's heading downtown (direction: Rialto or San Marco). Some boats only go as far as Rialto *(solo Rialto),* so check with the conductor.

Types of Trains

You'll encounter several types of trains in Italy. Along with the various pokey, milk-run trains *(regionali),* there are the slow IR *(interregionali)* and *diretto* trains, the medium *espresso,* the fast IC *(Intercity),* and the space-age ES *(Eurostar Italia).* All of these trains are fully covered by a railpass (except the ES, which requires railpass-holders to purchase a €15 seat reservation, €23 if you buy on board). You may need supplements on *diretto* and *IC* night trains if they have *cuccette* (sleeper berths). For point-to-point tickets, you'll pay more the faster you go—but even the fastest trains are still affordable (for example, a first-class Venice-to-Florence ticket costs about €45 including the express supplement; second-class is about €30). Before boarding the train, stamp your ticket in the machine on the platform. Purchasing seat reservations on the train comes with a nasty penalty. Buying them at the station can be a time-waster unless you use the automatic ticket machines. If you're on a tight schedule, you'll want to reserve a few days ahead for fast trains.

Schedules

Newsstands sell up-to-date regional and all-Italy train timetables (€4–5, ask for the *orario ferroviario).* On the Web, check http://bahn.hafas.de/bin/query.exe/en (Germany's excellent all-Europe website) or www.trenitalia.it. There is also a single all-Italy telephone number for train information (24 hours daily, tel. 892-021, Italian only, consider having your hotelier call for you).

At the station, the easiest way to check schedules is at the

Arrival in Venice

handy automatic ticket machines. Enter the date and time of your departure (to or from any Italian station) and you can view all your options. You can also check the low-tech printed schedules posted at the station—departure posters are always yellow. Note that your final destination may be listed in fine print as an intermediate destination. For example, if you're going from Venice to Verona, or Padua, scan the schedule and you'll notice that trains that go to Milan usually stop in Verona and/or Padua en route. Travelers who read the fine print end up with a far greater choice of trains.

Strikes are common and locals take them in stride. They generally last a day, and train employees will simply say, *"sciopero"* (strike). Still, sporadic trains—following no particular schedule—lumber down the tracks during most strikes.

From Venice by Train to: Padua (3/hr, 30 min), **Vicenza** (2/hr, 1 hr), **Verona** (2/hr, 1.5 hrs), **Ravenna** (hourly, 3–4 hrs, transfer in Ferrara, Faenza, or Bologna), **Florence** (roughly hourly, 3–3.5 hrs, may transfer in Bologna; often crowded so make reservations), **Dolomites** (to Bolzano about hourly, 3–4 hrs with transfer in Verona; catch bus from Bolzano into mountains), **Milan** (hourly, 3–4 hrs), **Cinque Terre/Monterosso** (8/day, 6–8 hrs, with 1–3 changes), **Cinque Terre/La Spezia** (20/day, 5–7 hrs, with 1–3 changes), **Rome** (hourly, 5–8 hrs, may transfer in Bologna, slower overnight), **Naples** (about hourly, with changes in Bologna or Rome, about 7–8 hrs), **Brindisi** (6/day, 10–12 hrs, most change in Bologna), **Bern** (6/day, change in Milan or Brig, 8 hrs), **Munich** (3–5/day, 7 hrs, may change in Verona), **Paris** (1 direct night train/day, 12.5 hrs, important to reserve ahead; 3/day, 4/night, 10–16 hrs with change in Milan), and **Vienna** (1 direct, 7 hrs; 3/day, 10–12 hrs with changes).

Marco Polo Airport

Venice's modern airport on the mainland, six miles north of the city, has a sleek wood-beam-and-glass terminal, with a TI (daily, 9:00–20:00), cash machines, car-rental agencies, and a few shops and eateries (airport info tel. 041-260-9250). Check with your hotel or in *Un Ospite di Venezia* (the free tourist information guide at fancy hotels) for phone numbers and websites for all airlines serving Marco Polo and nearby airports.

There are four ways for you to get between the airport and downtown Venice (described in detail below): the slow but reasonable Alilaguna boat, a faster and pricier Alilaguna boat (which goes nonstop to St. Mark's Square), the fastest and priciest water taxi, and the cheap shuttle bus to the edge of Venice (with easy connections to the Grand Canal *vaporetti*). Except for the fast boat and water taxi, expect a trip between the airport terminal and St. Mark's Square (San Marco) to take up to 90 minutes. When flying out of Venice, travelers are advised to get to the airport two or more hours before departure (even for flights within Europe), but I usually arrive about 90 minutes before takeoff and manage fine.

Alilaguna Water Bus: This is the simplest transportation to and from downtown Venice. A minor drawback is that you must walk (and carry your bags) eight minutes between the airport terminal and the boat dock (follow signs, level sidewalks are fine for wheeled bags).

The Alilaguna website (www.alilaguna.it) lists times and the various lines. These are the routes for the slow boats: The Blue (BLU) Line stops at Fondamenta Nuove and Ospedale (€6, on Venice's north shore), and San Zaccaria (€12, best for hotels east of St. Mark's Square); the Red Line stops at San Marco (St. Mark's Square) and then continues west to Zattere (€12, serving Dorsoduro hotels); and the Orange (ARANCIO) Line stops at Guglie near the train station (€12). From Venice to the airport, the first boat departs from San Marco–Giardinetti at 4:00 in the morning, with the last boat leaving at 22:25. Allow roughly 70–80 minutes for the trip, depending on your stop.

The fast Alilaguna Golden (ORO) Line zips nonstop to and from San Marco–Giardinetti in 35 minutes (€25, departs from San Marco–Giardinetti for the airport about hourly from 7:40–13:30).

Driving in Italy

Note: Your times may vary based on traffic, construction, and road conditions.

m = miles
h = hours

Buy Alilaguna tickets and get more schedule information at the airport's "Public Transport" desk (to the left as you exit baggage claim), at the airport dock, or at any other vaporetto stop in Venice that has Alilaguna service. You can also purchase tickets on board (tel. 041-523-5775).

Water Taxi: Luxury taxi speedboats zip directly between the airport and your hotel in 30 minutes for €90 for up to four people. This can be a smart investment—especially for small groups and those with an early departure. Arrange at the airport's water-taxi desk when you arrive, or through your hotel the day before you leave. You'll have to schlep your bags for the eight-minute walk between the dock and the airport.

Buses: Blue ATVO shuttle buses connect the airport and the Piazzale Roma vaporetto stop at the head of the Grand Canal (€3, buy from driver, 2/hr, 20 min; buses leave airport 8:20–24:00 from platform 1 directly outside arrivals terminal, leave Piazzale Roma 5:00–20:40 from far side of the lot from Hotel S. Chiara, www .atvo.it). At the Piazzale Roma vaporetto stop, the slow vaporetto #1 or faster #82 (€6 for either) head to St. Mark's Square (see

"Getting Around Venice," page 23).

Connecting to Padua: There's a cheap and easy SITA bus connection from Venice's airport to Padua's bus station (€4, buy tickets from SITA desk inside airport near TI or €5 from driver, €1/bag, 2/hr Mon–Fri, hourly on weekends, 1 hr; as you exit the airport, catch just beyond platform 3 at the far right of the buses).

Tips for Drivers

The freeway dead-ends at Venice, near several parking lots on the edge of the island. The most central lot, San Marco, is very busy and too expensive. Tronchetto (across the causeway and on the right) has a huge multistoried garage (€20/day, tel. 041-520-7555). From there, avoid the travel agencies masquerading as TIs, and head directly for the vaporetto docks for the boat connection (#2) to the town center. Don't let water taxi boatmen con you out of the relatively cheap €6 vaporetto ride.

Parking in Mestre is easy and cheap (open-air lots cost €5/day Mon–Fri, €10/day Sat–Sun, across from Mestre train station, easy shuttle-train connections to Venice's Santa Lucia Station—6/hr, 10 min). There are also huge and economical lots in Verona, Padua, and Vicenza.

DAY TRIPS
FROM VENICE

While Venice is just one of many towns in the Italian region of Veneto (VEN-eh-toh), few visitors venture off the lagoon. Three important towns and possible side trips, in addition to the lakes and the Dolomites, make zipping directly from Venice to Milan (or Florence) a route strewn with temptation.

The towns of Padua, Vicenza, and Verona are all good stops, for various reasons. Each town gives the visitor a low-key slice of Italy that complements the urbanity of Venice, Florence, and Rome.

Visiting Verona, Padua, and Vicenza couldn't be easier: All are roughly 30 minutes apart on the Venice–Milan line (hourly, 3 hrs). Spending a day town-hopping between Venice and Milan—with three-hour stops at Padua, Vicenza, and Verona—is exciting and efficient. Trains run frequently enough to allow flexibility and little wasted time.

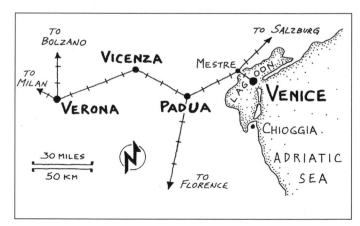

If you're Padua-bound, note that you need to reserve ahead to see the Scrovegni Chapel (see page 279). Also, note that most sights in Verona and Vicenza are closed on Monday.

PADUA
DAY TRIP

Padova

Living under Venetian rule for four centuries seemed only to sharpen Padua's independent spirit. Nicknamed "the brain of Veneto," Padua (Padova is the Italian spelling) has a prestigious university (founded in 1222) that hosted Galileo, Copernicus, Dante, and Petrarch. Padua's old town is elegantly arcaded, filled with students, and sprinkled with surprises. And Padua's museums and churches hold their own in Italy's artistic big league.

ORIENTATION

Padua's main tourist sights lie on a north-south axis through the heart of the city: from the train station to Scrovegni Chapel to the market squares (the center of town) to the Basilica of St. Anthony. It's roughly a 10-minute walk between each of these sights, or about 30 minutes from end to end.

Tourist Information

Padua has three TIs. At the train station TI, pick up a map, a list of sights, and the *Padova Today* entertainment listing (Mon–Sat 9:15–13:30 & 15:00–19:00, Sun 9:00–12:30, tel. 049-875-2077, www.turismopadova.it). Another TI is across the street from Caffè Pedrocchi (Mon–Sat 9:00–13:30 & 15:00–19:00, closed Sun, tel. 049-876-7927). You'll find a third TI at the Basilica of St. Anthony (daily April–Oct 9:00–13:30 & 15:00–18:00, closed Nov–March).

Padova Card: All the TIs sell the wonderful Padova Card (€14), which gives you 48 hours of unlimited bus travel, free parking, and entry to all the recommended sights, except the university's anatomy theater and the Basilica of St. Anthony's Oratory of St. George.

Arrival in Padua

By Train: Inside the station is the main **TI, WCs,** and **baggage deposit** (€4, daily 6:00–21:30, bring your passport, it's near track 1). An **ATM** and a **post office** (Mon–Sat 8:30–14:00, closed Sun) are outside the station, under the colonnade by the right exit. For any train business, head to a convenient travel agency, Leonardi Viaggi–Turismo, located half a block up the main drag in front of the station (Mon–Fri 8:45–19:00, Sat 9:00–13:00, closed Sun, Corso del Popolo 14, tel. 049-650-455).

By Bus: To get into town, buy a ticket (€1) for a **city bus.** These tickets are sold only from the kiosk in front of the train station, and buses leave from in front of the station. Buses #8, #12, and #18 go through town to the Basilica of St. Anthony (called "Santo" locally), departing from platform *(corsia)* #3. Get off at the end of Via Umberto I, just before Prato della Valle. If you're not sure where to get off, ask the driver, *"Santo?"* Due to pedestrian and car traffic, this relatively short distance can take up to 20 minutes. A taxi into town costs about €5. You'll see **hop-on, hop-off bus tours** around town. While these ubiquitous tourist transporters make sense in some towns, they're not worth it in Padua.

Long-distance buses (including buses from Venice's Marco Polo Airport—see page 265) arrive at the main bus station at Piazzale Boschetti, several blocks north of the Scrovegni Chapel. From there, Via Gozzi leads into town.

Helpful Hints

Internet Access: Oddly, for a college town, Padua has few Internet cafés. The TI offers free access for 15 minutes. You can also try **Internet Point** (Mon–Sat 10:00–24:00, Sun 16:00–24:00, Via Altinate 145, 5-min walk from Porta Altinate, tel. 049-659-292).

Bookstore: Feltrinelli's International Bookstore, with books in English, is near the university (Mon–Sat 9:00–13:00 & 15:30–19:30, closed Sun, Via San Francesco 1a, tel. 049-875-0792).

Laundry: Lava e Lava is about a 10-minute walk east of the Basilica of St. Anthony (daily 8:00–22:00, €12/load to wash and dry, self-service only, on the left just past the roundabout at Via San Massimo 5).

Local Guide: Charming **Cristina Pernechele** is a great teacher (€105/half-day, mobile 338-495-5453, c.pernechele@virgilio.it).

Best Gelato: Locals love the *gelateria* **Grom** for its fresh ingredients and honest flavors (on Via Roma).

Padua in Four Hours

Day-trippers can do a quick but enjoyable blitz of Padua—including a visit to the Scrovegni Chapel—in four hours. Your Scrovegni

Padua

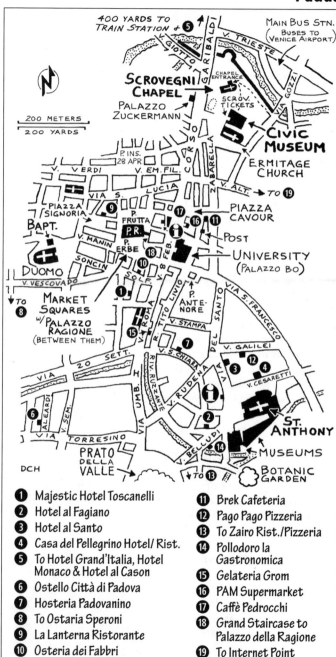

400 YARDS TO TRAIN STATION ⑤

MAIN BUS STN.
(BUSES TO VENICE AIRPORT)

SCROVEGNI CHAPEL

PALAZZO ZUCKERMANN

CHAPEL ENTRANCE

SCROV. TICKETS

CIVIC MUSEUM

ERMITAGE CHURCH

200 METERS
200 YARDS

P. INS. 28 APR

V. VERDI
V. EM. FIL.
VIA S. LUCIA
→ TO ⑲

PIAZZA SIGNORIA
BAPT.
⑨
P. FRUTTA
P.R.
⑰
⑯ ⑪
PIAZZA CAVOUR

V. MANIN
P. ERBE
⑱
⑩
POST

DUOMO
SONCIN
V. 8 FEB.
UNIVERSITY (PALAZZO BO)

V. VESCOVADO
V. SOLF.
①
P. ANTENORE

↓ TO ⑧
MARKET SQUARES w/ PALAZZO RAGIONE (BETWEEN THEM)

V. ROMA
R. TITO LIVIO
V. STAMPA
VIA S. FRANCESCO

⑮
V. S. CHIARA
⑦
VIA DEL SANTO
V. GALILEI
③ ⑫ ④
V. CESARETTI

VIA 20 SETT.
VIA ALEARDI
V. SEM.
RIV. RUZZANTE
VIA UMB.
V. RUDENA
①
ST. ANTHONY

⑥
VIA TORRESINO
PRATO DELLA VALLE
BELLUDI
②
⑭
MUSEUMS

DCH
↓ TO ⑬
BOTANIC GARDEN

① Majestic Hotel Toscanelli
② Hotel al Fagiano
③ Hotel al Santo
④ Casa del Pellegrino Hotel/ Rist.
⑤ To Hotel Grand'Italia, Hotel Monaco & Hotel al Cason
⑥ Ostello Città di Padova
⑦ Hosteria Padovanino
⑧ To Ostaria Speroni
⑨ La Lanterna Ristorante
⑩ Osteria dei Fabbri

⑪ Brek Cafeteria
⑫ Pago Pago Pizzeria
⑬ To Zairo Rist./Pizzeria
⑭ Pollodoro la Gastronomica
⑮ Gelateria Grom
⑯ PAM Supermarket
⑰ Caffè Pedrocchi
⑱ Grand Staircase to Palazzo della Ragione
⑲ To Internet Point

Chapel reservation will dictate the order of your sightseeing (see the booking procedure on page 279). Also, if you like markets, get an early start.

Here's one possible plan: Take the bus from the train station to the Basilica of St. Anthony at the south end of town, then walk back through the old town, sightseeing your way (using descriptions from this chapter) back to the Scrovegni Chapel, then on to the station.

Ready, set, go...

At zero hour: Arrive at the Padua train station (timing it so that you arrive three hours before your reservation for the Scrovegni Chapel). Check your bags and catch bus #3, #8, #12, or #18 to the Basilica of St. Anthony. Note that parts of the basilica close during lunch. Sightsee the basilica.

At one hour: Walk north along Via del Santo and turn left onto Via San Francesco, which leads to the huge Piazza delle Erbe and Palazzo della Ragione. The vibrant markets here start to shut down around 13:00. Visit the town center's sights (without actually touring the university): Caffè Pedrocchi and the university's courtyard.

At 2:15 hours: Walk 10 minutes to the Scrovegni Chapel. Pick up your pre-paid and reserved ticket first, then spend 30 minutes checking out the Civic Museum and its Multimedia Room . Get in line five minutes early for the Chapel.

At three hours: Visit the Scrovegni Chapel.

At 3:30 hours: Walk north to the train station (10–15 min) and reclaim your baggage.

At four hours: Catch your train. Ahhhh.

SIGHTS

▲▲Basilica of St. Anthony

Friar Anthony of Padua (1195–1231), "Christ's perfect follower and a tireless preacher of the Gospel," is buried here. For nearly 800 years, his remains and this impressive Romanesque Gothic church (building started immediately after the death of the saint in 1231) have attracted pilgrims to Padua.

Cost and Hours: The basilica is free and open daily in summer 6:30–19:45 (in winter 6:30–18:45). Note that these sights within the basilica close around lunchtime but are open daily (in summer): Chapel of the Reliquaries (daily 8:00–12:45

St. Anthony of Padua
(1195–1231)

One of Christendom's most popular saints, Anthony is known as a powerful speaker, a miracle worker, and the finder of lost articles.

Born in Lisbon to a rich, well-educated family, his life changed at age 25, when he saw the mutilated bodies of some Franciscan martyrs. Their sacrifice inspired him to join the poor Franciscans and dedicate his life to Christ. He moved to Italy and lived in a cave, studying, meditating, and barely speaking to anyone.

One day, he joined his fellow monks for a service. The appointed speaker failed to show up, so Anthony was asked to say a few off-the-cuff words to the crowd. He started slowly but, filled with the Spirit, he became more confident and amazed the audience with his eloquence. Up in Assisi, St. Francis heard about Anthony and sent him on a whirlwind speaking tour.

Anthony had a strong voice, knew several languages, had encyclopedic knowledge of theology, and could speak spontaneously as the Spirit moved him. It's said he even stood on the shores of the Adriatic Sea in Rimini and enticed a school of fish to listen. Anthony also was known as a miracle worker—healing a sick horse, protecting a crowd from the rain, and making poisoned food harmless.

In 1230, Anthony retired to Padua, where he founded a monastery and initiated reforms for the poor. An illness cut his life short at age 36. Anthony once said, "Happy is the man whose words issue from the Spirit and not from himself!"

& 14:30–19:30, shorter hours in winter), Sacristy (open daily), a multimedia exhibit (daily 9:00–12:30 & 14:30–18:00), the museum (daily 9:00–13:00 & 14:30–18:30, shorter hours and closed Mon in winter), and the Oratory of St. George, which costs €2.50 to enter (daily 9:00–12:30 & 14:30–19:00).

Information: In the basilica, a modest dress code is enforced. A helpful information desk with Anthony-related pamphlets is in the cloisters, located on the right side of the church (info desk open daily 8:30–13:00 & 14:00–18:30, public WC nearby). To find English versions of the pamphlets—one on the saint's life and another about the basilica—head to the Chapel of the Reliquaries and offer a donation.

There's a TI on the square facing the church (April–Oct daily 9:00–13:30 & 15:00–18:00, closed Nov–March). A 10-minute stroll north up Via del Santo takes you back into the center of town.

Exterior of Basilica

Nod to St. Anthony, who looks down from the redbrick facade and blesses us. He holds a book, a symbol of all the knowledge he accumulated as a quiet monk before starting his famous preaching career.

Guarding the church is Donatello's life-size equestrian statue of the Venetian mercenary general, Gattamelata. Though it looks like a thousand other man-on-a-horse statues, it was a landmark in Italy's budding Renaissance—the first life-size, secular, equestrian statue cast out of bronze in a thousand years. The church is technically outside of Italy. When you pass the banisters that mark its property line, you're passing into Vatican territory.

Interior

Entering the basilica, gaze down the nave, past the crowds and through the incense haze, to Donatello's glorious crucifix arising from the altar, and realize that this is one of the most important pilgrimage sites in Christendom.

Along with the crucifix, Donatello's bronze statues—Mary with Padua's six favorite saints—grace the high altar. Late in his career, the great Florentine sculptor spent a decade in Padua (1444–1455), creating the altar and Gattamelata.

St. Anthony's Tomb

Head to the left side of the nave. Here, pilgrims file slowly through a side chapel around the tomb of St. Anthony. Nine marble reliefs, Renaissance masterpieces from around 1500, show scenes and miracles from the life of the saint.

As you enter the chapel, the first relief on the left depicts St. Anthony receiving the Franciscan habit. In the next, Anthony's compassion miraculously revives a woman who has been stabbed to death by her jealous husband. Notice the etchings of familiar Paduan architecture at the top of the sculptures. In the third panel, the building with the hull-shaped roof is Palazzo della Ragione.

On the back wall of the chapel (the sixth panel), look for "the miracle of the miser's heart." Anthony dips his hand into a moneylender's side to demonstrate the absence of his heart. This relief illustrates the scriptural verse "for where your treasure is, there your heart will be also." The heart miraculously appears in the dead man's treasure chest.

The next relief shows Anthony holding the foot of a young man who confessed to kicking his mother. Upon hearing of this act, Anthony declared that anyone so disrespectful to his mother ought to have his foot cut off. The boy took Anthony's word literally. His hysterical mother implored Anthony's help, and Anthony's prayers to God enabled him to reattach the foot.

Stand in the corner for a moment observing the passionate devotion that pilgrims and locals alike have for Anthony. Touching his tomb or kneeling in prayer, the faithful here believe Anthony is their protector—a confidant and intercessor of the poor. And they believe he works miracles. The faithful place offerings, votives, and prayers to ask for help or to give thanks for miracles they believe he's performed. By putting their hand on his tomb while saying a silent prayer, pilgrims show devotion to Anthony and feel the saint's presence.

Popular Anthony is the patron saint of dozens of things: of travelers, amputees, donkeys, pregnant women, barren women, flight attendants, and pig farmers. Most pilgrims ask for his help in his role as the "finder of things"—from lost car keys to a life companion.

Continuing from this chapel around the corner into the next room, enter the oldest part of church—the original chapel, where Anthony was first buried in 1231. Note the fine (and impressively realistic for the 14th century) view of medieval Padua, with this church outside the wall (finished by 1300 and still looking as it looks today).

In a circa-1380 fresco, Anthony on his cloud promises he'll watch over his town. Because people wanted to be buried near a saint, graves lie all around. If you could afford it, this was about the best piece of real estate a dead person could want. (The practice was ended with Napoleonic reforms in 1806.)

Chapel of the Reliquaries

Continue your circuit of the church by going behind the altar into the apse, to the Chapel of the Reliquaries. The most prized relic is in the glass case at center stage—Anthony's tongue. When Anthony's remains were exhumed 32 years after his death (1263), his body had decayed to dust, but his tongue was found miraculously unspoiled and red in color. How appropriate for the multilinguist who, full of the Spirit, couldn't stop talking about God.

Working clockwise around the chapel, start in front of the staircase at St. Anthony's holy, and holey, tunic *(tonaca)*. His rough-hewn wood coffin is on the left wall. His pillow—a comfy rock—is up the stairs (in first glass case). The center display case contains (top to bottom) the Saint's lower jaw *(il mento)*, his uncorrupted tongue *(lingua)*, and, finally, his vocal chords *(apparato vocale,* discovered intact when his remains were examined in 1981). In the last display case, fragments of the True Cross *(la croce)* are held in a precious crucifix reliquary.

Cloisters

From the right side of the nave as you face the altar, follow signs to *chiostro;* from outside, find signs on the right side of the church. The main cloister is dominated by an exceptionally bushy magnolia tree, planted in 1810, and by the graves of the most illustrious Padovans (such as the scientists who gave their names to their discoveries: Fallopian tube and Eustachian tube).

Wander around the various cloisters. Picnic tables invite pilgrims and tourists to enjoy meals within the solitude of one of the cloisters (it's covered and suitable even when rainy, WCs in same cloister). A **multimedia exhibit** on the life of St. Anthony is presented in this cloister. Ask if they'll run the English version for you.

In the far end, a fascinating little **museum** is filled with votives and folk art recounting miracles attributed to Anthony. The abbreviation *PGR* you'll see on many votives stands for *per grazia ricevuta*—for answered prayers.

Oratory of St. George

The small but sumptuous oratory (which costs €2.50 to enter) faces the little square in front of the basilica. The oratory ("ora" means prayer) is not actually a church, though it's certainly a fine place to pray—it's filled with vivid, circa-1370 frescos and soft classical music. It's an understandably popular place for local wedding ceremonies.

Near the Basilica

Prato della Valle—The so-called "field without grass" is 150 yards southwest of the basilica (down Via Luca Belludi). Once a Roman theater and later Anthony's preaching grounds, this square claims to be the largest in Italy. It's a pleasant, 400-yard-long, oval-shaped piazza with fountains, walkways, dozens of statues of Padua's eminent citizens, and (yes) grass. It's also a **market** scene: A huge clothing, shoe, and household goods market encircles the

Prato on Saturdays (8:00–19:00). An antique market creaks into action on the third Sunday of every month (8:00–19:00).

Botanic Garden—Green thumbs appreciate this nearly five-acre botanical garden, which contains the university's vast collection of rare plants. It was founded in 1545 by the Faculty of Medicine to cultivate medicinal plants (€4, April–Oct daily 9:00–13:00 & 15:00–19:00, Nov–March Mon–Sat 9:00–13:00, closed Sun, entrance 150 yards south of Basilica of St. Anthony—with your back to the facade, take a hard left). A visitors center—in a little cottage to the right of the garden's entrance—houses models of the garden's layout and computer programs that describe the history and composition of the garden in English (same hours as the garden).

▲▲▲Scrovegni Chapel (Cappella degli Scrovegni)

You must make reservations in advance to see this glorious, recently renovated chapel. Wallpapered with Giotto's beautifully preserved

cycle of nearly 40 frescoes, the chapel holds scenes depicting the lives of Jesus and Mary. (See "Booking Your Reservation," below.)

Painted by Giotto and his assistants from 1303 to 1305 and considered by many to be the first piece of modern art, this work makes it clear: Europe was breaking out of the Middle Ages. A sign of the Renaissance to come, Giotto placed real people in real scenes, expressing real human emotions. These frescoes were radical for their 3-D nature, lively colors, light sources, emotion, and humanism.

The chapel was built out of guilt for white-collar crimes. Reginaldo degli Scrovegni (skroh-VEHN-yee) charged sky-high interest rates at a time when that practice was forbidden by the Church. He even caught the attention of Dante, who placed him in one of the levels of hell in his *Inferno*. When Reginaldo died, the Church denied him a Christian burial. His son Enrico tried to buy forgiveness for his father's sins by building this superb chapel. After seeing Giotto's frescoes for the Franciscan monks of St. Anthony, Enrico knew he'd found the right artist to decorate the interior (and, he hoped, save his father's soul).

Cost and Hours: €12 combo-ticket with Civic Museum. The chapel is open daily 9:00–22:00 (off-season until 19:00).

The Civic Museum (and its worthwhile *pinacoteca* and Multimedia Room) are included in your entry fee. During the times the Civic Museum is closed—after 19:00 and on Mon—tickets are €8. (The Multimedia Room , which is adjacent to the Civic Museum, is always open the same hours as the chapel.)

Entry Times: Every 15 minutes (at :00, :15, :30, and :45 past the hour during the day), the chapel opens for 15-minute visits. After 19:00, the chapel opens every 20 minutes for 20-minute visits (last entry at 21:40).

Booking Your Reservation: To protect the paintings from excess humidity, only 25 people are allowed in the chapel at a time.

Scrovegni Chapel

● Joachim Driven From the Temple
● Joachim Returns to the Sheepfold*
● Mary's Birth Announced to St. Anne
● Birth of Jesus
● Slaughter of the Innocents
● Jesus Astounding the Scholars

● Jesus Drives Out the Money Changers
● Last Supper
● Betrayal of Christ*
● Jesus Beaten and Humiliated
● Jesus Carrying the Cross
● Lamentation (Deposition)*
● Last Judgment*

*Described in text

Prepaid reservations are obligatory (booking office open Mon–Fri 9:00–19:00, Sat 9:00–13:00, closed Sun, provide your credit-card number and hotel telephone number where you can be reached the day before if necessary, call 049-201-0020—you may have to be persistent and call several times). You can also reserve faster and easier online at www.cappelladegliscrovegni.it.

Book your visit well in advance. It's sometimes possible to buy a ticket for the same day at the ticket office, but don't count on it. (A sign on the desk indicates the next available time.)

You'll be instructed to pick up your tickets at the ticket office at least an hour before your visit. In practice, I've found that you can arrive later, but give yourself at least 30 minutes to weather any commotion at the desk. Present your confirmation number, confirm your time, and pick up your ticket.

While you're waiting for your reserved time, blitz the museum and Multimedia Room. Read the section below before you enter, since you'll only have a short time in the chapel itself.

Be at the chapel doors (well-signed, 100 yards to the right of the ticket office as you exit) at least five minutes before your scheduled visit. The doors to the chapel are automatic, and if you're even a minute late, you'll forfeit your visit and have to rebook and repay to enter.

At your appointed time, you first enter an anteroom to watch a very instructive 15-minute video (with English subtitles) and to establish humidity levels before continuing into the chapel (no photos are allowed). Although you have only a short visit inside the chapel, it is divine. You're inside a Giotto time capsule, looking back at an artist ahead of his time.

Giotto's Frescoes in the Scrovegni Chapel

Giotto painted the entire chapel in 200 working days over two years, but you'll get only 15 minutes to see it.

As you enter the long, narrow chapel, look right down to the

far end—the rear wall is covered with Giotto's big *Last Judgment.* Christ in a bubble is flanked by crowds of saints and by scenes of heaven and hell. This is the final, climactic scene of the story told in the chapel's 38 panels—the three-generation history of Jesus, his mother Mary, and Mary's parents.

The story begins with Jesus' grandparents, on the long north wall (with the windows) in the upper-left corner. In the first frame, a priest scolds the man who will be Mary's father (Joachim, with the halo) and kicks him out of the Temple for the sin of being childless. In the next panel to the right, Joachim returns dejectedly to his sheep farm. Meanwhile (next panel), his wife is in the bedroom, hearing the miraculous news that their prayers have been answered—she'll give birth to Mary, the mother of Jesus.

From this humble start, the story of Mary and Jesus spirals clockwise around the chapel, from top to bottom. The top row (both north and south walls) covers Mary's birth and life.

Jesus enters the picture in the middle row of the north (windowed) wall. The first frame shows his birth in a shed-like manger.

Giotto di Bondone
(c. 1267–1337)

Though details of his life are extremely sketchy, we know that as a 12-year-old shepherd boy, Giotto was discovered painting pictures of his father's sheep on rock slabs. He became the wealthiest and most famous painter of his day. His achievement is especially remarkable because painters at that time weren't considered anything more than craftsmen and weren't expected to be innovators.

After making a name for himself by painting the life of St. Francis frescoes in Assisi, the Florentine tackled the Scrovegni Chapel (c. 1303–1305). At age 35, he was at the height of his powers. His scenes were more realistic and human than anything done for a thousand years. Giotto didn't learn technique by dissecting corpses or studying the mathematics of 3-D perspective. But he had innate talent, and his personality shines through in the humanity of his art.

The Scrovegni frescoes break ground by introducing nature—rocks, trees, animals—as a backdrop for religious scenes. Giotto's people, with their voluminous, deeply creased robes, are as sturdy and massive as Greek statues, throwbacks to the Byzantine icon art of the Middle Ages. But these figures exude stage presence. Their gestures are simple but expressive: A head tilted down says dejection, an arm flung out is grief, clasped hands are hope. Giotto created his figures not just by drawing outlines and filling them in with single colors, but as patchworks of lighter and darker shades, pioneering modern modeling techniques. Giotto's storytelling style is straightforward, and anyone with knowledge of the episodes of Jesus' life can read the chapel like a comic book.

The Scrovegni represents a turning point in European art and culture—away from scenes of heaven and toward a more down-to-earth, human-centered view.

In the next frame, the Magi arrive and kneel to kiss his little toes. Then the child is presented in the tiny temple. Fearing danger, the family gets on their horse and flees to Egypt. Meanwhile, back home, all the baby boys are slaughtered to try to prevent the coming of the Messiah (Slaughter of the Innocents).

Spinning clockwise to the opposite (south) wall, you see (in a badly damaged fresco) the child Jesus astounding the scholars with his wisdom. Next, Jesus is baptized by John the Baptist. His first miracle, at a wedding, is turning jars of water into wine. Next, he raises a mummy-like Lazarus from the dead. Riding a donkey, he enters Jerusalem triumphantly. In the temple, he drives the wicked money changers out.

Turning again to the north wall (bottom row), we see scenes from Jesus' final days. In the first frame, he and his followers gather at a table for a Last Supper. Next, Jesus kneels humbly to wash their feet. He is betrayed with a kiss and arrested. Jesus is tried. Then he is beaten and humiliated.

Finally (south wall, bottom row), he is forced to carry his own cross, crucified, and prepared for burial, while his followers mourn (Lamentation). Then he is resurrected, and ascends to heaven, leaving his disciples to carry on.

The whole story concludes on the rear wall, where Jesus reigns at the Last Judgment. The long north wall (ground level) features the Virtues that lead to heaven, while the south wall has the (always more interesting) Vices. And all this unfolds beneath the blue, starry sky overhead on the ceiling.

Some panels deserve a closer look:

Joachim Returns to the Sheepfold (north wall, upper left, second panel): Though difficult to appreciate from ground level, this oft-reproduced scene is groundbreaking. Giotto—a former shepherd himself—uses nature as a stage, setting the scene in front of a backdrop of real-life mountains, and adding down-home details like Joachim's jumping dog, frozen in mid-air.

Betrayal of Christ, a.k.a. *Il Bacio,* "The Kiss" (north wall, bottom row, center panel): Amid the crowded chaos of Jesus' arrest, Giotto focuses our eye on the central action, where Judas ensnares Jesus in his yellow robe (the color symbolizing envy), establishes meaningful eye contact, and kisses him.

Lamentation, a.k.a. *Deposition* (south wall, bottom row, middle): Jesus has been crucified, and his followers weep and wail over the lifeless body. John the Evangelist spreads his arms wide and shrieks, his cries echoed by anguished angels above. Each face is a study in grief. Giotto emphasizes these saints' human vulnerability.

Last Judgment (big west wall): Christ in the center is a glorious vision, but the action is in Hell (lower right). Satan is a Minotaur-headed ogre munching on sinners. Around him, demons give sinners their just desserts in a scene right out of Dante...who was Giotto's friend and fellow Florentine. Front and center is Enrico Scrovegni in a violet robe (the color symbolizing penitence), donating the chapel to the Church in exchange for forgiveness for his father's sins.

Before you're scooted out, take a look at the actual altar. While Enrico's father's tomb is lost, Enrico Scrovegni himself is in the tomb at the altar. The three statues are by Giovanni Pisano—Mary (in the center) supports baby Jesus on her hip with a perfectly natural, maternal, S-shape. She's flanked by no-name deacons.

Civic Museum (Musei Civici Eremitani)

This museum, next to the Scrovegni Chapel, was once an Augustinian hermit's monastery. Visit in order to see the *pinacoteca* and the Multimedia Room. The ground floor is a skippable archaeological museum with Roman and Etruscan artifacts and no English descriptions.

Cost, Hours, Information: €12 Scrovegni Chapel combo-ticket, €10 without the chapel. The Civic Museum is open Tue–Sun 9:00–19:00, closed Mon. The Multimedia Room is open at the same time as the Scrovegni Chapel (daily 9:00–22:00, off-season until 19:00). Another part of the museum, Palazzo Zuckermann, is open Tue–Sun 10:00–19:00, closed Mon. No photos are allowed, and there's a mandatory and free bag check (Piazza Eremitani, tel. 049-820-4551).

Pinacoteca

The museum's highlight is upstairs, in the *pinacoteca* (picture gallery). The collection has 13th- to 18th-century paintings by Titian, Tintoretto, Giorgione, Tiepolo, Veronese, Bellini, Canova, Guariento, and other Veneto artists. But I'd make a beeline for the room with the Giotto crucifix. Ask for it: *"La Croce di Giotto?"*

Originally hung in the Scrovegni Chapel between the Scrovegni family's private zone and public's worshipping zone, this crucifix is painted on wood by Giotto. If you actually sit on the floor and look up, the body really pops. The adjacent "God as Jesus" painting was the only painting in the otherwise frescoed chapel. (This is hung here for preservation concerns. Its copy is the only non-original art in the chapel.) Studying these two masterpieces affirms Giotto's greatness.

Behind the crucifix room is a collection of 14th- and 15th-century art. While the works here are exquisite—and came well after Giotto—they're clearly not as modern.

Multimedia Room

This room, dedicated to taking a closer look at the Scrovegni Chapel, is adjacent to the Civic Museum (in the same building). Rows of computer screens offer a virtual Scrovegni Chapel visit and provide cultural insights into daily life in the Middle Ages. There are explanations of the individual panels, Giotto's fresco technique, close-ups of the art, and a description of the restoration. They show a 12-minute video (English headphones available) that is similar—but not identical—to the one that precedes your chapel visit. For me, it's worth just taking some time to enjoy a second video that features a mesmerizing, slow montage of close-ups of the Giotto frescoes.

Between the museum and the chapel are the scant remains

of Roman Padua. The remnants are from the wall of an arena and nicely fitting pipes that once channeled water so that the arena could be flooded (which took place during the annual celebration of a great Roman naval victory over the Greeks in 302 B.C.).

Palazzo Zuckermann

This little-visited wing of the Civic Museum, just across a busy street, is included in the same ticket as the *pinacoteca* and Multimedia Room. Its first two floors offer a commotion of applied and decorative arts from the Venetian Republic (1600s–1700s). On the top floor, the Bottacin collection takes you to the 19th century with coins and delightful (but no-name) pre-Impressionist paintings.

More Sights in the Center

Palazzo della Ragione—This grand 13th-century palazzo, commonly called *il Salone* (great hall), once held the medieval law courts. The first floor consists of a huge hall—265 feet by 90 feet—that was at one time adorned with frescoes by Giotto. A fire in 1312 destroyed those paintings, and the palazzo was redecorated with the 15th-century art you see today: a series of 333 frescoes depicting the signs of the zodiac, labors of the month, symbols representing characteristics of people born under each sign, and, finally, figures of saints to legitimize the power of the courts in the eyes of the Church.

The hall is topped with a hull-shaped roof, which helps to support the structure without the use of columns—quite an architectural feat in its day, considering the building's dimensions. The curious stone in the right-hand corner near the entry is the "Stone of Shame," which was the seat of debtors being punished during the Middle Ages. Instead of being sentenced to death or prison (same thing back then), debtors sat upon this stone, surrendered their possessions, and denounced themselves publicly before being exiled from the city (€4, more if there's an exhibition, Feb–Oct Tue–Sun 9:00–19:00, closed Mon, Nov–Jan closes at 18:00, enter through north end of Piazza delle Erbe, up long staircase, tel. 049-820-5006, WCs just past the exit).

▲▲**Market Squares: Piazza delle Erbe and Piazza della Frutta**—The stately Palazzo della Ragione (described above) provides a dramatic backdrop for Padua's almost exotic-feeling market, filling the surrounding squares—Piazza delle Erbe and Piazza della Frutta—each morning and all day Saturday (Mon–Fri roughly 8:00–13:00, Sat 8:00–17:00, closed Sun). Second only to the produce market in Italy's gastronomic capital of Bologna, this market has been renowned for centuries as having the freshest and greatest selection of

herbs, fruits, and vegetables. And don't miss the ground floor of the Palazzo della Ragione, where you'll find various butchers, *salumerie* (delicatessens), cheese shops, bakeries, and fishmongers.

Explore this scene. Students gather here each evening, after the markets have closed, spilling out of colorful bars and cafés—drinks in hand—into the square. Pizza by the slice is dirt cheap. The drink of choice is a *spritz*, an aperitif generally made with Campari (liquor infused with bitter herbs), white wine, and sparkling water and garnished with a blood-orange wedge. The *spritz* most popular with women (less alcohol, lighter) is made with Aperol (orange-flavored liquor), rather than Campari.

Get your *spritz* to take away *(da portar via)*, and join the young people out on the piazza. This is a classic opportunity to enjoy a real discussion with smart, English-speaking students who see tourists not as pests, but as interesting people from far away. For an instant conversation starter, ask about the current political situation in Italy, the right-wing party's policy on immigrants, or the cultural differences between Italy's North and the South.

A typical snack stand selling all kinds of fresh, hot, and ready-to-eat seafood appetizers sets up in Piazza della Frutta between 17:00–20:30 (daily except Sun). Belly up to the bar with your drink and try whatever's being served.

Caffè Pedrocchi—This white-columned Neoclassical café is not just a café. A complex of meeting rooms and entertainment venues, it stirs the Italian soul (at least, patriotic Italian souls). Built in 1831 during the period of Austrian rule, the Caffè Pedrocchi was inaugurated for the fourth Italian Congress of Scientists, which convened during the mid–19th century to stir up nationalistic fervor as Italy struggled to become a united nation. As a symbol of patriotic hope, it was the target (no surprise) of a student uprising plot in 1848. You can still see a bullet hole in the wall of the Sala Bianca, where one of the insurgents was killed. Nowadays, you get more foam than fervor.

Each room is decorated and furnished in a different color: red, white, and green—representing the colors of the Italian flag. In the Sala Verde (Green Room), people are welcome to sit and enjoy the beautiful interior without ordering anything or having to pay—in fact, you can even bring your own food and eat it free. Otherwise, take a seat in the Red or White rooms and order from the menu of teahouse fare, including salads, sandwiches, and the writer Stendhal's beloved *zabaglione,* a creamy custard (June–Sept daily 9:00–24:00; Oct–May Sun–Wed 9:00–21:00, Thu–Sat 9:00–24:00; entrance is at intersection of Oberdan and VIII Febbraio, between Piazza delle Erbe and Piazza Cavour; tel. 049-878-1231).

Piano Nobile: This upper, "noble floor" is more elaborate. The rooms are all in different styles, such as Greek, Etruscan, or Egyptian, with good English descriptions throughout. These rooms were intended to evoke memories of the glory of past epochs, which a united Italy had hopes of reliving.

Museum of the Risorgimento: The Piano Nobile hosts a small museum that traces Padua's role in Italian history, from the downfall of the Venetian Republic (1797) to the founding of the Republic of Italy (1948). Exhibits, a few with English descriptions, include uniforms, medals, weaponry, old artillery, Fascist propaganda posters, and a propagandistic video (in Italian, continuous 30-min loop), which shows the town in the 1930s and, later, during WWII bombardments.

The war and propaganda posters in the last room are haunting. An old woman pleads to those who might question the Fascist-driven war effort: "Don't betray my son." Another declares, "The Germans are truly our friends." And another asks, "And you...what are you doing?" (€4, Tue–Sun 9:30–12:30 & 15:30–18:00, closed Mon, tel. 049-820-5007.) You can reach Piano Nobile by a stairway to the right of the Caffè's entrance.

▲**Baptistery**—If you're an art lover but can't get in to see the Scrovegni Chapel, Padua's Baptistery is a good alternative. Originally, it was the private chapel of Padua's ruling family. Then, in 1405, Venice took over, killing Padua's ruling family and making it a baptistery. Located next to the Duomo, the Baptistery was frescoed (c.1370, about 70 years after Giotto) by Giusto de' Menabuoi.

The complex design must have made perfect and cohesive sense to the faithful in centuries past: with almighty Christ in majesty on top; approachable Mary and the multitude of saints providing the devout with access to God; the world (as was known in the 14th century) kicking off a cycle of scenes illustrating creation; and the four evangelists (Matthew, Mark, Luke, and John) with their books and symbols in the corners. A vivid crucifixion scene faces a gorgeous annunciation (€2.50, daily 10:00–18:00).

University of Padua

The seat of this prestigious university is adjacent to Caffè Pedrocchi. Founded in 1222, it's one of the first, greatest, and most progressive

Graduation Antics in Padua

With 60,000 students, Padua's university graduates individuals on any given day. A constant trickle of happy grads and their friends and families celebrate the big event.

During the school year, every 20 minutes or so, a student steps into a formal room (upstairs, above the university courtyard) to formally meet with the leading professors of his or her faculty. When they're finished, the students are given a green laurel wreath. They pose for formal group photos and family snapshots. It's a sweet scene. Then, craziness takes over.

The new graduates replace their somber clothing with raunchy outfits as gangs of friends gather around them in the street in front of the university. The roast begins. The gang rolls out a giant butcher-paper poster with a generally obscene caricature of the student and a litany of *This Is Your Life* photos and stories. The new grad, subject to various embarrassing pranks, reads the funny statements out loud. The poster is then taped to the university wall for all to see (and allowed to stay there for 24 hours).

During the roast, the friends sing the catchy but obscene local university anthem reminding their newly esteemed friend not to get too huffy: *Dottore, dottore, dottore del buso del cul. Vaffancul, vaffancul* (loosely translated: "Doctor, doctor. You're just a Doctor of the a-hole...go f-off, go f-off"). After you've heard this song (with its fanfare and um-pah-pah catchiness) and have seen all the good-natured fun, you can't stop singing it.

universities in Europe. Back when the Church controlled university curricula, a group of professors and students broke free from the University of Bologna, creating this liberal school, independent of Catholic constraints and accessible to people of alternative faiths.

A haven for free thought, the university attracted intellectuals from all over Europe, including the great astronomer Copernicus, who realized here that the universe didn't revolve around him. And Galileo—notorious for disagreeing with the Church's views on science—called his 18 years on the faculty here the best of his life.

Today, students gather in ancient courtyards, surrounded by memories of illustrious alumni, including the first woman ever to receive a university degree (in 1678).

While the tour is more involved, anyone can pop into the university's 16th-century courtyard, the school's historic core. It's littered with the coats of arms of administrators. Classrooms, which open onto the square, are still used.

The big attraction among tourists is the university's historic anatomy theater, which you can visit only on a guided tour. Try to get a ticket, but keep in mind that it's not worth any heroics to catch.

Cost, Hours, Information: While it's free to visit the university, you must sign up for a 30-minute tour (€5) to see the anatomy theater. Only 30 people may enter at a time. Tours run three times a day (Mon, Wed, and Fri at 15:15, 16:15, and 17:15; Tue, Thu, and Sat at 9:15, 10:15, and 11:15, no tours on Sun). School groups often book the entire visit, and many of the guides speak no English.

Confirm tour times and availability by calling 049-827-3047 or stopping by the university bookstore (located inside the palace, on the right side of courtyard). If the tour isn't booked, you can buy tickets from the bookstore 15 minutes before the tour is due to start.

Anatomy Theater Tour

The first two rooms of the tour are underwhelming: One features the supposed "pulpit of Galileo" (c. 1550) and portraits of 40 famous alums. The second is the Aula Magna, a ceremonial room for festivities. Everywhere you look you see the coats of arms of important faculty and leaders of the university over ages.

The highlight is Europe's first great anatomy theater (from 1594). Despite the Church's strict ban on autopsies, more than 300 students would pack this theater to watch professors dissect human cadavers (the bodies of criminals from another town). This had to be done in a "don't ask, don't tell" kind of way, because the Roman Catholic Church has only allowed the teaching of anatomy through dissection since the late 1800s.

SLEEPING

In the Center

$$$ Majestic Hotel Toscanelli is a central, fancy hotel with 34 pleasant, air-conditioned rooms and a touch of charm, on a relatively quiet side street (Sb-€99–115, Db-€159–175, 10 percent discount with this book in 2008, superior rooms and suites available at extra cost, includes a wonderful breakfast, about 2 blocks south of Piazza delle Erbe at Via dell'Arco 2, tel. 049-663-244, fax 049-876-0025, www.toscanelli.com, majestic@toscanelli.com). From Piazza delle Erbe, head up Via dei Fabbri and take the first left, then turn right onto Via dell'Arco.

Near Basilica of St. Anthony

$ Hotel al Fagiano, located on a side street west of Piazza del Santo, has 30 bright and cheery air-conditioned rooms decorated with Rossella Fagiano's modern-art canvases (Sb-€57, Db-€80,

---

Sleep Code

(€1 = about $1.30, country code: 39)
S = Single, **D** = Double/Twin, **T** = Triple, **Q** = Quad, **b** = bathroom,
s = shower only. Unless otherwise noted, credit cards are accepted, English is spoken, and breakfast is included in these rates.

To help you easily sort through these listings, I've divided the rooms into three categories, based on the price for a standard double room with bath:

$$$ **Higher Priced**—Most rooms €130 or more.
$$ **Moderately Priced**—Most rooms between €95–130.
$ **Lower Priced**—Most rooms €95 or less.

Tb-€90, ask for special prices with this book through 2008, breakfast €3–6 extra; with your back to the Basilica of St. Anthony, take Via Belludi, then veer right onto Via Locatelli, #45 is under portico on the right; tel. & fax 049-875-3396, www.alfagiano.com, info @alfagiano.com). This hotel is all about the union of a man and a woman (quite romantic).

$ Hotel al Santo, run by the Tenan family, offers 15 rooms with all the comforts a few steps from the basilica (Sb-€60, Db-€90, Tb-€130, Qb-€145, double-paned windows, air-con, quieter rooms off street, some rooms have views of basilica, free Internet access, Via del Santo 147, tel. 049-875-2131, fax 049-878-8076, www.alsanto.it, alsanto@alsanto.it).

$ Casa del Pellegrino, with 160 spotless, cheap, institutional rooms, is home to the pilgrims who come to pay homage to St. Anthony in the basilica next door, but welcomes any visitor to Padua (S-€45, Sb-€58, D-€56, Db-€72, Tb-€78, Qb-€90, most rooms have air-con, ask for a room off the street, breakfast-€6, elevator, Via Cesarotti 21, tel. 049-823-9711, fax 049-823-9780, www.casadelpellegrino.com, info@casadelpellegrino.com). They have a modern wing with 30 better rooms at the same price—just request a room in the *dependenza*.

Hostel: **$ Ostello Città di Padova,** near Prato della Valle, is a well-run hostel with 90 beds in 4-, 6-, and 13-bed rooms (€17 beds with sheets and breakfast; 4-person family rooms-€69, with bath-€72; non-members pay €3 per night extra, laundry, bike rentals in summer and lockers, reception open 7:00–9:30 & 16:30–23:00, rooms locked during afternoon but reception staffed if you need to leave bags, 23:00 curfew; bus #3, #8, or #18 from station, get off at Prato della Valle, Via Aleardi 30; tel. 049-875-2219, www .ostellopadova.it, ostellopadova@ctgveneto.it).

Down by the Station

$$$ Hotel Grand'Italia offers four-star elegance, convenience, and prices. Housed in a palace, its 61 modern, business-class rooms are comfortable, and the breakfast room is bright and inviting (Db-generally €130 on Fri, Sat, and Sun; €165 otherwise but can be more during holidays and trade fairs, air-con, elevator, outside train station on the right side of main drag at Corso del Popolo 81, tel. 049-876-1111, fax 049-875-0850, www.hotelgranditalia.it, booking@hotelgranditalia.it).

$$ Hotel Monaco, a three-star hotel with 57 darkly decorated rooms, is a few doors away from the Grand'Italia and plain in comparison, but a heck of lot cheaper (Sb-€75, Db-€100–110, 10 percent discount with cash and this book through 2008, €5 optional breakfast, air-con, elevator, traffic noise; as you exit the station, it's to your right and across the street at Piazzale Stazione 3; tel. 049-664-344, fax 049-664-669, www.hotelmonacopadova .it, info@hotelmonacopadova.it, Adriana).

$$ Hotel al Cason, run by the Salmaso family, is a five-minute walk from the train station. It offers a good value for its 48 newly renovated and artistic rooms in a big, efficient, business-style hotel on a big, noisy, and forgettable street (Db-€98, air-con, elevator, Internet access, free parking, handy restaurant, tel. 049-662-636, fax 049-875-4217, leaving the station head to the right, Via Frà Paolo Sarpi #40, www.hotelalcason.com, info@hotelalcason.com).

EATING

The university population means cheap, good food abounds. My recommended restaurants are all centrally located in the historic core. You'd think there would be fine dining on the charming market squares, but on the piazzas it's a take-out-pizza-and-casual-bar scene (dominated by students after dark). It's a fun place but only for drinks, rather than for a meal. (La Lanterna, at the neighboring Piazza dei Signori, is the only good, on-square dining I've found.) The dreamily atmospheric neighborhood (just two blocks off the market squares) thrives after dark with trendy bars and a lively student *spritz* scene.

Romantic Dining in Padua

Hosteria Padovanino is very romantic, with a vanilla-candle-and-Titian-nude ambience. They serve traditional food with a creative twist, with an emphasis on fish (€15 pastas, €25 *secondi*, open Mon–Sat, closed Sun, Via Santa Chiara 1, tel. 049-876-5341, reservations wise).

Ostaria Speroni offers something even more intimate than Padovanino. Foodies may appreciate the special care brought by chef Gilberto. The trick here is to talk with Gilberto and design the meal of your dreams, which is especially easy if it includes a fish dish (€12 pastas, €20 *secondi*, open nightly, Via Sperone Speroni 32, tel. 049-875-3370).

Eating near the Center

La Lanterna has a forgettable interior, but a meal here includes a rare-in-Padua chance to sit in a grand square under the stars, surrounded by great architecture. It's fine for pizza and basic meals (€8 pastas and pizzas, €14 *secondi*, Fri–Wed 12:00–15:00 & 19:00–24:00, closed Thu, Piazza dei Signori 39, tel. 049-660-770, reservations smart).

Osteria dei Fabbri, with shared rustic tables, offers just the right mix of class and accessibility, quality and price. It's a great choice for a memorable meal (Mon–Sat 12:30–14:30 & 19:30–22:30, closed Sun, Via dei Fabbri 13, tel. 049-650-336).

Brek, tucked into a corner of Piazza Cavour 20, is an easy self-service *ristorante* with healthy and affordable choices. It's big, bright, practical, and family-friendly (daily 11:30–15:30 & 18:30–22:00, tel. 049-875-3788).

If the markets are closed, stock up on picnic items at the **PAM supermarket,** in a tiny *piazzetta* east of Caffè Pedrocchi (Mon–Sat 8:00–20:30, closed Wed evenings and all day Sun, Piazzetta Garzeria 3, tel. 049-657-006).

Eating near the Basilica of St. Anthony

Pago Pago dishes up €4–8 wood-fired Neapolitan pizzas (a local favorite), a variety of big €8 salads, and daily specials. Get there early for dinner or wait (Wed–Mon 12:00–14:00 & 19:00–22:30, pizza until 24:00, closed Tue; just 2 blocks from Basilica of St. Anthony, heading north on Via del Santo take the first right onto Via Galileo Galilei to #59; tel. 049-665-558).

Casa del Pellegrino Ristorante caters to St. Anthony pilgrims with simple, basic, and hearty meals, served in a cheery dining room, just north of the basilica (€3–4 pastas, €6–12 *secondi*, pizza served only in evening, daily 12:00–14:00 & 19:30–21:30, Sun lunch by reservation only, Via Cesarotti 21, tel. 049-823-9711).

Zairo is a huge *ristorante*/pizzeria with reasonable prices, delicious and homemade pastas, Veneto specialties, snappy service, and a local clientele (Tue–Sun 11:30–15:30 & 18:30–24:00, closed Mon, east side of Prato della Valle at #51, tel. 049-663-803).

Pollodoro la Gastronomica, a take-out deli near the basilica, sells roast chicken and will make sandwiches (Wed–Sat and Mon 8:30–14:00 & 17:00–20:00, Sun 8:30–14:00, closed Tue, 100 yards from basilica at Via Belludi 34; with your back to the basilica entrance, it's under the arches on the left; tel. 049-663-718). You can picnic at the nearby cloisters of the basilica.

TRANSPORTATION CONNECTIONS

From Padua by Train to: Venice (3/hr, 30 min), **Vicenza** (2/hr, fewer on weekends, 25 min), **Milan** (1–2/hr, generally leaving at :24 and :54 past the hour, 2.5 hrs), **Verona** (2/hr, 1 hr).

By Bus to: Venice's Marco Polo Airport (€5—buy ticket from driver, hourly from 5:25–22:25, 1 hr, €1/bag, departs from Padua's bus station in Piazzale Boschetti).

VICENZA DAY TRIP

To many architects, Vicenza (vih-CHEHN-zah) is a pilgrimage site. Entire streets look like the back of a nickel. This is the city of Andrea Palladio (1508–1580), the 16th-century Renaissance architect who gave us the Palladian style that is so influential in countless British country homes.

Palladio's real name was Andrea di Pietro della Gondola, but his genius was such that one of his patrons—responsible for the architect's liberal arts education—gave him the nickname of Palladio, an allusion to Pallas Athena, Greek goddess of wisdom and the arts.

The town's enthusiasm for its Palladian architecture is due partly to its aggressive subjugation by Venice. While little Vicenza couldn't buck Venetian rule, it could enjoy a bit of freedom in its art. Classicism was Vicenza's revenge against Venetian Gothic and Venice's ubiquitous winged lions. But as grandiose as Vicenza's Palladian facades may feel, there is little marble here. The city lacked the wealth to build with much more than painted wood and plaster.

For the casual visitor, a quick stop to Vicenza (on any day but Mon, when major sights are closed) offers plenty of Palladio—the last great artist of the Renaissance. And 2008 promises to be a great year for Vicenza as the town celebrates Palladio's 500th birthday (see www.andreapalladio500.it).

ORIENTATION

Tourist Information
The main TI is at Piazza Matteotti 12 (daily 9:00–13:00 & 14:00–18:00, tel. 0444-320-854, www.vicenzae.org); a second office is at Piazza dei Signori 8 (daily 10:00–14:00 & 14:30–18:30).

Vicenza

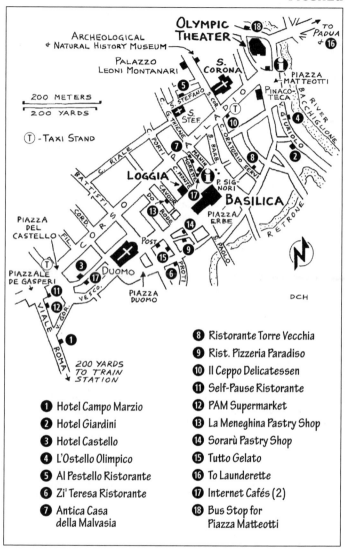

- ❶ Hotel Campo Marzio
- ❷ Hotel Giardini
- ❸ Hotel Castello
- ❹ L'Ostello Olimpico
- ❺ Al Pestello Ristorante
- ❻ Zi' Teresa Ristorante
- ❼ Antica Casa
    della Malvasia
- ❽ Ristorante Torre Vecchia
- ❾ Rist. Pizzeria Paradiso
- ❿ Il Ceppo Delicatessen
- ⓫ Self-Pause Ristorante
- ⓬ PAM Supermarket
- ⓭ La Meneghina Pastry Shop
- ⓮ Sorarù Pastry Shop
- ⓯ Tutto Gelato
- ⓰ To Launderette
- ⓱ Internet Cafés (2)
- ⓲ Bus Stop for
    Piazza Matteotti

The TI sometimes offers guided tours in English (April–Sept). Architecture fans appreciate the TI's *Vicenza Città e le Ville del Palladio nel Veneto* booklet (€2.50, in English).

Arrival in Vicenza

From the train station, it's a five-minute **walk** up wide Viale Roma to the bottom of Corso Palladio. Or it's a short **bus** ride to Piazza

Matteotti and the top of Corso Palladio. For a day trip, consider catching bus #1, #2, #5, or #7 from the train station to Piazza Matteotti and doing your sightseeing on the way back (€1.10, tickets sold at *tabacchi* shop in station, stop is immediately to your left as you exit the station). Validate your ticket in the machine as you board the bus. Get off at Piazza Matteotti, a skinny, park-like square in front of a white Neoclassical building. A **taxi** to Piazza Matteotti costs about €6. Vicenza has no official baggage check, but Hotel Campo Marzio will store your bags for free, even if you're not staying there.

Helpful Hints

Combo-Tickets: Most of Vicenza's sights are covered by a combo-ticket called **Card Musei** (€8/3 days, €12 Family Ticket, sold only at the Olympic Theater, which you can only enter with this card). The card also covers the Archaeological and Natural History Museum (next to the Church of Santa Corona), but doesn't cover the Palazzo Leoni Montanari or the villas outside of town. The pricier €11 combo-ticket (Biglietto Cumulativo) gets you into every sight in Vicenza except for exhibits in Basilica Palladiana.

Market Days: In the mornings (7:00–13:00), Vicenza hosts a Tuesday market on Piazza dei Signori, and a larger Thursday market on Piazza dei Signori, Piazza Duomo, Piazza del Castello, and Viale Roma.

Internet Access: Try **Vicenza.Com** (daily 10:00–13:00 & 16:00–19:30, next to TI at Piazza dei Signori 6, tel. 0444-540-430) or **Bar Michele** (Mon–Sat 7:00–19:30, closed Sun, near Piazza del Castello at Via San Francesco Vecchio 1).

Laundry: The self-service **Washing Point** is across the river, a couple of blocks from Piazza Matteotti (daily 8:00–22:00, Contrà XX Settembre 27).

Parking: Two cheap lots (Parcheggio Bassano and Parcheggio Cricoli, €2.20/day per person, not per car) are north and south of the city. At either lot, you can catch free shuttle bus #10 to the center.

Private Guide: Romina Rampazzo is a new, young guide with a command of both English and the hometown she loves (€80/half-day private tour, mobile 349-218-5656, romiramp@tin.it).

Best Gelato: Tutto Gelato is the local favorite, with natural colors and plenty of fresh and creative flavors (Tue–Sun 10:00–24:00, closed Mon, a block behind basilica at Contrà Frasche del Gambero 26).

SIGHTS

Central Vicenza

▲▲Olympic Theater (Teatro Olimpico)—Palladio's last work is one of his greatest. It was commissioned by the Olympic Academy, a society of Vicenzan scholars and intellectuals (including Palladio), for the purpose of staging performances and intellectual debates. Begun in 1580, shortly before Palladio died, the theater was actually completed by a fellow architect, Scamozzi.

Your visit includes three rooms: the first two rooms were frescoed in 1647 using Greek themes (glass cases display original 1585 oil lamps). The third is the actual theater.

Modeled after the theaters of antiquity, this theater is a wood-and-stucco festival of classical columns, statues, and an oh-wow stage bursting with perspective tricks. Behind the stage, framed by a triumphal arch, are five streets receding at different angles. The streets, depicting an idealized city of Thebes, were created for the gala opening of *Oedipus Rex,* the first play ever performed in the theater. While designed to seat 800 people, more than 2,000 attended on that opening night in 1585. In homage to Palladio, the theater has kept the original stage set.

Sit in the middle to enjoy the perspective. Rather than marble, the theater is all bricks and plaster with reinforcing iron inside. (That's a blessing—if it had been made of precious marble, Napoleon would have carted it all back to Paris.) Perspective tricks were a real turn-on back then. The main street is only 40 feet deep. To accentuate the illusion during the theater's debut, dwarves and smaller-than-normal oil lamps appeared in the fake distance.

Many of the statues in niches on the stage are modeled after the people who funded the work—junior members are portrayed as Roman soldiers of antiquity, senior members as senators. Panels at the top show the labors of Hercules, in keeping with the classical antiquity theme that was all the rage in the 16th century. In contrast to the stunning stage, the audience's wooden benches are simple and crude (entry possible only with €8 Card Musei, which covers other Vicenza sights—no separate theater ticket available; dense 45-min audioguide-€3 or €5/two people; Tue–Sun 9:00–17:00, closed Mon, July–Aug until 19:00, last entry 30 min before closing, occasionally closed when theater is in use, entrance to the left of TI, tel. 0444-222-800). When you step back outside, look up the town's main drag—named after Palladio. It's the same main street you saw in his theater.

Performances: One of the oldest indoor theaters in Europe and considered one of the world's best, it's still used for performances from April through June (jazz and classical music) and from September through October (Greek tragedies and dramas).

Shows start at 21:00 (for details, see www.vicenzae.org).

▲Church of Santa Corona—A block away from the Olympic Theater, this "Church of the Holy Crown" was built in the 13th century to house a thorn from the Crown of Thorns, given to the Bishop of Vicenza by the French King Louis IX (free, Mon 16:00–18:00, Tue–Sun 8:30–12:00 & 15:00–18:00). The church has two artistic highlights: the art embellishing its high altar and a fine Bellini painting.

Study the exquisite inlaid marble and mother-of-pearl work decorating the high altar (c. 1670). As Mary appears before Vicenza, you get a realistic peek at the town's skyline (at least as artists in 1670 thought the town had looked in 1426, the year Mary supposedly visited). Walk all around the altar. Find the Last Supper, the dramatic resurrection scene, Christ (in a scene as ugly as Abu Ghraib) being forced to wear the Crown of Thorns, and the King of France giving a thorn to the local bishop (the act this church was built to commemorate). Notice also the Florentine-style inlaid wood in the choir that shows off medieval Vicenza townscapes.

Giovanni Bellini's fine painting, *Baptism of Christ*, is nearby, on the left (south) side of the nave. A powerful vertical line connects the Father, Son, Holy Spirit, a cup dripping with water, and John the Baptist. Three women—clothed in radiant colors and symbolizing faith, hope, and charity—look on. It's pure Renaissance style as John realistically shifts his weight to one side. The frame is a festival of classic motifs and proportions (c. 1500, insert a €0.50 coin for light).

Archaeological and Natural History Museum—Located next door to the Church of Santa Corona, this museum has a ground floor featuring Roman antiquities (mosaics, statues, and artifacts excavated from Rome's Baths of Caracalla, plus swords) and a barbarian warrior skeleton complete with sword and helmet. Prehistoric scraps are upstairs, and there are a few English description sheets near exhibit entryways throughout (covered by €8 Card Musei—see page 296, Tue–Sun 9:00–17:00, closed Mon, last entry 15 min before closing, tel. 0444-320-440).

Palazzo Leoni Montanari—Across the street from the Church of Santa Corona, this small museum feels overlooked. It's a palatial riot of Baroque, with cherub-cluttered ceilings jumbled like a pre-school in heaven. A quick stroll shows off Venetian paintings and a floor of Russian icons (€3.50, Tue–Sun 10:00–18:00, closed Mon, Contrà Santa Corona 25).

Corso Andrea Palladio—From the Olympic Theater or Church of Santa Corona, stroll up Vicenza's main drag, Corso Andrea Palladio, and see why they call Vicenza "Venezia on terra firma." A steady string of Renaissance palaces and Palladian architecture

is peopled by Vicenzans (considered by their neighbors to be as uppity as most of their colonnades) and punctuated by fancy *gelaterie*. After a few blocks, turn left, and you'll see the basilica on Piazza dei Signori.
Piazza dei Signori—Vicenza's main square has been the center of town ever since it was the site of the ancient Roman forum. It's dominated by the commanding **Basilica Palladiana,** with its 270-foot-tall, 13th-century tower. This was not a church, but a meeting place for local big shots. It was young Palladio's proposal—to redo Vicenza's dilapidated Gothic palace of justice in the Neo-Greek style—that established him as Vicenza's favorite architect. The rest of Palladio's career was a one-man construction boom. Opposite the basilica, the brick-columned **Loggia del Capitaniato**—home of the Venetian governor and one of Palladio's last works—gives you an easy chance to compare early Palladio (the basilica) with late Palladio (the loggia).

The basilica, normally open to tourists during frequent special exhibitions, is likely to be closed throughout 2008 for restoration work (tel. 0444-322-196, see www.vicenzae.org for schedule). Even if the basilica is closed, you can climb the 15th-century stairway (unless it's blocked off for renovation). Halfway up the steps, there's a gargoyle-like lion's mouth (representing the long arm of the Venetian Republic). Centuries ago, people used to sneak notes into this mouth, anonymously reporting neighbors suspected of carrying communicable diseases that could bring on the plague. The arcaded upper floor contains the entrance to the huge basilica. The basilica's roof, shaped like an upside-down boat's hull, has a nautical feel, augmented by the porthole windows.

Outside, on Piazza dei Signori, note the two tall, **15th-century columns** topped by Jesus and the winged lion (a symbol of both St. Mark and Venice). When Venice took over Vicenza in the early 1400s, these columns were added—à la St. Mark's Square—

to give the city a Venetian feel.

If you're strolling through town back to the station, finish your walk, continuing along the Corso Palladio. At Piazzale de Gasperi (where you'll find the PAM supermarket, a handy place to grab a picnic for the train ride), dip into the park called **Giardino Salvi** (for one last Palladio-style loggia, closed to visitors but viewable from outside), and then walk five minutes down Viale Roma back to the station. Trains leave about every hour for Milan/Verona and Venice (less than an hour away).

Villas on the Outskirts of Vicenza

Vicenza is surrounded by dreamy Venetian villas. As Venice's commercial empire receded in the 1500s (when trade began to pick up along the Atlantic seaboard and dwindle in the Mediterranean), it redirected its economic agenda to terra firma—dominating the Veneto region. During the 16th century, Venice consolidated and incorporated Veneto into its economy. Rather than seagoing trade (Venice's forte), this area was busy with agribusiness—and that meant a need for lavish country villas. The region's many splendid villas were multifunctional. They provided a business headquarters, a suitable place to host VIP guests, warehouse facilities, and the family home of the farmer. The standard Palladian villa comes with three floors: kitchen and cellar in the cool basement; fancy ground-level *piano nobile*—the "noble floor"—where aristocrats lived and hosted friends among marvelous frescoes; and an upstairs, with rooms for the extended family and for storing goods. The most famous villa here, Villa la Rotonda, is an exception. It was the home not of a wealthy farmer, but of a retired church official.

The following two villas are worth a visit for architecture buffs (even with limited time). Both houses are furnished with period pieces and come with good English descriptions. Pick up the free English brochure on Palladio's villas from the TI if you plan to visit.

Villa la Rotonda—Thomas Jefferson's Monticello was inspired by Palladio's Rotonda (a.k.a. Villa Almerico Capra). Started by Palladio in 1566, it was finished by his pupil, Scamozzi. The white, gently domed building with grand colonnaded entries is built to look as if it popped out of the grassy slope. Palladio, who designed a number of country villas, had a knack for using the natural setting for dramatic effect. This private—but sometimes open for tours—residence is on the edge of Vicenza (€5 to enter grounds, mid-March–mid-Oct Tue–Sun 10:00–12:00 & 15:00–18:00, closed Mon, shorter hours off-season, confirm hours before heading out; €10 for interior—open only Wed 10:00–12:00 & 15:00–18:00; Via Rotonda 45, tel. 0444-321-793). To get to the villa from Vicenza's train station, hop a bus (#8, 2/hr, stop is to the left of the station as you're facing it on Viale Venezia—ask the driver or a local where to get off) or take a taxi. For a quick round-trip any time of day, you can zip out by cab (about €8, 5-min ride from train station) to see the building sitting regally atop its hill, and then ride the same cab back.

Villa Valmarana ai Nani—The 17th-century "Villa of the Dwarves"

is just up the street from Villa la Rotonda. This makes a convenient stop if you want to see a villa interior. The elegant Neoclassical estate features panoramic views and 18th-century murals by Tiepolo.

The villa's name comes from the local legend of an ancient manor house owned by a nobleman whose daughter was born a dwarf. Her father surrounded her with dwarf servants so she wouldn't realize she was small. One day as she was looking out the window, she saw a handsome prince ride by on his horse. Realizing she was a dwarf, she killed herself in anguish. Her servants—so saddened by her death that they turned to stone—now line the wall of the villa like petrified sentries.

The rooms in the main house include frescoes with scenes from the Trojan War, classical myths, and Italian lyrical poems. The frescoes in the guest house *(foresteria)* are nearly all by Tiepolo's son, Giandomenico, whose themes highlight 18th-century gentrified culture—the idealized tranquility of peasants, the exotic fashion and styles of the Chinese from a Western perspective, and scenes from Carnevale (€6, Tue–Sun 10:00–12:00 & 15:00–18:00, closed Mon; from Villa la Rotonda, head a few steps downhill, then up the slope on Stradella Valmarana about 200 yards; tel. 0444-321-803).

SLEEPING

Vicenza is so easy to visit from Venice or Padua that few people actually sleep here. If you do, keep in mind that several annual trade fairs cause hotel prices to skyrocket (in 2008: Jan 13–20, May 17–21, and Sept 6–10).

$$$ Hotel Campo Marzio, a four-star, American-style, pricey place, has 35 rooms with all the comforts facing a park on a busy street (Db-€169–184, pricier rooms are bigger with more amenities, air-con, elevator, free bikes, free parking, a few minutes' walk in front of train station at Viale Roma 21, tel. 0444-545-700, fax 0444-320-495, www.hotelcampomarzio.com, info@hotelcampomarzio.com).

Sleep Code

(€1 = about $1.30, country code: 39)
S = Single, **D** = Double/Twin, **T** = Triple, **Q** = Quad, **b** = bathroom. Unless otherwise noted, credit cards are accepted, English is spoken, and breakfast is included in these rates. Prices can be higher during trade fairs.

To help you easily sort through these listings, I've divided the rooms into three categories, based on the price for a standard double room with bath.

$$$ **Higher Priced**—Most rooms €150 or more.
$$ **Moderately Priced**—Most rooms between €110–150.
$ **Lower Priced**—Most rooms €110 or less.

$$ Hotel Giardini, with three stars and 17 sleek rooms, has splashy pastel colors and a refreshing feel (Sb-€83, Db-€114, air-con, elevator, on busy street but has double-paned windows, across from bus stop a block away from Piazza Matteotti/Olympic Theater on Via Giuriolo 10, tel. & fax 0444-326-458, www.hotelgiardini.com, info@hotelgiardini.com, Stefano).

$$ Hotel Castello, on Piazza del Castello, has 18 homey, artsy, quiet rooms, and lots of stairs (Sb-€90–120, Db-€120–149 depending on trade fairs, air-con, rooftop terrace, Contrà Piazza del Castello 24, tel. 0444-323-585, fax 0444-323-583, www.hotelcastelloitaly.com, info@hotelcastelloitaly.it). It's a five-minute walk from the train station (turn right after Hotel Campo Marzio, head up hill to square, in an alley to right of Ristorante agli Schioppi).

$ *Hostel:* **L'Ostello Olimpico,** just a few years old, is wonderfully central on Piazza Matteotti, a few steps from the Olympic Theater (85 beds, 4- to 6-bed rooms-€18 per person, Db and family rooms-€23 per person, includes sheets and breakfast, non-members pay €3/night extra, closed 9:30–16:15, curfew-24:00; best to reserve several weeks in advance by fax or email, Viale Giuriolo 7/9, tel. 0444-540-222, fax 0444-547-762, www.ostellovicenza.com, ostello.vicenza@tin.it).

EATING

The local specialty is marinated cod, called *baccalà alla Vicentina.*

In **Al Pestello**'s casually elegant dining room, owner Fabio patiently and lovingly describes his historic *cucina Vicentina* (including *baccalà*) from a menu written in dialect. The day's offerings are created from the freshest seasonal ingredients to complement an extensive list of local and national wines (€9 pastas, €14 *secondi,* Mon 19:30–22:30, Tue–Sat 12:30–14:30 & 19:30–22:30, closed Sun, a block from Church of Santa Corona at Contrà Santo Stefano 3, tel. 0444-323-721).

Zi' Teresa is a favorite among locals for its romantic ambience and moderately priced traditional cuisine and pizzas (€6 pizzas, €7 pastas, €13 *secondi,* Thu–Tue 11:45–14:30 & 18:30–23:00, closed Wed; a couple blocks southeast of Piazza dei Signori, at intersection with Contrà Proti, Contrà S. Antonio 1; tel. 0444-321-411).

Antica Casa della Malvasia, an *osteria* since 1210, is a popular, atmospheric, cavernous joint serving up affordable regional favorites and homemade pastas (daily 12:00–15:30 & 19:00–23:30, just off Piazza dei Signori on a little alley directly across from bell tower at Contrà delle Morette 5, tel. 0444-543-704). The attached *enoteca* offers wines (€0.80–3.50/glass) and snacks (closes at 21:30 in winter).

Ristorante Torre Vecchia is an appealing, old-time bistro with Art Nouveau decor, bedecked with Gibson Girl portraits and 19th-century lovers' photos. Sample creatively prepared, reasonably priced local specialties (€6 *antipasti,* €6 pastas, €10 *secondi*) paired with great, affordable local wines (Mon–Sat 19:00–22:00, closed Sun, near the basilica at Contrà Oratorio dei Servi 19, tel. 0444-320-001).

Ristorante Pizzeria Paradiso, with indoor and outdoor seating on a narrow square, offers dozens of inexpensive options, including pasta, wood-fired pizzas, and a €5–10 seafood or veggie buffet (daily 12:00–14:30 & 19:00–23:00, closed Mon in winter, south of Piazza dei Signori and Piazza Erbe at Via Pescherie Vecchie 5, tel. 0444-322-320).

Cheap Eats: The delicatessen **Il Ceppo** whips up pasta salads, roasted meats and vegetables, lasagna, savory crepes, and sandwiches to go. To get your meal heated, request *"Riscaldare, per favore"* (Thu–Tue 8:00–13:00 & 16:00–19:30, closed Wed, Corso Palladio 196, a few steps from Piazza Matteotti, tel. 0444-544-414). Take your picnic to the nearby park (next to the Olympic Theater) or to Piazza dei Signori.

A cheap, self-service **Self-Pause Ristorante** is just off Piazza del Castello, where Corso Andrea Palladio meets Viale Roma. Expect self-service cafeteria dining for lunch; for dinner, there's a limited buffet of pizzas, pastas, salads, and dessert for €7.60 (Tue–Sat 12:00–14:30 & 19:00–22:00, Mon lunch only, Sun dinner only, Corso Andrea Palladio 10, tel. 0444-327-829).

A few steps away is the **PAM supermarket** for all your picnic needs (Mon–Tue and Thu–Sat 8:00–20:00, Wed 8:00–14:00, closed Sun, follow the curve of the road just outside the city wall).

Pastry: **La Meneghina** is an atmospheric pastry shop (Tue–Sun 8:00–24:00, closed Mon, pricey meals 12:00–16:00 &

20:00–23:00 in summer, until 22:00 in winter; on Contrà Cavour 18, a short street between Piazza dei Signori and Corso Andrea Palladio; tel. 0444-323-305).

The tiny **Sorarù** pastry shop, nearby on Piazza dei Signori, has lots of sidewalk tables within tickling distance of the Palladio statue (Thu–Tue 8:30–13:00 & 15:30–20:00, closed Wed; next to the basilica in Piazzetta Palladio, tel. 0444-320-915).

TRANSPORTATION CONNECTIONS

From Vicenza by Train to: Venice (roughly 2/hr, 1 hr), **Padua** (roughly 2/hr, 20 min), **Ravenna** (about hourly, 3–4 hours, depending on train, with changes in Padua and Ferrara or Bologna), **Verona** (2/hr, 40 min).

VERONA DAY TRIP

Romeo and Juliet made Verona a household word. Alas, a visit here has nothing to do with those two star-crossed lovers. You can pay to visit the house that falsely claims to be Juliet's (with an almost-believable balcony and a courtyard swarming with tour groups), join in the tradition of rubbing the breast of Juliet's statue to help find a lover (or pick up the sweat of someone who can't), and even make a pilgrimage to what isn't "La Tomba di Giulietta."

Despite the fiction, the town has been an important cross-roads for 2,000 years and is therefore packed with genuine history. R and J fans will take some solace in the fact that two real feuding families, the Montecchi and the Capellos, were the models for Shakespeare's Montagues and Capulets. And, if R and J had existed and were alive today, they would recognize much of their "hometown."

Verona's main attractions are its wealth of Roman ruins; the remnants of its 13th- and 14th-century political and cultural boom; its 21st-century, quiet, pedestrian-only ambience; and a world-class opera festival each summer (www.arena.it). After Venice's festival of tourism, the Veneto's second city (in population and in artistic importance) is a cool and welcome sip of pure Italy, where dumpsters are painted by schoolchildren as class projects and public spaces are the domain of locals, not tourists. If you like Italy but don't need blockbuster sights, this town is a joy.

ORIENTATION

The vibrant and enjoyable core of Verona is along Via Mazzini between Piazza Brà (pronounced "bra") and Piazza Erbe, Verona's market square since Roman times. Head straight for Piazza Brà—and stroll. While Via Mazzini attracts mob scenes during the *passeggiata* (evening stroll), don't neglect the parallel Corso Porta Borsari. All sights of importance are located within an easy walk through the old town, which is defined by a bend in the river. For a good day trip to Verona, visit the Roman Arena and take my self-guided walk (see page 308).

Tourist Information

Verona has two TIs: at the train station (daily 8:00–19:00, tel. 045-800-0861) and at Piazza Brà (Mon–Sat 9:00–19:00, Sun 9:00–15:00; facing the large yellow-white building, the TI is across the street to your right; tel. 045-806-8680, www.tourism.verona.it, public WC on Piazza Brà). At either TI, pick up the free city map for a list of sights and opening hours, and confirm the walking-tour schedule. If you're staying the night, ask about concerts or pick up a monthly entertainment guide (either *Carnet Verona* or *Verona Live*) for about €1 at any newsstand.

Verona Card: This tourist card covers bus transportation and entrance to all the recommended Verona sights, except for the manicured garden named Giardino Giusti (€8/day or €12/3 days, sold at participating sights and at *tabacchi*—tobacco shops—in the city center). If you arrive at the train station, it makes sense to buy the card at the station TI, because it'll cover your bus ride to and from the city center and nearly all of your sightseeing for one painless price.

Arrival in Verona

By Train: Get off at Verona's Porta Nuova station. On the far left as you emerge from the passage are pay WCs, phones, an ATM, and baggage storage (€4/5 hrs, daily 7:00–23:00). From the main lobby—where the ticket windows are—a smaller hall branches off to the right, where you'll find a TI, train information desk, and another ATM.

Avoid the boring 15-minute walk from the station to Piazza Brà by catching the bus. Buses leave from directly in front of the station. To cover your trip into town, either get a Verona Card (listed above) or buy an individual ticket before boarding from a *tabacchi* shop inside the station (€1/1 hr; €3.10 valid until midnight).

Confirm the route by asking *"Per centro?"* (pehr CHEN-troh). You'll probably have a choice of bus #11, #12, or #13, leaving from Platform A (buses are orange or green-and-purple). If you have an individual ticket, validate it by stamping it in the machine in the middle of the bus. Buses stop on Piazza Brà, the square with the can't-miss-it Roman Arena. The TI is just a few steps beyond the bus stop (located along the medieval walls). Buses return to the station from the bus stop just outside the city wall (on the right), where Corso Porta Nuova hits Piazza Brà.

Verona

Taxis pick up only at taxi stands (at Piazza Brà and train station) and cost about €7 for the quick ride between the train station and Piazza Brà.

By Car: Drivers will find cheap parking at the stadium, at the long-term parking near the train station and city walls, and across the river from the Basilica of San Zeno Maggiore. There are a few free spaces across the river from the fortress/castle called Castelvecchio (on Lungoadige Cangrande). The most central lot is behind the Roman Arena on Piazza Cittadella (guarded, €1/hr). Street parking costs €1.50 per hour (buy ticket at *tabacchi* shop to put on dashboard, spaces marked with blue lines). The town center is closed to traffic, but if you're staying here, your hotel can get you permission to drive in—ask when you book. Otherwise your license plate could be photographed and you could have a €100 ticket waiting for you in the mail when you get home.

By Plane: From Verona's airport, catch a shuttle bus to the train station (€4.50, buy tickets on board, daily 6:30–23:30, 3/hr, 15 min). If going *to* the airport, catch the shuttle just to the left of the train station entrance (daily 5:40–23:10).

Helpful Hints

Sightseeing Schedules: Many sights are closed on Monday and are free on the first Sunday of every month.

Opera: In July and August, Verona's opera festival brings crowds and higher hotel prices (upper-level seats about €25, book tickets either online at www.arena.it or by calling 045-800-5151, box office open Mon–Fri 9:00–12:00 & 15:15–17:15, Sat–Sun 9:00–12:00; in opera season, it's open daily 10:00–17:45, or until 21:00 on days when there's a show).

Internet Access: Try **Internet Train** (Mon–Fri 10:00–22:00, Sat–Sun 14:00–20:00, Via Roma 17A, a couple of blocks off Piazza Brà toward Castelvecchio, tel. 045-801-3394) or **Internet Etc.** (Tue–Sat 10:30–20:00, Sun–Mon 15:30–20:00, off Via Mazzini on Via Quattro Spade 3B, tel. 045-800-0222).

Post Office: The post office is at Via Cattaneo 23E (Mon–Sat 8:30–18:30, closed Sun, near Piazza Brà).

TOURS

Walking Tours—The TI on Piazza Brà organizes 75-minute tours daily in English for €10 per person (April–Nov daily at 17:30; Sat–Mon also at 11:30; confirm schedule and meeting point at TI, call 045-810-3173 or 333-219-9645, or visit www.julietandco.com or www.venetoguide.it).

Private Guides—Two excellent and enthusiastic Verona guides enjoy giving private tours of the town and region to readers of this book (€105/half-day per group, tours tailored to your interests—villas, wine-tasting, etc.). They are Marina Menegoi (tel. 045-801-2174, mobile 328-958-1108, milanit@libero.it) and Valeria Biasi (mobile 348-9034-238, www.veronatours.com, valeria @veronatours.com).

SELF-GUIDED WALK

Welcome to Verona Town Walk

This walk covers the essential sights in the town core, starting at Piazza Brà and ending at the cathedral. Allow 90 minutes (including the tower climb and dawdling, but not the optional detours).

❶ Piazza Brà

If you're wondering where the name came from, it's a local dialect for open space. A generation ago this piazza was noisy with cars. Now it's open and people-friendly—the community family room and natural festival grounds. The big statue is of Italy's first king, Victor Emmanuel, and celebrates Italian unity, won back in the 1860s.

Piazza Brà is all about strolling...the *passeggiata* is a national sport in Italy. The broad, shiny sidewalk was named the "Liston" (ribbon) by 17th-century Venetians who made it big and wide (better for promenading socialites to see and be seen in all their finery). Just after World War II, opera singer Maria Callas lived above the Brek restaurant. As a starlet, she performed in the town's opera festival and found her husband in Verona (and likely never ate at Brek).

❷ Roman Arena

Just as modern stadiums are usually located outside of downtown districts today, Romans built this stadium outside the town walls.

With 72 aisles, this elliptical 466-by-400-foot amphitheater is the third-largest in the Roman world. Most of the stone you see is original. Dating from the first century A.D., it looks great in its pink marble. Over the centuries, crowds of up to 25,000 spectators have cheered Roman gladiator battles, medieval executions, and modern plays (including the popular opera festival, held every July and August, which takes advantage of the arena's famous acoustics). There's little to see inside except for the impressive stonework and great city views—if you climb to the top (€4, Tue–Sun 8:30–19:30,

Verona

200 YARDS
200 METERS

𝖵 VIEW

ROMAN BRIDGE

CASTEL SAN PIETRO

DUOMO

⑪ PIETRA

ROMAN THEATER

⑫ END

VIA CAPP.

VIA DUOMO

PIGNA

ROSA

FORTI

⑩

SANT' ANASTASIA

GARIBALDI

PAVINO

ADIGE

SAN FRAN.

BORSARI

S. MARIA

SOTTORIVA

VITT.

CORSO P.

⑧

⑨

NUOVA

S. LORENZO

⑥

④

⑤

CATULLO

4 SPADE

VIA MAZZINI

PALAZZO RAGIONE, TORRE LAMBERTI & WC

⑦

CORSO CAVOUR

OBERDAN

MARIO

③

VIA SCALA

V. ANEL.

HOUSE OF JULIET

CAPELLO

CATT.

LISTON

WC

①

② ARENA

(ARROW SHOWS ENTRANCE)

DOGANA

NAVI

PIAZZA BRÀ START

OLD CITY WALLS

MACELLO

CORSO PORTA NUOVA

PIAZZA CITTA- DELLA

ⓘ

PALLONE

ALEARDI

D C H

N

TO TRAIN STATION

① Piazza Brà
② Roman Arena
③ Devotional Column
④ Porta Borsari & Corso Porta Borsari
⑤ Enoteca Oreste
⑥ Piazza Erbe
⑦ House of Juliet
⑧ Piazza dei Signori
⑨ Tombs of the Scaligeri Family
⑩ Church of Sant'Anastasia
⑪ Ponte Pietra & River View
⑫ Duomo

Verona

Mon 13:30–19:30, closes at 14:00 during opera season, last entry 1 hour before closing, WC near entry, tel. 045-800-3204).

❸ Devotional Column

In the Middle Ages, this column blessed a marketplace held here. Ten yards in front of it, a bronze plaque in the sidewalk shows the Roman city plan—a town of 20,000 placed strategically in the bend of the river, which provided protection on three sides. A wall enclosed the peninsula. The center of the grid was the forum, today's Piazza Erbe. (If you look down Via Mazzini, the busy main pedestrian drag, the bell tower in the distance marks Piazza Erbe.)

• *From the bronze plaque, face Via Mazzini and go left (past Restaurant Rubiani) down Via Oberdan to an ancient gate, Porta Borsari.*

❹ Porta Borsari and Corso Porta Borsari

You're standing before the main entrance to Roman Verona. It functioned as a toll booth (*borsari* means purse, referring to the collection of tolls here). Now cross into the ancient city and walk down Corso Porta Borsari, the ancient main drag, toward what was the forum. As you walk, discover bits of the town's illustrious past—chips of Roman columns, medieval reliefs, fine old facades, fossils in marble—as well as its elegant present of fancy shops in a setting that prioritizes pedestrians over cars.

• *A block before you reach Piazza Erbe, at Vicolo San Marco in Foro, detour right following the* Posso dell'Amore *sign. Twenty yards off Corso Porta Borsari, you'll find...*

❺ Enoteca Oreste

This funky wine and *grappa* bar is still run by Oreste (with his Chicagoan wife, Beverly) like a 1970s, old-style *enoteca*. Browse, munch, sample. There's no formal food, but an abundance of fun and hearty bar snacks instead. This historic *enoteca* was once the private chapel of the archbishop of Verona. Traces of the past hide between the bottles—ask Beverly to tell you the story (daily 8:00–20:00, Vicolo San Marco in Foro 7, tel. 045-803-4369). For romantics, the Posso dell'Amore (Well of Love) is in a cul-de-sac 30 yards farther along.

• *Return to Corso Porta Borsari and continue on until you hit a big square.*

❻ Piazza Erbe

This bustling market square is a photographer's delight. Its pastel buildings corral the fountains, pigeons, and people who have congregated here since Roman times, when this was a forum. Notice the Venetian lion hovering above the square, reminding locals of their conquerors since 1405. During medieval times, the stone canopy in the center held the scales where merchants measured the weight of goods they bought and sold, such as silk, wool, and wood. The fountain has bubbled here for 2,000 years. Its statue, originally Roman, had lost its head and arms. After a sculptor added a new head and arms, the statue became Verona's Madonna. She holds a small banner that reads: "I want justice and I bring peace." The city once had a San Gimignano–type skyline of noble family towers. The big families of the day erected tall towers to show off and provide protection. Each (often feuding) local family had its own tower until the Scaligeri family (a.k.a. della Scala) took control and required its rivals to chop the tops off of their towers.

At the far end of Piazza Erbe, a market column featuring St. Zeno, the patron of Verona, oversees the action.

• *St. Zeno faces the much-appreciated House of Juliet (100 yards down Via Cappello to #23—just follow the crowds). Side-trip there now (but watch your wallet—it's a pickpocket's haven).*

❼ House of Juliet

This bogus house is Verona's touristic claim to fame. The tiny, admittedly romantic courtyard is a spectacle in itself, with tourists from all over the world posing on the balcony, Nebraskans polishing Juliet's bronze breast, and amorous graffiti everywhere. Hang out and savor the spectacle. The information boxes offer a good history (€1 for two people: "While no documentation has been discovered to prove the truth of the legend, no documentation has disproved it either.") The "museum," which displays art inspired by the love story,

plus costumes and the bed from Franco Zeffirelli's film *Romeo and Juliet,* is certainly not worth the €4 entry fee (Tue–Sun 8:30–19:30, Mon 13:30–19:30, tel. 045-803-4303).

Was there a Juliet Capulet? You just walked down the street of the cap makers (Via Cappello). Above the courtyard entry (looking out) is a coat of arms featuring a hat—representing a family that made hats and which would be named, logically, Capulet. Every day, 10 volunteers at Verona's Juliet Club (www.julietclub.com) respond to countless letters addressed simply to Juliet, Verona, Italy.

• *Return to Piazza Erbe. From the center, head right, downhill toward the river on Via della Costa (which becomes Via Santa Maria Antica after Piazza dei Signori, below).*

*The street is marked by an **arch** with a whale's rib suspended from it. It was likely a souvenir brought home by a traveling merchant, reminding the townspeople of a big world out there. On your left is...*

❽ Piazza dei Signori

Literally the "square of the lords," this is Verona's sitting room, more quiet and harmonious than Piazza Erbe. The buildings—which span five centuries—define the square and are all linked by arches. The long portico on the left is inspired by Brunelleschi's Hospital of the Innocents (considered the first Renaissance building) in Florence.

Locals call the square Piazza Dante for the statue of the Italian poet Dante Alighieri that dominates it. Dante—always pensive, never smiling—seems to wonder why the tourists choose Juliet over him. Dante was expelled from Florence for political reasons and was granted asylum in Verona by the Scaligeri family. With the whale's rib behind you, you're facing the brick, crenellated, 13th-century Scaligeri residence. Behind Dante is the yellowish, 15th-century, Venetian Renaissance–style Portico of the Counsel. In front of Dante—and to his right (follow the white *WC* signs) is the 12th-century Romanesque **Palazzo della Ragione.**

Enter the courtyard. The impressive staircase—which goes nowhere—is the only surviving Renaissance staircase in Verona. For a grand city view, you can climb to the top of the 13th-century **Torre dei Lamberti** (€2 for stairs, €3 for elevator, Tue–Sun 8:30–19:30, Mon 13:30–19:30, last entry 45 min before closing). The elevator saves you 245 steps—but you'll still need to climb about 45 more to get to the first viewing platform. It's not worth continuing up the endless spiral stairs to the second viewing platform.

• *Exit the courtyard the way you entered and turn right, continuing downhill. Within a block, you'll find the...*

❾ Tombs of the Scaligeri Family

These exotic and very Gothic 14th-century tombs, with their fine, original, wrought-iron protective cages, evoke the age when one family ruled Verona. The Scaligeri family was to Verona what the Medici family was to Florence. Notice the dogs' heads near the top of the tombs. On the first tomb, the dogs peer over a shield displaying a ladder. The Scaligeri family got rich making ladders, but money can't buy culture. When Marco Polo returned from Asia boasting of the wealth of Kublai Khan, the Scaligeri wanted to be associated with this powerful Khan by name. But misunderstanding Khan as *"cane"* (dog), one Scaligero changed his name to Can Grande (big dog), and another to Can Signore (lord dog).

• *Continue 20 yards to the next corner and take a left on Vicolo*

Cavalletto. At the first corner, turn right and walk to the big, unfin-
ished brick facade of Verona's largest church.

❿ Church of Sant'Anastasia

This church was built from the late 13th century through the 15th
century, but the builders ran out of steam and the facade was never

finished. The highlights of the
interior are the grimacing hunch-
backs holding basins of holy water
on their backs (near entrance at
base of columns) and Pisanello's
fragmented fresco of *St. George*
and the Princess (above chapel to
right of altar). Ask for the English
brochure, which describes the
story of the church (€2.50 entry,
March–Oct Mon–Sat 9:00–18:00, Sun 13:00–18:00; Nov–Feb Sun
13:00–17:00 only).

• *Facing the church, go right and walk along its length. Take a left*
on Via Sottoriva. In a block, you'll reach a small riverfront park that
usually has a few modern-day Romeos and Juliets gazing at each other
rather than the view. Get up on the sidewalk right next to the river.

⓫ Ponte Pietra and a River View

The white stones of the Ponte Pietra are from the original Roman
bridge that stood here. After the bridge was bombed in World
War II, the Veronese fished the marble chunks out of the river to
rebuild it. From here, you can see the Roman Theater, built into
the hillside behind the green hedge (see sight listing, below). Way
above the theater is the fortress, Castello San Pietro.

Continue up the river toward the bridge. You'll pass
Gelateria Ponte Pietra (at #23), where Mirko dishes out fine
gelato (try the *riso*, open Fri–Wed 14:30 until late, closed Thu).
Then walk to the high point on the bridge. For some exercise,
break away, cross the bridge, and visit the Roman Theater or
head up to the Castello for an expansive city view (at the end
of the bridge, go up the little road called Scalone Castello San
Pietro at the end of the bridge, or climb the stairs to the left of
the theater). Me? I'll just enjoy the view from here.

• *From the bridge, look back 200 yards at the tall spire...that's where*
you're heading.

⓬ Duomo

Started in the 12th century, this church was built over a period
of centuries. Its fine facade features Romanesque carvings, while
its bright interior demonstrates a mishmash of styles and lack of

harmony. The highlights are Titian's *Assumption* (left side of nave, Mary calmly rides a cloud—direction up—to the shock and bewilderment of the crowd below), and the ruins of an older church (last wooden door, just left of high altar). These ruins are the 10th-century foundations of the Church of St. Elena (closed Nov–Feb), turned intriguingly into a modern-day chapel. Get the English description at the entrance (April–Sept Mon–Sat 10:00–17:30, Sun 13:30–17:30, shorter hours off-season and closed Mon Nov–Feb). The peaceful Romanesque cloister is to the right as you leave the church, with mosaics from a fifth-century Christian church exposed below the walk.

SIGHTS AND ACTIVITIES

▲▲**Evening *Passeggiata***—For me, the highlight of Verona is the *passeggiata* (stroll)—especially in the evening. Make a big circle from Piazza Brà through the old town on Via Mazzini (one of Europe's many "first" pedestrian-only streets) to the colorful Piazza Erbe, and then back up Corso Porta Borsari to Piazza Brà. Consider a small town, where people know each other, all out on parade. Like peacocks, the young and nubile spread their wings. The classy shop windows are integral to the *passeggiata* as, for the ladies, shopping is a sport. Their never-finished wardrobes are considered a work in progress. This is when they gather ideas.

▲ **Castelvecchio**—Verona's powerful Scaligeri family built this castle (1343–1356) as both a residence and a fortress. Today, this 14th-century brick fantasy is a museum showing off Verona's glory days (€4, free first Sun of month, Mon 13:30–19:30, Tue–Sun 8:30–19:30, last entry 45 min before closing, good English descriptions on sheets throughout, audioguide-€3.60 or €5.25/2 people). Locals simply appreciate the elegant and balanced design of the building. Many drop in for a stroll on the Sundays it's free. The pedestrian bridge behind the castle is a favorite for wedding-day photos.

The **ground floor** houses early Christian statues that were once vibrantly colored (notice faint traces of paint). The homier first floor held the castle's residential rooms (original wooden ceilings, traces of frescoes, religious paintings).

The **second floor** takes you out of the Middle Ages and into the Renaissance (paintings now have secular themes). Displayed on this floor are fine ancient bronze and gold artifacts and a collection of hair-raising medieval weaponry—pikes, halberds, helmets, breastplates, and enormous broadswords. Climb the skinny stairway on the far side of the armaments exhibit for a grand view from the battlements.

▲ **Basilica of San Zeno Maggiore**—This church is dedicated to the patron saint of Verona, whose remains are buried in the crypt under the main altar. In addition to being a fine example of Italian Romanesque, the basilica features Mantegna's *San Zeno Triptych* (which will probably be on the road through 2008), with its marvelous perspective, peaceful double-columned cloisters, and a set of 48 paneled 11th-century bronze doors nicknamed "the poor man's Bible." Pretend you're an illiterate medieval peasant and do some reading. Facing the altar, on the walls of the right-side aisle, you can see frescoes painted on top of other frescoes and graffiti dating from the 1300s. These were done by people who fled into the church in times of war or flooding and scratched prayers into the walls. Druidic-looking runes are actually decorated letters typical of the Gothic period, like those in illuminated manuscripts (March–Oct Mon–Sat 8:30–18:00, Sun 13:00–18:00; Nov–Feb Sun 13:00–18:00 only).

Roman Theater (Teatro Romano)—Dating from the first century A.D., this ancient theater was discovered in the 19th century and

restored. Admission includes the Roman Museum (high in the building above the theater, reach it via elevator—start at the stage and walk up the middle set of stairs, then continue straight on the path through the bushes).

The museum displays a model of the theater, a small Jesuit chapel, and Roman artifacts, including mosaic floors, busts and other statuary, clay and bronze votive figures, and architectural fragments. You'll find helpful English information sheets throughout (€3, free first Sun of month, Tue–Sun 8:30–19:30, Mon 13:30–19:30, last entry 45 min before closing, theater across the river near Ponte Pietra, tel. 045-800-0360). From mid-June through August, the theater stages Shakespeare plays—only a little more difficult to understand in Italian than in Elizabethan English.

Giardino Giusti—If you'd enjoy a Renaissance garden with manicured box hedges and towering cypress trees, you might find this worth the walk and fee (€5, daily 9:00–20:00, off-season 9:00 until sunset; cross river at Ponte Nuovo, continue up Via Carducci, turn left on Via Giardino Giusti).

SLEEPING

I've listed rates you'll pay in regular season. Prices soar above these in late June, July, and August (during opera season), the first week of April (during the Vinitaly wine festival), and any time of year during a trade fair or holiday. Hotel Aurora and Hotel Torcolo are my favorites for their family-run feeling.

Near Piazza Erbe

$$ Hotel Aurora, just off Piazza Erbe, has friendly family management, a terrace overlooking the piazza, and 19 fresh, air-conditioned rooms (S-€62, Sb-€100, Db-€120, Tb-€140, Qb-€200, cheaper off-season, reserve with traveler's check or personal check for deposit, elevator, nearby church bells ring the hour early, Piazza Erbe, tel. 045-594-717, fax 045-801-0860, www.hotelaurora.biz, info@hotelaurora.biz, Rita).

$ L'Ospite, a 10-minute walk from Piazza Erbe, has six cozy, immaculate, fully equipped apartments and lots of stairs. The rooms, which sleep up to four, include air-conditioning and free use of the washing machine. Kind manager Federica Rossi, who doesn't gouge during the opera season, can also help you get opera tickets (Db-€85, Qb-€140; about €35–55/person, depending on length of stay; prefers longer stays but will take one-night stands when possible; on west side of Ponte Navi bridge, a few steps past San Paolo church on the left at Via XX Settembre 3; tel. 045-803-6994, mobile 329-426-2524, www.lospite.com, info@lospite.com).

$ Hotel Arena is located in a peaceful courtyard off a busy street just west of Castelvecchio, and offers 17 very basic, institutional, quiet, and economical rooms (S-€48, Sb-€56, D-€77, Db-€87, cash only, no opera season gouging, breakfast, no air-con, a few free parking spaces—request when you reserve, 100 yards from Piazza Brà at Stradone Porta Palio #2, tel. & fax 045-803-2440,

Verona

Sleep Code

(€1 = about $1.30, country code: 39)

S = Single, **D** = Double/Twin, **T** = Triple, **Q** = Quad, **b** = bathroom, **s** = shower only. Hotels accept credit cards and provide breakfast unless otherwise noted. Everyone speaks English.

To help you easily sort through these listings, I've divided the rooms into three categories, based on the price for a standard double room with bath:

  $$$ Higher Priced—Most rooms €140 or more.
    $$ Moderately Priced—Most rooms between €100–140.
     $ Lower Priced—Most rooms €100 or less.

Verona Hotels and Restaurants

1 Bus to Station
2 Bus from Station
3 Hotel Aurora
4 To L'Ospite Apartments
5 To Hotel Arena
6 Hotel Bologna
7 Hotel Giulietta e Romeo
8 Hotel Europa
9 Hotel Torcolo
10 Locanda Catullo
11 To Villa Francescatti Hostel

12 Osteria al Duca
13 Ristorante Greppia
14 Bottega del Vin
15 Osteria le Vecete &
   Pizzeria Du de Cope
16 Enoteca Can Grande
17 Trattoria al Pompiere
18 Rist. Olivo & Brek Cafeteria
19 PAM Supermarket
20 Internet Cafés (2)

www.albergoarena.it, info@albergoarena.it).

Near Piazza Brà

You'll find several options in the quiet streets just off Piazza Brà, within 200 yards of the bus stop. From the square, yellow signs point you to the hotels.

$$$ Hotel Bologna, located a half block of the Roman Arena, has 30 bright, classy, and well-maintained rooms; attractive public areas; and an attached restaurant (Sb-€100, Db-€140, Tb-€175, air-con, Piazzetta Scalette Rubiani 3, tel. 045-800-6830, fax 045-801-0602, www.hotelbologna.vr.it, hotelbologna@tin.it).

$$$ Hotel Giulietta e Romeo is on a quiet side street just 50 yards behind the Roman Arena. Its 30 well-designed rooms (nine with balconies) are decorated in dark colors, but on the plus side, they have non-smoking rooms and don't take tour groups (Sb-€80–120, Db-€105–190, prices vary with season, air-con, elevator, free loaner bikes, laundry, garage-€16/day, Vicolo Tre Marchetti 3, tel. 045-800-3554, fax 045-801-0862, www.giuliettaeromeo.com, info@giuliettaeromeo.com).

$$ Hotel Europa offers sleek, modern comfort. Nearly half of its 46 rooms are non-smoking and a few rooms have little balconies overlooking the *piazzetta* below (Db-€130, off-season mention this book through 2008 when you reserve for a discount, air-con, elevator, Via Roma 8, tel. 045-594-744, fax 045-800-1852, www.veronahoteleuropa.com, hoteleuropavr@tiscali.it).

$ Hotel Torcolo offers 19 comfortable, lovingly maintained, non-smoking rooms (Sb-€65, Db-€100, €8–13 breakfast is optional except during opera season, air-con, fridge in room, elevator; standing on Piazza Brà with your back to the gardens and the Roman Arena over your right shoulder, head down the alley to the right of #16 and walk to Vicolo Listone 3; tel. 045-800-7512, fax 045-800-4058, www.hoteltorcolo.it, hoteltorcolo@virgilio.it, well-run by Silvia, Diana, and helpful Caterina).

Between Piazza Brà and Piazza Erbe

$ Locanda Catullo is an inexpensive, quiet, and quirky place deep in the old town, with 21 basic rooms up three flights of stairs. Prices are always the same. To book during the opera season—when they enforce a three-night minimum—you must prepay the entire amount by personal check or bank transfer (they'll explain the procedure). Otherwise, they generally have space and will hold a room with a phone call the day before (S-€40, D-€55, Db-€65, Q-€105, Qb-€125, cash only, no breakfast; go left off Via Mazzini onto Via Catullo, down an alley between 1D and 3A at Via Valerio Catullo 1; tel. 045-800-2786, fax 045-596-987, locandacatullo@tiscali.it, a leetle English spoken).

Hostel

$ Villa Francescatti is a good hostel (€14–16 beds with breakfast, 6-, 8-, and 10-bed rooms, some family rooms with private bathrooms, €8 dinners, launderette, rooms closed from 9:00 to 17:00 but reception open all day, 24:00 curfew; bus #73 from train station on weekdays or #90 at night and Sun to Piazza Isolo stop, walk over the river beyond Ponte Nuovo at Salita Fontana del Ferro 15; tel. 045-590-360, fax 045-800-9127).

EATING

Osteria al Duca is a fun, family-run place with a lively atmosphere and a winning formula. Locals line up twice a night (seatings at 19:30 and 21:30) for its affordable, two-course, €15 fixed-price meal. I much prefer their ground floor (*piano terra*—worth requesting). Reservations are a must—easier at 19:30 (closed Sun, half-block from Scaligeri family tombs at Via Arche Scaligere 2, tel. 045-594-474).

Ristorante Greppia serves typical *cucina Veronese* outside on a quiet courtyard or inside its elegant dining room (€8 pastas, €12 *secondi*, Tue–Sun 12:00–14:30 & 19:00–22:30, closed Mon, Vicolo Samaritana 3, first left off Via Mazzini if you're coming from Piazza Erbe, tel. 045-800-4577).

Bottega del Vin is pricey, venerable, and proud to have a sister establishment in New York City. Under a high ceiling and walls of wine bottles, brisk black-vested waiters match traditional dishes (polenta, duck, game) with glasses of fine wine. Choose from 50 open bottles—glasses range from €1 to €14. The wait staff, ambience, and food have deep roots in local culture. I like their front room best. Reservations are smart (€10 pastas, €20 *secondi*, Wed–Mon 12:00–15:00 & 19:00–24:00, closed Tue, good daily specials, take second left off Via Mazzini as you're coming from Piazza Erbe, Via Scudo di Francia 3, tel. 045-800-4535).

Osteria le Vecete consists of just one room under open beams and walls of wine. It has an enjoyable, intimate pub setting. Choose from a dozen or so daily specials of homemade pastas and Veronese specialties—as well as simpler *bruschette* and salads—or select a few of the elaborately dressed *tartine farcite* (little open-faced *crostini* sandwiches, €1.20 each) available in the case. The blackboard lists a good selection of wine by the glass (€8 pastas, €16 *secondi*, kitchen open daily 12:30–14:30 & 18:30–22:30, drinks and snacks are served between mealtimes and until late; buried in an alley between Via Mazzini and Corso Sant'Anastasia: from Piazza Brà, go down Via Mazzini and turn left onto Via Quattro Spade, then right onto Via Pelliciai—restaurant is about a half-block down on your left at #32A; tel. 045-594-748).

The Wines of Verona

Wine connoisseurs love the high-quality wines of this area. The hills to the east are covered with grapes to make Soave; to the north is Valpolicella country; and Bardolino comes from vineyards to the west.

Valpolicella grapes, which are used to make the fruity, red Valpolicella table wine (found everywhere), are also used to make the full-bodied red Amarone and the sweet dessert wine, Recioto. To produce Amarone, grapes are partially dried (*passito*) before fermentation, then aged for a minimum of four years in oak casks, resulting in a rich, velvety, full-bodied red. Recioto, which in local dialect means "ears," uses only the grapes from the top of the cluster (so they sort of look like the ears of a face). Because these grapes get the most sun, they mature the fastest and have the highest concentration of sugar. The grapes are dried for months until all moisture has gone out before pressing, and aged for one to three years.

Bardolino, from the vineyards near Lake Garda, is a light, fruity wine, like a French Beaujolais. It's a perfect picnic wine.

Soave, which might be Italy's best-known white wine, goes well with seafood and risotto dishes. While Soave can vary widely in quality, the best are called "Soave Classico" and come from the heart of the region, near the Soave Castle. Soave is sometimes aged in oak casks, giving it a mellow, rounded flavor.

Sample these and many others at the numerous *enoteca*s (wine-tasting bars) or any restaurant around town. The first week of every April, Verona hosts Vinitaly, the most important international convention of domestic and international wines. Vintners vie for prestigious awards for the past year's vintage. Tourists are welcome to attend at the end of the week, and are shuttled to the convention hall from Piazza Brà. Hotels book up months in advance. Check with the TI for more details.

If you're visiting the area in the fall, consider a day trip to nearby Monteforte d'Alpone, east of Verona. The town hosts a fun, raucous wine festival in September—ask at the TI for more information on this and other regional wine festivals.

Pizzeria Du de Cope buzzes with smartly attired young waiters and locals who consider the pizza to be the best in town. This high-energy, trendy place feels like the casual sidekick of a Michelin star restaurant—which, in fact, it is (big €9 salads, €9 pizzas, Wed–Mon 12:00–14:30 & 18:30–23:00, closed Tue, flamboyant desserts, family-friendly, no reservations, sit inside or out, next to Osteria le Vecete at Galleria Pellicciai 10, tel. 045-595-562).

Enoteca Can Grande enjoys turning people on to great, well-matched food and wine. Their cold plates, designed for wine appreciation, make a fine main dish. I'd trust Giuliano and Corrina with a creative meal (just set a limit, such as €25 per person plus wine). A festival of *antipasti* treats, followed by a creative pasta with a sampling of top wines by the glass, can be a gourmet experience for a reasonable price (Wed–Mon 12:00–15:30 & 18:00–24:00, closed Tue, a block off Piazza Brà at Via Dietro Liston 19D—if the equestrian statue jogged slightly right, he'd head straight here, tel. 045-595-022).

Trattoria al Pompiere, which has a commitment to regional traditions, is a favorite of foodies and has earned its huge local following. Amid the bustle (contained by walls plastered with photos of local big shots), Stefano and his gang serve gourmet meats and cheeses as *antipasti,* ideal for a mixed plate to complement the huge selection of fine wines. There's not a bad table in this grand, old-style dining room. Reservations are wise (€11 pastas, €14 *secondi,* Mon–Sat 12:30–14:00 & 19:30–22:30, closed Sun, lady's menus without prices, very nice house wine, Vicolo Regina d'Ungheria 5, tel. 045-803-0537).

Eating on Piazza Brà: A cancan of nondescript restaurants line the *passeggiata* action along Piazza Brà. Of course, you sacrifice service, value, and quality for the view—but the view can make it a great deal. Survey the scene and grab a table to enjoy the floodlit Roman Arena and Verona on parade. **Ristorante Olivo,** with a small menu and decent prices, is a good bet. For fast food with a superb view of Verona's main square, consider **Brek,** a modern and well-run self-service cafeteria (daily, breakfast and sandwiches from 9:30, full menu 11:30–15:00 & 18:30–22:00, indoor/outdoor seating, cheap salad plates, right on the square between historic city gate and equestrian statue at Piazza Brà 20, tel. 045-800-4561).

Eating Cheap near Piazza Brà: PAM supermarket is just outside the historic gate on Piazza Brà (daily 8:00–20:30, exit Piazza Brà through the gate and take the first right). The döner kebab place—just behind Hotel Europa and a few steps off Via Roma—is cheap, fast, and not Italian (great €4 meals).

TRANSPORTATION CONNECTIONS

From Verona by Train to: Venice (2/hr, 90 min), **Padua** (2/hr, 1 hr), **Florence** (about hourly with transfer in Bologna, 3 hrs, note that all Rome-bound trains stop in Florence—listed as *Firenze* on train schedules), **Bologna** (nearly hourly, 2 hrs), **Milan** (hourly, 1.5–2 hrs), **Rome** (4/day, 5–6 hrs, more with transfer in Bologna or Padua), **Bolzano** (hourly, 1.5–2 hrs; note that Brennero-bound trains stop in Bolzano).

VENETIAN HISTORY

SAILING THE SEVEN SEAS— THE RISE OF A GRAND CITY

People didn't live on the islands of the Venetian lagoon in Roman times. But the region had many important mainland cities. Convoys of Roman ships connected the major ports of Ravenna and Aquileia (then the fourth-largest Roman city) by navigating a series of lagoons they called "the Seven Seas" (hence the term we use today).

In the fifth century, when Rome fell, barbarian Visigoths and Huns ravaged the farmers of this area. Hoping the barbarians didn't like water, the first "Venetians" took refuge in the lagoon. For centuries there was no Venice as such...just a series of about a dozen principal refugee settlements.

The lagoon is a delta littered with tiny, muddy islands created by sediment deposited by rivers. As refugees squatted on this wet and miserable land, they kept certain streams from silting, and these streams gradually became canals. A motley collection of about 120 natural islands would eventually become Venice.

From the start, these former farmers harvested salt and fish for their livelihood. Later, using business savvy gained from the salt-and-fish business, they began trading up the rivers. With the expansion of Byzantium into Italy, East–West trade grew, and Ravenna became the western capital of a briefly united East and West under Byzantine Emperor Justinian. After Ravenna fell, Venetians filled the void as middlemen, selling goods from the East to consumers in the West.

In the sixth century, another wave of barbarians (the Lombards) plundered the mainland. This time attacking cities, they sent a new kind of refugee into the lagoon: shopkeepers,

---

Venetian History in a Seashell

In the Middle Ages, the Venetians became Europe's clever middlemen for East–West trade, creating a great trading empire ruled by a series of doges. By smuggling in the bones of St. Mark (San Marco, A.D. 828), Venice gained religious importance as well. With the discovery of America and new trading routes to the Orient, Venetian power ebbed. But as Venice fell, her appetite for decadence grew. Throughout the 17th and 18th centuries, Venice partied on the wealth accumulated in earlier centuries as a trading power.

---

clergymen, artisans, and nobles.

Previously, the farmers had subsisted without much need to organize. But with the arrival of aggressive noble families, the lagoon became political. To sort out the squabbles, a local duke, or doge, was elected in 726. This began an 1,100-year period of doge rule, ending only with the arrival of Napoleon in 1797.

The doge needed a capital, and he chose the town of Rialto (the future Venice) for its easy-to-defend position. Over time, the most important trading nobles built their palaces in Rialto to be near the doge.

Because nobles settled on their own little islets, palaces are scattered all over the current city. Eventually, island communities decided to join, or "bridge," with others. Building bridges required shoring up the canals. Soon, paved canal-side walks appeared. And by the 12th century, the government provided oil and required that streets be lit—a first in Europe.

Feudalism didn't really work in the lagoon economy. The natural entrepreneurial energy of the nobility instead created the "noble merchant." Trade, which became the exclusive privilege of the upper classes, grew, thus supporting a larger, wealthier population. Suddenly, people (like both the Byzantine and Holy Roman emperors) were noticing Venice. Charlemagne, the Holy Roman Emperor (c. 800), eyed the region hungrily.

Venetians wanted to keep their freedom, but knew that they would have to choose: Byzantium or the Holy Roman Empire. Byzantium—its capital in far-away Constantinople (now called Istanbul)—was preferable. On a distant fringe of that empire, Venice would be subjugated only in name. Arranging an alignment with Byzantium also involved Church politics.

In about A.D. 800, the bishop who resided in the mainland city of Aquileia, and who was loyal to the Holy Roman Emperor, was given Venice as part of his ecclesiastical domain. This subjected the people of the lagoon to the influence of the Holy Roman

Venice's Place in History

LONDON

BRUGES

PARIS

VIENNA

GENOA

VENICE

RAVENNA

PISA

FLORENCE   ROME

GIBRALTAR

CON-
STAN-
TIN-
OPLE

DCH

LEPANTO

CRETE

BLACK AREA SHOWS VENETIAN
EMPIRE AT ITS PEAK –
THE 15TH CENTURY

TO HOLY LAND
& ALEXANDRIA

Emperor. To avoid this, the Venetians accepted a rival bishop who was loyal to Byzantium.

To legitimize their split with Aquileia, the Venetians of the lagoon decided they needed just the right holy relics. This area had a strong affinity for St. Mark (he traveled here as Peter's translator), the man credited with bringing Christianity to the region. Knowing the power of actually possessing the relics of St. Mark, the Venetians managed to smuggle his remains from Egypt to Rialto in 828. Overnight, it became clear: Venice was a religious power. This underscored Venice as part of the Byzantine Empire, saving it from European control. To seal the city's oriental orientation, Venetian leaders had the grand St. Mark's Basilica built in a distinctly Eastern style.

As the home of both the doge and St. Mark, and with its easily defensible position, Venice emerged as a regional powerhouse. The miscellaneous communities in the lagoon coalesced around what is now Venice. Though technically part of the Byzantine Empire, the city was so remote that, in practice, it was practically free.

Venetian merchants ran a profitable trading triangle: timber from Venice's mainland to Egypt for gold to Byzantium for luxury goods to Venice. As this went round and round, Venice amassed lots of capital, and its merchant fleet grew to be the biggest in the Mediterranean. Back then, a fleet was essentially the same as a navy, making Venice a military power. Venice agreed, quite cleverly, to defend Byzantine and Crusader ports in return for free-trade privileges. This made the eastern Mediterranean a virtual free-trade zone for a very aggressive Venetian trading community to exploit.

As Venetian nobles grew wealthy, they built lavish palaces. While their mainland counterparts fortified compounds with tall towers, Venetian merchants built palazzos—with a natural lagoon defense—that were luxurious rather than fortified. Palaces in Venice came complete with loading docks, warehouses, and, eventually, chandeliered ballrooms.

Later, Venice expanded its economy beyond trade. Picking up techniques from the East, it established strong local industries. Having mastered the art of making glass, Venice was on the cutting edge of the new science of grinding lenses for eyeglasses and telescopes. Understanding medicine as a chemical rather than an herbal business, the city developed Europe's first real pharmaceutical industry. Making Europe's first cheap paper from rags rather than from sheepskins (parchment) and offering the first patent protection (in 1474), the Venetian paper and printing industry boomed. Already clever at trading products from other countries, now Venice peddled its own stuff...more profitably than ever.

By 1104, Venice was running Europe's first industrial complex, the Arsenale. With more than 1,000 workers using an early form of assembly-line production, the Arsenale could produce about one warship a day. This put the "fear of Venice" into visiting rulers. When France's King Henry III dropped by the Arsenale, Venice entertained him with a shipbuilding spectacle: from ribs to finished product in four hours. Then the ship was completely outfitted before gliding down the exit canal.

With mountains of capital, plenty of traders with ready ships, and a sophisticated system of insurance, joint ventures, and money drafts, Venice's traveling merchants eventually became resident merchants and bankers. By the 15th century, Venice was a commercial powerhouse—among the six biggest cities in Europe. Of its estimated 180,000 citizens, nearly 1,000 were of Rockefeller-esque wealth and power.

But Venice's power peaked. With the Ottoman defeat of the Byzantine emperor (messing up established trading partners and patterns), Vasco da Gama's voyage to India (opening up trade routes that skirted Venetian control), the rise of English and Dutch shipping in the Mediterranean, and devastating plagues, Venice began to decline.

When Napoleon rolled into Venice, he brought with him (in theory, at least) the ideals of the French Revolution. In light of French ideas of citizens' rights, the Venetian populace re-evaluated its 1,000-year aristocratic rule, and in 1797, the last doge abdicated. A period of French and Austrian rule lasted until 1866, when Venice joined the kingdom of Italy.

TIMELINE OF VENETIAN HISTORY

A.D. 500–1000: Rome Falls, Venice Rises

With Rome's infrastructure crumbling and Italy crawling with barbarians, coastal folk fled to marshy islands in the Adriatic. They sank pilings in the mud in order to build. Fishermen became sea traders.

A.D. **476**   The last Roman emperor abdicates.

540   Byzantine Emperor Justinian reconquers Italy from the barbarians, briefly reestablishing the Roman Empire with Ravenna as its capital.

568   Lombards invade northern Italy, driving mainlanders onto sparsely populated islands in the Venetian lagoon. The Byzantine Empire in Constantinople gives aid and protection to the refugees.

697   According to legend, the first doge, Pauluccio Anafesto, is elected at Eraclea.

726   The first documented doge, Orso Ipato, begins his rule.

800   Charlemagne controls northern Italy.

828   Venice acquires St. Mark's relics from Alexandria. Possession of the famous relics gives Venice religious stature, tempering the influence of the Holy Roman Emperor.

c. 850   Tiny Venice is effectively an independent, self-ruling country.

Representative Sights

- Gondolas and the network of canals
- Old crypt under San Zaccaria Church
- San Moisè Church
- Church on Torcello Island

1000–1500: Medieval Growth as a Seafaring Trading Power

Well-located between northern Europe and the eastern Mediterranean, Venetian sea traders established trading outposts in Byzantine and Muslim territories to the east. At home, a stable, constitutional government ran an efficient, state-operated multinational corporation. Grand buildings reflected Venice's wealth.

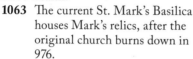

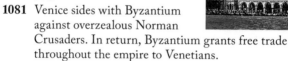

1063 The current St. Mark's Basilica houses Mark's relics, after the original church burns down in 976.

1081 Venice sides with Byzantium against overzealous Norman Crusaders. In return, Byzantium grants free trade throughout the empire to Venetians.

c. 1150 Constitutional limits are placed on the doges. The Republic is ruled by an oligarchy of wealthy families.

1204 During the Fourth Crusade, Venetian troops join other Crusaders in attacking and looting Christian Constantinople (partly to retaliate against Byzantine harassment of Venetian merchants). The booty boosts Venice further.

1261 Venice's seafaring rival, Genoa, helps the Byzantines retake Constantinople. Genoa is rewarded with trading rights in the Byzantine Empire, thus sparking a century of war over markets with Venice.

c. 1300 To avoid political coups d'état, the Venetian Senate sets constitutional limits restricting political power only to established (read: wealthy) families.

1381 Venetian ships rout Genoa's fleet at Chioggia (on the south end of the lagoon). Venice rules the waves and the sea-trade of the eastern Mediterranean.

c. 1420 After military victories in northern Italy, Venice is at the height of its power, with mainland possessions and a powerful overseas trading empire to the east. As the Turks rise in the East, a period of conflict begins, which lasts off and on until 1718.

1423 Doge Francesco Foscari starts disastrous, money-draining wars against Milan. Fending off challenges from other trading rivals such as Pisa and Amalfi takes a toll. Meanwhile, the Turks chip away at Venice's trading cities on the eastern front.

History

1453 The Turks take Constantinople. Venice suffers major losses in its eastern markets.

1454 Venice finally makes peace with Milan. Other European powers join to prey on a weakened Venice.

1492 Columbus sails the ocean blue, heading west through the Straits of Gibraltar and establishing trade in a World that's New.

1498 Vasco da Gama circles around Africa's Cape of Good Hope, finding a new sea-trade route to eastern markets. Venice's sea-trade monopoly is threatened.

Noteworthy Residents

Dandolo, Enrico (r. 1192–1205): Doge during the Fourth Crusade, when Venetian crusaders looted Constantinople, helping to enrich Venice.

Polo, Marco (1254–1324): Traveler to far-away China whose journal, *The Book of Marvels*, many dismissed as fiction.

Veneziano, Paolo (1310–1358): Painter who mastered the Byzantine gold-icon style, then added touches of Western realism.

Foscari, Francesco (1373–1457): Doge at Venice's peak of power, whose ill-advised wars against Milan and Turks started the Republic's slow fade.

Bellini, Jacopo (c. 1400–1470): Father of painting family. His training in Renaissance Florence brought 3-D realism to Venice.

Bellini, Gentile (c. 1429–1507): Elder son of painting family, known for straightforward, historical scenes of Venice.

Representative Sights

- Doge's Palace
- St. Mark's Basilica
- Frari Church
- Buildings decorated in ornate Venetian Gothic style
- Doge paraphernalia and city history at Correr Museum
- Glass and lace industries
- Arsenale shipbuilding complex

1500–1600: Renaissance and Slow Fade

Europe's richest city-state poured money into the arts...even as her power was waning. Venice established a reputation as a luxury-loving, exotic, cosmopolitan playground.

c. 1500 Though waning in power, Venice is a Renaissance cultural capital. Titian, Tintoretto, Sansovino, and Palladio all call her home.

1509 Pig pile on Venice—a European alliance of the pope, northern Italians, and northern Europeans defeat Venice at Agnadello. Meanwhile, the Turks keep pecking away in the east.

1571 At the Battle of Lepanto, Venice and European allies score a temporary victory over the Turks. Unfortunately, it's only a moral victory, as Venice's navy suffers major damage, and the city loses more trading rights. Spain, England, and Holland, with their ocean-going vessels, emerge as superior traders in a more global economy.

1669 Crete, the last major Venetian outpost, falls to the Turks.

Noteworthy Residents

Bellini, Giovanni (c. 1430–1516): The most famous son in the painting family, whose glowing, colorful, 3-D Madonna-and-Childs started the Venetian Renaissance. Teacher of Titian and Giorgione.

Carpaccio, Vittore (c. 1460–1525): Painter of realistic, secular scenes.

Giorgione (c. 1477–1511): Innovative painter whose moody realism influenced Bellini (his teacher) and Titian (his friend and fellow painter).

Sansovino, Jacopo (1486–1570): Renaissance architect who redid the face of Venice (especially St. Mark's Square), introducing sober, classical columns and arches to a city previously full of ornate Gothic.

Titian (Tiziano Vecellio, 1488–1576): Premier Venetian Renaissance painter. Master of many styles, from teenage Madonnas to sober state portraits to exuberant mythological scenes to centerfold nudes.

Palladio, Andrea (1508–1580): Influential architect whose classical style was much-imitated around the world, resulting in villas, government buildings, and banks that look like Greek temples.

Tintoretto (Jacopo Robusti, c. 1518–1594): Painter of dramatic religious scenes, using strong 3-D, diagonal compositions, twisting poses, sharp contrast of light and shadow, and bright, "black velvet" colors (late Renaissance/Mannerist style).

Veronese, Paolo (1528–1588): Painter of big, colorful canvases, capturing the exuberance and luxury of Renaissance Venice.

Representative Sights
- St. Mark's Square facades and other work by Sansovino
- Palladio's classical facades on churches of San Giorgio Maggiore and Il Redentore
- Titian (Accademia, Frari Church, Doge's Palace, others)
- Giovanni Bellini (Accademia, Frari Church, San Zaccaria Church, Correr Museum)
- Giorgione (Accademia)
- Tintoretto (Accademia, Scuola San Rocco, many churches)
- Jewish Ghetto and Jewish Museum

1600–1800: Elegant Decline

New trade routes, new European powers, and belligerent Turks drained Venice's economy and shrank its trading empire. At home, however, Venice's reputation for luxury—and decadence—still made it a popular tourist destination for Europe's gentry.

1718 The Turks drive Venetians from southern Greece. Venice's once-great trading empire in the eastern Mediterranean is over.

1797 Napoleon invades Venice and deposes the last doge.

Noteworthy Residents

Monteverdi, Claudio (1567–1643): The composer and *maestro di capella* at St. Mark's Basilica who wrote in a budding new medium—opera.

Longhena, Baldassare (1598–1682): Architect of the Baroque-style La Salute Church.

Vivaldi, Antonio (1678–1741): Composer of *Four Seasons* ("Dah dunt-dunt-duh dutta dah-ah-ah").

Tiepolo, Giovanni Battista (1696–1770): Painter of mythological subjects in colorful, Rococo ceilings.

Canaletto, Antonio (1697–1768): Painter of photo-realist Venice views.

Goldoni, Carlo (1707–1793): Comic playwright who brought refinement to *Commedia dell'Arte* buffoonery.

Guardi, Francesco (1712–1793): Painter of proto-Impressionist Venice views.

Casanova, Giovanni Giacomo (1725–1798): Gambler, womanizer, and adventurer whose exaggerated memoirs inspired Romantics.

Tiepolo, Giovanni Domenico (1727–1804): Painter son of

the famous Giovanni Battista Tiepolo.

Da Ponte, Lorenzo (1749–1838): Mozart's librettist who popularized Venice's sophisticated and decadent high society.

Canova, Antonio (1757–1822): Neoclassical sculptor whose polished, white, beautiful statues were especially popular in Napoleon's France.

Representative Sights

- Ca' Rezzonico (Museum of 18th-century Venice)
- La Salute Church
- Masks of the Carnevale tradition
- Old cafés (e.g., the Florian and the Quadri)
- La Fenice opera house
- Baroque interiors in many churches
- Canova sculpture (Correr Museum, Frari Church)
- G. B. Tiepolo paintings (Accademia, Doge's Palace, Ca' Rezzonico)
- Paintings of Canaletto, Guardi, and G. D. Tiepolo (Ca' Rezzonico)

1800–2007: Modern Venice

Conquered by Napoleon, then placed under Austrian rule, the Venetians joined Italy's Risorgimento movement, resulting in the unified, democratic nation of Italy. Because little new building was done in the city, Venice remained a museum piece for foreigners—one increasingly threatened by mainland pollution, floods, and hordes of tourists.

1815 After the Battle of Waterloo, Europe's kings put Venice under Austrian rule. Young aristocrats visit Venice on the Grand Tour; British culture dominates.

1846 A two-mile railroad causeway links Venice to the mainland.

1848 Daniele Manin, an influential lawyer, briefly establishes an independent, democratic Venetian Republic, but the revolution is soon crushed by Austrian troops.

1866 After Prussia defeats Austria, Venice is freed to join the new, modern, democratic kingdom of Italy.

1932 A highway running parallel to the causeway is built, bringing cars to Venice's edge.

c. 1950 Unbridled industrialization on the mainland produces pollution (sulfuric acid) and threatens Venice's stone monuments.

1966 Venice suffers a disastrous flood.

c. 1985 Plans are made to control flooding with a sea barrier (the Moses Project). The project was funded in 2003...but no construction has occurred yet.

1996 La Fenice opera house burns down.

2003 After an international reconstruction effort, La Fenice reopens

2008 You arrive in Venice to add to the city's illustrious history.

Noteworthy Residents

Manin, Daniele (1804–1857): Rebel who led Venetian revolt (1848) against the city's Austrian rulers, eventually leading to united, democratic, modern Italy.

Guggenheim, Peggy (1898–1979): American-born art collector, gallery owner, and friend of modern art and artists.

Representative Sights

- Correr Museum's Risorgimento wing
- Statue of Daniele Manin
- Motorized *vaporetti* and taxis
- Train station (1954)
- Peggy Guggenheim Collection
- The Biennale International Art Exhibition
- Pollution from the mainland city of Mestre, Burger King

History

APPENDIX

CONTENTS

RESOURCES

Tourist Offices in the US

Before you go, you can contact the nearest Italian tourist office (abbreviated **TI** in this book) in the US to briefly describe your trip and request information. You'll get the general packet and, if you ask for specifics (city map, calendar of festivals, etc.), an impressive amount of help. If you have a specific problem, they're a good source of sympathy. Their website is www.italiantourism.com.

Their offices are...

In New York: Tel. 212/245-5618, brochure hotline tel. 212/245-4822, fax 212/586-9249, enitny@italiantourism.com; 630 Fifth Ave. #1565, New York, NY 10111.

In Illinois: Tel. 312/644-0996, fax 312/644-3019, enitch @italiantourism.com; 500 N. Michigan Ave. #2240, Chicago, IL 60611.

In California: Tel. 310/820-1898, fax 310/820-6357, enitla @italiantourism.com; 12400 Wilshire Blvd. #550, Los Angeles, CA 90025.

Websites on Venice: Good online resources include www .turismovenezia.it (Tourist Board of Venice), www.veniceforvisitors .com, www.museiciviciveneziani.it (civic museums in Venice), www.venicexplorer.net (interactive maps), www.meetingvenice.it, and www.aguestinvenice.com.

Websites on Italy: Consider visiting www.italiantourism.com (Italian Tourist Board in the US), www.museionline.it (museums in Italy), and www.trenitalia.com (train info and schedules).

More Resources from Rick Steves

Guidebooks and Online Updates

This book is updated every year—but as soon as you pin Italy down, it wiggles. For the latest, visit www.ricksteves.com/update. Also at my website, you'll find a valuable list of reports and experiences—

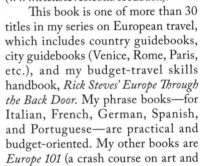

good and bad—from fellow travelers (www.ricksteves.com/feedback).

This book is one of more than 30 titles in my series on European travel, which includes country guidebooks, city guidebooks (Venice, Rome, Paris, etc.), and my budget-travel skills handbook, *Rick Steves' Europe Through the Back Door*. My phrase books—for Italian, French, German, Spanish, and Portuguese—are practical and budget-oriented. My other books are *Europe 101* (a crash course on art and history, newly expanded and in full color), *European Christmas* (on traditional and modern-day celebrations), and *Postcards from Europe* (a fun memoir of my travels over 25 years, offering an insight into Florentine culture that you won't find in guidebooks). For a complete list of my books, see the inside of the last page of this book.

Public Television and Radio Shows

My TV series, *Rick Steves' Europe,* covers European destinations in 70 shows, with 13 episodes on Italy. My weekly public radio show, *Travel with Rick Steves,* features interviews with travel experts from around the world, including several hours on Italy and Italian culture. All the TV scripts and radio shows (which are easy and free to download to an MP3 player) are at www.ricksteves.com.

Free Audio Tours for Venice

New for 2008, Rick Steves and Gene Openshaw (the co-authors of this book) have produced a free series of self-guided audio tours—of the Grand Canal, St. Mark's Square, and St. Mark's Basilica—for users of iPods and other MP3 players.

Begin Your Trip at www.ricksteves.com

At our travel website, you'll find a wealth of free information on European destinations, including fresh monthly news and

helpful tips from thousands of fellow travelers.

Our **online Travel Store** offers travel bags and accessories specially designed by Rick Steves to help you travel smarter and lighter. These include Rick's popular carry-on bags (wheeled and rucksack versions), money belts, totes, toiletries kits, adapters, other accessories, and a wide selection of guidebooks, planning maps, and DVDs.

Choosing the right **railpass** for your trip—amidst hundreds of options—can drive you nutty. We'll help you choose the best pass for your needs, plus give you a bunch of free extras.

Rick Steves' Europe Through the Back Door travel company offers **tours** with more than two dozen itineraries and 450 departures reaching the best destinations in this book... and beyond. Our Italy tours include "the best of" in 17 days, Village Italy in 14 days, South Italy in 13 days, Sicily in 12 days, Venice–Florence–Rome in 10 days, and week-long city tours (one for Rome and one for Florence). You'll enjoy great guides, a fun bunch of travel partners (with small groups of generally around 25), and plenty of room to spread out in a big, comfy bus. You'll find European adventures to fit every vacation length. For all the details, and to get our Tour Catalog and a free *Rick Steves Tour Experience* DVD (filmed on location during an actual tour), visit www.ricksteves.com or call us at 425-608-4217.

Appendix

The tours, based on this book, allow you to focus on what you're seeing rather than what you're reading. Additional walking tours are available for Florence, Rome, and Paris, covering the greatest sights of these magnificent cities.

These free tours are available through iTunes and at www.ricksteves .com after January 2008. Simply download them onto your computer and transfer them to your iPod or MP3 player. (Don't forget to bring a Y-jack

and extra set of ear buds for your travel partner.)

Maps

The maps in this book are drawn by Dave Hoerlein, who is well-traveled in Italy. Dave's maps help you locate recommended places and get to the tourist information offices, where you can pick up a more in-depth map (usually free) of the city or region. More detailed maps are also sold at newsstands and bookstores—look before you buy to be sure the map has the level of detail you want. For drivers, I'd recommend a 1:200,000- or 1:300,000-scale map.

Other Guidebooks

For most travelers, this book is all you need. But when you consider the improvements they'll make in your $3,000 vacation, $25 or $35 for extra maps and books is money well spent. The Access guide (which combines Venice and Florence) is well-researched, organized by neighborhood, and color-coded for sights, hotels, and restaurants. Focusing mainly on sights, the colorful Eyewitness guide (on Venice and Veneto) is fun for its great graphics and photos, but it's relatively skimpy on content and weighs a ton. (Their *Top 10 Venice* book, which features top-10 lists, is lighter.) You can buy these in Venice (no more expensive than in the US) or simply borrow them for a minute from other travelers at certain sights to make sure you're aware of that place's highlights. In Venice, local guidebooks (sold at kiosks) are cheap and give you a map and a decent commentary on the sights.

Recommended Books and Movies

To get the feel of Venice past and present, consider reading some of these books or seeing these films:

Non-Fiction

A History of Venice (Norwich) covers the city from its beginnings until Napoleon ended the Republic's independence. *Venice: A Maritime Republic* (Lane) explains how dominance on the high seas brought in piles of riches. *Venice: Lion City* (Wills), another city history, has a more academic tone. *Francesco's Venice* (da Mosto), based on a BBC series, balances history with coffee-table-book illustrations.

Filled with stories of a woman abroad, *Venice Observed* rings with Mary McCarthy's engaging voice. *The City of Falling Angels,* by bestselling author John Berendt, hinges on a devastating fire at La Fenice Opera House. Based on once-hidden letters found in a palazzo, *A Venetian Affair* (di Robilant) tells a true love story. *Venice: A Cultural and Literary Companion* (Garrett) also covers the nearby islands, while *A Literary Companion to Venice* (Littlewood) includes walking tours of the city, as does *Strolling Through Venice* (Freely). For a traveler's insight into Venice, consider picking up Barrie Kerper's *Venice: The Collected Traveler.*

Fiction
Henry James set many of his best books in Venice, including *The Wings of the Dove, Italian Hours,* and *The Aspern Papers and Other Stories.* Thomas Mann also chose this city for his doomed tale *Death in Venice.*

Invisible Cities (Calvino) takes place during the era of Genghis Khan and Marco Polo, while *The Palace: A Novel* (St. Aubin de Terán) has the Italian Risorgimento as its backdrop. Set in the Napoleonic era, *The Passion* (Winterson) is both a complex love story and a work of literary fiction. *In the Company of the Courtesan* (Dunant) is a novel that chronicles the drama and romances of Renaissance Venice.

Venice's murky waters make a perfect setting for intrigue. Mystery fans will enjoy *Dead Lagoon* (Dibdin), *Dirge for a Doge* (Eyre), *Stone Virgin* (Unsworth), and *The Haunted Hotel* (Collins). In *Death at La Fenice,* one of a dozen of her novels set in Venice, Donna Leon chronicles the adventures of detective Guido Brunetti and his wife Paola.

Films
Summertime (1955) sends melancholy Katherine Hepburn to Venice for romance. *Death in Venice* (1971), based on the book (see above), shows the devastating impact of a troubling infatuation.

Only You (1994) is a cute (and even sappy) love story, while *Bread and Tulips* (2000)—equally romantic, but firmly grounded in reality—shows the power of Venice in reviving a wounded soul. *Dangerous Beauty* (1998), meanwhile, keeps love out of the picture in the story of a 16th-century prostitute.

The 2003 version of *The Italian Job* begins its fluffy, fun crime caper in Venice (before ending in L.A.). Shakespeare fans will appreciate *The Merchant of Venice* (2004), which won raves for Al Pacino. The Woody Allen musical *Everyone Says I Love You* (1997) is partially set in Venice. Another recent Hollywood flick filmed here is *Casanova* (2005), starring Heath Ledger as the master of *amore.*

TELEPHONES, EMAIL, AND MAIL
Telephones
Smart travelers learn the phone system and use it daily to reserve or reconfirm rooms, get tourist information, reserve restaurants, confirm tour times, or phone home.

Types of Phones

You'll encounter various kinds of phones on your trip:

Card-operated phones—where you insert a locally bought phone card into a public pay phone—are common in Europe.

Coin-operated phones, the original kind of pay phone, require you to have enough change to complete your call.

Hotel room phones are sometimes cheap for local calls (confirm at the front desk first), but can be a rip-off for long-distance calls unless you use an international phone card (described below). But incoming calls are free, making this a cheap way for friends and family to stay in touch, provided they have a good long-distance plan for calls to Europe.

American mobile phones work in Europe if they're GSM-enabled, tri-band or quad-band, and on a calling plan that includes international calls. They're convenient but pricey. For example, with a T-Mobile phone, you'll pay $1 per minute for calls.

European mobile phones run about $75 (for the most basic models) and come without contracts. If you don't speak Italian, the mechanics of using these phones is almost impossible, but any young Italian can bail you out in a snap. These phones are loaded with prepaid calling time that you can recharge as you use up the minutes. As long as you're not "roaming" outside the phone's home country, incoming calls are free. If you're traveling to multiple countries within Europe, make sure the phone is electronically "unlocked," so that you can swap 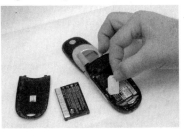 out its SIM card (a fingernail-sized chip that holds the phone's information) for a new one in other countries.

Using Phone Cards

Get a phone card for your calls. Prepaid phone cards come in two types: international and insertable (both described below). Neither type of card works outside of Italy. While traveling, you can share either type of card with your companions (and, in the case of an international phone card, your buddy doesn't even need the actual card—just the numbers on it). If you have time left on a card when you leave the country (as you likely will), simply give it to another traveler—anyone can use it.

You'll get the best deal with an **international phone card.** It enables you to make calls to the US for as little as two cents per minute, and also works for local calls. You can use these cards from any phone, including the one in your hotel room (check to make sure your phone is set on tone instead of pulse, and ask the hotel

---

Important Phone Numbers

Consulates and Embassies
Nearest US Consulate: tel. 02-290-351 (Via Principe Amedeo 2/10, Milan, http://milan.usconsulate.gov)
Nearest Canadian Embassy: tel. 06-854-441 (Via Zara 30, Rome, www.canada.it)

Emergency
Emergency (English-speaking police help): 113
Ambulance: 118
Road Service: 116

Assistance
Telephone Help (in English; free directory assistance): 170
Directory Assistance (for €0.50, an Italian-speaking robot gives the number twice, very clearly): 12

---

about hidden fees on toll-free calls). You can buy the cards at small newsstand kiosks, *tabacchi* (tobacco) shops, Internet cafés, hostels, and hole-in-the-wall long-distance phone shops. Because there are so many brand names, simply ask for an international phone card (*carta telefonica prepagata internazionale*, KAR-tah teh-leh-FOHN-ee-kah pray-pah-GAH-tah in-ter-naht-zee-oh-NAH-lay). Tell the vendor where you'll be making most calls (*"per Stati Uniti"*—to America), and he'll select the brand with the best deal. Buy a lower denomination in case the card is a dud. I've had good luck with the Europa card, which offers 220 minutes from Italy to the US for €5.

To use an international phone card, dial the toll-free number listed on the card; you'll reach an automated operator. When prompted, dial in a scratch-to-reveal code number. Then dial your number (start with 001 for calls to the US).

Generally, you'll get more minutes—sometimes up to five times as many—if you do two things: use your international phone card from your hotel room, rather than from a pay phone, and use the local access number (if you're in that city), rather than the toll-free number (which uses up the card more quickly).

An **insertable phone card** can only be used at a pay phone. These Telecom cards, considered "official" because they're sold by Italy's phone company, give you the best deal for calls within Italy and are reasonable for international calls.

You can buy Telecom cards (in denominations of €5 or €10) at *tabacchi* shops, post offices, and machines near phone booths (many phone booths have signs indicating where the nearest phone-card sales outlet is located).

European Calling Chart

Just smile and dial, using this key:
AC = Area Code, LN = Local Number.

European Country	Calling long distance within...	Calling from the US or Canada to...	Calling from a European country to...
Austria	AC + LN	011 + 43 + AC (without the initial zero) + LN	00 + 43 + AC (without the initial zero) + LN
Belgium	LN	011 + 32 + LN (without initial zero)	00 + 32 + LN (without initial zero)
Bosnia-Herzegovina	AC + LN	011 + 387 + AC (without initial zero) + LN	00 + 387 + AC (without initial zero) + LN
Britain	AC + LN	011 + 44 + AC (without initial zero) + LN	00 + 44 + AC (without initial zero) + LN
Croatia	AC + LN	011 + 385 + AC (without initial zero) + LN	00 + 385 + AC (without initial zero) + LN
Czech Republic	LN	011 + 420 + LN	00 + 420 + LN
Denmark	LN	011 + 45 + LN	00 + 45 + LN
Estonia	LN	011 + 372 + LN	00 + 372 + LN
Finland	AC + LN	011 + 358 + AC (without initial zero) + LN	999 + 358 + AC (without initial zero) + LN
France	LN	011 + 33 + LN (without initial zero)	00 + 33 + LN (without initial zero)
Germany	AC + LN	011 + 49 + AC (without initial zero) + LN	00 + 49 + AC (without initial zero) + LN
Greece	LN	011 + 30 + LN	00 + 30 + LN
Hungary	06 + AC + LN	011 + 36 + AC + LN	00 + 36 + AC + LN
Ireland	AC + LN	011 + 353 + AC (without initial zero) + LN	00 + 353 + AC (without initial zero) + LN

Appendix

European Country	Calling long distance within ...	Calling from the US or Canada to ...	Calling from a European country to ...
Italy	LN	011 + 39 + LN	00 + 39 + LN
Montenegro	AC + LN	011 + 382 + AC (without initial zero) + LN	00 + 382 + AC (without initial zero) + LN
Netherlands	AC + LN	011 + 31 + AC (without initial zero) + LN	00 + 31 + AC (without initial zero) + LN
Norway	LN	011 + 47 + LN	00 + 47 + LN
Poland	LN	011 + 48 + LN (without initial zero)	00 + 48 + LN (without initial zero)
Portugal	LN	011 + 351 + LN	00 + 351 + LN
Slovakia	AC + LN	011 + 421 + AC (without initial zero) + LN	00 + 421 + AC (without initial zero) + LN
Slovenia	AC + LN	011 + 386 + AC (without initial zero) + LN	00 + 386 + AC (without initial zero) + LN
Spain	LN	011 + 34 + LN	00 + 34 + LN
Sweden	AC + LN	011 + 46 + AC (without initial zero) + LN	00 + 46 + AC (without initial zero) + LN
Switzerland	LN	011 + 41 + LN (without initial zero)	00 + 41 + LN (without initial zero)
Turkey	AC (if no initial zero is included, add one) + LN	011 + 90 + AC (without initial zero) + LN	00 + 90 + AC (without initial zero) + LN

- The instructions above apply whether you're calling a land line or mobile phone.
- The international access codes (the first numbers you dial when making an international call) are 011 if you're calling from the US or Canada, or 00 if you're calling from virtually anywhere in Europe (except Finland, where it's 999).
- To call the US or Canada from Europe, dial 00, then 1 (the country code for the US and Canada), then the area code and number. In short, 00 + 1 + AC + LN = Hi, Mom!

Rip off the perforated corner to "activate" the card, and then physically insert it into a slot in the pay phone. It displays how much money you have remaining on the card. Then just dial away. The price of the call is automatically deducted while you talk.

Using Hotel-Room Phones, Metered Phones, VoIP, or US Calling Cards

The phone in your **hotel room** is convenient...but expensive. While incoming calls (made by folks back home) may be the cheapest way to keep in touch, charges for *outgoing* calls can be a very unpleasant surprise. Make sure you understand all the charges and fees associated with outgoing calls before you pick up that receiver.

Dialing direct from your hotel room—without using an international phone card (described above)—is usually quite expensive for international calls. Always ask first how much you'll be charged, even for local and (supposedly) toll-free calls.

If your family has an inexpensive way to call Europe, either through a long-distance plan or prepaid calling card, have them call you in your hotel room. Give them a list of your hotels' phone numbers before you go. Then, as you travel, send them an email or make a quick pay-phone call to set up a time for them to give you a ring.

Metered phones are sometimes available in bigger post offices. You can talk all you want, then pay the bill when you leave—but be sure you know the rates before you have a lengthy conversation.

If you're traveling with a laptop, consider trying **VoIP (Voice over Internet Protocol).** With VoIP, two computers act as the phones, allowing for a free Internet-based call. The major providers are Skype (www.skype.com) and Google Talk (www.google.com/talk).

US Calling Cards (such as the ones offered by AT&T, MCI, or Sprint) are the worst option. You'll nearly always save a lot of money by paying with a phone card (see above).

How to Dial

Calling from the US to Europe, or vice versa, is simple—once you break the code. The European calling chart on page 340 will walk you through it.

Dialing Within Italy

Italy has a direct-dial phone system (no area codes). To call anywhere within Italy, just dial the number. For example, the number of one of my recommended Venice hotels is 041-520-5764. That's the number you dial whether you're calling it from Venice's train station or from Rome. Keep in mind that Italian phone numbers vary in length; a hotel can have, say, an eight-digit phone number and a nine-digit fax number.

Italy's toll-free numbers start with 800 (like US 800 numbers, though in Italy you don't dial a 1 first). In Italy, these 800 numbers—called *freephone* or *numero verde* (green number)—can be dialed free from any phone without using a phone card or coins. Note that you can't call Italy's toll-free numbers from America, nor can you count on reaching America's toll-free numbers from Italy.

Dialing Internationally

If you want to make an international call, follow these three steps:

1) Dial the international access code (00 if you're calling from Europe, 011 from the US or Canada). If you see a phone number that begins with +, you have to replace the + with the international access code.

2) Dial the country code of the country you're calling (39 for Italy, or 1 for the US or Canada).

3) Dial the local number. Note that in most European countries, you have to drop the zero at the beginning of the local number—but in Italy, you dial it.

So, to call the Venice hotel from the US, dial 011 (the US international access code), 39 (Italy's country code), then 041-520-5764. To call my office in Edmonds, Washington, from Italy, I dial 00 (Europe's international access code), 1 (the US country code), 425 (Edmonds' area code), and 771-8303.

Email and Mail

Email: Many travelers set up a free email account with Yahoo, Microsoft (Hotmail), or Google (Gmail). Email use among European hoteliers is quite common. Internet cafés and little hole-in-the-wall Internet-access shops (offering a few computers, no food, and cheap prices) are popular in most cities. More and more hotels now offer Internet access in their lobbies for guests, and some even have wireless connections (Wi-Fi) for travelers with laptop computers. Ask if your hotel has access. If it doesn't, your hotelier will direct you to the nearest place to get online.

Because of a recent anti-terrorism law in Italy, you may be asked to show your passport (carry it in your money belt) when using a public Internet terminal at an Internet café or in a hotel lobby. The proprietor will likely make a copy of your passport.

Mail: While you can arrange for mail delivery to your hotel (allow 10 days for a letter to arrive), phoning and emailing are so easy that I've dispensed with mail stops altogether.

Mail service in Italy has improved over the last few years, but even so, mail nothing precious from Italy....Federal Express makes pricey two-day deliveries.

MONEY MATTERS

Damage Control for Lost Cards

If you lose your credit, debit, or ATM card, you can stop people from using your card by reporting the loss immediately to the respective global customer-assistance centers. Call these 24-hour US numbers collect: Visa (410/581-9994), MasterCard (636/722-7111), and American Express (623/492-8427).

At a minimum, you'll need to know the name of the financial institution that issued you the card, along with the type of card (classic, platinum, or whatever). Providing the following information will allow for a quicker cancellation of your missing card: full card number, whether you are the primary or secondary cardholder, the cardholder's name exactly as printed on the card, billing address, home phone number, circumstances of the loss or theft, and identification verification (your birth date, your mother's maiden name, or your Social Security number—memorize this, don't carry a copy). If you are the secondary cardholder, you'll also need to provide the primary cardholder's identification-verification details. You can generally receive a temporary card within two or three business days in Europe.

If you promptly report your card lost or stolen, you typically won't be responsible for any unauthorized transactions on your account, although many banks charge a liability fee of $50.

Tipping

Tipping in Italy isn't as automatic and generous as it is in the US, but for special service, tips are appreciated, if not expected. As in the US, the proper amount depends on your resources, tipping philosophy, and the circumstances, but some general guidelines apply.

Restaurants: Check the menu to see if the service is included (*servizio incluso*—generally 15 percent); if not, you could tip 5 to 10 percent for good service, though be advised that Italians rarely tip.

Taxis: To tip the cabbie, round up. For a typical ride, round up to the next euro on the fare (to pay a €4.50 fare, give €5). If the cabbie hauls your bags and zips you to the airport to help you catch your flight, you might want to toss in a little more. But if you feel like you're being driven in circles or otherwise ripped off, skip the tip.

Special Services: It's thoughtful to tip a couple of euros to someone who shows you a special sight and who is paid in no other way. Tour guides at public sites sometimes hold out their hands for tips after they give their spiel; if I've already paid for the tour, I don't tip extra, though some tourists do give a euro or two, particularly for a job well done. I don't tip at hotels, but if you do, give the porter a euro for carrying bags and leave a couple of euros in your room at the end of your stay for the maid if the room was kept clean. In general, if someone in the service industry does a super job for you, a tip of a couple of euros is appropriate...but not required.

When in doubt, ask. If you're not sure whether (or how much) to tip for a service, ask your hotelier or the tourist information office; they'll fill you in on how it's done on their turf.

Getting a VAT Refund

As is the case throughout the European Union, wrapped into the purchase price of your Italian souvenirs is a Value Added Tax (VAT) of about 20 percent. If you purchase more than €155 (about $200) worth of goods at a store that participates in the VAT-refund scheme, you're entitled to get most of that tax back. Getting your refund is usually straightforward and, if you buy a substantial amount of souvenirs, well worth the hassle. If you're lucky, the merchant will subtract the tax when you make your purchase. (This is more likely to occur if the store ships the goods to your home.) Otherwise, you'll need to:

Get the paperwork. Have the merchant completely fill out the necessary refund document, called a "cheque." You'll have to present your passport.

Get your stamp at the border or airport. Process your cheque(s) at your last stop in the EU with the customs agent who deals with VAT refunds. It's best to keep your purchases in your carry-on for viewing, but if they're too large or dangerous (such as knives) to carry on, track down the proper customs agent to inspect them before you check your bag. You're not supposed to use your purchased goods before you leave. If you show up at customs wearing your new leather shoes, officials might look the other way—or deny you a refund.

Collect your refund. You'll need to return your stamped document to the retailer or its representative. Many merchants work with a service, such as Global Refund (www.globalrefund.com) or Premier Tax Free (www.premiertaxfree.com), which have offices at major airports, ports, or border crossings. These services, which extract a 4 percent fee, can refund your money immediately in your currency of choice or credit your card (within two billing cycles). If the retailer handles VAT refunds directly, it's up to you to contact the merchant for your refund. You can mail the documents from home, or, even quicker, from your point of departure (using a stamped, addressed envelope you've prepared or one that's been provided by the merchant)—and then wait. It could take months.

Customs for American Shoppers

You are allowed to take home $800 worth of items per person duty-free, once every 30 days. The next $1,000 is taxed at a flat 3 percent. After that, you pay the individual item's duty rate. You can also bring in duty-free a liter of alcohol (slightly more than a standard-size bottle of wine; pack carefully in checked bag; you must be at least 21), 200 cigarettes, and up to 100 non-Cuban cigars. Cans or sealed jars of food are okay if no meat is included. Some, but not all, types of cheese are allowed, but fresh fruits and vegetables are not. To check customs rules and duty rates before you go, visit www.cbp.gov, and click on "Travel" then "Know Before You Go."

HOLIDAYS AND FESTIVALS

Festivals in Venice

Venice's most famous festival is **Carnevale,** the celebration Americans call Mardi Gras (Jan 25–Feb 5 in 2008, www.carnevale .venezia.it). Carnevale, which means "farewell to meat," originated centuries ago as a wild two-month-long party leading up to the austerity of Lent. In Carnevale's heyday—the 1600s and 1700s—you could do pretty much anything with anybody from any social class if you were wearing a mask. These days it's a tamer 10-day celebration, culminating in a huge dance lit with fireworks on St. Mark's Square. Sporting masks and costumes, Venetians from kids to businessmen join in the fun. Drawing the biggest crowds of the year, Carnevale has nearly been a victim of its own success, driving away many Venetians (who skip out on the craziness to go skiing in the Dolomites).

Every odd year (next in 2009), the city hosts the **Venice Biennale International Art Exhibition,** a world-class contemporary art fair spread over the Arsenale and sprawling Castello Gardens. Artists representing 70 nations from around the world offer the latest in contemporary art forms: video, computer art, performance art, and digital photography, along with painting and sculpture (generally June–Oct; take vaporetto #1 or #82 to Giardini–Biennale; for details and an events calendar, see www .labiennale.org).

Other typically Venetian festival days filling the city's hotels with visitors and its canals with decked-out boats are **Feast of the Ascension Day** (May 1 in 2008), **Feast and Regatta of the Redeemer** (third Sun in July and the preceding evening), and the **Historical Regatta** (old-time boats and pageantry, first Sat and Sun in Sept). Smaller regattas include the **Murano Regatta** (early July) and the **Burano Regatta** (mid-September).

2008

JANUARY
S	M	T	W	T	F	S
		1	2	3	4	5
6	7	8	9	10	11	12
13	14	15	16	17	18	19
20	21	22	23	24	25	26
27	28	29	30	31		

FEBRUARY
S	M	T	W	T	F	S
					1	2
3	4	5	6	7	8	9
10	11	12	13	14	15	16
17	18	19	20	21	22	23
24	25	26	27	28	29	

MARCH
S	M	T	W	T	F	S
						1
2	3	4	5	6	7	8
9	10	11	12	13	14	15
16	17	18	19	20	21	22
23/30	24/31	25	26	27	28	29

APRIL
S	M	T	W	T	F	S
		1	2	3	4	5
6	7	8	9	10	11	12
13	14	15	16	17	18	19
20	21	22	23	24	25	26
27	28	29	30			

MAY
S	M	T	W	T	F	S
				1	2	3
4	5	6	7	8	9	10
11	12	13	14	15	16	17
18	19	20	21	22	23	24
25	26	27	28	29	30	31

JUNE
S	M	T	W	T	F	S
1	2	3	4	5	6	7
8	9	10	11	12	13	14
15	16	17	18	19	20	21
22	23	24	25	26	27	28
29	30					

JULY
S	M	T	W	T	F	S
		1	2	3	4	5
6	7	8	9	10	11	12
13	14	15	16	17	18	19
20	21	22	23	24	25	26
27	28	29	30	31		

AUGUST
S	M	T	W	T	F	S
					1	2
3	4	5	6	7	8	9
10	11	12	13	14	15	16
17	18	19	20	21	22	23
24/31	25	26	27	28	29	30

SEPTEMBER
S	M	T	W	T	F	S
	1	2	3	4	5	6
7	8	9	10	11	12	13
14	15	16	17	18	19	20
21	22	23	24	25	26	27
28	29	30				

OCTOBER
S	M	T	W	T	F	S
			1	2	3	4
5	6	7	8	9	10	11
12	13	14	15	16	17	18
19	20	21	22	23	24	25
26	27	28	29	30	31	

NOVEMBER
S	M	T	W	T	F	S
						1
2	3	4	5	6	7	8
9	10	11	12	13	14	15
16	17	18	19	20	21	22
23/30	24	25	26	27	28	29

DECEMBER
S	M	T	W	T	F	S
	1	2	3	4	5	6
7	8	9	10	11	12	13
14	15	16	17	18	19	20
21	22	23	24	25	26	27
28	29	30	31			

Venice's patron saint, **St. Mark,** is commemorated every April 25. Venetian men celebrate the day by presenting roses to the women in their lives (mothers, wives, and lovers).

Every November 21 is the **Feast of Our Lady of Good Health.** On this local "Thanksgiving," a bridge is built over the Grand Canal so that the city can pile into La Salute Church and remember how Venice survived the gruesome plague of 1630. On this day, Venetians eat smoked lamb from Dalmatia (which was the cargo of the first ship admitted when the plague lifted).

Venice is always busy with special musical and artistic events. The free monthly *Un Ospite di Venezia* lists all the latest in English (free from fancy hotels). For a comprehensive list of festivals, contact the Italian tourist information office in the US (see page 333) and visit www.turismovenezia.it.

Italian Holidays in 2008

These national holidays (when many sights close) are observed throughout Italy. Note that this isn't a complete list; holidays strike without warning.

Jan 1: New Year's Day
Jan 6: Epiphany
March 23: Easter Sunday
March 24: Easter Monday
April 25: Liberation Day, St. Mark's Day (Venetian patron saint)
May 1: Labor Day and Ascension Day
June 2: Anniversary of the Republic
Aug 15: Assumption of Mary
Nov 1: All Saints' Day
Nov 21: Feast of Our Lady of Good Health
Dec 8: Feast of the Immaculate Conception
Dec 25: Christmas
Dec 26: St. Stephen's Day

CONVERSIONS AND CLIMATE

Numbers and Stumblers

- Europeans write a few of their numbers differently than we do. 1 = 1, 4 = 4, 7 = 7.
- In Europe, dates appear as day/month/year, so Christmas is 25/12/08.
- Commas are decimal points and decimals commas. A dollar and a half is 1,50, and there are 5.280 feet in a mile.
- When pointing, use your whole hand, palm down.
- When counting with fingers, start with your thumb. If you hold up your first finger to request one item, you'll probably get two.
- What Americans call the second floor of a building is the first floor in Europe.
- On escalators and moving sidewalks, Europeans keep the left "lane" open for passing. Keep to the right.

Roman Numerals

In the US, you'll see Roman numerals—which originated in ancient Rome—used for copyright dates, clocks, and the Super Bowl. In Italy, you're likely to observe these numbers chiseled on statues and buildings. If you want to do some numeric detective work, here's how: In Roman numerals, as in ours, the highest numbers (thousands, hundreds) come first, followed by smaller numbers. Many numbers are made by combining numerals into sets: V = 5, so VIII = 8 (5 plus 3). Roman numerals follow a subtraction principle for multiples of fours (4, 40, 400, etc.) and nines (9, 90, 900, etc.); the number four, for example, is written as IV (1 subtracted from 5), rather than IIII. The number nine is IX (1 subtracted from 10).

Rick Steves' Venice 2008—written in Roman numerals—would translate as *Rick Steves' Venice MMVIII*. Big numbers such as dates can look daunting at first. The easiest way to handle them is to read the numbers in discrete chunks. For example, Michelangelo was born in MCDLXXV. Break it down: M (1,000) + CD (100 subtracted from 500, or 400) + LXX (50 + 10 + 10, or 70) + V (5) = 1475. It was a very good year.

M = 1000	XL = 40
CM = 900	X = 10
D = 500	IX = 9
CD = 400	V = 5
C = 100	IV = 4
XC = 90	I = duh
L = 50	

Metric Conversions (approximate)

1 foot = 0.3 meter	1 square yard = 0.8 square meter
1 yard = 0.9 meter	1 square mile = 2.6 square kilometers
1 mile = 1.6 kilometers	1 ounce = 28 grams
1 centimeter = 0.4 inch	1 quart = 0.95 liter
1 meter = 39.4 inches	1 kilogram = 2.2 pounds
1 kilometer = 0.62 mile	32°F = 0°C

Appendix

Venice's Climate

First line, average daily high; second line, average daily low; third line, days of no rain.

J	F	M	A	M	J	J	A	S	O	N	D
42°	46°	53°	62°	70°	76°	81°	80°	75°	65°	53°	46°
33°	35°	41°	49°	56°	63°	66°	65°	61°	53°	44°	37°
25	21	24	21	23	22	24	24	25	24	21	23

Temperature Conversion: Fahrenheit and Celsius

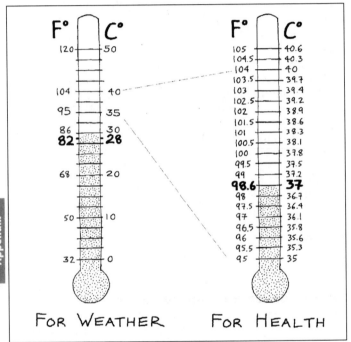

FOR WEATHER   FOR HEALTH

Europe takes its temperature using the Celsius scale, while we opt for Fahrenheit. For a rough conversion from Celsius to Fahrenheit, double the number and add 30. For weather, remember that 28°C is 82°F—perfect. For health, 37°C is just right.

Essential Packing Checklist

Whether you're traveling for five days or five weeks, here's what you'll need to bring. Remember to pack light to enjoy the sweet freedom of true mobility. Happy travels!

- ❑ 5 shirts
- ❑ 1 sweater or lightweight fleece jacket
- ❑ 2 pairs pants
- ❑ 1 pair shorts
- ❑ 1 swimsuit (women only—men can use shorts)
- ❑ 5 pairs underwear and socks
- ❑ 1 pair shoes
- ❑ 1 rainproof jacket
- ❑ Tie or scarf
- ❑ Money belt
- ❑ Money—your mix of:
  - ❑ Debit card for ATM withdrawals
  - ❑ Credit card
  - ❑ Hard cash in US dollars
- ❑ Documents (and backup photocopies)
- ❑ Passport
- ❑ Airplane ticket
- ❑ Driver's license
- ❑ Student ID and hostel card
- ❑ Railpass/car-rental voucher
- ❑ Insurance details
- ❑ Daypack
- ❑ Sealable plastic baggies
- ❑ Camera and related gear
- ❑ Empty water bottle
- ❑ Wristwatch and alarm clock
- ❑ Earplugs
- ❑ First-aid kit
- ❑ Medicine (labeled)
- ❑ Extra glasses/contacts and prescriptions
- ❑ Sunscreen and sunglasses
- ❑ Toiletries kit
- ❑ Soap
- ❑ Laundry soap (if liquid and carry-on, limit to 3 oz.)
- ❑ Clothesline
- ❑ Small towel
- ❑ Sewing kit
- ❑ Travel information
- ❑ Necessary map(s)
- ❑ Address list (email and mailing addresses)
- ❑ Postcards and photos from home
- ❑ Notepad and pen
- ❑ Journal

Hotel Reservation

To: _____   _____
         hotel   *email or fax*

From: _____   _____
            name   *email or fax*

Today's date: _____ /_____ /_____
                      day   *month*   *year*

Dear Hotel _____ ,
Please make this reservation for me:

Name: _____

Total # of people: _____   # of rooms: _____   # of nights: _____

Arriving: _____ /_____ /_____   My time of arrival (24-hr clock): _____
             day   *month*   *year*   (I will telephone if I will be late)

Departing: ____ /____ /_____
              day   *month*   *year*

Room(s): Single____   Double ____   Twin ____   Triple ____   Quad____

With: Toilet ____   Shower_____   Bath ____   Sink only ____

Special needs: View____   Quiet____   Cheapest ____   Ground Floor____

Please email or fax confirmation of my reservation, along with the type of room reserved and the price. Please also inform me of your cancellation policy. After I hear from you, I will quickly send my credit-card information as a deposit to hold the room. Thank you.

_____
Name

_____
Address

_____
City   *State*   *Zip Code*   *Country*

Before hoteliers can make your reservation, they want to know the information listed above. You can use this form as the basis for your email, or you can photocopy this page, fill in the information, and send it as a fax (also available online at www.ricksteves.com/reservation).

Italian Survival Phrases

English	Italian	Pronunciation
Good day.	**Buon giorno.**	bwohn JOR-noh
Do you speak English?	**Parla inglese?**	PAR-lah een-GLAY-zay
Yes. / No.	**Sì. / No.**	see / noh
I (don't) understand.	**(Non) capisco.**	(nohn) kah-PEES-koh
Please.	**Per favore.**	pehr fah-VOH-ray
Thank you.	**Grazie.**	GRAHT-seeay
I'm sorry.	**Mi dispiace.**	mee dee-speeAH-chay
Excuse me.	**Mi scusi.**	mee SKOO-zee
(No) problem.	**(Non) c'è un problema.**	(nohn) cheh oon proh-BLAY-mah
Good.	**Va bene.**	vah BEHN-ay
Goodbye.	**Arrivederci.**	ah-ree-vay-DEHR-chee
one / two	**uno / due**	OO-noh / DOO-ay
three / four	**tre / quattro**	tray / KWAH-troh
five / six	**cinque / sei**	CHEENG-kway / SEHee
seven / eight	**sette / otto**	SEHT-tay / OT-toh
nine / ten	**nove / dieci**	NOV-ay / deeAY-chee
How much is it?	**Quanto costa?**	KWAHN-toh KOS-tah
Write it?	**Me lo scrive?**	may loh SKREE-vay
Is it free?	**È gratis?**	eh GRAH-tees
Is it included?	**È incluso?**	eh een-KLOO-zoh
Where can I buy / find...?	**Dove posso comprare / trovare...?**	DOH-vay POS-soh kohm-PRAH-ray / troh-VAH-ray
I'd like / We'd like...	**Vorrei / Vorremmo...**	vor-REHee / vor-RAY-moh
...a room.	**...una camera.**	OO-nah KAH-meh-rah
...a ticket to ___.	**...un biglietto per ___.**	oon beel-YEHT-toh pehr
Is it possible?	**È possibile?**	eh poh-SEE-bee-lay
Where is...?	**Dov'è...?**	DOH-veh
...the train station	**...la stazione**	lah staht-seeOH-nay
...the bus station	**...la stazione degli autobus**	lah staht-seeOh-nay DAYL-yee OW-toh-boos
...tourist information	**...informazioni per turisti**	een-for-maht-seeOH-nee pehr too-REE-stee
...the toilet	**...la toilette**	lah twah-LEHT-tay
men	**uomini, signori**	WOH-mee-nee, seen-YOH-ree
women	**donne, signore**	DON-nay, seen-YOH-ray
left / right	**sinistra / destra**	see-NEE-strah / DEHS-trah
straight	**sempre diritto**	SEHM-pray dee-REE-toh
When do you open / close?	**A che ora aprite / chiudete?**	ah kay OH-rah ah-PREE-tay / keeoo-DAY-tay
At what time?	**A che ora?**	ah kay OH-rah
Just a moment.	**Un momento.**	oon moh-MAYN-toh
now / soon / later	**adesso / presto / tardi**	ah-DEHS-soh / PREHS-toh / TAR-dee
today / tomorrow	**oggi / domani**	OH-jee / doh-MAH-nee

In the Restaurant

I'd like...	**Vorrei...**	vor-REHee
We'd like...	**Vorremmo...**	vor-RAY-moh
...to reserve...	**...prenotare...**	pray-noh-TAH-ray
...a table for one / two.	**...un tavolo per uno / due.**	oon TAH-voh-loh pehr OO-noh / DOO-ay
Non-smoking.	**Non fumare.**	nohn foo-MAH-ray
Is this seat free?	**È libero questo posto?**	eh LEE-bay-roh KWEHS-toh POH-stoh
The menu (in English), please.	**Il menù (in inglese), per favore.**	eel may-NOO (een een-GLAY-zay) pehr fah-VOH-ray
service (not) included	**servizio (non) incluso**	sehr-VEET-seeoh (nohn) een-KLOO-zoh
cover charge	**pane e coperto**	PAH-nay ay koh-PEHR-toh
to go	**da portar via**	dah POR-tar VEE-ah
with / without	**con / senza**	kohn / SEHN-sah
and / or	**e / o**	ay / oh
menu (of the day)	**menù (del giorno)**	may-NOO (dayl JOR-noh)
specialty of the house	**specialità della casa**	spay-chah-lee-TAH DEHL-lah KAH-zah
first course (pasta, soup)	**primo piatto**	PREE-moh peeAH-toh
main course (meat, fish)	**secondo piatto**	say-KOHN-doh peeAH-toh
side dishes	**contorni**	kohn-TOR-nee
bread	**pane**	PAH-nay
cheese	**formaggio**	for-MAH-joh
sandwich	**panino**	pah-NEE-noh
soup	**minestra, zuppa**	mee-NEHS-trah, TSOO-pah
salad	**insalata**	een-sah-LAH-tah
meat	**carne**	KAR-nay
chicken	**pollo**	POH-loh
fish	**pesce**	PEH-shay
seafood	**frutti di mare**	FROO-tee dee MAH-ray
fruit / vegetables	**frutta / legumi**	FROO-tah / lay-GOO-mee
dessert	**dolci**	DOHL-chee
tap water	**acqua del rubinetto**	AH-kwah dayl roo-bee-NAY-toh
mineral water	**acqua minerale**	AH-kwah mee-nay-RAH-lay
milk	**latte**	LAH-tay
(orange) juice	**succo (d'arancia)**	SOO-koh (dah-RAHN-chah)
coffee / tea	**caffè / tè**	kah-FEH / teh
wine	**vino**	VEE-noh
red / white	**rosso / bianco**	ROH-soh / beeAHN-koh
glass / bottle	**bicchiere / bottiglia**	bee-keeAY-ray / boh-TEEL-yah
beer	**birra**	BEE-rah
Cheers!	**Cin cin!**	cheen cheen
More. / Another.	**Ancora un po.' / Un altro.**	ahn-KOH-rah oon poh / oon AHL-troh
The same.	**Lo stesso.**	loh STEHS-soh
The bill, please.	**Il conto, per favore.**	eel KOHN-toh pehr fah-VOH-ray
tip	**mancia**	MAHN-chah
Delicious!	**Delizioso!**	day-leet-seeOH-zoh

For hundreds more pages of survival phrases for your trip to Italy, check out *Rick Steves' Italian Phrase Book & Dictionary* or *Rick Steves' French, Italian, and German Phrase Book.*

INDEX

Travel smart…carry on!

The latest generation of Rick Steves' carry-on travel bags is easily the best—benefiting from two decades of on-the-road attention to what really matters: maximum quality and strength; practical, flexible features; and no unnecessary frills. You won't find a better value anywhere!

Rick Steves' Convertible Carry-On $99.⁹⁵

Our roomy, versatile 9" x 21" x 14" carry-on has a large 2600 cubic-inch main compartment, plus four outside pockets (small, medium and huge) that are perfect for often-used items. Wish you had even more room to bring home souvenirs? Pull open the full-perimeter expando-zipper and its capacity jumps from 2600 to 3000 cubic inches. When you want to use it as a suitcase or check it as luggage (required when "expanded"), the straps and belt hide away in a zippered compartment in the back. It weighs just 3 lbs.

Rick Steves' Classic Back Door Bag $79.⁹⁵

This ultra-light (1½ lbs.) version of our Convertible Carry-On features the same 9" x 21" x 14" dimensions and hideaway straps, but does not include a waistbelt or expandability. This is the bag that Rick lives out of for three months a year!

Rick Steves' 21" Roll-Aboard $139.⁹⁵

Our sturdy 21" Roll-Aboard is rucksack-soft in front, but the rest is lined with a hard ABS-lexan shell to give maximum protection to your belongings. We've spared no expense on moving parts, splurging on an extra-long button-release handle and big, tough inline skate wheels for easy rolling on rough surfaces. It features the same 9" x 21" x 14" carry-on dimensions, pocket configuration and expandability as our Convertible Carry-On—and at 7 lbs. it's the lightest roll-aboard in its class.

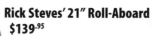

Prices and features are subject to change.

For great deals on a wide selection of travel goodies, begin your next trip at the Rick Steves Travel Store!

Visit the Rick Steves Travel Store at
www.ricksteves.com

FREE-SPIRITED TOURS FROM
Rick Steves

Small Groups
Great Guides
No Grumps

**Best of Europe ■ Family Europe
Italy ■ Village Italy ■ South Italy
Sicily ■ France ■ Eastern Europe
Adriatic ■ Prague ■ Scotland
Britain ■ Ireland ■ Scandinavia
Germany-Austria-Switzerland ■ Spain ■ Turkey ■ Greece
London-Paris ■ Paris ■ Rome ■ Venice-Florence-Rome…and more!**

Looking for a one, two, or three-week tour that's run in the Rick Steves style? Check out Rick Steves' educational, experiential tours of Europe.

Rick's tours are an excellent value compared to "mainstream" tours. Here's a taste of what you'll get…

- **Small groups:** With just 24-28 travelers, you'll go where typical groups of 40-50 can only dream.

- **Big buses:** You'll travel in a full-size 40-50 seat bus, with plenty of empty seats for you to spread out and be comfortable.

- **Great guides:** Our guides are hand-picked by Rick Steves for their wealth of knowledge and giddy enthusiasm for Europe.

- **No tips or kickbacks:** To keep your guide and driver 100% focused on giving you the best travel experience, we pay them well—and prohibit them from accepting tips and merchant kickbacks.

- **All sightseeing:** Your tour price includes all group sightseeing, with no hidden extra charges.

- **Central hotels:** You'll stay in Rick's favorite small, characteristic, locally-run hotels in the center of each city, within walking distance of the sights you came to see.

- **Visit www.ricksteves.com:** You'll find all our latest itineraries, dates and prices, be able to reserve online, and request a free copy of our Rick Steves Tour Experience DVD!

Rick Steves' Europe Through the Back Door, Inc.
130 Fourth Avenue North, PO Box 2009, Edmonds, WA 98020 USA
Phone: (425) 771-8303 ■ Fax: (425) 771-0833 ■ www.ricksteves.com

Start your trip at
www.ricksteves.com

Rick Steves' website is packed with over 3,000 pages of timely travel information. It's also your gateway to getting FREE monthly travel news from Rick—and more!

Free Monthly Travel News

Fresh articles on Europe's most interesting destinations and happenings. Rick will even send you an email every month (often direct from Europe) with his latest discoveries!

Timely Travel Tips

Rick Steves' best money-and-stress-saving tips on trip planning, packing, transportation, hotels, health, safety, finances, hurdling the language barrier…and more.

Travelers' Graffiti Wall

Candid advice and opinions from thousands of travelers on everything listed above, plus whatever topics are hot at the moment (discount flights, politics, nude beaches, scams…you name it).

Rick's Guide to Eurail Passes

The clearest, most comprehensive guide to the confusing array of railpass options out there, and how to choo-choose the railpass that best fits your itinerary and budget.

Great Gear at Our Travel Store

In the past year alone, more than 50,000 travelers have enjoyed great online deals on Rick's guidebooks, maps, DVDs—and his custom-designed carry-on bags, day packs, and light-packing accessories.

Rick Steves Tours

This year, 12,000 lucky travelers will explore Europe on a Rick Steves tour. Learn about our 28 different one- to three-week itineraries, read uncensored feedback from our tour alums, and get our free Tour Experience DVD.

Rick on TV, Radio and Podcasts

Read the scripts from the popular Rick Steves' Europe TV series, and listen to or download your choice of over 100 hours of our Travel with Rick Steves radio show.

Respect for Your Privacy

Whether you buy something from us or subscribe to Rick's monthly Travel News emails, we'll never share your name or email address with anyone else. You won't be spammed!

Have fun raising your Travel I.Q. at
www.ricksteves.com

Rick Steves®

More *Savvy*. More *Surprising*. More *Fun.*

COUNTRY GUIDES

Croatia & Slovenia
England
France
Germany & Austria
Great Britain
Ireland
Italy
Portugal
Scandinavia
Spain
Switzerland

CITY GUIDES

Amsterdam, Bruges & Brussels
Florence & Tuscany
Istanbul
London
Paris
Prague & The Czech Republic
Provence & The French Riviera
Rome
Venice

BEST OF GUIDES

Best of Eastern Europe
Best of Europe

As the #1 authority on European travel, Rick gives you inside information on what to visit, where to stay, and how to get there—economically and hassle-free.

www.ricksteves.com

PHRASE BOOKS & DICTIONARIES

French
French, Italian & German
German
Italian
Portuguese
Spanish

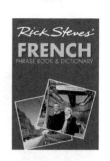

MORE EUROPE FROM RICK STEVES

Europe 101
Europe Through the Back Door
Postcards from Europe

RICK STEVES' EUROPE DVDs

All 70 Shows 2000–2007
Britain
Eastern Europe
France & Benelux
Germany, The Swiss Alps & Travel Skills
Ireland
Italy
Spain & Portugal

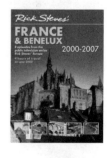

PLANNING MAPS

Britain & Ireland
Europe
France
Germany, Austria & Switzerland
Italy
Spain & Portugal

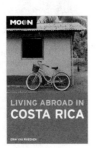

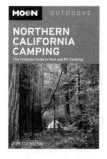
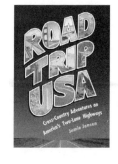

CREDITS

Researcher
To help update this book, Rick relied on the help of…

Heidi Sewell
Heidi lived in Italy for two years, learning to speak Italian and roll her own pasta. When she's not leading tours and scouring the Italian peninsula for Back Doors worthy of Rick Steves' guidebooks, she resides in Seattle with her husband Ragen.

Rick Steves' Guidebook Series

Country Guides

Rick Steves' Best of Europe
Rick Steves' Croatia & Slovenia
Rick Steves' Eastern Europe
Rick Steves' England
Rick Steves' France
Rick Steves' Germany & Austria
Rick Steves' Great Britain
Rick Steves' Ireland
Rick Steves' Italy
Rick Steves' Portugal
Rick Steves' Scandinavia
Rick Steves' Spain
Rick Steves' Switzerland

City and Regional Guides

Rick Steves' Amsterdam, Bruges & Brussels
Rick Steves' Florence & Tuscany
Rick Steves' Istanbul
Rick Steves' London
Rick Steves' Paris
Rick Steves' Prague & the Czech Republic
Rick Steves' Provence & the French Riviera
Rick Steves' Rome
Rick Steves' Venice

Rick Steves' Phrase Books

French
German
Italian
Spanish
Portuguese
French/Italian/German

Other Books

Rick Steves' Europe Through the Back Door
Rick Steves' Europe 101: History and Art for the Traveler
Rick Steves' Postcards from Europe
Rick Steves' European Christmas

(Avalon Travel Publishing)

Avalon Travel
a member of the Perseus Books Group
1700 Fourth Street
Berkeley, CA 94710, USA

Text © 2007 by Rick Steves
Maps © 2007 by Europe Through the Back Door
Printed in the United States of America by Worzalla
Third printing April 2008

Portions of this book were originally published in **Rick Steves' Mona Winks** © 2001, 1998, 1996, 1993, 1988 by Rick Steves and Gene Openshaw, and in **Rick Steves' Italy** © 2007, 2006, 2005, 2004, 2003, 2002, 2001, 2000 by Rick Steves.
ISBN (10): 1-56691-869-3
ISBN (13): 978-1-56691-869-5
ISSN: 1538-1595

For the latest on Rick's lectures, guidebooks, tours, public radio show, and public television series, contact Europe Through the Back Door, Box 2009, Edmonds, WA 98020, tel. 425/771-8303, fax 425/771-0833, www.ricksteves.com, rick@ricksteves.com.

Europe Through the Back Door Managing Editor: Risa Laib
ETBD Editors: Cathy McDonald, Gretchen Strauch, Jennifer Madison Davis, Jennifer Hauseman (Senior Editor), Cameron Hewitt (Senior Editor)
Avalon Travel Senior Editor and Series Manager: Madhu Prasher
Avalon Travel Project Editor: Kelly Lydick
Copy Editor: Jennifer Malnick
Proofreader: Kay Elliott
Indexer: Laura Welcome
Cover Design: Kari Gim, Laura Mazer
Cover Design Manager: Laura VanDeventer
Maps & Graphics: David C. Hoerlein, Laura VanDeventer, Lauren Mills, Barb Geisler, Mike Morgenfeld
Production & Typesetting: McGuire Barber Design
Research Assistance: Heidi Sewell
Photography: Rick Steves, David C. Hoerlein, Dominic Bonuccelli, Elizabeth Openshaw, Gene Openshaw, Andrea Johnson, Karen Kant
Front Cover Photos: Front image: View of La Salute © David C. Hoerlein; Back image: Venice Laundry © Carol Ries
Front Matter Color Photos: p. i, Grand Canal, Venice, Italy © Rick Steves